The Concept of Active Defence in China's Military Strategy

THE CONCEPT OF ACTIVE DEFENCE IN CHINA'S MILITARY STRATEGY

Amrita Jash

Centre for Land Warfare Studies

PENTAGON PRESS LLP

The Centre for Land Warfare Studies (CLAWS), New Delhi, is an independent Think Tank dealing with contemporary issues of national security and conceptual aspects of land warfare, including conventional and sub-conventional conflicts and terrorism. CLAWS conducts research that is futuristic in outlook and policy-oriented in approach.

CLAWS Vision: To establish CLAWS as a leading Think Tank in policy formulation on Land Warfare, National Security and Strategic Issues.

Centre for Land Warfare Studies
RPSO Complex, Parade Road, Delhi Cantt, New Delhi-110010
Phone: 011-25691308 • CLAWS ARMY NO : 33098 • Fax: 011-25692347
email: landwarfare@gmail.com • website: www.claws.in

First Published in 2021

ISBN 978-93-90095-30-8

DISCLAIMER: The views expressed and suggestions made in the book are solely of the author in his/her personal capacity and do not have any official endorsement of CLAWS, Indian Army or the Government of India. Attributability of the contents lies purely with the author.

Published by
PENTAGON PRESS LLP
206, Peacock Lane, Shahpur Jat,
New Delhi-110049
Phones: 011-64706243, 26491568
Telefax: 011-26490600
email: rajan@pentagonpress.in
website: www.pentagon-press.com

Printed at Aegean Offset Printers, Greater Noida, U.P.

For my loving Ma, Baba and Di

Contents

Foreword

The India-China stand-off in Eastern Ladakh since early May 2020 brings into perspective the imperative need to reassess China's military strategy. Given the opacity attached, China's military strategy is largely one of the most debated issues. It is commonly argued that China plays by the rule book of Sun Tzu's *The Art of War,* wherein, 'deception, concealment and surprise' are the key battle winning strategy. While one cannot dismiss this aspect but it also holds true that 'deception' is just an element in China's military strategy. Thus, the question that demands significant attention: *What is China's Military Strategy? Or, What constitutes China's Military and Strategic Thinking?*

Officially, China maintains to have a defensive posture; however, its actions transcending from being assertive to that of becoming aggressive suggest otherwise. This is exemplified by China's unilateral dispositions, well-witnessed in the case of South China Sea, East China Sea and most recently, in changing the status-quo along the India-China border. These actions call for scepticism over Chinese intentions. For the assumption is that there is a design in every Chinese action. Thus, all is not 'defensive'.

What significantly adds to the debate on China's military strategy and its defensive posturing is the aspect of 'Active Defence'. Simplistically, it suggests that 'China will attack only when attacked'. Highlighting the relevance of "active defence" in China's military thinking, the 2015 Defence White Paper on "China's Military Strategy" pronounced "active defence" as the "essence of CPC's military strategic thought". This perspective brings forth the need to enquire: *What is "active defence"? Is it only defensive in nature? What is the role of "active defence" in China's military strategy?*

These queries are significant for the very fact that examining the concept of "Active Defence" acts as the key in understanding the Chinese military thinking. While the existing literature is scant and no detailed study available, this book offers a conceptual and analytical understanding to the 'Concept of Active Defence' . In providing a comprehensive perspective, the book makes a detailed study on China's military and strategic thinking by assessing China's military doctrine; military modernisation and reforms of the People's Liberation Army and; China's military capabilities in terms of the defence budget, the defence industry and weapon and weapon systems. Furthermore, the book also outlines China's behavioural assessment by making a detailed study of China's boundary dispute with India. Thus, underlying China's growing military activism.

Given that India is faced with the 'China Challenge', the imperative lies in going back to the drawing board in assessing China - primarily from a military perspective. Indeed, it is time to deliberate on China's hard power thinking!

In this regard, the book makes a comprehensive read both in terms of understanding and assessment of China's Military Strategy. Offering an in-depth analyses, the book deconstructs the concept of active defence and its relevance in China's military thinking. With its all-encompassing outlook, Dr. Amrita Jash, an Indian scholar, makes a timely and valuable contribution on a pertinent subject that interests the global audience at large.

The book on "The Concept of Active Defence in China's Military Strategy" makes a significant value addition to the field of Chinese Studies and mainly to the studies on the People's Liberation Army. It makes an important read for policy makers, strategic analysts, academia and mainly for the Armed Forces- both at home and abroad.

My appreciation and compliments to Dr. Amrita Jash for her keen sense of commitment and endeavour to put it all together in a lucid, cogent and comprehensive way.

New Delhi
December 2020

Lt Gen (Dr.) VK Ahluwalia
PVSM, AVSM**, YSM, VSM (Retd)
Director, Centre for Land Warfare Studies
(Former Army Commander, Central Command; Former Member Armed Forces Tribunal, Jaipur)

Acknowledgements

A look back at December 2017, and I see how far I have traversed since I undertook this study at the Centre for Land Warfare Studies (CLAWS). Standing at the destination, I can certainly say that a study of this nature is a culmination of the goodwill of many people the institutional support. It has been a lengthy process that came with its own kind of lows but, in the end, the journey has been immensely rewarding.

Being trained in Chinese studies, working on the Chinese military was indeed a learning experience. Even before I ventured into writing, I had to first educate myself on the subject. In the process, I developed a deep interest in the field of defence and strategic studies and mainly on the People's Liberation Army. This experience was not just intellectually stimulating but also complex and fascinating. It demanded that one be constantly updated and rewrite the texts based on newer research and emerging perspectives, which appeared to be a never-ending saga.

In pursuit of this study, I have greatly benefitted from the interactions with members of the Indian Armed Forces and the Veterans, the Chinese academics and practitioners as well as Indian and Western scholars. What added to the process was my Visiting Fellowship at POLIS, University of Cambridge, in 2019, where I was a Pavate Fellow. This gave me an opportunity to interact with scholars and practitioners as well as get to access the resource-rich Cambridge Library: besides benefitting from various lectures, conferences and discussions held at the University during my stay. Cambridge will always hold a special place in shaping this project.

What greatly added to the study was my time of ideation, as in debating the issues, I published various papers at CLAWS, some of which have been adapted in this book. Also, making presentations at the Army War College, Mhow, further enhanced my understanding of the subject.

As I see it now, I am more convinced to say that 'This was meant to be'. Especially, in the testing times of the India-China relations amidst the COVID-19 Pandemic, this book only seems to be a *Manifest Destiny*.

With this note, I would first like to thank Lt Gen B. S. Nagal, former Director of CLAWS and Lt Gen (Dr.) V. K. Ahluwalia, Director CLAWS, for expressing their confidence in me to pursue research in an area that is not just challenging but comes with an added responsibility. A special note of thanks to Lt Gen Ahluwalia for the insightful Foreword and his valuable suggestions on the overall subject and mainly on the India-China boundary dispute that helped me improve the study.

I would like to extend my sincere gratitude to Brig Narender Kumar for his time and patience in reading the complete manuscript and offering valuable and trenchant suggestions. His critical feedback immensely helped in sharpening my arguments, fine tuning the manuscript, and thus preventing me from making grievous errors.

Taking this opportunity, I would also like to thank Professor Srikanth Kondapalli, who was my doctoral supervisor and has also mentored me in Chinese Studies. This pursuit is very much a product of the training I received in the China Programme at the Jawaharlal Nehru University. I am also grateful to Sir for his encouraging words for the book.

A special note of gratitude to Gen Deepak Kapoor, former Chief of the Army Staff and Lt Gen Ranbir Singh, former GOC-in-C Northern Command, for their valuable thoughts and kind appreciation of the book. Their words only make me humble as this study came with great responsibility and utmost sincerity.

This study could not have materialised without the institutional support. A special note of thanks to Brig H. S. Burn and Col Amit Hajela who have always encouraged, supported and trusted me in this pursuit. I would also like to thank Col P. S. Ranawat and Col S. K. Singh for their kind support.

I would be guilty of ingratitude if I neglect the people who helped me to successfully complete this research. I am very thankful to CLAWS Librarian, Nitesh Khandelwal, for providing me with valuable resources,

Dharmender Bansiwal for all the official assistance, and the entire administrative staff of CLAWS for their tacit support. I would also like to convey my gratitude to Shreya for facilitating the publication in a timely manner, and the editorial and publication Team of Pentagon Press LLP for their meticulous efforts. A special note of thanks to all my friends and colleagues at CLAWS for their support in various capacities.

Not to forget, the most important part of this journey came with the challenges. But the strength to fight the odds came from the unconditional love and support of my family and friends. No other time would be better than this to express my deepest gratitude to Ma, Baba, and Di, to whom I dedicate this book. With friends being more like family, I would like to specially acknowledge the bond shared with Sabu, Minks, Sonam, Anju, Zo, Gullak, Rinch, Amali and Saniya for being there and believing in me at all times, as we walked this far in thick and thin. I cannot fail to cite Anu for her excitement on the book since the very beginning and for believing in me more than myself, Rose for going an extra mile in making the beautiful illustration for the cover of this book, Arnab for being there as my pillar of strength as a younger brother, Manjari for being a comrade-in-arms, and my beloved nephew Rishaan for his unconditional love and affection. They kept me going, when the going got tough!

And finally, I extend my prayers and gratitude to the Almighty for giving me the strength and patience to overcome all odds and successfully complete this study. I bear full responsibility for the contents of this book. It is not unusual for such a study of depth to not have errors or issues of assessments - for any such errors, I bear full responsibility.

This journey has been a learning process, both personally and professionally, and will always be treasured.

New Delhi
December 2020

Amrita Jash

Abbreviations

ADD	Annual Defence Dialogue
ADIZ	Air Defence Identification Zone
AECC	Aero Engine Corporation of China
AEW	Airborne Early Warning
AI	Artificial Intelligence
AIIB	Asian Infrastructure Investment Bank
AMS	Academy of Military Science
ASW	Anti-Submarine Warfare
ATT	Arms Trade Treaty
AUV	Autonomous Underwater Vehicle
AVIC	Aviation Industry Corporation of China
BDCA	Border Defence Cooperation Agreement
BECA	Basic Exchange and Cooperation Agreement
BPM	Border Personnel Meeting
BRI	Belt and Road Initiative
C2	Command and Control System
CAEP	Chinese Academy of Engineering Physics
CASC	China Aerospace Science and Technology Corporation
CASIC	China Aerospace Science and Industry Corporation
CATTB	Combined Arms Tactical Training Bases
CBM	Confidence Building Measure
CETC	China Electronics Technology Group Corporation
CGTN	China Global Television Network
C4ISR	Command, Control, Communications, Computers, Intelligence, Surveillance, and Reconnaissance

CMC	Central Military Commission
CNP	Comprehensive National Power
CNSC	Central National Security Commission
COVID-19	Coronavirus Disease 2019
COSTIND	Commission for Science, Technology and Industry for National Defense
CPC	Communist Party of China
CPEC	China-Pakistan Economic Corridor
CPPCC	National Committee of the Chinese People's Political Consultative Conference
CSGC	China South Industries Group Corporation
CSIC	China Shipbuilding Industry Corporation
CSIS	Center for Strategic & International Studies
CSSC	China State Shipbuilding Corporation Ltd
DBO	Daulat Beg Oldi
DF	Dong Feng
DIA	Defense Intelligence Agency
DoD	Department of Defense
DSDBO	Darbuk- Shyok- Daulat Beg Oldi
EU	European Union
GA	Group Army
GAD	General Armaments Department
GDP	Gross Domestic Product
GNP	Gross National Product
GPS	Global Positioning Satellite
GSD	General Staff Department
HADR	Humanitarian Assistance and Disaster Relief
HGV	Hypersonic Glide Vehicles
IOR	Indian Ocean Region
IPOE	Intelligence Preparation of the Environment
IISS	International Institute for Strategic Studies
JOCC	Joint Operations Command Center
KMT	Kuomintang
LAC	Line of Actual Control
LDUUV	Large Displacement Unmanned Underwater Vehicle
LoC	Line of Control
MCF	Military-Civil Fusion

MEA	Ministry of External Affairs
MIC	Military-Industrial Complex
MIIT	Ministry of Industry and Information Technology
MIRV	Multiple Independent Reentry Vehicle
MND	Ministry of National Defense
MoD	Ministry of Defence
MOOTW	Military Operations Other Than War
MR	Military Region
NDU	National Defense University
NEO	Non-Combatant Evacuation Operation
NMO	National Military Objective
NMR	National Military Resource
NMS	National Military Strategy
NMSC	National Military Strategic Concept
NORINCO	China North Industries Group Corporation Limited
NPC	National People's Congress
NSS	National Security Strategy
OTH-T	Over The Horizon-Targeting
PAP	People's Armed Police
PBSC	Politburo Standing Committee Members
PLA	People's Liberation Army
PLAA	People's Liberation Army Army
PLAAF	People's Liberation Army Air Force
PLA JLSF	People's Liberation Army Joint Logistics Support Group
PLAN	People's Liberation Army Navy
PLARF	People's Liberation Army Rocket Force
PLASSF	People's Liberation Army Strategic Support Force
PME	Professional Military Education
PoK	Pakistan Occupied Kashmir
PRC	People's Republic of China
RMA	Revolution in Military Affairs
RMB	Renminbi
SASTIND	State Administration for Science, Technology and Industry for National Defense
SCO	Shanghai Cooperation Organization
SFA	Striving for Achievement
SLBM	Sea-Launched Ballistic Missile

SOE	State Owned Enterprise
SoS	System-of-Systems
S&T	Science and Technology
SIPRI	Stockholm International Peace Research Institute
SRBM	Short Range Ballistic Missile
TAR	Tibet Autonomous Region
TC	Theatre Command
TMC	Tibet Military Command
TTR	Teeth-To-Tail Ratio
UAV	Unmanned Aerial Vehicles
UCAV	Unmanned Combat Aerial Vehicles
UFWD	United Front Work Department
UK	United Kingdom
UNPKO	United Nations Peacekeeping Operations
USA/US	United States of America/Unites States
USD	United States Dollar
UT	Union Territory
UUV	Unmanned Underwater Vehicle
WMCC	Working Mechanism for Consultation & Coordination on India-China Border Affairs
WTC	Western Theatre Command
XMC	Xinjiang Military Command

List of Figures and Tables

FIGURES

TABLES

Introduction

Does China have a Military Strategy? This pertinent question has been a longstanding query given the People's Republic of China's (PRC) ambiguous posture in delineating its military approach. What calls for this ambiguity is the absence of a Chinese equivalent of a 'national military strategy' document as issued by the USA, resulting in an 'opacity' that favours China. Being conspicuous by its absence, the veiled nature of China's strategic intentions has been the core factor in raising suspicion and concerns over China's military actions. Furthermore, whether or not China openly declares its motives behind its military development, but its actions do imply preparedness for a conflict situation. *Therefore, the worry!*

Given the opacity, decoding China's military strategy has become one of the key quandaries of the global strategic community. This is validated by China's expanding military capabilities, a result of rapid modernisation and robust reforms of the People's Liberation Army (PLA). While China's stated policy suggests that it favours "international peace and an equitable international order"; however, its actions suggest otherwise - implying an aggressive and assertive China. Besides, China's 'Wolf Warrior diplomacy' under the COVID-19 pandemic and most importantly, China's expansionist designs in Eastern Ladakh that led to a military stand-off with India, have resurfaced the debate: *What entails China's rise?*

While China maintains that it holds a defensive military posture; however, it is the very 'defensive' standing that signals the red alarm of a 'China threat'. This aspect brings into perspective the caveat that needs attention. That is, while considerable efforts have been made to analyse China's military advancement but, the understanding of Chinese strategic military thinking is still limited. In this context, the starting point lies in the query: *Why is it important to understand a country's strategy?*

In Barry Posen's view, the understanding of 'strategy' helps view a state's behaviour from two perspectives: First, whether a particular state's behaviour will contribute to stability or instability in the international system; and second, will it provide clues about how the state in question will perform in a military conflict.[1] In view of this, to understand China's national military strategy, the first step lies in understanding its 'national strategy', as it is embedded in its 'national strategic goals and objectives'. For instance, the PLA is currently tasked with ensuring the rejuvenation of the Chinese nation- the ultimate goal of the Chinese Dream.

In this regard, to understand China's strategic thinking, the logic lies in going beyond the counting of the number of PLA troops and weapon systems. Rather, the imperative lies in understanding the 'military thinking' as represented by the strategy. Here, the essence lies in understanding China's definition of the opponent and how it would use force as well as its military preparedness and force projection capabilities. This would explain: *What are China's intentions?*

Assessing from this point of query helps connect China's national military strategy to the PLA's intentions, motivations and ambitions regarding the use of military power and the drive for modernisation and reforms. In this regard, to gain a perspective on assessing China's next move, it becomes imperative to decode the strategic rationale of China's proclaimed 'Military Strategy'. As on 26 May 2015, the State Council Information Office of the PRC issued a Defence White Paper on "China's Military Strategy", providing a blueprint of China's military motivations.[2] Being the ninth since 1998, this white paper marked a significant departure from the previous eight as it pronounced PRC's military strategy, by categorically stating:

> "The strategic concept of active defense is the essence of the CPC's military strategic thought. [...] Shortly after the founding of the PRC in 1949, the Central Military Commission (CMC) established the military strategic guideline of active defence, and later, in line with the developments and changes in the national security situation, had made a number of major revisions of it".[3]

PRC's denomination of "active defence" as the "strategic concept" highlights the need to explore as to what constitutes China's military strategy. This very insight makes it imperative to de-mystify two key aspects: First, is "active defence", the core of China's military strategy; and second, has "active defence" been a constant factor in China's military thinking. What makes these queries significant is that given the lack of an official Chinese document on 'national military strategy', it is the PLA's "strategic guidelines" or the concept of "active defence" that has often been perceived as 'China's military strategy'—thus, calling for an error in assumption. To explain, on one end, since the founding of the PRC in 1949, China has adopted nine such "guidelines" that have witnessed major departures and minor adjustments over the years; while on the other end, the strategic concept of "active defence" has been a constant reference point in indicating China's 'defensive' military posture—predominantly perceived as China's military strategy. However, bringing a clarity to such assumptions, the 2015 White Paper clearly defined "active defence" as a "strategic concept"—thereby, lifting the veil over China's military strategy. While it is clear that 'active defence' is a concept, but what remains unclear, as going by the 'name': *How defensive is the concept of "active defence"?*

Simplistically put, Beijing's growing military capabilities and quest for power projection highlight an 'offensive' intent—an ability to attack and not just respond, when attacked.

To argue so, as China's bold and confident posture in the changing dynamics of the international system indicates its departure from Deng Xiaoping's dictum of "Keeping a low profile". More importantly, while "active defence" calls for the PLA to 'not attack unless attacked, but surely counterattack when attacked', one cannot ignore the scope of 'pre-emption' that exists. In this context, it becomes imperative to decode the underpinnings of the 'Chinese Military Strategy'. For, with changes in China's assessment of threats and its place in the world, its military strategy too has witnessed a significant change; no more inward-looking but more focused on addressing threats, both at home and beyond its immediate periphery. This is witnessed in China's evolving military superiority with "anti-intervention" (*fanjieru*; 反介入) capabilities that include ballistic and anti-ship cruise missiles, submarines, air defence systems, and counter-C4ISR (command, control, communication, computer, intelligence, surveillance, and reconnaissance) capabilities in space, cyber and electronic warfare.

In this regard, it is of interest to trace the evolution of the key concepts such as "active defence" that define and shape China's military strategy in connection with China's national strategy and national security strategy in a broader sense. In view of this, the book is mainly based on the study of China's doctrinal documents, the concept of national interests, perception and key principles of modern warfare, and the priority objectives of military modernisation and the PLA reforms.

Purpose and Scope of the Study

No single work can fill the analytical gap that exists in the understanding of the concept of 'active defence'. However, this study represents more of a beginning than an end to the discussion. In doing so, the interest lies in advancing the debate by providing a broad spectrum of understanding and assessment of data as available to date. In this regard, the study makes several arguments and sub-arguments, with the overarching thesis centered on offering a comprehensive perspective on China's strategic military thinking.

Broadly, the study addresses the following key questions: (a) What is the Chinese understanding of 'strategy'? (b) What is the nature and significance of "active defence" in shaping China's Military Strategy? (c) What are China's strategic interests, intentions and military objectives? (d) What are China's military capabilities and how does it impact China's strategic behaviour? And (e) What are the implications of China's military strategy, both regionally and globally?

Given the vastness of the subject, the scope of the book is limited and mainly concentrated on analysing some of the core issues. In this respect, the book examines the concept of 'active defence' in PRC's national military strategy from the perspective of: its basic notions, the concept of national and core interests and the main goals of maintaining it, and aspects of its implementation. This study seeks to understand the 'concept' under the various components that shape China's Military Strategy, such as: China's threat analysis; military doctrine/strategic military guidelines; PLA's force structure, readiness, and training; military budget, arms sales, defence industry and others.

More specifically, the crux of this study lies in assessing the element of 'offensive defence' of "active defence" by providing critical assessments of China's military modernisation and trend analyses of the PLA's military capabilities, its intentions and its implications. It does so by examining the current state of the PLA in terms of its doctrine, command and control structures, military spending, and weapons and weapon systems. Furthermore, the study makes a critical assessment of China's strategic behaviour in the context of the India-China boundary dispute, with special focus on the Eastern Ladakh stand-off, based on events that unfolded until 31 December 2020. Thus, this book makes a critical assessment of China's strategic military thinking and the implications of it for the world at large, and India in particular.

Methodology of the Study

Understanding a state's strategic intentions is always based on assumptions. In the case of China, its strategic intentions have been broadly and mainly assessed on the basis of its military modernisation process and military capabilities. The rationale of this study is to fill this speculative gap by using strategy as a method of assessment. Thus, it cannot be treated as an equivalent. In the case of China, the puzzle lies in understanding two key aspects: Is "active defence" China's Military Strategy? Is it purely defensive or has an element of offence? In this case, the study is focused on examining China's national military strategy based on PLA's threat perception, its intentions, and its military capabilities. This study extrapolates the nature of "active defence" by examining China's military objectives, military capabilities and the ways in which it is implemented by the PLA.

The foundation of this study is based on the core understanding that the Chinese perception of strategy is not in the same vein as that of Western thinking. In doing so, examining Chinese terminologies has been the key methodology used in this study to highlight the distinction, if/ as it exists. Here, it is important to note that a study of this kind is often faced with the caveat of lack of availability of many official, original copies of Chinese government documents that are significant for the assessment.

However, to fill the gap, this study relies on content analyses of key Chinese authoritative sources of strategic guidance, as issued by the Communist Party of China (CPC), the Chinese Government and the PLA. These consist of the Constitution of the PRC; documents issued by

Chinese institutions such as the Ministry of National Defense of the PRC; the Defence White Papers published every two to three years and other White Papers as issued by the State Council Information Office of the PRC; speeches by paramount Chinese leaders, such as Mao Zedong, Deng Xiaoping, Jiang Zemin, Hu Jintao, Xi Jinping and others; National Party Congress Reports and Work Reports; and PLA texts such as *The Science of Military Strategy* and others, as published by the Academy of Military Science (AMS) and the PLA National Defense University (NDU), and other relevant PLA documents. This is guided by the logic that the understanding of China's national military strategy should be based on documents issued by the central authorities of the PRC, as this then provides the essence of the strategic guidance and governing philosophies issued by China's military authorities to the PLA.

In addition, Chinese perspectives are also drawn from data available in the websites such as *China Military Online* and *China.org.cn*; and leading Chinese newspapers such as *People's Daily, Xinhua, Global Times, China Global Television Network (CGTN), China Daily* and others. Furthermore, assessments are also drawn from references and secondary source descriptions of Chinese-language sources as well as western literature on the subject.

On the whole, in this study, the subject of enquiry is approached in an analytical framework using both descriptive sources and empirical data. The aim of this book is to make a value addition to the literature on China's Military Strategy and the PLA.

Organisation of the Book

In delving deeper into the subject of enquiry, this book systematically details and discusses the concept of "active defence" in five parts.

Chapter 1 conceptualises China's approach to 'strategy' or '*zhanlue*'. In doing so, the chapter offers a thorough understanding of how China defines strategy and most importantly, how it comprehends strategy in its broader understanding of 'grand strategy' to that of 'national security strategy'. Here, the objective lies in adopting a top-down approach to the understanding of China's military strategy, drawing from the broad conception of China's national/grand strategy.

Chapter 2 examines the concept of 'active defence' in China's military strategy. It aims at examining two key perspectives: First, identifying and explaining the key Chinese constructs and their components that comprise the equivalent of Chinese military strategy. And second, explaining the key features that constitute China's military strategy based on the assessment of its evolution and the main drivers associated with it.

Chapter 3 explores China's military modernisation from two key perspectives: First, based on the PLA's perception of modern warfare; and second, the way the PLA seeks to deploy its military capabilities in various scenarios. In view of this, the chapter examines three key aspects: First, what explains China's rapid and robust military modernisation? Second, what are the significant reforms undertaken by the PLA? And third, what kind of operations the PLA wants to conduct in fighting future wars?

Chapter 4 examines China's military capabilities from two key perspectives: the increasing trend of China's defence expenditure and the exponential growth of China's defence industry. The crux of this chapter lies in the assessment of three key fundamental aspects: First, the ambiguity over China's official defence budget; second, the status of China's military-industrial complex (MIC); and third, the composition and capabilities of China's advanced weaponry.

Chapter 5 studies China's strategic behaviour in dealing with its unresolved boundary dispute with India. In doing so, it examines the patterns in PLA's behaviour at the LAC as well as its force projection capabilities. Here, the crux lies in assessing: China's perceptions with respect to the boundary; its military actions in the name of safeguarding its core interests; and its implications for India.

Finally, the conclusion reviews the key findings of the study and makes some significant claims on the implications of China's military strategy for the future.

NOTES

1. Barry R. Posen (1984), *The Sources of Military Doctrine: France, Britain, And Germany Between the World Wars*, Ithaca, NY: Cornell University Press.
2. The State Council of the People's Republic of China (2015), "China's Military Strategy", 27 May 2015, http://english.gov.cn/archive/white_paper/2015/05/27/content_281475115610833.htm, accessed online 11 May 2020.
3. Ibid.

1

Understanding *Zhanlue*

"Strategy is the art and science of using and strengthening power to achieve long-term political goals".

—Lieutenant General Li Jijun[1]

"West focuses on power in strategy, whereas the Chinese focus on using stratagems. In the US definition of strategy, the emphasis is on the use of resources and forces to achieve the objective. China seeks to use the situation to adapt strategy. War becomes fight of stratagems against resources".

—Colonel Xue Guo[2]

With the turn of the 21st century, China's rapid economic rise and development have raised significant concerns. This has been compounded with China's military rise which is manifested in the form of robust military modernisation and accelerated reforms to the PLA under the leadership of President Xi Jinping. This is indicative of China's increasing political power that is accompanied with development of an effective military deterrent. Wherein, the ambition of the 'Chinese Dream' permeates into China's national security strategy with the PLA's enhanced role in supporting the Communist Party's strategic objectives, which are mainly to ensure security, promote modernisation, and preserve China's socialist system. Given this context, the constant quest has been 'how to interpret China correctly', mainly in terms of its strategic intentions and choices. This very quest makes it imperative to reassess China's national military strategy.

Bringing a halt to the long-held debate on PLA reforms, the 18th National Congress of the CPC set the pace for moving forward with structural, organisational and other readjustments to China's armed forces. The major strides came with the transformation from seven Military Regions (MRs) to that of establishment of five Theatre Commands (TCs); a significant reduction of 300,000 personnel in force size; setting up of a new service under PLA Strategic Support Force (PLASSF); and upgrading the Second Artillery to PLA Rocket Force. (PLARF). Given these dynamics, more changes are foreseen; however, the trajectory to it remains uncertain given the opacity of China's defence system. This uncertainty then demands significant attention to two key queries: (a) What are the PLA's ambitions in the 21st century? (b) What blueprint does the PLA seeks to follow in achieving its strategic ends? The answer to these questions lies in deciphering the core, that is the Chinese understanding of military strategy, which is often under debate.

To provide some transparency to China's military thinking, in May 2015, the Information Office of the State Council of the PRC issued a Defence White Paper titled "China's Military Strategy" that categorically stated that '[t]he strategic concept of "active defence" is the essence of the CPC's military strategic thought'.[3] Being ninth in order of defence white papers as published since 1998, the 2015 White Paper marks a difference. Unlike its predecessors, the ninth White Paper for the first time spelt out China's so-called 'military strategy' which has long been an issue of curiosity and debate. What adds to this military outlook is China's Ministry of National Defense (MND) official statement that the PRC implements a military strategy of "active defence".[4] Furthermore, the 2019 White Paper on "China's National Defense in the New Era" pointedly mentions that the military strategic guideline for a new era "adheres to the principles of defence, self-defence and post-strike response, and adopts active defence".[5]

What makes these official statements a significant point of enquiry is that unlike the USA, China does not officially issue a 'National Military Strategy' document. Should the 'absence' be then be inferred that the PRC has no such military strategy. However, in case of China, to make such a linear assumption will indeed be an error of assessment. On the contrary, one needs to question whether such an ambiguity is by a Chinese design. That is, what China wants the world to believe and what it practises on the ground. This very aspect makes the understanding of China's military strategy a critical subject of enquiry.

Given that there is no clear and cohesive document that reflects the Chinese national military strategy, the starting point lies in drawing from its corollaries. Here, the 'Chinese terminology' acts as the key. Owing to this concept of terminology, it then becomes imperative to understand the core of the subject of assessment, which in this case, is 'strategy'. To argue so, a country's national military strategy represents the intersection between national and military levels of strategy.[6] Here, the key to understanding is pivoted on three principle concepts, namely: strategy/national strategy, national security strategy and national military strategy.

In this perspective, the chapter attempts to examine China's approach to 'strategy' or '*zhanlue*' (as the Chinese call it) primarily from a conceptual understanding. In doing so, this chapter offers a thorough understanding of how China defines strategy and most importantly, how it comprehends strategy in its broader understanding of 'grand strategy' which further breaks down to 'national security strategy'. Here, the objective lies in adopting a top-down approach to the understanding of China's military strategy—drawing from the broad conception of China's national/grand strategy.

The Concept of Strategy/National Strategy

In 1981, during his visit to the U.S. Army War College, General Maxwell D. Taylor characterised 'strategy' as comprising of objectives, ways and means. In expressing Taylor's characterisation into an equation, Colonel Arthur F. Lykke Jr. describes it as: *Strategy = Ends + Ways + Means*.[7]

Table 1.1: Lykke's Model

Component	*Definition*
Ends	Objectives towards which one strives
Ways	Course of action
Means	Instruments by which some end can be achieved

Source: Adapted from Lykke.[8]

The definition of 'strategy', as approved by the U.S. Joint Chiefs of Staff, is stated as: "A prudent idea or set of ideas for employing the instruments of national power in a synchronized and integrated fashion to achieve theatre, national, and/or multinational objectives".[9]

However, owing to Lykke's model, the three important aspects that need consideration are:[10] First, the three components of a strategy—ends, ways and means—are interdependent. That is, each of the components must be appropriate to the whole and in proper balance with the others if the strategy is to be successful. Second, applying this model to study someone else's strategy, focusing on only one component of the strategy without an understanding of the other two may lead to incorrect or incomplete conclusions. And third, this model can be used to formulate any kind of strategy (military, political, economic or others) depending upon the element of national power employed,[11] making it universal in applicability and not just limited to military affairs.[12]

Given this concept of 'strategy', what underpins a country's 'national (grand) strategy' becomes the key point of enquiry. As defined, national strategy is: "The art and science of developing and using the political, economic, and psychological powers of a nation, together with its armed forces, during peace and war, to secure national objectives".[13] National Strategy, then involves all the elements of national power, which if broken down on a horizontal plane encompasses political, economic, psychological, and military aspects, as described in Figure 1.1 below.

Figure 1.1: National Strategy: The Horizontal Plane

Source: Adapted from Bartholoomes Jr. (2010).[14]

In this horizontal model, it is the "military instrument of power" that acts as the "linchpin" of national strategy, as it emerged since World War I.[15] This makes national strategy the 'overarching strategy' that provides authoritative direction for all elements of national power regarding the achievement of national level goals and objectives set by the central leadership.[16] A grand strategy reflects the vision that a state has for itself and for its desired position in the international system. Thereby, a state's 'national or grand strategy' becomes a "top-down approach", that is "assumed to be sustained over a long period of time, and it seeks to mobilise and integrate all the available domestic resources and instruments of national power (not just military but also diplomatic, economic, financial, intellectual, cultural and political)".[17]

China's National Strategy

In the case of China, the very query about understanding its strategic intent is often attributed to a two-fold perspective: wherein, the majority argue that China pursues an aggressive and expansionist policy; while others question the very aspect of China having a national strategy, more specifically, denying that China has a national strategy. Here, the primary debate dwells on the very question: Does China have a 'grand strategy' (*da zhanlue*; 大战略)?

This query demands an understanding of the term 'grand strategy'. The two dominant perspectives are mainly: First, Paul Kennedy's conception, which contends that:

> "The crux of grand strategy lies therefore in *policy*, that is, in the capacity of the nation's leaders to bring together all of the elements, both military and non-military, for the preservation and enhancement of the nation's long-term (that is, in wartime *and* peacetime) best interests".[18]

Second, by Barry Posen, who argues that "a state's theory is about how it can best 'cause' security for itself".[19] To this twin perspective, Hal Brands' elaboration of the conception of grand strategy posits that:

> "At its best, then, a grand strategy represents an integrated scheme of interests, threats, resources, and policies. It is the conceptual framework that helps nations determine where they want to go and how they ought to get there; it is the theory, or logic, that guides leaders seeking security in a complex and insecure world".[20]

This holistic viewpoint of national power thus, distinguishes the concept of 'grand strategy' from its components in terms of security strategy and military strategy as well as foreign policy and statecraft.

In view of the above definitions, Wang Jisi, in his 2011 article titled "China's Search for a Grand Strategy", in *Foreign Affairs* pointedly states: "Any country's grand strategy must answer at least three questions: What are the nation's core interests? What external forces threaten them? And what can the national leadership do to safeguard them?".[21] Furthermore, in calling grand strategy a "field still to be ploughed" by China, Wang strongly argues that "Whether China has any such strategy today is open to debate." [... and that], the Chinese government has yet to disclose any document that comprehensively expounds the country's strategic goals and the ways to achieve them".[22]

In view of this, the very absence of a national strategy document compounded with the fact that China has not formally issued a national strategy leads to the conclusion that China lacks a national strategy. However, although there exists no direct reference of China's national strategy, certain concepts officially used by the Chinese authorities in terms of the Party's and the PRC's general line, general guidelines and overall policy in the domestic situation; comprehensive use of political, military, economic, scientific and technological culture; and others help to fill the existing gap. Owing to which, some suggest that debates on understanding China's national strategy have "overlooked" an important source - the 'national strategy as formulated by China's leaders themselves'.[23]

What explains this neglect is that observers often conclude that any attempt to deduce such a strategy from disparate CPC writings can "only produce contrived and artificial results", laden with "anachronistic Marxist jargon".[24] However, in doing so, one fails to take into account the key sources that create the foundation of China's strategic intent. Thereby, in an attempt to fill this gap by drawing from government documents, China's "national strategy" can be defined as "the party's guidance on the nation's desired end state and supporting objectives, ways, and means".[25] The CPC's "national-level strategic guidance" acts as the coherent equivalent of China's national strategy drawn from diverse sources, mainly the Party Constitution, the Party Congress Work Reports and others such as the speeches by the Politburo Standing Committee Members (PBSC) and analysis in authoritative Communist Party organs. To note, Chinese leaders are extremely ambitious and have a documented history of formulating long-term plans and devising strategies for implementing these grand goals.[26] For example, Mao Zedong's "Great Leap Forward", Deng Xiaoping's "Reform and Opening Up", or Xi Jinping's "Chinese Dream" – all emphasise on a larger national goal.

These official sources are essential indicators of Chinese thinking, such as: First, the CPC Constitution is important for two reasons—first, it provides the definitive version of the party theory; and second, it outlines the national strategy's desired end state.[27] As the 1982 Constitution states:

> "Under the leadership of the Communist Party of China and the guidance of Marxism-Leninism and Mao Zedong Thought, the Chinese people of all nationalities will continue to adhere to the people's democratic dictatorship and follow the socialist road, steadily improve socialist institutions, develop socialist democracy, improve the socialist legal system and work hard and self-reliantly to modernize industry, agriculture, national defence and science and technology step by step to turn China into a socialist country with a high level of culture and democracy".[28]

Furthermore, the Constitution stipulates adherence to the Four Cardinal Principles in the course to socialist modernisation in order to avoid any form of "bourgeoisie liberalisation".[29] Continuing with the tradition, the Constitution, as revised and adapted in 2017, maintains that:

> "The Four Cardinal Principles—to keep to the path of socialism, to uphold the people's democratic dictatorship, to uphold the leadership of the Communist Party of China, and to uphold Marxism-Leninism and Mao Zedong Thought—form the foundation for building the country".[30]

Drawing relevance from the above statements as outlined in the Constitution, it can be argued that, in the current context, it is the CPC Constitution that outlines how the Party views "national rejuvenation", which then serves as the functional equivalent of the "desired strategic end state" toward which the national strategy is oriented.[31]

Second, it is the Party Congress Work Reports that provide the main content of the supporting interim objectives and guidance on the "ways and means" to obtain the strategic end state.[32] What makes it so, as Alice Miller contends, is that 'Work Reports' are established at the highest authority, reflecting the party's "consensus line on virtually all policy sectors that the party leadership will be addressing in the five years until the next Party Congress convenes".[33]

Third, the PBSC members' speeches elaborate on existing guidance or introduce new guidance on behalf of the party leadership and hold significance in guiding the party in between Congresses. In view of this, the White Papers act as an important source of the authoritative party guidance blended with statements of PRC government policy for consumption by domestic and foreign audiences.[34] And finally, other important sources, such as the *People's Daily* (*Renmin Ribao*), which is officially known as the 'CPC's mouth piece' and *Seeking Truth* (*Qiushi*), represent high-level party organs that provide aid for analysts seeking to understand the logic and implications of the political guidance of the Chinese leadership.[35]

From these sets of the PRC's official sources, two key perspectives can be drawn that seemingly act as the base of China's national strategy: First, the Constitution notes the Party's "highest ideal and ultimate goal is the realization of communism";[36] second, the Constitution focuses on the idea of China's national rejuvenation (*zhonghua minzu fuxing*) as a more proximate and feasible end state. The 'basic line' states that the party seeks to oversee the development of a "prosperous, strong, democratic, culturally advanced, and harmonious modern socialist state" (*fuqiang minzhu wenming hexie de shehui zhuyi xiandaihua guojia*) under Communist Party control.[37] As the 2017 Constitution categorically states that:

> "The basic line of the Communist Party of China in the primary stage of socialism is to lead all the people of China together in a self-reliant and pioneering effort, making economic development the central task, upholding the Four Cardinal Principles, and remaining committed to reform and opening up, so as to see China becomes a great modern socialist country that is prosperous, strong, democratic, culturally advanced, harmonious, and beautiful".[38]

The Constitution envisions attaining the desired end state by 2049 at the centenary of the founding of the PRC, as promoted under the vision of 'the China Dream'—the aspiration to 'restore' China to a position of strength, prosperity, and leadership on the world stage. These documents outline the national strategic objectives (*guojia zhanlue mubiao*) that constitute fundamental strategic principles, concepts and priorities that guide China's foreign and defence policy, as derived from the basic line on Chinese domestic and external relations set by the Party leadership. That is, they represent the legal, philosophical and moral values that are embodied in China's national purpose that encompasses the nation's domestic and global needs.

In view of this, the main elements of China's national strategy include the basic focus of the national security strategy and the national development strategy.[39] This is based on the principles of the path to Socialism with Chinese Characteristics, adherence to peaceful development, the unity of the rich countries and the strong military to create a favourable environment conducive to China's national security and development and ensures that the national government consolidates social stability with the larger objective of long term-peace and stability, the goal of fully building a well-off society and the great rejuvenation of the Chinese nation.[40] These elements therefore, act as fundamental precursors to risk assessment when formulating China's national strategy.

What is also noteworthy is that there is a continuity with reference to the key phrase "Socialism with Chinese Characteristics", as witnessed in various official documents such as Party Congress Reports, Central Committee plenary documents, speeches by leaders as well as in official media outlets such as *Xinhua*, *People's Daily*, and others. That is to suggest, although China does not use the term "national strategy"; however, the construct of "Socialism with Chinese Characteristics" as used by the central authorities, can be seen as a functional equivalent to what can be identified as 'China's national strategy'.[41]

Table 1.2: Linkage between Strategy and Concept

Strategy	*Key Strategic Concept*
China's National Strategy	Chinese Dream of the Great Rejuvenation of the Chinese Nation
China's National Security Strategy	Core Interests
China's National Military Strategy	Active Defence

Source: Author.

Therefore, China's national strategy is far more pronounced and embodied in the formal planning documents formulated and major official speeches articulated by the paramount leader or set of senior leaders at the apex of power. To cite an example, on 1 October 2019, Xi Jinping, in his speech on the 70th anniversary of the founding of the PRC, remarked:

> "The Chinese people managed to stand up on their feet and embark on a great journey of national rejuvenation [...] Today a socialist China is standing in the east of the world and there is no force that can shake the foundation of this great nation".[42]

China's Quest for *Zhongguo Meng*: Shift from *Tao Guang Yang Hui* to *Fen Fa You Wei*

Since 2002, China's national strategy has sought to elevate the standard of living of its people and realise the nation's revitalisation as a great power by the mid-21st century.[43] What is noteworthy is that the starting point to this debate was provided by Deng Xiaoping's "Reform and Opening Up", wherein Deng called for a "three-stage development plan" in 1987 with a strategic objective to make China a mid-level developed country by 2050. In this, the first stage was to double GDP and GDP per capita by the late 1980s; the second stage was to double GDP and GDP per capita again by the end of the 20th century and the third stage would only be achieved in another 50 years.[44] What dominated the discourse is Deng's dictum of "keeping a low profile" (*tao guang yang hui;* 韬光养晦).

In assessing China's strategic thinking, Wang Jisi identifies 'four changes' that may suggest the foundations for a new grand strategy. Here, "changes" refer to: a more comprehensive understanding of security and transnational problems (such as terrorism or piracy); a more multilateral and issue-oriented Chinese diplomacy (such as on energy security or nuclear non-proliferation); a greater focus on social issues arising out of China's economic development; and, greater attention to the "cultural soft power of the nation" (China's international image).[45]

Given the "changes", what is noted that there is a continuity from Deng Xiaoping's "three-stage development plan" to Xi Jinping's "two-staged development plan" under fulfilling the Chinese Dream (*zhongguo meng;* 中国梦). This encompasses two centenary goals (*liangge yibainian mubiao;* 两个一百年目标): First, 'a moderate well-off society' (*xiaokang shehui;* 小康社会) by 2021 (the 100th anniversary of the CPC) and; second, becoming a 'rich and strong socialist country' (*fuqiang de shehuizhuyi guojia;* 富强的社会主义国家) by 2049, the 100th anniversary of the founding of the PRC. The twin goals are guided by the principle of "Socialism with Chinese Characteristics" (*zhongguo tese shehuizhuyi;* 中国特色社会主义) under the command of the CPC. This very theoretical construct has come to define "Xi Jinping's Thought". In his speech at the 19th Party Congress, Xi contextualised the changing dynamics of Chinese politics under the thematic framework that "Socialism with Chinese Characteristics has entered a new era", in which he categorically stated:

> "Remain true to our original aspiration and keep our mission firmly in mind, hold high the banner of socialism with Chinese

> characteristics, secure a decisive victory in building a moderately prosperous society in all respects, strive for the great success of socialism with Chinese characteristics for a new era, and work tirelessly to realize the Chinese Dream of national rejuvenation".[46]

What motivates these ambitious goals are Beijing's dramatic economic and military rise that is strongly informed by China's growing concerns with respect to its role and influence in the Asian region as well as the international system. Primarily, it is argued to be catalysed by: Beijing's internal economic imperatives; its heightened desire for the "geopolitical strategic rights" and national glory that are due to it as a major power; a sharp increase in popular nationalism and "triumphalism" within the country; and its much more militant and ambitious armed forces.[47] What justifies the role of the 'Chinese Dream' in shaping China's national strategy is the identity factor, as argued:

> "a state's attitude towards international society and its international behaviour are rooted in its identity. States with different identities have different world-views, which, in turn, make different impacts upon its foreign policies and strategies".[48]

This suggests that Xi's 'two-stage' plan is primarily the third stage of Deng's longer-term vision reflecting the continuity in China's grand plan, if not 'grand strategy'. To further substantiate, in 2015, Xi put forward his political theory of "Four Comprehensives", a four-pronged approach to: "comprehensively build a moderately prosperous society, comprehensively deepen reform, comprehensively govern the nation according to law and comprehensively be strict in governing the party" – further adding to the national strategy driven by the concept of the "Chinese Dream".[49]

This brings into perspective the shift in China's strategic thinking from "keeping a low profile" to that of "striving for achievement" (*fen fa you wei;* 奋发有为; SFA).[50] Under this new policy, China seems to be shifting from passively adapting to changes in the external environment to that of actively shaping the external environment—a shift from "responsive diplomacy" (*fanying shi waijiao;* 反应式外交) to "proactive diplomacy" (*zhudong shi waijiao;* 主动式外交).[51] This strategy is strongly informed by China's new concepts and initiatives such as "New Type of Great Power Relations", the "Belt and Road Initiative" (BRI) and others. Given these perceptual changes, China's new SFA policy comprises four elements—"*qin* (being close), *cheng* (credible), *hui* (benefiting) and *rong* (inclusive)" against the 'low profile' policy's emphasis on "undertake no leadership, insist on non-alliance and give first priority to relations with the United States".[52]

In this perspective, China's shift from *tao guang yan hui* to that of *fen fa you wei* can be explained in a two-fold perspective: First, domestically, the low-profile approach is vulnerable to the charge that PRC is too soft, especially when security issues become acute. This has been further aggravated with the surge in China's nationalist feelings that demand a hard-line approach. And second, maintaining a low profile is no longer an appropriate policy in the current era given that China is far more powerful.[53]

Thereby, in keeping with the CPC's tradition of linking theory to practice, Xi Jinping has deeply integrated the idea of the "Chinese Dream" in Beijing's overall strategic outlook. For instance, in his address at the 19th Party Congress, Xi posited:

> "The dream of the Chinese people is closely connected with the dreams of the peoples of other countries; the Chinese Dream can be realized only in a peaceful international environment and under a stable international order. [...] and [China] will foster new thinking on common, comprehensive, cooperative, and sustainable security".[54]

In this regard, the link between the "Dream" and China's policy of *fen fa you wei* can be rightly assessed from Chinese State Councillor Yang Jiechi's article "Implementing the Chinese Dream",[55] wherein Yang clearly posits that:

> "The Chinese dream requires a peaceful and stable international and neighbouring environment, and China is committed to realizing the dream through peaceful development. Since the Chinese dream is closely linked with the dreams of other peoples around the world, China is committed to helping other countries, developing countries and neighbouring countries in particular, with their development while achieving development of its own. China will share more development opportunities with other countries so as to facilitate their efforts to realize their dreams. China hopes to see win-win cooperation and common development with the rest of the world".[56]

For Beijing, the major risk is not war with USA, but rather military confrontation with some of its neighbours, especially Japan and India, with which it has unresolved territorial and maritime disputes. As China grows increasingly stronger than its neighbours, the SFA could be easily perceived as an aggressive strategy.[57] This is justified by China's actions in terms of: establishment of the Asian Infrastructure Investment Bank (AIIB); the launch of the Belt and Road Initiative; building of artificial islands in the South China Sea; development of the first Chinese overseas military base in Djibouti; and launching of the great global political campaign under "Made in China 2025" to expand China's global influence and "Amazing China",[58] that demonstrate the self confidence of the CPC.

This reflects an image of a confident China which, as Yang Jiechi argues, is ready to "shoulder its responsibility as a major country" and build a global network of partnerships, while simultaneously it is resolved and uncompromising as it upholds its sovereignty and security interests.[59]

These dispositions further exemplify that China's national strategy is strongly embedded in two key perspectives. First, the key concept of 'Chinese Dream', wherein, 'keeping a low profile' is no more a viable option in Chinese strategic thinking. This is well-witnessed in Xi's statement at the 19th Party Congress that China is "moving closer to centre stage" to achieve the "great rejuvenation of the Chinese nation".[60] Second, by non-conforming to a normative framework, China has developed a new ideal for international relations based on non-interference in the affairs of other states, which Xi articulated as:

> "We should abide by the principle of non-interference in other countries' internal affairs, respect the independent choice of development path and social system by people of other countries, promote peaceful resolution of differences and disputes between countries through dialogue and consultation, and oppose the wilful use or threat of force".[61]

Against this background, China's grand strategy is argued to be neither "assertive" nor "cooperative", but gets displayed as being more "calculative".[62] This approach is characterised by "an outward-oriented pragmatism", which is designed to rapidly improve the PRC's domestic social conditions, increase the legitimacy of its governing regime, enhance its national economic and technological capabilities, and ultimately strengthen its military prowess and improve its standing and influence in the international political order.[63]

However, this calculative strategy has gradually transformed into becoming increasingly assertive.[64] However, in Chinese view, it is not a violent China but a China that is discontented with the international system and seeks to shape the international environment that affects its national strategy of strengthening its comprehensive national power (*zonghe guoli*, 综合国力; CNP). Here, CNP refers to the measure of strength of a nation which, in the view of Yan Xuetong is derived from the sum of a country's military, economic, and soft power multiplied by its political power (CNP=(M+E+C)×P).[65] In the case of China, CNP comprises the following power indexes, as outlined in Table 1.3.

Table 1.3: PLA Academy of Military Science Subsystems and Subindices of China's Comprehensive National Power

SUBSYSTEM	*SUBINDEX*
Political power	• national security goals • political stability • policy level • the nation's leadership, organisation, and decision-making capability • national embodiment power
Foreign affairs power	• foreign political relations • foreign economic relations • foreign military relations • diplomatic activities capability • international contribution capability
Science and Technology power	• Science and technology troops (scientists and engineers, technological personnel) • investment in science and technology (total, proportion of the GNP) • science and technology level (high science and technology, general science and technology) • science and technological progress speed • scientific and technological progress contribution • scientific and technological results and applications
National defence power	• Standing army (nuclear, conventional) and reserve forces • national defence investment • national defence science and technology and national defence industry • national defence bases and installations • strategic material reserves and logistics safeguards • national defence education and training • national defence system establishment • national defence ideology of the people and troop morale

Source: Adapted from Golden (2011).[66]

This derivation makes the status or position of a country in the international community integral to the rise and fall of its national power which is directly linked to the increase and decrease of its strategic resources. In Chinese understanding, 'grand strategy', as noted by the U.S. Department of Defense, is defined as:

> "'...overall strategy of a nation or alliance of nations which brings into play the whole of the nation's strength to achieve political goals, especially those related to national security and development. ... There are two key issues in the Chinese conception of how to achieve this balance of priorities: the idea of 'CNP' and the 'strategic configuration of power' or [shi; 勢]. Wherein, CNP is how China's strategists evaluate and measure national power in their own country, in comparison with that of others, including the quantitative and qualitative extent of territory, natural resources, economic power, diplomatic influence, military capabilities and cultural influence. ... The 'strategic configuration of power'—*shi*—is roughly equivalent to the concept of the foreign 'alignment of forces' whose challenges, threats and opportunities must be properly assessed in order to readjust the national strategy".[67]

Therefore, it can be argued that China so far has had four grand strategies since the founding of the PRC in 1949: revolution (1949–1977), recovery (1978–1989), building comprehensive national power (1990–2003), and rejuvenation (2004–present), as noted in Table 1.4.

Table 1.4: China's Grand Strategies Since 1949

Vision	*Revolution*	*Recovery*	*Building CNP*	*Rejuvenation*
Dates	1949-1977	1978-1989	1990-2003	2004-present
Key threats	Superpower-centric (military and political)	Economic weakness (underdeveloped)	Military & political weakness	Superpower-centric (hard and soft power)
Ways	*External:* • Autarky • Confrontation *Internal:* • Mobilization • Stability	• Reform and opening • Cooperation • Low profile	• Build hard power • Do something • Internal control	*External:* • Assertive • High profile *Internal:* • Control • Struggle
Means (in rank order)	1. Political 2. Military 3. Economic	1. Economic 2. Political 3. Military	1. Military 2. Economic 3. Political	Hard and soft power resources

Source: Adapted from Scobell et al. (2020).[71]

China's National Security Strategy

The term "national security strategy" or "security strategy" is most commonly used in the context of a nation's military concerns or military-related issues.[68] According to the definition used by the U.S. Joint Chiefs of Staff, "A National Security Strategy (NSS) will refer to the development, application and coordination of all the elements of national power (political/diplomatic, economic, informational, military, sociological/cultural) to achieve a nation's objectives in domestic and international affairs in peace as well as in war".[69] To pursue the national objectives set forth in the NSS, will then encompass multiple strategies such as an economic strategy, a political strategy, a diplomatic strategy, a social strategy, and a military strategy, at the very least.[70]

Owing to this broader definition of NSS, in the case of China, it exists as a "subset and "important part" of its national strategy".[72] This makes China's security strategy to mainly aim at pursuing the reduction in vulnerabilities, cope with threats, and support the nation's revitalisation – that includes shaping an international environment more favourable to the exercise of growing Chinese power in addition to enhancing protection of its core interests related to national security, territory, sovereignty, and economic development.[73]

PRC's such an understanding of NSS is drawn from Deng Xiaoping's strategic vision, wherein national security is about creating a peaceful and stable strategic environment and a favourable situation; and providing strong security protection for the nation's development.[74] Likewise, in ways to build national security, Deng dismissed the old idea of seeking military power and rather suggested development of comprehensive power of the country.[75] He argued that national security lies in the overall development of the country, and national security strength should be thoroughly strengthened.[76] In relation to the function of national security strategy, Deng posited that, at first, the effort should be to prevent the breakout of war and have crisis situations under control; maintain peace to ensure national economic development; uphold China's independence and sovereignty; and defend the socialist cause - to ensure that China enjoys a long period of peace and stability.[77]

This analogy still continues to be prevalent in the Chinese understanding, as the 2011 version of the PLA dictionary defines that national security strategy is the "set of *fangzhen* and tactics that 'guide actions to ensure comprehensive security for the nation's survival and development'".[78] That is to suggest, at the broadest level, China's national security strategy outlines how security should be conceived and how it is to be realised to support the national strategy.[79] Furthermore, this makes national interest the highest criterion in handling the question of China's military strategy. For Beijing, the anxiety over safeguarding its national security is greatly compounded by: China's increasing strategic ambitions; its rapid economic growth and development; the existence of unresolved territorial and maritime claims; the increasing suspicion towards the intention of the West; and above all, China's growing internal political and social instabilities—the factors that define China's external behaviour, both politically as well as militarily. In this perspective, it becomes imperative to understand the Chinese perception of the concept of 'national security' (*guojia anquan*), and whether there is any difference from the Western perspective. Such an assessment provides an understanding of three key perspectives: First, how China perceives the international environment; second, what China perceives to be as 'threats' to its national interests; and finally, how China seeks to achieve its national objectives in peacetime, crisis, and military conflict.

To note, unlike the Western narrative, Beijing's understanding of securitisation is centred on the concept of "political security".[80] Wherein, security is primarily hinged on safeguarding the legitimacy of the Communist Party, thus, making 'regime survival' the core of China's political security.[81] That is, the concerns of political security hold tantamount importance for China's CPC regime – making it imperative for China's national security to "safeguard the political security, the people's security and social stability" (*baowei guojia zhengzhi anquan, renmin anquan he shehui wending*; 保卫国家政治安全、人民安全和社会稳定). However, in this process, the element of 'value judgement' that Beijing attaches to its national security discourse draws similarity with the Western perspective, which argues that "security is a value and serves as an instrumental value to realise the expectations of individuals, groups and states to secure them".[82] That is, the ideational value is state-centric with individual (human) security as a subordinated 'offshoot' of state security.[83]

What makes this 'value judgement' principle important to the CPC can be argued in the following ways:[84] First, the security discourse creates identity categories, which are exclusionary by nature. Second, the national security discourse constitutes part of a nation's strategic culture that defines patriotism, loyalty and belonging. For instance, in China's strategic culture, the 100-year humiliation acts as a defining feature of a security-insecurity complex. And finally, in practice, the national security discourse transcends conceptualisation and under constructivist guidance leads to concrete national security policy actions to protect the CPC's ideational goals.[85] Thereby, in the Chinese perspective, national security as Xi Jinping categorically notes, "is the cornerstone of peace and stability of our country [China], and safeguarding it is in the fundamental interests".[86] This very essence of 'national security' acts as the bedrock in shaping China's national security strategy.

What is important to note is that for long, China has failed to have any form of formal national security strategy. In PRC's political tradition, the Chinese leaders' predominant understanding of their country's history was drawn from their persistent sensitivity to domestic disorder caused by foreign threats. This can be explained under the political evolution of China under three key stages, such as: First, in ancient times, the ruling regime was brought down by a combination of internal uprising and external invasion; second, the Qing dynasty's collapse was a result of internal revolts combined with invasion by Western and Japanese forces; and finally, the collapse of Kuomintang (KMT) rule and founding of the PRC by an indigenous revolution inspired by the Soviet Union-led international communist movement.[87] Wherein, in all the three phases, there was an absence of a concrete national security strategy.

Owing to this way of thinking, as argued, under Mao Zedong's leadership (1949-1976), China had never formally applied the concept of "national interest" to delineate its strategic aims, but its international strategies were dominated by political and military security threats, often framed by ideological principles such as "proletarian internationalism".[88] In this process, China's strategic thinking was drawn from the Leninist view of "dividing the world into political camps, such as: archenemies, secondary enemies, political allies and revolutionary forces".[89] To add further, China's perception of the international order under Mao was predominantly shaped by the "Three World's Theory" wherein China perceived the world in three spheres. As noted in a *People's Daily* article on "Chairman Mao's Theory of the Differentiation of the Three Worlds Is a Major Contribution to Marxism-Leninism", published on 1 November

1977, Mao Zedong in his talk with the leader of a Third World country in February 1974, stated:

> "In my view, the United States and the Soviet Union form the first world. Japan, Europe and Canada, the middle section, belong to the second world. We are the third world [...]. The third world has a huge population. With the exception of Japan, Asia belongs to the third world. The whole of Africa belongs to the third world, and Latin America too".[90]

While the "Three-Worlds Theory" was officially pronounced by Deng Xiaoping at the Sixth Special Session of the UN General Assembly on 10 April 1974, it can be said that the "Three-Worlds Theory" was a simplified model adopted by Mao to assess the main contradictions in the international order, that acted as "a geopolitical compass for China to establish its rightful place in the world", as to explain:[91]

> "Stripped to its core, Mao's Three-Worlds Theory is a theory of anti-hegemonism designed to strengthen the weak and the poor (including China) to overcome the strong and the rich. It envisions a united front strategy, derived from China's own revolutionary experience that has been extrapolated to the global setting to pit the nations of the Third World against those of the First in an unfolding struggle to transform the post war international system. Although the theory calls for a dual-adversary approach directed against both superpowers, in practice the Soviet Union has often been singled out as the greater threat to world peace".[92]

In taking a departure from Mao, China under Deng Xiaoping in the 1980s, emphasised on China's national interests as the guiding force, wherein Deng singled out economic development as the key objective. However, although economic interests became a major driver of China's behaviour on the international scene, traditional security concerns and the need to guard against Western political interference remained important.[93] This was predominantly witnessed in the event of the Tiananmen Square incident of 1989 that led to the West's sanctions against Beijing, serving as "an alarming reminder" to China's leaders that internal and external troubles could easily intertwine.[94] This phase saw the evolution in Chinese strategic thinking, as Beijing "resolutely refused to consider adopting Western-type democratic institutions" and most importantly, "insisted that it would never give up the option of using force if Taiwan tried to secede"—a significant change in Beijing's attitude from that under Mao.[95]

This also suggests that Chinese thinking began to be framed explicitly in terms of national interests only in the 1980s under Deng Xiaoping. The "interest-based thinking" represented one of the defining characteristics of policy change during this period – highlighting a "major transformation", as China under Mao had been preoccupied with its security interests related to state survival, autonomy and sovereignty.[96]

In succession, a somewhat formal perspective on the national security was provided with the Central Committee's idea of a "new security concept"(*xin anquan guandian*) as put forward in 1996 under the leadership of Jiang Zemin,[97] in the aftermath of the collapse of the Soviet Union and the end of the Cold War that altered the context of Chinese strategic thinking; and prompted China to replace the Cold War antagonistic relations with a policy of security through diplomatic and economic interactions. This concept thereby, expanded the definition of security to include political, defence, diplomatic and, above all, economic considerations, which in the Chinese perspective, as Wu Baiyi argued:

> "[w]hat China pursues now is a security of sustained development. The change is a landmark...The nature of its security policy, therefore, is accommodative, rather than confrontational.. Compared to past policies, the current concept signifies two major changes [...] For the first time economic security is treated as equally important with those of 'high politics'. Second, it focuses more on the interrelationship between external and internal security challenges".[98]

Officially, the "New Concept of Security" entered into the Chinese political lexicon with the 1998 Defence White Paper on "China's National Defense". Wherein, the concept was featured in the very first section titled "The International Security Situation", which posited that:[99]

> "In the new international security environment, while stressing the settlement of disputes through political, economic and diplomatic means, most countries still regard military means and the reinforcement of military strength as important ways to safeguard their own security and national interests".[100]

In view of this, David Finkelstein argues that the "New Concept of Security" clearly was a direct Chinese reaction to three main factors: First, dissatisfaction and frustration with the unfolding international system as China hoped for a multipolar world with the end of the Cold War; second, policies and actions by the USA that Beijing perceived as threatening, especially Washington's strengthening of its military alliances; and finally, it constituted a concerted attempt by Beijing to present a kinder and gentler face within the region (especially in Southeast Asia).[101] But what is noteworthly is that China's attempt to define its new security concept also defined the role of its national military establishments, although not explicitly as:

> "From the viewpoint of military security, the security concept requires: The military force shoulders the important mission of defending a state's territorial sovereignty and integrity, resisting foreign aggression, and safeguarding state unification. Therefore, it is necessary to strengthen army building, develop armaments, and reform military organizations. The defence policies and military strategies of all countries should be defensive, be based on avoiding conflicts and wars, preventing crises, and checking the escalation of conflicts. The military forces of all countries should play a role in the broader scope such as cracking down on terrorism and drug trafficking, rescue work, and [sic, providing] humanitarian aid. All countries should not and are not allowed to pursue the doctrine of military interference and resort to military force at every turn. The military cooperation and munitions trade between countries should be based on the principle which is "not aimed at any third party".[102]

However, the formalisation and most importantly, institutionalisation of the concept of national security in Chinese thinking came into existence with the establishment of the Central National Security Commission (CNSC) (*zhongyang guojia anquan weiyuanhui*; 中央国家安全委员) in January 2014, as announced in connection with the Third Plenum of the 18th Central Committee in November 2013.[103] By establishing a unified national security system, PRC exhibited a departure from its old national security decision-making structure – which was formerly divided among many departments across the CPC, the government, the military, and the Chinese society.

In view of this, the objective behind the creation of the CNSC, as initially stated, suggested the Chinese need to safeguard sovereignty, security and development interests overseas, and maintain domestic political security and social stability. However, at the first meeting of the CNSC on 15 April 2014, Xi in his address on "A holistic view of national security" stated:

> "The aim of the establishment of the Council [sic, Commission] is to better handle new developments and new tasks in the realm of

> national security, and build a national security system which is centralized, integrated, highly efficient, and authoritative, so as to improve leadership over the work of national security".[104]

Owing to this perspective, the CNSC has mainly three tasks:[105] First, to advise the Politburo, which oversees the Communist Party and the highest levels of leadership in matters of strategy and security. Second, to carry out strategic coordination between the different departments; and to unify the departments throughout the party, the government, the military, and the society. And third, to conduct crisis management and risk management for both internal and external security threats.[106] What is noteworthy is that although the Commission is inspired by the US National Security Council, the Chinese CNSC is an administrative coordination agency. Wherein, unlike its American counterpart[107] (but similar to its Russian equivalent), the CNSC oversees several specific working departments, including bureaus involved with strategy, intelligence, security, and administrative affairs; acts as an inter-ministerial body that coordinates the National People's Congress (NPC) and the Committee of the Chinese People's Political Consultative Conference (CPPCC), as well as serves as a planning agency with connections to think tanks.[108]

Here, it is important to note that in China's NSS, an important role is played by Beijing's so-called "three warfares" strategy (*san zhong zhanfa*, 三战).[109] The "three warfares" mainly deals with: public opinion (media) warfare (*yulun zhan*, 舆论战), psychological warfare (*xinli zhan*, 心理战), and legal warfare (*falu zhan*, 法律战). Officially, it is China's Political Work Department (政治工作部) that handles this strategy with the aim to safeguard the legitimacy of CPC's political power from any international as well as domestic threat. In addition, the Party's United Front Work Department (UFWD) also monitors and maintains checks and balances over 'anti-China' narratives purported and perceived outside China that might seek to threaten CPC's control. This brings into perspective the fact that political warfare is a crucial part of Chinese security strategy and foreign policy, that helps formulate the Chinese discourse. With this strategy, Beijing seeks to:

> "influence emotions, motives, objective reasoning, and behaviour of foreign governments, organisations, groups, and individuals in a manner favourable to one's own political-military objectives".[110]

In doing so, the "three warfares", although interrelated, but each has a significant role to play. That is: First, public opinion or media warfare, aims to shape public opinion both domestically as well as internationally. The means used are that of materials delivered to public audiences through established news services, informal internet sites, and other social media to influence domestic and international perspectives associated with ongoing disputes involving the PRC's interests.[111] For instance, in demanding absolute loyalty to the Party, Xi stated that the "[n]ation's media outlets are essential to political stability" and that they need to "love the party, protect the party, and closely align themselves with the party leadership in thought, politics and action" as "guiding public opinion is crucial to governance of the country".[112]

Second, psychological warfare, aims at shaping of international image of China by influencing foreign decision-makers perception and their approach towards China. It is operated by means of pre-conflict posturing of military/paramilitary forces or application of other national capabilities (diplomatic, economic, cultural) with the intention of intimidating adversaries and encouraging acquiescence to PRC-desired outcomes.[113] In view of this, the five tasks associated with psychological warfare are: presenting one's own side as just; emphasising on one's own advantages; undermining the opposition's will to resist; encouraging dissension in the enemy's camp; and implementing psychological defences.[114]

Third, legal warfare, aims at offering a legal justification for China's assertive actions or policies. It is operated by means of exploiting national and international legal systems. This is done by leveraging the existing legal regimes and processes to constrain adversary behaviour, contest disadvantageous circumstances, confuse legal precedent, and maximise advantage in situations related to the PRC's core interests.[115]

In practice, China's "three warfares strategy" is mainly focused on: control of public opinion (舆论控制); blunting an adversary's determination (意志挫伤); transformation of emotion (情感转化); psychological guidance (心智诱导); collapse of (an adversary's) organisation (组织瓦解); psychological defence (心理防御); and restriction through law (法律制约).[116] Especially, in the current context, under the guidance of "uniting with friends and disintegrating enemies," CPC's such a political warfare strategy aims at promoting the "rise of China within a new international order and defend against perceived threats to state security".[117]

With such a strategy, China seeks to mould and influence the perception of others towards itself - that of friends and adversaries. One of the significant implications of this is witnessed in the military dimension, wherein with propaganda carried out both during peacetime and in armed conflict, China is able to maximise the outcome given it either "amplifies or attenuates the political effects of the military instrument of national power".[118] Hence, in this way China's national security strategy percolates down to its military strategy.

The Idea of 'Core Interests' in China's National Security Strategy

In formulation of the NSS, on 23 January 2015, for the first time ever, the Politburo of the CPC adopted a "national security strategy guideline", wherein the statement issued noted that "risks were unpredictable so the country [China] must always be mindful of potential dangers".[119] In protecting China's national security, the strategy will follow:

> ""a pattern [consistent] with Chinese characteristics", firmly protect its core interests—with the safety of its people as its main mission—and safeguard national security through reform and economic development".[120]

Building up further on the specifics of China's national security strategy, on 1 July 2015, the Chinese government passed a new "National Security Law" to further add to China's national security policy.[121] As per the 'new law', "national security" is described as:

> "the country's state power, sovereignty, unity, and territorial integrity; its people's wellbeing; its sustainable economic and social development; and other major interests are comparatively in a state of being in no danger and free of any threat from both within and without, and that the aforementioned state can be constantly guaranteed".[122]

China's overall national security perspective regards—people's security as the tenet, political security as the fundamental, economic security as the basis and, military, cultural, and social security as the safeguard.[123] Given this perspective, China now defines national interest to include two major parts: national security and national development interest.[124] The very aspect of 'national development interest' further exemplifies the broadened scope of China's national interest, wherein anything that undermines China's development can be perceived to be a threat.

This newly expanded understanding of national security reflects the shift in the way China perceives its threats, which unlike the past, is no more limited to the physical border rather has become more diversified. To argue so, as the very understanding of "absence of international or domestic threats" is mainly focused on safeguarding the legitimacy of the CPC. To which, even the PLA's primary task lies in protecting China's national interest which at the foremost entails providing "strategic support for consolidating the leadership of the CPC and the socialist system".[125] PLA's such a dictum follows from Mao Zedong's understanding that "the Chinese Red Army is an armed body for carrying out the political tasks of the revolution"[126]—wherein, PLA is the Party's army tasked with maintaining the political power. Here, the objectives are twofold: First, to ensure the continuation of Party's control; and second, to prevent any form of external interference in China's foreign and domestic affairs.

These perspectives thereby, suggest that China's official narrative on its national security priorities is fundamentally drawn from the concept of its 'core interests' (*hexin liyi*; 核心利益). Where, the notion of China's 'core interests' is a product of its rise to a certain level in the post Mao era, given the term "core interests" entered the Chinese political parlance sometime around 2004 with reference to China's sovereignty issues, including Taiwan, Tibet, and Xinjiang.[127] In general Chinese understanding, 'core interests' are defined as those national interests that China would never "'compromise or trade' and that which take 'first priority' in a hierarchy of China's national interests, with repercussions for the 'entire system'".[128] Given the intensity attached to its meaning, safeguarding the core interests, as many Chinese argue "acts as the 'benchmark' to distinguish between a patriot and a traitor" - clarifying that Beijing would be willing to resort to force to defend its interest.[129] However, this is not to suggest that China would necessarily use force, but the consideration of 'use of force' will surely be an option, if needed.

In dispelling the ambiguity over the understanding of 'core interests', in 2009, Chinese State Councillor Dai Bingguo officially interpreted the term "China's core interests" in three aspects: (a) fundamental system and state security; (b) state sovereignty and territorial integrity; and (c) the stable development of the economy and society.[130] Since then, the scope of China's core interests has been broadening. It was in 2011 that the White Paper on "China's Peaceful Development" categorically listed six "core interests", namely: state sovereignty, national security, territorial integrity and national reunification, China's political system established by the Constitution and overall social stability, and the basic safeguards for ensuring sustainable economic and social development.[131] What each of these core interests entail is summarised in Table 1.5.

Table 1.5: China's Core Interests

Core Interest	*Description and Threats/Dangers*
"State sovereignty"	• Refers to the exercise of authority over all state assets and the right to dignity and independence from foreign control • Threats include cyber activity that threatens China's sovereign control of its cyber domain, as well as any action by any actor that Beijing deems an affront to the dignity of its people
"National security"	• Refers to the basic security of the nation • Dangers include nuclear war, invasion, separatism, and other threats to the nation's cohesion and survival
"Territorial integrity and national reunification"	• Speaks of the exercise of the Chinese government's authority over all claimed geographic features • Threats include any action by an actor that imperils the integrity of China's borders or the government's control of those features
"China's political system and overall social stability"	• Refers to the Chinese Communist Party–led government and political system • China's leaders regard anything that endangers Chinese Communist Party control and anything that threatens to provoke unrest and instability to be a major threat
"The basic safeguards for ensuring sustainable economic and social development"	• Refers to major sea lines of communication, natural resources, markets, and other economic and financial assets needed for economic growth • Threats include piracy and other threats to Chinese access to its goods

Source: Adapted from Bonds et al. (2017).[132]

With respect to the evolving nature of China's core interests, Kevin Rudd summarises it under seven aspects:[133] (a) maintaining the ruling party position and the socialist system; (b) keeping national unity of mainland China and Tibet, Xinjiang, Inner Mongolia, and Taiwan; (c) promoting sustainable economic development; (d) developing stable relations with 14 neighbouring countries; (e) expanding China's sea power including the South China Sea and the East China Sea; (f) deepening win-win cooperation with developing countries and; (g) continuing to play roles in reforming the current Western liberal order led by the USA.[134] Although the 'interests' keep evolving, however, what has remained constant is that all aspects of China's core/national interests must serve the interest of the Party—contributing to the survival of the CPC regime.

Hence, the query: What makes the Chinese conception of "core interests" significant? Such an identification clarifies the Chinese intention on the issues it is 'willing to go for war, if need be'. Of which, the most commonly encountered list consists of three broad groupings:[135] First, security - preserving China's basic political system and national security. This concerns the maintenance of China's one-party rule under CPC in the face of potential domestic challenges such as increasing social unrest, natural disasters, and public health crises and others.

Second, sovereignty - protecting national sovereignty, territorial integrity, and national unification. This is mainly attributed to China's sensitivity towards Taiwan, Tibet and Xinjiang. As noted, officially, China's core national interests explicitly link the term 'territorial integrity' to these three contested regions with respect to concerns over Taiwan independence, Tibet independence and East Turkistan independence. For instance, the 2012 White Paper stated that the "threats posed by "three forces," namely, terrorism, separatism and extremism, are on the rise,[136] while the 2015 White Paper mentions that "[r]egional terrorism, separatism and extremism are rampant."[137]

Third, development - maintaining international conditions for China's economic development. This concerns the economic and other interests deemed vital for ensuring the sustained growth of the Chinese economy with reference to protection of resources such as economic raw materials, markets, sea lines of communication (SLOCs), and others critical to sustaining China's development.[138]

Under this three-tier framework, China argues its security needs in terms of the protection or defence of its 'core interests'. As the 18th Party Congress Work Report clearly states: "We [CPC] are firm in our resolve to uphold China's sovereignty, security and development interests and will never yield to any outside pressure".[139] Being the single-most important public document that lays the principal policy goals, this central agenda clearly hinted of an 'uncompromising China'. That is, the pledge to "never yield to outside pressure" is reflective of the attitudinal change, wherein China no more remains submissive to the outside world. This further exemplifies China's decisive departure from the old dictum of "keeping a low profile".

In view of this, what is noteworthy is that in the case of China, the notion of 'national interest' is compounded with the idea of 'core interests'. To which, priorities as encapsulated in Article 2 of the new law, formally describes them as: safeguarding "the political regime (国家政权), the sovereignty (主权), the unity and territorial integrity of the nation (统一和领土完整), people's livelihoods (人民福祉), sustainable economic development of society (经济社会可持续发), and the country's other major interests (国家其他重大利益)".[140] This suggests that China practises an "outward-oriented security" posture and continues to be strongly conditioned by Party leaders' concerns for "state or regime security," and a persistent focus on matters of sovereignty and territorial integrity related to Taiwan, Tibet and Hong Kong along with defensive concerns related to dealing with US-China security competition by building asymmetric deterrence and crisis management capabilities.[141]

As noted, in recent times there has been a significant addition to China's national security policy with the need to protect Chinese citizens and assets from overseas risks. For instance, Xi Jinping in his address at the Central Conference on Work relating to Foreign Affairs (中央外事工作会议) in November 2014 called for 'protecting China's overseas interests and improving the capacity to provide such protection'.[142] In prioritising this aspect of security, the 2015 White Paper highlighted "protecting China's overseas interests" as one of the strategic "missions and tasks" for the PLA to execute.

These new additions suggest a notable policy shift concerning China's stance regarding its core interests, wherein Beijing has increasingly hardened its position under the "bottom line principle" (*disiansiwei*, 底线原则). In 2013, Xi pledged that China would not "compromise an inch" of any of its territorial and sovereignty claims, which he regarded as the "bottom line" for policy. Owing to this policy, Xi in his work report at the 19th Party Congress, categorically stated: "We [China] must put national interests first" and "resolutely safeguard China's sovereignty, security, and development interests"[143] – clearly articulating China's non-compromising attitude in safeguarding its interests. Furthermore, Xi also strongly asserted that:

> "China will never pursue development at the expense of others' interests, but nor will China ever give up its legitimate rights and interests. No one should expect China to swallow anything that undermines its interests".[144]

This 'bottom line principle' in Chinese national security perspective entails three key implications, as argued:[145] First, it calls for the consideration of the 'worst-case scenarios' and making preparations on that basis. Second, it brooks no crossing of China's baselines; typically, these allude to China's core national interests. And third, it commits China to respond accordingly if these bottom lines are violated.[146]

This fundamental position has become a benchmark of Chinese national security strategy since the 18th Party Congress, given that Xi vowed to "never give up" legitimate rights, or sacrifice core interests, by stating: "No country should presume that we will engage in trade that will place our core interests at risk or that we will swallow the 'bitter fruit' of harming our sovereignty, security or development interests".[147] To note, this was the first time that China categorically stated that its peaceful development would not come at the cost of its 'core national interests'. The precedent to China's such a stance was set by the 18th Party Congress Report, which suggested that China will "uphold" its interests and "never yield to any outside pressure".[148] In concurrence, Yang Jiechi in his article on "Xi Jinping's Thought on Diplomacy" contends that by demonstrating China's resolve to uphold its sovereignty and security interests, Xi has drawn "a clear line of what is unacceptable, and acted forcefully to defend our core interests as well as legitimate rights".[149] What calls for such a distinction? As Yang explains:

> "We [China] should be on high alert against potential danger and effectively uphold China's sovereignty, security and development interests. Upholding core national interests is the noble mission of China's diplomacy. We will continue to uphold China's national interests as the starting point and basic goal of China's external work, and be firm in defending China's territorial sovereignty and legitimate maritime rights and interests".[150]

Undoubtedly, China's emphasis on safeguarding its national interests—sovereignty and territorial integrity—lies at the core. What makes it so, as Qin Yaqing argues, is that "legitimacy" of the Chinese state and political system rests very much on whether the system can "protect" the country's sovereignty, of which, territorial integrity continues to be the most conspicuous and tangible dimension.[151] Highlighting on its growing importance in recent years, Qin draws links to that of public opinion which has criticised the Chinese government for being too 'soft' over issues involving China's sovereignty and territorial integrity.[152]

The implication of this is felt in Xi's policy that is premised on "hardening the hard, softening the soft" (*yingde gengying, ruande gengruan*) - a concept that situates China's assertiveness within a strategic context.[153] This two-pronged Chinese strategic approach can be understood as: One, a tougher and more uncompromising policy towards issues that China regards as its core interests or connecting to its core interests; and two, a more flexible and cooperative position towards other more negotiable interests that, while valuable, are of relative secondary importance.[154]

Simplistically put, 'core interests' serve as the "red line" determining whether the nation (China) goes to war or not, with no middle ground between these two choices; while for the 'non-core interests', there is room for negotiation.[155]

Chinese Perception of the Security Environment: Key Influencer in Shaping China's National Security Strategy

What explains the Chinese distinction of 'core and national' interests under its national security strategy? This very query demands an understanding of the way the Chinese leadership perceives Beijing's security environment, which is predominantly argued to be faced with 'new security challenges and vulnerabilities' – mainly linked to the geopolitical setting. This assessment stands essential as China's overarching national strategy and security strategy as mentioned earlier, is primarily derived from the way the Chinese leaders' assess and perceive Beijing's security environment, both in the present as well as in the past. In this regard, the shift in Chinese perception of the security situation can be assessed from the way it was interpreted in the Chinese white papers on national defence over the years. The White Papers play a significant role in offering a summary of China's strategic view of the world, at a given point in time, as noted in Table 1.6.

Table 1.6: China's Defence White Papers (1995-2019)

Year/White Paper	*Chinese Perception of the International Security Situation*
November 1995 *China: Arms Control and Disarmament*	Given the new international situation, the importance of arms control and disarmament has become ever more apparent to the inter-national community, both as a component of national security policies and as an effective measure to reduce the danger of war.
July 1998 *China's National Defense*	Peace and development are the major themes of the present era. The striving for peace and cooperation, and the promotion of develop-ment have become irresistible

Year/White Paper	*Chinese Perception of the International Security Situation*
	historical trends. In general, the present international security situation has continued to tend toward relaxation. With the end of the Cold War, a tendency toward multi-polarity has further developed both globally and regionally in the political, economic and other fields as various world forces are experiencing new splits and realignments.
October 2000 *China's National Defense in 2000*	Peace and development remain the two major themes in today's world. The trend toward multipolarity and economic globalization is gaining momentum, and the international security situation, in general, continues to tend toward relaxation.
December 2002 *China's National Defense in 2002*	The international situation is undergoing profound changes as the world has entered the new century. World multi-polarization and economic globalization are developing amid twists and turns. Science and technology are advancing with each passing day. [...] Peace and development remain the themes of the present era.
December 2004 *China's National Defense in 2004*	The current international situation continues to undergo profound and complex changes. Peace and development remain the dominating themes of the times. Although the international situation as a whole tends to be stable, factors of uncertainty, instability and insecurity are on the increase.
December 2006 *China's National Defense in 2006*	Peace and development remain the principle themes in today's world, and the overall international security environment remains stable. But, uncertainties and destabilizing factors are on the increase, and new challenges and threats are continuously emerging. World peace and security face more opportunities than challenges. The world is at a critical stage, moving toward multi-polarity.
2008 (Issued in January 2009) *China's National Defense in 2008*	With the advent of the new century, the world is undergoing tremendous changes and adjustments. Peace and development remain the principal themes of the times, and the pursuit of peace, development and cooperation has become an irresistible trend of the times. However, global challenges are on the increase, and new security threats keep emerging.
2010 (Issued in March 2011) *China's National Defense in 2010*	The international situation is currently undergoing profound and complex changes. [...] The current trend toward peace, development and cooperation is irresistible. But, international strategic competition and contradictions are intensifying, global challenges are becoming more prominent, and security threats are becoming increasingly integrated, complex and volatile. On the whole, the world remains peaceful and stable.

Year/White Paper	*Chinese Perception of the International Security Situation*
2012 (Issued in April 2013) *The Diversified Employment of China's Armed Forces*	Since the beginning of the new century, profound and complex changes have taken place in the world, but peace and development remain the underlying trends of our times. [...] The balance of international forces is shifting in favour of maintaining world peace, and on the whole the international situation remains peaceful and stable. Meanwhile, however, the world is still far from being tranquil. There are signs of increasing hegemonism, power politics and neo-interventionism.
May 2015 *China's Military Strategy*	Profound changes are taking place in the international situation, as manifested in the historic changes in the balance of power, global governance structure, Asia-Pacific geostrategic landscape, and international compete-tion in the economic, scientific and technological, and military fields. The forces for world peace are on the rise, so are the factors against war.
July 2019 *China's National Defense in the New Era*	The world today is undergoing profound changes unseen in a century. [...] Nonetheless, there are prominent destabilizing factors and uncertainties in international security. The world is not yet a tranquil place.

Source: Annotated by the Author with reference to data accessed from the website of Ministry of National Defense, PRC.[156]

The security situation as noted above, exemplify the significant shifts in China's perception of the world—from being perceived as peaceful to that of becoming uncertain. Apart from highlighting the Chinese perceptions, it is also argued that the White Papers, if not an equivalent of the US National Security Strategy, but are instrumental in shaping the foreign perceptions of Chinese military modernisation.[157] This is well-witnessed in the way the White Papers provide information about how the PLA wants the world to perceive it, as noted in the three dominant themes that entail:[158]

First, China is becoming more comfortable with a greater global role and with a PLA that is more involved in promoting and implementing, if not shaping, Chinese foreign policy. This is evident from Xi Jinping's policies on national rejuvenation, the BRI, and policy towards building a new type of major power relations and others, that exemplify two key aspects: One, China is no longer keen on 'hiding and biding'; and two, the PLA has a legitimate role to play on the global stage - an extension of Chinese interests across the world.

Second, China wants to present itself as a force of peace and USA as an instigator of strategic competition. As the 2019 White Paper points, the PRC's military developments are 'peaceful, defensive, and rational'; with the PLA contributing to the global good through United Nations Peacekeeping Operations (UNPKO), Humanitarian Assistance and Disaster Relief (HADR), joint exercises, major security dialogues, and multilateral treaties – highlighting that China 'can and should' play a leadership role in the international order.

Third, while on one end, the White Papers attempt to alleviate international concerns about China's military modernisation; on the other end, they provide justification for China's assertive behaviour, which in the Chinese view, is protection of what Beijing sees as its interests, such as territorial integrity. This is mainly witnessed in the case of Taiwan, South China Sea and Diaoyu/Senkaku Islands, which Beijing considers to be "inalienable parts" of Chinese territory, as noted in Table 1.7 below.[159]

Table 1.7: China's Key Security Challenges as stated in Defence White Papers (1998-2019)

	South Asia Instability	*Afghanistan Instability*	*U.S. Alliances Strengthening*	*Korean Peninsula Instability*	*Taiwan Independence*	*Uighur/Tibetan Independence*	*Diaoyu/Senkakus Infringement*	*Japan Militarization*	*South China Sea Infringement*	*Australia Strengthening Alliances*
1998	X									
2000			X	X	X			X	X	
2002	X	X	X	X	X					
2004			X	X	X			X		
2006		X	X	X	X			X		
2008			X		X	X				
2010		X	X	X	X	X				
2013			X		X	X	X			
2015			X	X	X	X		X	X	
2019			X	X	X	X		X		X

Source: Adapted from Wuthnow (2020).[160]

Presently, as noted in the 2019 White Paper, the four key Chinese perceptions include:[161] First, the fight against separatists is becoming more acute. Second, China's homeland security still faces threats. Third, China's overseas interests are endangered by immediate threats such as international and regional turmoil, terrorism, and piracy. And fourth, threats to outer space and cyber security loom large and the threat of non-traditional security issues posed by natural disasters and major epidemics is on the rise.[162] Owing to this broad framework, the 2013 and 2015 White Papers categorically mention that the key security threats and challenges to China's interests mainly include: the USA adjusting its Asia-Pacific strategy to strengthen alliances and expand military presence; a Japanese threat to territorial sovereignty and maritime rights; Taiwan "separatism"; natural disasters, security accidents, and public health incidents; factors affecting social harmony and stability; increasing risk to China's overseas investments; and major powers developing more sophisticated space and cyber technologies.[163] Given this distribution of threats, one needs to ask: What calls for this security assessment in Chinese eyes?

In providing an understanding of China's perception of the security environment, in May 2014 the Chinese Academy of Social Sciences published a "Research Report on China's National Security" under the title *Blue Book on National Security*.[164] Being the first such book ever published in China, the report made a clear distinction between China's domestic and international security, wherein the domestic security identified concerns over terrorism, unemployment and societal unrest, security of political rule and political power, environmental security and food safety; while international security entailed challenges resulting from strategic competition, as well as US, Russian and EU attitudes and policies towards China serving to endanger the country's territorial and maritime interests.[165]

Given this distinction, a noted assessment remains that the concepts of volatility and risks have increasingly become the dominant aspects in the Chinese leadership's description of the emerging security environment that confronts the PRC. As China's 2015 National Security Guidelines argued that "volatility" and "turbulence" characterise the current state of international affairs.[166] Furthermore, in 2016, Chinese Foreign Minister Wang Yi categorically pointed at the "unprecedented changes" and "unexpected problems" in China's security environment.[167] While in Xi Jinping's perception, China's security environment is faced with "Three Trends" (*sange qiansuo weiyou*; 三个前所未有) and "Three Major Dangers" (*sange weixian*; 三个危险).[168] The "Three Trends" exemplify the external environment, the international situation that is constantly changing and new opportunities and challenges that are continually emerging; while the "Three Major Dangers" are that of China being "invaded, toppled and separated".[169] Therefore, these Chinese perspectives on the uncertain security environment help justify the expanding nature of China's national interests. Taking a holistic view, Xi proposed "an overall security outlook" in dealing with 11 types of national security concerns, which entail: politics, territory, military, economy, culture, society, science and technology, information, ecology, and nuclear and natural resources.[170]

In view of the above, it can be argued that China's security strategy is heavily conditioned by four fundamental features of its security environment, which are:[171] First, a long, and in many places, geographically vulnerable border. For instance, out of the 14 land borders of China, 12 remain resolved, except those with India and Bhutan; while maritime disputes have become more volatile as witnessed in the case of the South China Sea and the East China Sea. Second, the increasing presence of potential threats, both nearby and distant. Third, a domestic political system marked by high levels of elite internecine conflict at the apex and weak institutions or processes for mediating and resolving such conflict. And fourth, a great power self-image, which is mainly bolstered by the aspiration of taking a pre-eminent place in the world at large, and among neighbouring Asian states in particular.[172]

This suggests that China's security goals are mainly two-fold: preserving domestic order and well-being, and deterring external threats to Chinese territory. However, the pursuit of these twin goals often overlaps in Chinese strategic thinking. To argue so, as on one end, for China, the maintenance of domestic order and well-being is viewed as the *sine qua non* for the defence of Chinese territory against outside threats.[173] That is, in the Chinese perception, a "weak, divided and conflictual, or "unjust" (that is, highly coercive and corrupt) leadership and an impoverished, disgruntled populace" are seen as causal factors of domestic instability that can result in weakening of China's defences, and invariably invite foreign manipulation and aggression.[174] On the other end, it is perceived by China that maintaining a strong defence, eliciting political deference from the periphery, preserving the broader goal of Chinese regional centrality, and influencing the actions of more distant powers, are an absolute necessity to ensure not just regional order and deter or prevent foreign aggression and territorial dismemberment, but also to avert internal social unrest.[175] However, it is interesting to note that in the Chinese calculus, often the maintenance of domestic order and well-being takes precedence over the external threat factor—wherein, survival of the CPC regime acts as the PRC's key strategic objective that automatically permeates into China's other security imperatives.

Given this prioritisation, the challenge for China lies in drawing a balance between its internal and external security demands. This very factor then determines the type of security strategy that China needs to adopt. In this process, the variables that influence the strategic decision-making can be understood under three perspectives:[176] First, the capability and outlook of the central government; as measured by the unity, integrity, and security priorities of its leadership and the extent of control it exercises over the government bureaucracy and military. Second, the level and origin (external or internal) of resources available to the state for national defence versus internal security and social welfare. And finally, the capabilities and dispositions of potential foes, particularly those located along China's periphery, as well as more distant major powers.[177]

Owing to these Chinese perceptions, it can be invariably argued that China's security strategy is a by-product of a multitude of factors, which mainly attributes to the shifts in China's overall security environment and leadership outlook. This assessment of the security environment then helps to draw the threat perceptions, the definition of the external and the internal security concerns and thus, the requirements to pursue security strategies for maintenance of domestic order and well-being and to quell the risks of external threats.

In an overall assessment, four key deductions can be drawn in the understanding of China's national security strategy, that includes: First, China's 'holistic' approach to security exemplifies the expanding scope of China's security strategy, making it all-encompassing and constantly evolving in nature. Second, China's national security strategy is increasingly adapting a comprehensive and flexible approach resulting from substantial shifts in Beijing's security perceptions. Third, China's security strategy is highly centralised in order to maintain a balance between competing security objectives and to control the emanating risks. And finally, there is a visible recognition of the need to protect China's overseas interests against the changing dynamics of the emerging security threats. These aspects play a decisive role in designing China's military strategy and more precisely, in charting the role of the PLA in the 21st century.

Thus, China's national security strategy is based on pursuing a comprehensive security outlook in order to achieve a favourable domestic and international security environment for China, given that national security is instrumental in safeguarding and fulfilling the Chinese Dream of the great national rejuvenation. As national security acts as the cornerstone of internal peace and stability of governance in China, the ultimate goal of PRC's national security strategy is embedded in safeguarding the leadership of the CPC, which further permeates into defining the PLA's role in supporting the Party. To explain, in putting forward the "New Historic Missions" (*xin de lishi shiming*; 新的历史使命) of the Armed Forces, Hu Jintao stated:

> "We must continuously enhance our sense of political responsibility, and always place the task of defending national sovereignty, security and territorial integrity and safeguarding the interests of national development above anything else".[178]

These "new historic missions" otherwise known as the "three provides, and one role" entail:[179] (1) providing an important guarantee of strength for the party to consolidate its ruling position, (2) providing a strong security guarantee for safeguarding the period of important strategic opportunity for national development, (3) providing a powerful strategic support for safeguarding national interests, and (4) playing an important role in safeguarding world peace and promoting common development. These "historic missions" have broadened the Chinese definition of security and have further expanded the scope of the PLA's role in traditional security to now include non-traditional security as well. This continues to define PLA's strategic role in China's National Strategy in the current context, as the 18th Party Congress report affirmed, that the military "would carry out historic missions of the armed forces to meet the new requirements for national development".[180] To this transition, Chinese military thinkers now claim that:

> "The armed forces need to cope with traditional security threats, and also need to cope with non-traditional security threats; need to safeguard the state's survival interests, and also need to safeguard the state's development interests; need to safeguard the homeland security, and also need to safeguard the overseas interests security; need to safeguard the overall state interests of reform, development, and stability, and also need to safeguard world peace and promote common development".[181]

Therefore, these new dimensions exemplify the evolution in Chinese strategic thinking, which has departed from Mao's idea of conducting 'people's war' to that of becoming focused on 'fighting and winning informationised local wars' in the 21st century.

Conclusion

At the foremost, the Chinese understanding of strategy brings into perspective that lack of an official Chinese document on 'strategy' or 'military strategy' should not be treated as lack of a 'strategy'. Such simplistic deductions only call for ill-informed ideas. Especially, in the case of China, the starting point lies in decoding the Chinese formulation of national strategy, which unlike the West is not available as an official document. But, China has its own way of projecting its 'strategy'.

What lies at the apex is China's national strategy that seeks to realise "the great rejuvenation of the Chinese nation" under the umbrella of "Socialism with Chinese Characteristics". This very goal has set the course of China's policy milestones and laid out objectives for China to fulfill in terms of its overall economic and social development, strengthening of its armed forces, and enhancing its global role—politically, economically and militarily.

Drawing from this larger perspective, China's national security strategy aims to safeguard sovereignty, security and development interests. To which, China's military strategy seeks to protect China's national and core interests. What links the three is China's national defence policy that aims to uphold national security and unity, and ensure the interests of national development. Therefore, it highlights the interconnectedness of China's national strategy to national security and national military strategy, wherein the realisation of the Chinese Dream of the 'great rejuvenation' is complemented by building a 'strong PLA'.

NOTES

1. Cited in "The Sources of Chinese Military Strategy", *Classics of Strategy and Diplomacy*, 19 May 2015, https://www.classicsofstrategy.com/2015/05/the-sources-of-chinese-military-strategy-timothy-l-thomas.html, accessed online 20 May 2019.
2. Ibid.
3. The State Council of the People's Republic of China (2015), "China's Military Strategy", 27 May 2015, http://english.gov.cn/archive/white_paper/2015/05/27/ content_281475115610833.htm, accessed online 11 May 2019.
4. Ministry of National Defense of the People's Republic of China (2019), "Defense Policy", http://eng.mod.gov.cn/defense-policy/index.htm, accessed online 11 May 2019.

5. "Full Text: China's National Defence in the New Era", *Xinhuanet*, 24 July 2019, http://www.xinhuanet.com/english/2019-07/24/c_138253389.htm, accessed online 02 August 2019.
6. Timothy R. Heath (2016), "An Overview of China's National Military Strategy" in Joe McReynolds (ed.) *China's Evolving Military Strategy*, Washington, DC: The Jamestown Foundation, p. 1.
7. Colonel Arthur F. Lykke Jr. (1989), "Defining Military Strategy = E + W + M", *Military Review*, Vol. LXIX, No. 5, May 1989, http://cgsc.contentdm.oclc.org/cdm/ref/collection/p124201coll1/id/504, accessed online 14 May 2019, p. 3.
8. Arthur F. Lykke Jr. (1993), "Toward an Understanding of Military Strategy", in Arthur F. Lykke Jr. (ed.) *Military Strategy: Theory and Application*, Carlisle Barracks: U.S. Army War College, p. 179.
9. Joint Publication 1-2: Department of Defence Dictionary of Military and Associated Terms, 8 November 2010 (As amended through 15 February 2016), https://fas.org/irp/doddir/dod/jp1_02.pdf, accessed online 14 May 2019, p. 227.
10. David M. Finkelstein (1999), "China's National Military Strategy", in James Mulvenon and Richard Yang (eds.) *The People's Liberation Army in the Information Age*, Santa Monica, CA: RAND Corporation, https://www.rand.org/pubs/conf_ proceedings/CF145.html, accessed online 14 May 2019, p. 101.
11. Colonel Arthur F. Lykke Jr. (1989), "Defining Military Strategy = E + W + M", n. 7, p. 3.
12. David M. Finkelstein (1999), "China's National Military Strategy", n. 10, p. 101.
13. Quoted in Colonel Arthur F. Lykke Jr. (1989), "Defining Military Strategy = E + W + M", n. 7, p. 3.
14. J. Boone Bartholomees, Jr. (2010), *The U.S. Army War College Guide to National Security Issues*, Volume I: *Theory of War and Strategy* (4th Edition), July 2010, p. 9, https://www. hsdl.org/?view&did=20955, accessed online 14 May 2019.
15. Ibid.
16. Timothy R. Heath (2016), "An Overview of China's National Military Strategy", n. 6, p. 11.
17. Nadege Rolland (2017), "The Belt and Road Initiative: China's Grand Strategy", European Council on Foreign Relations, 18 October 2017, https://www.ecfr.eu/publications/summary/grands_designs_does_china_have_a_grand_strategy, accessed online 14 May 2019.
18. Paul Kennedy (1991), "Grand Strategy in War and Peace: Toward a Broader Definition," in *Grand Strategies in War and Peace*, (ed.) Paul Kennedy, New Haven, CT: Yale University Press, p. 5.
19. Barry R. Posen (2014), *Restraint: A New Foundation for U.S. Grand Strategy*, Ithaca, NY: Cornell University Press, p. 1.
20. Hal Brands (2014), *What Good Is Grand Strategy? Power and Purpose in American Statecraft from Harry S. Truman to George W. Bush*, Ithaca, NY: Cornell University Press, p. 3.
21. Wang Jisi (2011), "China's Search for a Grand Strategy", *Foreign Affairs*, Vol. 90, Issue 2, p. 68.
22. Ibid.
23. Timothy R. Heath (2012), "What Does China Want Discerning the PRC's National Strategy", *Asian Security*, Vol. 8, No. 1, p. 54.
24. Ibid.
25. Ibid.

26. Andrew Scobell et al. (2020), *China's Grand Strategy: Trends, Trajectories and Long-Term Competition*, Santa Monica, CA: RAND Corporation, p. 10.
27. Ibid., p. 57.
28. See, Constitution of the People's Republic of China (Adopted on December 4, 1982), https://www.purdue.edu/crcs/wp-content/uploads/2014/04/Constitution.pdf, accessed online 08 August 2019.
29. Constitution of the Communist Party of China, revised and adopted at the 19th National Congress of the Communist Party of China on October 24, 2017, http://www.china.org.cn/20171105-001.pdf, accessed online 20 May 2019, p. 4.
30. Ibid.
31. Timothy R. Heath (2012), "What Does China Want", n. 23, p. 57.
32. Ibid.
33. Ibid.
34. Ibid., pp. 57-58.
35. Ibid., p. 58.
36. Constitution of the Communist Party of China, n. 28, p. 1.
37. Timothy R. Heath (2012), "What Does China Want", n. 23, p. 57.
38. Constitution of the Communist Party of China, n. 28, p. 4.
39. *The Science of Military Strategy* (China 2013), (English Translation), Beijing: Military Strategic Research Department, AMS, p. 7.
40. Ibid.
41. Timothy R. Heath (2016), "An Overview of China's National Military Strategy", n. 6, p. 11.
42. Quoted in Office of the Secretary of Defense (2020), "Annual Report to Congress: Military and Security Developments involving the People's Republic of China 2020", p. 1, https://media.defense.gov/2020/Sep/01/2002488689/-1/-1/1/2020-DOD-CHINA-MILITARY-POWER-REPORT-FINAL.PDF, accessed online 4 September 2020.
43. Timothy R. Heath (2016), "An Overview of China's National Military Strategy", n. 6, p. 11.
44. Zhong Feiteng (2018), "China's grand strategy in a new era", East Asia Forum, 5 March 2018, https://www.eastasiaforum.org/2018/03/05/chinas-grand-strategy-in-a-new-era/, accessed online 14 May 2019.
45. Wang Jisi (2011), "China's Search for a Grand Strategy", n. 21, pp. 74-77.
46. Xi Jinping (2017), "Secure a Decisive Victory in Building a Moderately Prosperous Society in All Respects and Strive for the Great Success of Socialism with Chinese Characteristics for a New Era", Delivered at the 19th National Congress of the Communist Party of China, 18 October 2017, http://www.xinhuanet.com/ english/download/Xi_Jinping's_report_at_19th_CPC_National_Congress. pdf, accessed online 20 July 2019.
47. Shi Yinhong (2015), "China's complicated foreign policy", Commentary, European Council on Foreign Relations (ECFR), 31 March 2015, http://www.ecfr.eu/article/commentary_chinas_complicated_foreign_policy311562, accessed online 2 August 2019.
48. Qin Yaqing (2010), "Struggle for Identity: A Political Psychology of China's Rise", in Brantly Womack (ed.) *China's Rise in Historical Perspective*, New York: Rowman & Littlefield, p. 265.
49. John Ross (2015), "'Four Comprehensives' pillars of Xism", China.org.cn, 15 April

2015, http://www.china.org.cn/opinion/2015-04/15/content_35325730.htm, accessed online 6 August 2019.

50. Yan Xuetong (2014), "From Keeping a Low Profile to Striving for Achievement", *The Chinese Journal of International Politics*, Vol. 7, No. 2, pp. 153-184.
51. Gudrum Wacker (2015), "The Irreversible Rise. A New Foreign Policy for a Stronger China", in Alessia Amighini and Axel Berkofsky (eds.) *Xi's Policy Gambles: The Bumpy Road Ahead*, Milano: ISPI, p. 66.
52. Yan Xuetong (2014), "From Keeping a Low Profile", n. 50, p. 167.
53. Ibid.
54. Xi Jinping (2017), "Secure a Decisive Victory in Building a Moderately Prosperous Society", n. 46, p. 22.
55. Yang Jiechi (2013), "Implementing the Chinese Dream", *The National Interest*, 10 September 2013, http://nationalinterest.org/commentary/implementing-the-chinese-dream-9026?page=2, accessed online 15 July 2019.
56. Ibid.
57. Yan Xuetong (2014), "From Keeping a Low Profile", n. 50, p. 184.
58. *Amazing China*, a film released on March 2, 2018 by China's state broadcaster CCTV, to highlight China's achievements over the past five years, and now the all-time top grossing documentary in the country. The 90-minute documentary is part of a sweeping propaganda blitz that elevates the ruling Communist Party's successes and Xi's role in driving progress. For details, see Tianyu M. Fang (2018), "'Amazing China,' A Documentary Extolling Xi Jinping, Is The Movie That Officials Want People To Love", *SupChina*, 16 March 2018, https://supchina.com/2018/03/16/amazing-china-a-documentary-extolling-xi-jinping/, accessed online 08 August 2019.
59. Quoted in Defence Intelligence Agency (2019), "China Military Power: Modernizing a Force to Fight and Win", https://www.dia.mil/Portals/27/Documents/ News/ Military%20Power%20Publications/China_Military_Power_FINAL_5MB_20190103.pdf accessed online 05 December 2019, p. 13.
60. Xi Jinping (2017), "Secure a Decisive Victory in Building a Moderately Prosperous Society", n. 46.
61. "Xi eyes more enabling int'l environment for China's peaceful development (2)", *Xinhua*, 30 November 2014, http://en.people.cn/n/2014/1130/c90883-8815967-2.html, accessed online 3 August 2019.
62. Michael D. Swaine and Ashley Tellis (2000), *Interpreting China's Grand Strategy: Past, Present and Future*, Santa Monica, CA: RAND Corporation, p. 112.
63. Ibid.
64. Ashley Tellis (2010), "Session 1: First Paper" in Maj Gen PJS Sandhu (ed.) *China's Quest for Global Dominance: Reality or Myth*, New Delhi: Vij Books India, p. 25.
65. Yan Xuetong (2011), *Ancient Chinese Thought, Modern Chinese Power*, Princeton: Princeton University Press, p. 101.
66. Sean Golden (2011), "China's Perception of Risk and the Concept of Comprehensive National Power", *The Copenhagen Journal of Asian Studies*, Vol. 29, No. 2, p. 98.
67. Ibid., pp. 96-97.
68. David M. Finkelstein (1999), "China's National Military Strategy", n. 8, p. 101.
69. Ibid.
70. Ibid.
71. Andrew Scobell et al. (2020), *China's Grand Strategy*, n. 26, p. 14.

72. Timothy R. Heath (2016), "An Overview of China's National Military Strategy", n. 6, p. 12.
73. Timothy R. Heath et al. (2016), *The PLA and China's Rejuvenation: National Security and Military Strategies, Deterrence Concepts and Combat Capabilities*, Santa Monica, CA: RAND Corporation, p. viii, https://www.rand.org/content/dam/rand/pubs/research_reports/RR1400/RR1402/RAND_RR1402.pdf, accessed online 20 October 2019.
74. See Peng Guangqian (1998), "Deng Xiaoping's Strategic Thought", in Michael Pillsbury (ed.) *Chinese Views of Future Warfare*, New Delhi: Lancer Publishers, p. 7.
75. Ibid.
76. Ibid.
77. Ibid.
78. Timothy R. Heath (2016), "An Overview of China's National Military Strategy", n. 6, pp. 12-13.
79. Ibid., p. 13.
80. You Ji (2016), "China's National Security Commission: theory, evolution and operations", *Journal of Contemporary China*, Vol. 25, No. 98, p. 179.
81. Ibid.
82. Ibid., p. 180.
83. Ibid.
84. Ibid.
85. Ibid.
86. Xi Jinping (2017), "Secure a Decisive Victory in Building a Moderately Prosperous Society", n. 46, p. 44.
87. Wang Jisi (2011), "China's Search for a Grand Strategy", n. 21, p. 69.
88. Ibid.
89. Ibid.
90. Editorial Department of *Renmin Ribao* (People's Daily): Chairman Mao's Theory of the Differentiation of the Three Worlds is a Major Contribution to Marxism-Leninism", https://www.marxists.org/history/erol/ncm-5/theory-3-worlds/section1. htm, accessed online 6 August 2019.
91. Samuel S. Kim (1984), "China and the Third World: In Search of a Neorealist World Policy", in S. S. Kim (ed.), *China and the World: Chinese Foreign Policy in the Post Mao Era*, Boulder: Westview Press, p. 183.
92. Ibid.
93. Wang Jisi (2011), "China's Search for a Grand Strategy", n. 21, p. 70.
94. Ibid.
95. Ibid.
96. Feng Zhang (2012), "Rethinking China's grand strategy: Beijing's evolving national interests and strategic ideas in the reform era", *International Politics*, Vol. 19, Issue 3, p. 322.
97. See, Ministry of Foreign Affairs of the People's Republic of China (2002), "China's Position Paper on the New Security Concept", 31 July 2002, https://www.fmprc.gov.cn/ce/ceun/eng/xw/t27742.htm, accessed online 6 August 2019.
98. Quoted in Carlyle A. Thayer (2003), "China's 'New Security Concept' and Southeast Asia" in David W. Lovell (ed.) *Asia-Pacific Security: Policy Challenge*, Singapore: Asia Pacific Press, p. 89.
99. Information Office of the State Council of the People's Republic of China (1998),

"China's National Defense", July 1998, http://www.china.org.cn/e-white/5/index.htm, accessed online 6 August 2019.

100. Ibid.
101. David M. Finkelstein (2003), "China's "New Concept of Security"", in Stephen Flanagan and Michael Marti (eds.) *People's Liberation Army and China in Transition*, Washington, DC: Institute for National Strategic Studies, pp. 199-201.
102. Ibid., p. 202.
103. It is important to note that the first attempt to establish an NSC was made by President Jiang Zemin in 1997. The idea was said to have been inspired by the National Security Council of the USA. However, Jiang's idea was rejected by other PBSC senior members, resulting in a compromise with the founding of the National Security Leading Small Group (NSLSG) to coordinate national security affairs in 2000. NSLSG remains a supplementary coordination body that is mostly responsible for responding to irregular major crises.
104. Shichen Wang (2017), "Xi Jinping's Centralisation of Chinese Foreign Policy Decision-Making Power", *East Asian Policy*, Vol. 9, No. 2, p. 40.
105. Zhao Keijin (2015), "China's National Security Commission", Carnegie-Tsinghua Centre for Global Policy, 14 July 2015, https://carnegietsinghua.org/2015/07/09/china-s-national-security-commission/id7i, accessed online 8 August 2019.
106. Ibid.
107. In the United States, the National Security Council serves as the President's personal advisory body. It is formally chaired by the President and used to coordinate policy among various government agencies and departments.
108. Zhao Keijin (2015), "China's National Security Commission", n. 105.
109. In 2003, the Communist Party's Central Committee and the Central Military Commission (CMC) put forward the concept of the "Three Warfares" for the PLA as it revised the "*Political Work Guidelines of the People's Liberation Army*".
110. Mark Stokes and Russell Hsiao (2013), "The People's Liberation Army General Political Department: Political Warfare with Chinese Characteristics", Project 20149 Institute, 14 October 2013, p. 3, https://project2049.net/wp-content/uploads/ 2018/04/P2049_Stokes_Hsiao_PLA_General_Political_Department_Liaison_101413.pdf, accessed online 23 September 2019.
111. Doug Livermore (2018), "China's "Three Wars" in Theory and in the Practice in South China Sea", Georgetown Security Studies Review, 25 March 2018, https://georgetownsecuritystudiesreview.org/2018/03/25/chinas-three-warfares-in-theory-and-practice-in-the-south-china-sea/, accessed online 19 September 2019.
112. Tom Phillips (2016), "'Love the party, protect the party': How Xi Jinping is bringing China's media to heel", *The Guardian*, 28 February 2016, https://www.theguardian.com/world/2016/feb/28/absolute-loyalty-how-xi-jinping-is-bringing-chinas-media-to-heel, accessed online 19 September 2019.
113. Doug Livermore (2018), "China's "Three Wars" in Theory", n. 111.
114. Dean Cheng (2013), "Winning Without Fighting: The Chinese Psychological Warfare Challenge", The Heritage Foundation, 12 July 2013, https://www.heritage.org/global-politics/report/winning-without-fighting-the-chinese-psychological-warfare-challenge, accessed online 20 September 2019.
115. Doug Livermore (2018), "China's "Three Wars" in Theory", n. 111.
116. Elsa Kania (2016), "The PLA's Latest Strategic Thinking on the Three Warfares", China

Brief, Vol. 16, Issue 13, 22 August 2016, https://jamestown.org/program/the-plas-latest-strategic-thinking-on-the-three-warfares/, accessed online 25 September 2019.

117. Mark Stokes and Russell Hsiao, "The People's Liberation Army General Political Department", n. 110.
118. Ibid.
119. "China adopts national security strategy guideline", China.org.cn, 23 January 2015, http://www.china.org.cn/china/2015-01/23/content_34640926.htm, accessed online 15 July 2019.
120. Ibid.
121. The first national security law took effect in 1993 and primarily regulated the work of national security agencies whose major duty is counterespionage.
122. "Xinhua Insight: China adopts new law on national security", *Xinhua*, 1 July 2015, http://en.people.cn/n/2015/0701/c90000-8914113.html, accessed online 6 August 2019.
123. "National Security Law", China Law Translate, 1 July 2015, https://www.chinalaw translate.com/en/2015nsl/, accessed online 17 September 2019.
124. Tasha Wibawa, "China's national security and the 'three warfares': How Beijing decides who or what to target", ABC News, 26 February 2019, https://www.abc.net. au/ news/2019-02-26/chinas-three-warfares-how-does-beijing-decide-who-or-what-to / 10825448, accessed online 19 September 2019.
125. "China issues white paper on national defence in new era", *Xinhuanet*, 24 July 2019, http://www.xinhuanet.com/english/2019-07/24/c_138253180.htm, accessed online 19 September 2019.
126. "On Correcting Mistaken Ideas in the Party", Selected Works of Mao Zedong, December 1929, https://www.marxists.org/reference/archive/mao/selected-works/ volume-1/mswv1_5.htm, accessed online 19 September 2019.
127. The rhetoric of core interests first appeared in Chinese diplomatic discourse as an expression and response to China's concerns over Taiwan's growing independence movement. In 2007, the concept became more formalised, becoming part of the official language of Chinese foreign affairs documents and activities.
128. Hoo Tiang Boon (2017), "Hardening the Hard, Softening the Soft: Assertiveness and China's Regional Strategy", *Journal of Strategic Studies*, Vol. 40, No. 5, p. 647.
129. Ibid.
130. Jinghao Zhou (2019), "China's Core Interests and Dilemma in Foreign Policy Practice", *Pacific Focus*, Vol. XXXIV, No. 1, p. 33.
131. The State Council of the People's Republic of China (2011), "China's Peaceful Development", September 2011, http://english.www.gov.cn/archive/white_paper/2014/09/09/content_281474986284646.htm, accessed online 03 August 2019.
132. Timothy M. Bonds et al. (2017), *What Role Can Land-Based, Multi-Domain Anti-Access/ Area Denial Forces Play in Deterring or Defeating Aggression?*, Santa Monica, CA: RAND Corporation, p. 16, https://www.rand.org/content/dam/rand/ pubs/research_reports/RR1800/RR1820/RAND_RR1820.pdf, accessed online 20 June 2019.
133. Jinghao Zhou (2019), "China's Core Interests and Dilemma", n. 130, p. 34.
134. Ibid.
135. Timothy R. Heath et al. (2016), *The PLA and China's Rejuvenation*, n. 73, pp. 14-15.
136. Ministry of National Defense of the People's Republic of China (2013), "The Diversified Employment of China's Armed Forces", April 2013, http://eng.mod. gov.cn/ Database/WhitePapers/2012.htm, accessed online 15 July 2019.

137. The State Council of the People's Republic of China (2015), "China's Military Strategy", n. 3.
138. Timothy R. Heath et al. (2016), *The PLA and China's Rejuvenation*, n. 73, p. 15.
139. The 18th National Congress of the Communist Party of China (CPC) (2012), "Report of Hu Jintao to the 18th CPC National Congress", 8 November 2012, http://www.china.org.cn/china/18th_cpc_congress/2012-11/16/content_27137540.htm, accessed online 3 August 2019.
140. Mikko Huotari et al. (2017), "China's emergence as a global security actor: Strategies for Europe", Merics Papers on China, No. 4, July 2017, p. 23, https://www.merics.org/sites/default/files/2018-07/170705_MPOC_04_China%27s_Emergence_as_a_Global_ Security_Actor_web.pdf, accessed online 15 July 2019.
141. Ibid.
142. Ministry of Foreign Affairs of the People's Republic of China (2014), "The Central Conference on Work Relating to Foreign Affairs was held in Beijing", 29 November 2014, https://www.fmprc.gov.cn/mfa_eng/zxxx_662805/t1215680.shtml, accessed online 25 August 2019.
143. Xi Jinping (2017), "Secure a Decisive Victory in Building a Moderately Prosperous Society", n. 46, p. 21.
144. Ibid., p. 54.
145. Hoo Tiang Boon (2017), "Hardening the Hard, Softening the Soft," n. 128, p. 646.
146. Ibid.
147. "Xi vows no surrender on 'legitimate rights, core interests'", *China Daily*, 30 January 2013, http://www.chinadaily.com.cn/china/2013-01/30/content_16185761.htm, accessed online 15 August 2019.
148. The 18th National Congress of the Communist Party of China (CPC) (2012), "Report of Hu Jintao", n. 139.
149. "Full text of Chinese state councillor's article on Xi Jinping's Diplomacy Thought", *Xinhuanet*, 19 July 2017, http://www.xinhuanet.com/english/2017-07/19/c_136456009.htm, accessed online 20 August 2019.
150. Ibid.
151. Qin Yaqing (2014), "Continuity through Change: Background Knowledge and China's International Strategy", *The Chinese Journal of International Politics*, Vol. 7, No. 3, p. 310.
152. Ibid.
153. Hoo Tiang Boon (2017), "Hardening the Hard, Softening the Soft", n. 128, p. 641.
154. Ibid.
155. Andrew Scobell et al. (2020), *China's Grand Strategy*, n. 26, p. 12.
156. See, Ministry of National Defence of the People's Republic of China, "White Papers", http://eng.mod.gov.cn/Database/WhitePapers/, accessed online 20 August 2019.
157. Oriana Skylar Mastro (2019), "China's Military Modernization Program: Trends and Implications", *American Enterprise Institute*, 04 September 2019, p. 9, https://www.uscc.gov/sites/default/files/Panel%20II%20Mastro_Written%20Testimony.pdf, accessed online 20 October 2019.
158. Ibid.
159. Ibid.
160. Joel Wuthnow (2020), "System Overload: Can China's Military Be Distracted in a War over Taiwan?", in Philip C. Saunders (ed.) *China Strategic Perspectives*, No. 15, Washington, D.C.: National Defence University Press, p. 9.
161. "Full Text: China's National Defence in the New Era", *Xinhuanet*, n. 5.

162. Ibid.
163. Cortez A. Cooper III (2018), *PLA Military Modernization: Drivers, Force Restructuring, and Implications*, Santa Monica, CA: RAND Corporation, p. 5, https://www.rand. org/content/dam/rand/pubs/testimonies/CT400/CT488/RAND_CT488.pdf, accessed online 20 May 2019.
164. Kristi Raik et al. (2018), "The Security Strategies of the US, China, Russia and the EU: Living in Different Worlds", FIIA Report 56, 15 June 2018, pp. 28-29, https://www.fiia.fi/wp-content/uploads/2018/06/fiia_report56_web_security-strategies.pdf, accessed online 2 December 2019.
165. Ibid.
166. Mikko Huotari et al. (2017), "China's emergence as a global security actor", n. 140, p. 27.
167. Ibid.
168. Sun Jianguo (2015), "Upholding the Chinese Approach to National Security", China Institute of International Studies, 11 June 2015, http://www.ciis.org.cn/english/2015-06/11/content_7983173.htm, accessed online 20 July 2019.
169. Ibid.
170. "China to follow specific national security strategy", China.org.cn, 17 April 2014, http://www.china.org.cn/opinion/2014-04/17/content_32121236.htm, accessed online 28 July 2019.
171. Michael D. Swaine and Ashley Tellis (2000), *Interpreting China's Grand Strategy: Past, Present and Future*, Santa Monica, CA: RAND Corporation, p. 9, https://www.rand.org/pubs/monograph_reports/MR1121.html, accessed online 20 June 2019.
172. Ibid.
173. Ibid. p. 17.
174. Ibid.
175. Ibid.
176. Ibid., p. 18.
177. Ibid.
178. "Hu Jintao urges army to perform "historic mission"", *People's Daily Online*, 14 March 2005, http://en.people.cn/200503/14/eng20050314_176695.html, accessed online 19 August 2019.
179. James Mulvenon (2009), "Chairman Hu and the PLA's "New Historic Missions", *China Leadership Monitor*, No. 27, p. 2, https://media.hoover.org/sites/default/files/documents/CLM27JM.pdf, accessed online 20 August 2019.
180. The 18th National Congress of the Communist Party of China (CPC) (2012), "Report of Hu Jintao to the 18th CPC National Congress", n. 139.
181. Quoted in Dr. Eric C. Anderson and Mr. Jeffrey G. Engstrom (2009), "Capabilities of the Chinese People's Liberation Army to Carry Out Military Action in the Event of a Regional Military Conflict", Science Applications International Corporation, March 2009, p. 11, https://www.uscc.gov/sites/default/files/Research/CapabilitiesoftheChinesePeople'sLiberationArmytoCarryOutMilitaryActionintheEventofaRegionalConflict.pdf, accessed online 20 October 2019.

2

De-coding *Jiji Fangyu*

"Active defence is also known as offensive defence, or defence through decisive engagements. [...] the only real defence is active defence [...]".

—Mao Zedong (1936)[1]

"China implements a military strategy of active defence. Strategically, it adheres to the principle of featuring defensive operations, self-defence and striking and getting the better of the enemy only after the enemy has started an attack".

—China's Defence White Paper (2008)[2]

The idea of 'winning victory by stratagem' has been central to traditional Chinese strategic thinking. This is concentrated on making use of limited force to achieve victory or realise the aim of the war. For instance, one of the key proposition's by Sun Tzu in *The Art of War*, is attributed to 'when to engage in a confrontation and when not to'. In view of which, one of the "five essentials for victory"[3] underpins the requisite, "[he] will win who knows when to fight and when not to fight".[4] Thereby, in attacking the enemy, Sun Tzu recommends that one should adopt a defensive position while waiting for an opportune moment to attack. Here, the logic is:

> "The good fighters of old first put themselves beyond the possibility of defeat, and then waited for an opportunity of defeating the enemy. [...] Security against defeat implies defensive tactics; ability to defeat the enemy means taking the offensive".[5]

In applying Sun Tzu's maxim to the current Chinese military context, it becomes imperative to understand the defensive and offensive element attached to China's military strategy. What makes it even more important is the fact that in the case of China, there is no publicly available single document for guiding PLA's military operations as that of the United States' comprehensive 'national military strategy' document. However, it was with the 2015 White Paper that the PRC released for the first time an official document on 'China's Military Strategy', which pledged "active defence" as the essence of 'CPC's military strategic thought'. For the first time, the PRC also officially narrowed in specifically on strategy by exemplifying the concept of 'active defence' in China's military thinking. In a nutshell, the 2020 U.S. Department of Defense (DoD) annual report categorically states:

> "China's military strategy is based on active defence, a concept that adopts the principles of strategic defence in combination with offensive action at the operational and tactical levels. Active defence is neither a purely defensive strategy nor limited to territorial defence. Active defence encompasses offensive and pre-emptive aspects".[6]

In the past, China issued eight Defence White Papers titled "China's National Defense" in 1998, 2000, 2002, 2004, 2006, 2008, 2010 and 2012, that mainly offered broader facts and figures of the country's military and scantily provided official insights into, and explanations of what, can be anticipated or expected to comprise China's military strategy; however, on the whole, the white papers failed to provide any concrete understanding of China's national military strategy under which the PLA operates. While there is no official Chinese document to clarify Beijing's military thinking; however, some clues can be drawn from the term "active defence" which has often been a point of reference in the PRC's military thinking since 1949. Here, the caveat lies in the existing ambiguity over the understanding of whether 'active defence' is China's military strategy or is it a military doctrine. This then makes it worth examining whether "active defence" is a constant aspect or has China moved beyond "active defence" in its strategic military thinking.

In this perspective, given the absence of an official Chinese document, the need lies in inferring China's military thinking from a combination of several documents and guidelines at different command levels of the armed forces, united into a hierarchical system that the Chinese refer to as "The Science of Military Strategy".[7] At the top of this hierarchy is the

"Military Strategic Guidelines" that provide direction on the current and future development of the PLA. Here, the crux lies in understanding two key aspects: First, what is the Chinese understanding of a military strategy? Second, what comprises China's national military strategy? These questions make critical points of enquiry for evaluating the Chinese armed forces- specifically, to assess the intentions and actions of the PLA.

In this context, the chapter studies the concept of 'active defence' and the way it applies to China's military strategy. It aims to examine two key perspectives: First, to identify and explain the key Chinese constructs and their components that comprise the equivalent of Chinese military strategy. And second, to analyse the key features that constitute China's military strategy based on the assessment of its evolution and the main drivers associated with it.

National Military Strategy: A Chinese Perspective

As noted in Chapter 1, within the larger umbrella of 'strategy', military strategy forms the military component of the overarching national security strategy. More specifically, National Military Strategy (NMS) comprises the set of ideas that a military organisation holds for fighting future wars, making the military strategy a part of, but not the same as, a state's grand strategy.[8] Broadly, NMS is described as a high-level military doctrine, a state's military strategy that explains or outlines how its armed forces will be employed to achieve military objectives that advance the state's political goals.[9] It is the 'strategy' that connects 'means with ends' by describing which forces (means) are necessary and the manner or way in which they will be used, shaping all aspects of force development.[10] Commonly, at the basic level, NMS of any country is characterised by six key features, as noted in Table 2.1.

Table 2.1: Key Features of National Military Strategy

Represent authoritative guidance that set the azimuth for actual planning or action.
Provide direction on how the military element of national power should support larger national objectives and, in varying degrees of detail, how it will do so.
Articulated in broad directives and large concepts.
Serve as planning guidelines across a spectrum of near-term, mid-term, or long-term horizons.
Address the issues of ends, ways, and means.
Informed by analytic assessments of threat perceptions or likely contingencies, capabilities-based assessments, larger-order strategic assessments, or domestic factors driving or constraining the strategy.

Source: Annotated by the Author with reference to Finkelstein (2007).[13]

Furthermore, in applying the equation of "ends + ways + means" to the NMS, the equation is rewritten to reflect the national level of military strategy wherein, *National Military Strategy = National Military Objectives (NMOs) + National Military Strategic Concepts (NMSCs) + National Military Resources (NMRs).*[11] As per the equation, the NMOs will be derived from the NSS; the NMSCs will articulate the courses of action that will be undertaken to achieve the ends, and the NMRs will entail the types of capabilities that will be required to be on hand or be developed to enable the NMSCs, as explained in Figure 2.1.[12]

Figure 2.1: The Elements in the Making of National Military Strategy

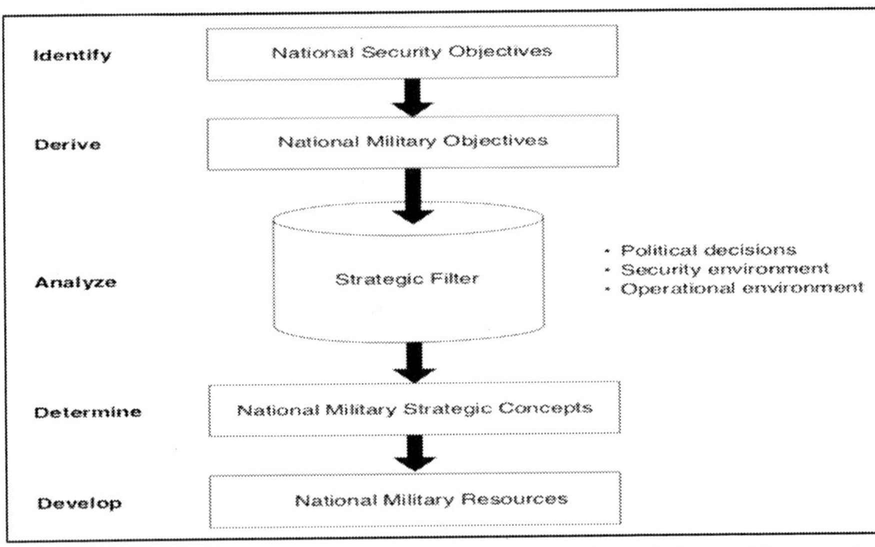

Note: The "strategic filter" identifies the imperatives of conflict and the possible constraints planners may have to consider. At minimum, the strategic filter: (1) considers political decisions handed down to military planners or brokered between military and civilian leaders; (2) assesses the current and projected security environments (conflict with whom? when?); and (3) performs an analysis of the operational environment (what kinds of conflicts?).

Source: Adapted from Finkelstein (1999).[14]

Owing to this understanding, as Lykke notes, military strategies will be either operational or force-development based.[15] Wherein, the former is capability-based and will be driven by near-term contingencies (making the ways driven by means; and in the latter, an assessment of future threats will dictate the development of resources (probably not available at the moment) to enable strategic concepts of a very different nature than currently employed.[16]

What calls for attention is that in the case of China, the terms 'strategy' (*zhanlue*; 战略) and 'military strategy' (*junshi zhanlue*; 军事战略) are used interchangeably. Rather it is noted that writers will only use 'strategy' when they mean "military strategy".[17] This highlights the fact that the Chinese usage of strategy is primarily denominated with a military aspect – with strategy seen as an abbreviation of military strategy. This makes it imperative to clarify two aspects: First, what is the Chinese understanding of strategy/military strategy? Second, what are the key components that define China's military strategy? These queries bring into perspective the ambiguity in Chinese perception.

To fill the void, clarity over the Chinese understanding of the concept of 'strategy/military strategy' can be drawn from books that provide 'authoritative statements' on 'strategy/military strategy' representing the PLA's approach and China's military strategy at different points in time. Some of the key texts are listed below (Table 2.2).

Table 2.2: Key Authoritative Texts on Chinese Military

Year	*Name of the Text*	*Publisher*	*Key Theme*
1987	Science of Military Strategy (*Zhanluexue*; 战略学)	AMS	Endorsed Deng Xiaoping's shift from preparing for total war to preparing for local war.
1999	Science of Military Strategy (*Zhanluexue*; 战略学)	NDU, PLA	Highlighted the shift to preparing for Local Wars Under Modern High Tech Conditions.
2001	Science of Military Strategy (*Zhanluexue*; 战略学)	AMS	Discusses the Chinese strategy of Local Wars Under Modern High Tech Conditions
2002	Study Guide for Strategic Theory (*Zhanlue Lilun Xuexi Zhinan*; 战略理论学指南)	NDU, PLA	Provides clarification on several aspects of China's current strategic thinking pertaining to definition of strategy, the role of active defence and the operational arts.
2013	Science of Military Strategy (*Zhanluexue*; 战略学)	AMS	Adapts to the changed conditions of the world and focuses on "learning" to "learn" and strives to adapt to China's strategic situation.

Source: Annotated by the Author from various Chinese and western sources.

These texts act as baseline reflections of the PLA's understanding of military strategy as an organisation and also illustrate the dominant approaches that shape China's military thinking. In drawing from one of the primary authoritative texts, the 1999 book on *Science of Military Strategy* by the NDU,[18] strategy is defined as:

> "planning and guidance for the overall situation of military struggle, including planning, deploying and guiding the construction and use of military force, to reach the effective achievement of a stated political goal".[19]

While in the PLA's *Military Encyclopaedia*, strategy is viewed as:

> "the analytical judgment of such factors as international conditions, hostilities in bilateral politics, military economics, science and technology, and geography as they apply to the preparation and direction of the overall military/war plan. It is advantageous: to study the occurrences and developments in war forecasting/ predictions; to formulate strategic policy, strategic principles, and strategic plans; to make warfare preparations; and to put into place directives on the actual principles and methods of warfare".[20]

Similarly, the 2011 edition of the PLA's glossary of military terms defines strategy as "the principles and tactics for planning and guiding the overall situation of war", that includes both offensive and defensive strategies.[21] While the term "military strategy" is defined as a "set of *fangzhen* and stratagems that guides the comprehensive war effort".[22]

Table 2.3: Chinese Definitions of Strategy/Military Strategy

Strategy is the highest division in military academia; it studies methods of leading and engaging in warfare for the entire armed struggle (the 1956 *Standardization of Military Terms*).
Strategy is the planning and guidance of warfare (1972 *Chinese People's Liberation Army Military Terminology*, 1985 *Course on the Science of Strategy*).
Strategy is the general plan for guiding the overall war situation (1987 Military Science Academy's *Science of Strategy*).
Strategy is also called military strategy; it is the general plan for planning and guiding the overall war situation (1997 *Chinese People's Liberation Army Military Technology*).
Strategy is also called military strategy; it is the planning and guidance of the overall situation of military combat (1999 NDU's *Science of Strategy*).
Strategy is the planning and guidance of warfare and the general plan for the overall building and use of armed strengths (2005 *Chinese Military Encyclopedia*, second edition, general outline articles and volume on categories).
Military strategy is the planning and guidance of the building and use of armed strengths as well as the general plan for the overall situation of military combat. It is abbreviated as strategy (2007 *Chinese Military Encyclopedia*, second edition, volume on military strategy).
Strategy is: (1) An abbreviation for military strategy. The guidelines and plaoys for planning and guiding the overall war situation. It is divided into offensive strategy and defensive strategy. (2) It generally refers to guidelines and ploys for major issues that are comprehensive in nature, that are high-level, and that are long-term. Examples are national strategy, national security strategy, and economic development strategy (2011 *Chinese People's Liberation Army Military Technology*).

Source: Annotated by the Author with reference to *The Science of Military Strategy* (2013).[23]

The above definitions clarify that the Chinese practice of the use of 'strategy' and 'military strategy' interchangeably is driven from the fact that unlike the USA, China does not have separate terms for 'strategy', 'national security strategy', 'national defence strategy', and 'national military strategy'. This lack of a distinction highlights two aspects of Chinese thinking: First, the monolithic perception that is all-encompassing; and second, the element of ambiguity given the various Chinese interpretations of 'strategy/military strategy'. To argue so, as what is apparent from the above definitions, is that unlike the PLA writings (as noted above) that limits the understanding of strategy to mainly planning and guidance of conduct of war; the NDU's definition of strategy provides a broad perspective that includes threat assessments, overall strategic goals, the main strategic direction, basic principles for conducting military struggle as well as the main means, methods and coordination of military struggle.

Owing to the caveat of being 'ambiguous' as noted earlier, the NDU's definition of strategy holds greater significance for not limiting the understanding of strategy to that of war; but also highlighting the military struggle and thereby, clarifying that the objective of any military struggle is always a political goal and that military strategy ultimately serves such a goal - that is, the 'national interest'. This then clarifies the logic that the military strategy is an important component of a nation's overall strategy and must not be viewed as independent of it although it is part of, but distinct, from the state's 'grand strategy'. To substantiate, the 2013 *Science of Military Strategy* describes strategy as the "*fangzhen* and stratagems for planning and guiding the overall construction and employment of military power, centred on war" which "proceeds from international strategy and the general situation of national development," and thus "must be subservient to and serve the general situation of national development".[24]

These definitions validate Finkelstein's framework as noted in Figure 2.1, as military strategy in the Chinese perception is the guide for military modernisation and military activities in pursuit of larger national objectives (national security strategy). In this perspective, to say that China lacks a military strategy based on the absence of a single unified official document will be a myopic argument. In providing a "notional view" as the PRC has not published a detailed national military strategy, Finkelstein[25] in 1999 argued that the closest equivalent to China's national military strategy is to be found in the concept of what China calls its "strategic guideline" (*zhanlue fangzhen*; 战略方针), which after 1988, has been described as the "military strategic guidelines" (*junshi zhanlue fangzhen*; 军事战略方针). In congruence, Taylor Fravel has stated that the guidelines provide the closest analogue to the operational doctrine in Western strategic parlance, pertaining to the strategic level of war as opposed to the campaign or tactical levels,[26] making it an important politico-military document. Hence, this makes it imperative to understand the Chinese perspectives on the military strategic guidelines – to assess whether it qualifies to be considered as the equivalent to China's national military strategy.

Junshi Zhanlue Fangzhen in China's Military Strategy

China's military preparedness is nested within the concept of "military strategic guidelines", which the Chinese interpret as '*junshi zhanlue fangzhen*'. David Finkelstein argues that China does in fact have the equivalent of a national military strategy, the elements of which are contained in the "military strategic guidelines" issued to the PLA;[27] while Taylor Fravel calls the 'guidelines', the "basis for China's national military strategy".[28]

Since 1949, the guidelines have been issued and periodically revised to provide authoritative guidance from the Central Military Commission of the CPC to the PLA on all aspects of combat-related activities. Specifically, it provides guidance on the overall direction for PLA's modernisation and is translated into specific objectives in areas such as weapons acquisition, operational planning, force structure, and training.[29] Here, the essence lies in understanding the concept, the components and the shifts in China's military strategic guidelines.

I. The Concept & Its Components

In PRC, the "military strategic guidelines"[30] act as the cornerstone in defining China's military strategy. It denotes the highest level of national guidance and direction to the armed forces of China.[31] As Chinese Marshal Peng Dehuai in 1957 stated: "The strategic guideline relates to the fundamental nature of army building, troop training, and war preparations".[32] Besides, Deng Xiaoping in 1977 stated, "Without a clear strategic guideline, many matters cannot be handled well".[33]

In the Chinese perception, as the PLA's glossary of military terms defines, the military strategic guideline is the "core and collected embodiment of military strategy"; and in particular, it contains "the program and principles for planning and guiding the overall situation of war in a given period".[34] As explained by the Army Building Research Department of the PLA's NDU:

> "The military strategic guidelines are the fundamental military policies (*junshi zhengce*) of the party and the nation. They are the overall principles (*zong yuanze*) and guiding principles (*zong gangling*) for planning and guiding the development and utilization of the armed forces".[35]

Similarly, in the 1999 *Science of Military Strategy*, published by the NDU, the guidelines are defined as the "general principles and general programs for guiding the overall situation of military struggle" that stipulate how to complete a strategic mission and realise the strategic goal by identifying the key points of struggle, the main strategic directions and related strategic deployments, making it the "principal part and heart of [China's] strategy".[36] In this regard, the scope of the guidelines includes both general principles about the whole process of military operations and specific principles for certain types of operations, providing an outline of 'how China plans to wage its next war'.[37] This suggests that the military strategic guidelines issued to the PLA, and the detailed plans and programs that are subsequently developed to implement them, constitute China's national military strategy. More precisely, as there is no closest equivalent to "doctrine" in Chinese, the "military strategic guidelines" serve as the closest equivalent to the Western "basic doctrine".[38]

The underlying principle of China's "military strategic guidelines" is based on the "strategic thoughts" (*zhanlue sixiang*; 战略思想), which form the foundation for Chinese writings on strategy. They can be termed as both 'strategic thoughts and strategic concepts', that are mainly "the basic viewpoints for guiding and planning the overall situation of military struggle"- comprising of foundational principles and concepts of war-fighting and military struggle; but not any specific guidelines or rules for conducting military operations.[39] For instance, some of the strategic thoughts that have been dominant in shaping China's military thinking are witnessed in Mao Zedong's ideas such as active defence (*jiji fangyu*; 积极防); people's war (*renmin zhanzheng*; 人民战争), protracted war (*chijiuzhan*; 持久战), guerrilla warfare (*youji zhanzheng*; 游击战争), and others.

In this regard, in outlining the military strategic guidelines for any particular period, the "strategic thoughts" are instrumental in providing guidance, in terms of:[40] First, the ideological and political basis for the military strategic guidelines; second, assessment of the international environment and its impact on China's security; third, China's overall national security objectives, its domestic objectives, and the relationship of military objectives to other national objectives; fourth, the most likely type of conflict for which the PLA must prepare (either a capabilities-based assessment, a contingency-based assessment, or both); and fifth, broad guidance to the PLA on how it will prepare, reform, or adjust to meet the challenges of the new situation. For instance, under Mao Zedong the "strategic thought" was guided by 'war and revolution' which, under Deng Xiaoping, underwent a fundamental shift to entail 'peace and development'. Here, the essence lies in understanding the key components of China's military strategic guidelines.

China's strategic military guidelines are promulgated based on certain key "strategic issues" (*zhanlue wenti*), or questions. However, the bottom line is grounded on two fundamental questions: "What kinds of conflicts must the PLA be prepared to fight?" and "How should the PLA modernisation and reform programs adjust to comport with the new operational imperatives?"[41] In view of this, Finkelstein identifies six key "strategic issues/concerns" that are contained in China's military strategic guidelines, which are:[42] First, the strategic assessment (*zhanlue panduan*), which comprises both a political assessment and a military assessment based on perceived: (a) changes in the international order; (b) changes in the security environment and China's security situation; (c) changes in China's domestic situation; and (d) changes in the nature of warfare itself.[43] Second, adjustment of the content (*nei rong*) of the "active defence strategy", to establish a set of broad strategic concepts and principles, and a set of very general operational concepts, for prosecuting war at the strategic level of conflict.[44] Third, articulation of strategic missions (*zhanlue renwu*) and strategic objectives (*zhanlue mubiao*) of the armed forces, which are set down in the broadest of terms, and are derived from the "strategic assessment" as well as the PRC's larger security objectives.[45]

Fourth, guidance for military combat preparations (*junshi douzheng zhunbei*), refers to the type of warfare the PLA must be prepared to fight; and therefore also constitutes an official assessment of the next *type of war* the PLA must be prepared to fight. To cite an example, such as directing the PLA to prepare to fight: (a) total war versus limited or local war; (b) local wars "under normal conditions" versus "local wars under modern high-tech conditions"; or (c) conventional warfare versus nuclear warfare, and others.[46] Fifth, identification of the 'main strategic directions' (*zhuyao zhanlue fangxiang*), a contingency-based assessment that informs both war fighting (the actual prosecution of a war in progress)[47] and war planning during peacetime.[48] Most PLA writings focus on its application as a war fighting concept.[49] And sixth, determination of the focus for army building (*jundui jianshe*), entails PLA's modernisation efforts in terms of: (a) development, procurement, acquisition, and fielding of new weapons systems, technologies, and combat capabilities; (b) institutional, structural, systemic, and personnel reforms; and (c) doctrinal adjustments, and others.[50]

On a similar understanding, Taylor Fravel has identified four key components, which entail:[51] First, identification of the "strategic opponent" (*zhanlue duishou*; 战略对手). This is based on an assessment of China's international environment and the perceived threats to China's national interests. The specific military threat posed by the strategic opponent then determines the operational target (作战对象). Second is the component of "primary strategic direction" *(zhuyao zhanlue fangxiang)*, which refers to the geographic focal point for a potential conflict and provides the basis for prioritising the allocation of resources and effort. This factor then decisively shapes the overall conflict as well as military deployments and war preparations. The third component is the core that entails the "basis of preparations for military struggle" (*junshi douzheng zhunbei de jidian*; 军事斗争准备的基点), which describes the characteristics of wars that China will need to fight in the future. This is usually based on an assessment of the "form of war" (*zhanzheng xingtai*; 战争形态) or the conduct of warfare at any point in time and the "form of operations" (*zuozhan xingtai*; 作战样式) that would outline how war will be waged. And, the fourth component is the basic guiding thought (*jiben zhidao sixiang*; 基本指导思想) for the use of military force to be applied for campaigns and operations, which refers to general operational principles for the PLA to use in future wars it might fight.

Taking into account both Finkelstein's and Fravel's framework, out of all the components listed, in terms of war planning during peacetime,' identification of the main/primary strategic direction' serves as a "worst-case scenario" planning tool for developing forces and capabilities, making force deployment decisions and making other preparations should conflict erupt. As Senior Colonel Ouyang Wei of China's NDU describes:

> "If [our] military strategy has determined the main strategic direction, it usually is necessary to deploy fairly strong military strengths strategically, striving to achieve superiority along this direction, to give the primary operational units a fairly small [that is, well-defined] area for operations, and to carry out relatively complete battlefield preparations and strategic prepositioning, in order to facilitate the completion of the corresponding missions [that is, tasks]".[52]

In addition to the 'main strategic directions', there are also secondary strategic directions (*ciyao zhanlue fangxiang*; 次要战略方向), where forces would have to prepare for less severe challenges. Dennis Blasko identifies them as "important strategic directions" [*zhongyao zhanlue fangxiang*; 重要战略方向] in the Northwest, Southwest, and Korean Peninsula.[53] To cite examples, during the Cold War, China continuously adjusted the main strategic direction several times depending on the specific regions that one anticipated as an American or Soviet invasion - as noted by Yuan Dejin and Guo Zhigang (Table 2.4) in their assessment of the development and adjustment of the main strategic directions under Mao Zedong (1949 to mid-1970s).

Table 2.4: Shifts in China's "Main Strategic Direction" (1949 to mid-1970s)

Dates	*Context*	*Main Threats*	*Main Strategic Direction*
1949-1950	Conclusion of Chinese Civil War	Kuomintang, the USA	Southeast Coast
1950-1953	Korean War	USA	Northeast
1953-early 1960s	Cold War	USA and Japan	Liaodong and Shandong peninsulas
Mid-to-late 1960s	Cold War	USA	East Coast
Late 1960s to mid-1970s	Sino-Soviet Split	Soviet Union	"Three Northerns" (Northeast, North, Northwest)

Source: Adapted from Wuthnow (2020).[54]

Owing to the component of 'strategic direction', it is noteworthy that in current times, China perceives that its national security is challenged from many directions and in many forms. As an article in the journal of the Central Party School notes:

> "Entering a new era, with the profound changes in the content of [our] national interests, various strategic directions may have security problems that infringe on national interests, which in turn cause serious harm and consequences to the overall development of the country. This makes any strategic direction likely to be the main strategic direction. Only by scientifically coordinating the use of military forces can we effectively respond to security threats in all directions and ensure the balance and stability of the overall strategy".[55]

Given this manifold perspective of 'security threat', the PLA is faced with the critical challenge of how to manage the multiple strategic directions.

The above components essentially highlight two key aspects: the nature of future warfare, and how to prepare for it – qualifying 'military strategic guidelines' as the Chinese variant of military doctrine. However, the "military strategic guidelines" can also be designated as the functional equivalent to China's national military strategy due to its components, that encompass: threat perceptions pertaining to both international and domestic security; the likely contingencies and 'type of future war'; capability and contingency-based assessments compounded with larger strategic assessments; and the ways to develop force structure, military education, training and others. Hence, as one or more of these components undergo changes, this calls for shifts in the military strategic guideline, which invariably implies a change to China's national military strategy.

II. Shifts in China's Military Strategic Guidelines (1949 onwards)

The changes in the components can bring about both major (dramatic departure from China's past strategy) and minor (an adjustment to the existing strategy) shifts to military strategic guidelines. Since 1949, the PRC has had nine unique military strategies or strategic guidelines (as noted in Table 2.5), wherein the PLA has pursued major changes in its military strategy in 1956, 1980 and 1993, while the others have constituted minor changes. As opposed to the minor changes, the major changes require a military to alter how it prepares to fight future wars; which necessitates changes in a military's operational doctrine, force structure, and training.

What calls for the shift in the PLA's military strategic guidelines? The change in the 'guidelines' as noted in Table 2.5 can be mainly attributed to two key factors: First, the perception of new threats to

Table 2.5: China's Military Strategic Guidelines Since 1949

		Guideline Components				*Indicators of Major Change*		
Year	*Name*	*Operational Target*	*Primary Direction*	*Basis of Preparation for Military Struggle*	*Main Form of Operations*	*Operational Doctrine*	*Force Structure*	*Training*
1956	"Defending the mother-land"	USA	Northeast	US amphibious assault	Positional defence and mobile offence	Drafting of operations regulations begins (1958)	Creation of new branches and combat arms; reduction of 3.5 m troops; formation of general staff system; creation of military regions	Draft training programme issued (1957)
1960	"Resist in the north, open in the south"	USA	Northeast	US amphibious assault	Positional defence and mobile offence (north of Xingshan Bay)	Operations regulations issued (1961)	—	—
1964	"Luring the enemy in deep"	USA	—	US amphibious assault	Mobile and guerrilla warfare	Drafting of operations regulations begins (1970)	Creation of Second Artillery; Expansion to 6.3 m troops	—
1977	"Active defence, luring the enemy in deep"	Soviet Union	North-central	Soviet armoured and airborne assault	Mobile and guerrilla warfare	Operations regulations issued (1979)	—	Training programme issued (1978)
1980	"Active defence"	Soviet Union	North-central	Soviet armoured and airborne assault	Positional warfare of fixed defence	Operations regulations drafted and issued (1982-87)	Transition from army corps to combined arms group armies; 3m troop reductions (1980, 1982, 1985)	Training programme issued (1980)

1988	"Dealing with local wars and military conflicts"	—	—	—	—	—	—	Training programme issued (1989)
1993	"Winning local wars under high-technology conditions"	Taiwan	Southeast	Warfare under high technology conditions	Joint operations	Operations regulations and campaign outlines drafted and issued (1995-99)	Shift to brigades; creation of GAD; 700,000 troop reductions (1997 and 2003)	Training programme issued (1995 and 2001)
2004	"Winning local wars under informationization conditions"	Taiwan (USA)	Southeast	Warfare under informationised conditions	Integrated joint operations	Drafting of operations regulations begins (2004)	Further shift to brigades	Training programme issued (2008)
2014	"Winning informationized local wars"	Taiwan (USA)	Southeast and maritime	Informationised warfare	Integrated joint operations	?	Reorganisation of command and management structures (2016); creation of Strategic Support Force; 300K troop reduction (2017)	Training programme issued (2018-19)

Source: Adapted from Fravel (2019).[56]

China's national security; and second, the perception that the form of war and thus the basis of preparations for military struggle has undergone an important shift. Owing to these two tenets, since 1949, there have been three major changes in China's military strategy as witnessed in 1956, 1980 and 1993, which are explained below. In contrast, to cite an example of a 'minor change', it is interesting to note that in 2014, the adjustment consisted of dropping only four characters from the 2004 guideline, changing from "winning local wars under the conditions of informatization" (打赢信息化条件下的局部战争) to "winning informationized local wars" (打赢信息化局部战争), which in the Chinese viewpoint indicates that "a qualitative change has occurred".[57]

In rationalising the doctrinal shift towards "winning informationized local wars", Yan Wenhua, a researcher from the AMS, argues:

> "The adjustment is necessary as long-range, precise, smart, stealthy and unmanned weapons and equipment are becoming increasingly sophisticated, and outer space and cyberspace have become new command posts".[58]

These changes in the Military Strategic Guidelines further impact the PLA's operational readiness. The linkage to which can be explained from the Figure 2.2.

Figure 2.2: Components of the PLA's Strategy and Doctrine

Source: Adapted from Kania (2016).[59]

The Three Major Shifts in China's Strategic Guidelines

1. 1956 Strategic Guideline of "Defending the Motherland"

In March 1956, on behalf of the CMC, Peng Dehuai introduced the new strategy in a report titled "On the Strategic Guideline for Defending the

Motherland and National Defence Building". The strategy focussed on the single contingency of a major war with the USA, mainly aimed at defending China against an American amphibious invasion in the northeast. Peng's report noted that this is "the strategic guideline that our military [the PLA] should adopt when the enemy in the future engages in a large-scale and direct attack of our country".[60] China's perception was driven by basis of preparations for military struggle against a surprise attack by the USA. To argue so, as Mao Zedong in his 'strategic assessment' posited that:

> "Internationally, conditions at present are favourable to our socialist construction. The socialist camp headed by the Soviet Union is strong and its ranks are united, while the imperialist camp is weak and beset by numerous insurmountable contradictions and crises. Even so, we should realize that we [PRC] are still surrounded by imperialist forces and must be prepared against all possible emergencies. If the imperialists should unleash a war in the future, very likely they would launch a surprise attack, as in World War II. Therefore, we must be prepared, mentally and materially, to avoid being caught unawares by such a sudden turn".[61]

The above statement by Mao highlights two key aspects: First, China did not perceive an imminent threat from the USA. Second, China's military planning was primarily driven by the assessment of the 'worst case scenario' based on the experiences from World War II and the Korean War. As a result of which, China was anticipating a surprise US amphibious invasion, most likely on the Shandong or Liaodong peninsulas. To avert this contingency, China's military strategy called for 'forward defence' of coastal areas during the first six months of a US invasion. In this regard, China's new guideline identified the USA as the "strategic opponent", and outlined that the PLA "should be able to offer a powerful counterattack and resist the enemy's invasion in areas with prepared defences".[62] As Peng Dehuai posited,

> "the basic content of our army's active defence strategic guideline" is to "stabilize the front, smash the enemy's plans for a rapid attack and victory, and compel the enemy to engage in protracted operations with our military so that we can gradually strip them of their strategic initiative and have it gradually transferred to our military, that is, transitioning from strategic defence to strategic offence".[63]

What makes the 1956 strategy significant and exemplifies a strategic shift in China's military thinking are two aspects: First, it spelt out that the core of China's military strategy lies in 'active defence' and, as noted, for the first time the strategic concept of 'active defence' was intertwined with the 'military strategic guidelines'. Second, taking a departure from guerrilla and mobile warfare, the new guideline emphasised on a new 'form of operations' for the PLA, namely, 'combining positional defensive warfare with mobile offensive warfare' for forward defence. The aspect of 'positional warfare'[64] marked a new thinking in the PLA's way of fighting, calling for the PLA's military preparedness to conduct combined arms operations.

To adapt to the new conditions, the reforms undertaken by the PLA were witnessed in three key aspects: First, operational regulations/ doctrine (第五代作战条令);[65] wherein in 1958, the AMS was founded to draft PLA's own military science, the operational doctrine. In May1961, China's CMC issued the first two sets of regulations: General Combat Regulations for a Combined Army (*hecheng jundui zhandou tiaoling gaize*) and Infantry Combat Regulations (*bubing zhandou tiaoling*).[66] Thereafter, in 1965, eighteen other combat regulations were issued by the services and branches for the air force, navy and the artillery; communications, chemical defence, engineering, and railway units. This marked the PLA's "first generation" of operational regulations, followed by second and third generations issued in the 1970s and 1980s, respectively.[67]

Second, the PLA's force structure underwent significant changes as the strategy called for creating a combined force (*hecheng jundui*), causing a shift from light infantry to a more balanced composition with emphasis on quality over quantity. The marked changes comprised of:[68] (a) From 1950 to 1958, personnel in the air force and navy grew from almost none to constitute 12.2 per cent and 5.8 per cent of the PLA, respectively. (b) Personnel in artillery and armoured units constituted 4.8 per cent and 2.3 per cent, respectively.[69] (c) Personnel in infantry units declined from 61.1 per cent to 42.3 per cent. (d) The size of the force was reduced to roughly 2.4 million between 1956 and 1958.

Third, to pursue combined arms operations, the PLA adjusted its approach to training. In 1957, the PLA's first training program was written, which was issued in draft form in January 1958. The purpose of the new program was for troops to "learn combat skills for modern conditions [to] deal with emergencies at any time" and stated that future training should "continue to raise modern military skills and learn combined arms operations under nuclear, chemical, missile and other complicated conditions".[70] To aid the process of training, the PLA established the Advanced Military Academy (*gaodeng junshi xueyuan*) in 1957,[71] and furthermore, to enhance the PLA's combat capabilities, China began conducting large-scale combined arms exercises on a yearly basis.[72]

2. 1980 Strategic Guideline of "Active Defence"

The strategic guideline adopted in September 1980, known as "active defence", marked the second major change in the PRC's military strategy. The guideline outlined a strategy to counter a Soviet invasion and prevent a strategic breakthrough. In this regard, according to the new guideline, the basis of preparations for military struggle was a 'surprise attack by the Soviet Union', wherein the primary strategic direction was China's northern border (also known as "three norths") that covers the area from Heilongjiang province in the east to Xinjiang in the west. This strategic assessment was driven by the 1969 border clash with the Soviet Union over Zhenbao (Damansky) Islands that raised the prospects of a major war with Moscow. Although a war did not unfold; however, the Chinese strongly perceived a Soviet military threat shaped by suspicion over Soviet intentions to invade China.[73]

In this scenario, the Chinese perceived a Soviet invasion to be characterised by rapid, deep strikes of tank columns with airborne operations in rear areas, to seek a swift and decisive victory. This assessment was based on the perceived shift in the conduct of warfare drawn from the observations of the 1973 Arab-Israeli War, in which clients of the USA and the Soviet Union employed advanced weapons in new ways. Despite the Soviet Union being a threat since 1960, the change in the guideline in 1980 was caused due to two key factors that entailed: First, the Chinese assessment of the kinds of operations that the Soviets would conduct in the background of the 1973 Arab-Israeli War. And second, Deng Xiaoping's consolidation of power as PRC's paramount leader in 1979.

Given these changes, in departing from the past tradition of 'luring the enemy in deep and strategic retreat', the 1980 strategy emphasised on 'forward defence' based on positional warfare supplemented by small-scale mobile warfare based on strategic defence. Wherein, as per the Chinese calculation, once the Soviet Union invaded, then China would respond in a three-stage manner: First, adopt forward defence on the northern border (potential invasion routes being Zhangjiakou or Jiayuguan) to prevent any strategic breakthrough and bide time for a nationwide mobilisation. Then follow up with the second strategy of combining the defence of strategic interior lines with offensive campaigns and operations on exterior lines to create a stalemate. And finally, once the invading force was sufficiently weakened, PLA would launch a strategic counterattack.

To adapt to the new conditions, the reforms undertaken by the PLA were witnessed in three key aspects:[74] First, operational regulations/doctrine, the 1980 strategy identified 'positional warfare', specifically, "positional warfare of fixed defence" (*jianshoufangyu de zhendizhan*) as the main form of operation; while downplaying mobile warfare at the strategic level, limiting it to small and medium sized offensive operations close to the defensive positions that the PLA would try to hold. This required the PLA to master the art of conducting combined arms operations. In this regard, in 1982, the PLA began to draft the "third generation" of combat regulations, which were finished in 1987. In addition, the drafting of the Science of Campaign Outlines, the PLA's first text on the operational level of war, restarted in 1980 and was published in 1987 with the first edition of the *Science of Military Strategy*.

Second, in terms of force structure, to make a nimble and effective force given that Deng Xiaoping in 1975 had called it "bloated", the 1980 guideline resulted in three major force reductions conducted in 1980, 1982 and 1986 that reduced the PLA from more than 6 million soldiers in 1979 to 3.2 million when completed in 1987. Furthermore, the 11 military regions were consolidated into seven military regions along with the transformation of 25 armies into 24 combined arms group armies composed of infantry, artillery, tank, rocket, and anti-aircraft artillery units. The force reduction and reorganisation aimed at improving the flexibility and overall effectiveness that would enable the PLA to conduct combined arms operations.

Third, in September 1980, the General Staff Department (GSD) issued a new training program with an emphasis on combined arms operations. In addition, the PRC renewed emphasis on military exercises; wherein in September 1981, the PLA held its largest campaign-level exercise in the Beijing Military Region dubbed as "802" meeting representing the PLA's largest exercise since 1949. It involved more than 110,000 troops from eight divisions and simulated defence against a Soviet armoured invasion to "implement the strategic guideline".[75]

3. 1993 Strategic Guideline of "Winning Local Wars under High-Technology Conditions"

On 13 January 1993, Jiang Zemin, Chairman of the CMC, put forward a new set of military strategic guidelines, officially called the "Military Strategic Guidelines for the New Period" (新时期国家军事战略方针), marking the third major change in China's military strategy since 1949. Introducing the new strategy, Jiang posited that the PLA "must place the basis of preparations for future military struggles on winning local wars that may occur under modern technology, especially under high-technology conditions", premised on the assessment that "as soon as a war breaks out, it is likely to be a high-technology confrontation".[76] As Jiang in his speech noted:

> "Since the beginning of the 1980s, the scope of high-tech competition throughout the globe has intensified by the day. Now, each country is readjusting their own development strategies, making the development of modern and especially high technology a crucial measure of strengthening their comprehensive national power and national defence strength, striving to take hold of the strategic initiative. [...] The facts of the Gulf War have shown that along with the utilization of high technology in the military arena [...]. In the present world, if a country does not work hard to strengthen its national defence power alongside its economic and social development, enhancing its military quality and the level of its weapons and equipment, its operational capabilities will not be strong under modern high-tech conditions. As soon as a war breaks out, it will be in a passive position and suffer attacks, with its national interest, the people's dignity, and its international prestige all suffering greatly. Because of this, many countries in the world are [...] readjusting their military strategy in order to adapt to the needs of developments to the international situation and the situation of military combat".[77]

This change in the Chinese perception was motivated by the 'Gulf War', as the then deputy director of AMS noted:

> "[it] marked a big step forward in both military theory and practice. For instance, strategy and the battles were closely interwoven, with the latter playing a major role, sometimes overlapping with strategy and tactics".[78]

Here, at the core, was the need to incorporate the use of new technologies in China's military preparedness. What called for this strategic shift in the Chinese perception? It is surprising to note that the change was administered despite the dominant perception that China's regional security environment was in "the best period" since 1949. As Jiang categorically stated:

> "The contemporary world is in a historic period of momentous change. Overall, the present international situation is beneficial to our country's development. First, for a relatively long time to come, it is probable that the international environment will be peaceful with new world wars being avoided. This is an extremely important strategic assessment [here quoting Deng]: "The increase in the forces for peace in the world is surpassing the increase in the forces for war." [...] Moreover, compared with other regions of the world, the Asia-Pacific region has maintained a relative degree of stability with economic contacts and cooperation between countries becoming closer by the day with many traditional hot spots either already resolved or in the process of realizing a political resolution. *Our country's peripheral security environment is continuing to improve and friendly relations with neighbouring countries have entered their best period since the founding of the nation.* (Emphasis added) [...] These conditions and factors mentioned above provide a relatively good external environment for us to consolidate our energy on developing the national economy".[79]

Against this 'favourable' security environment, China primarily perceived no threat of invasions, thus lowering the prospects of a war; however, there loomed a concern to "prevent a major incident of 'Taiwan independence' from occurring", which required the PLA to "prepare to deal with sudden incidents" (*zuohao yingbian zhubei*).[80]

Jiang's perceived need to issue a new set of military strategic guidelines was driven by three key assessments:[81] First, a major change to the international order following the Soviet Union's demise and the collapse of other communist regimes in Eastern Europe. Second, evolving domestic concerns, mainly caused by China's continued effort to "reform and opening up"; a priority on economic development; Beijing's requirement for a stable domestic, international, and peripheral environment to succeed; and the PLA's requirement to modernise within the context of other national objectives. And third, the most important factor was the changing nature of warfare and the PLA's acknowledged inadequacies for successfully operating within this new environment. To explain, the USA's Operation DESERT STORM that entailed 'application of high technology on the battlefield' provided a reality check to China on the PLA's lack of capabilities in modern warfare; thus, calling for a major adjustment to China's national military strategy.

In this regard, the "Military Strategic Guidelines of the New Period" outlined five key strategic-level missions and objectives for the PLA:[82] (a) defending national territory and sovereignty; (b) securing the nation's maritime rights and interests; (c) maintaining China's unity; (d) ensuring internal stability; and (e) maintaining a secure and stable external environment, particularly on China's periphery. These goals were driven by the strategic guiding thought: "Foster strength and avoid weaknesses, be flexible in handling emergencies, deter wars, and win wars" (*yangchangbiduan, linghuoyingbian, ezhizhanzheng, dayingzhanzheng*).[83]

In view of this, the PLA's reforms comprised of: First, on operational regulations/doctrine, the PLA rewrote the operational doctrine around joint operations and the basic guiding principle for operations of "integrated operations, key point strikes" (*zhengti zuozhan, zhongdian daji*).[84] To which, in January 1999, the PLA officially announced "new-generation operational regulations" (新一代作战条令) which were the fourth generation of operational regulations[85] (accounting for 89 regulations—three times more than the third generation); and issued seven campaign outlines (*zhanyi gangyao*), including the first-ever campaign outline for joint operations.[86]

Second, in terms of force structure, the strength of the force underwent two downsizings in 1997 and 2003 that cut 700,000 soldiers, to increase the PLA's effectiveness. The air force and the navy each declined by 11.4 and 12.6 per cent, respectively; while the ground forces underwent the largest cut by 18.6 per cent.[87] For instance, the 1997 downsizing led to reorganisation of 30 divisions into smaller brigades to increase the flexibility of the force.[88] Besides, to strengthen weapons design and procurement, a fourth general department called the General Armaments Department (GAD) was created in 1998.[89]

Third, in terms of training, in 1995 the GSD issued a new, army-wide training program that included the ground forces, navy, air force, Second Artillery, Commission for Science, Technology and Industry for National Defence (COSTIND), and the People's Armed Police (PAP).[90] This was followed by the promulgation of a second training programme in 2001 and implemented in January 2002 as 'military training and evaluation program' (*junshi xunlian yu kaohe dagang*)—emphasising on standards for the evaluation of training.[91] In addition, the military training also called for field exercises, such as in 1996, during the Taiwan Strait crisis, the PLA conducted its first major joint exercise.[92]

Therefore, the 1993 military strategic guideline highlights a significant departure in Chinese military thinking, with the orientation shifted towards technological advancement and concern for information exchange, logistics, long-range attacks, and increased firepower and others. This set the precedent for the PLA's military preparedness to fight a modern war, more specifically, learning the 'art of information warfare'. As noted, the 1993 guideline still continues to serve as the foundation, with minor adjustments made to the strategy based on re-characterisation of the type of future warfare resulting in the shifts: "Winning Local Wars Under Informationized Conditions" in 2004 and "Informationized Local Wars" in 2014, with 'information' continuing to act as the constant.

Thus, these periodic shifts only represent an adjustment to the military strategic guidelines of the new era and do not highlight a drastic change in China's 'national military strategy'. As the PLA's official newspaper, *Liberation Army Daily* (*Jiefangjun Bao*) in 2006 stated, it is an "enrichment and improvement" of the old guidelines, not a new set.[93] This is well-witnessed in the PLA's modernisation efforts which aim at developing 'information age' combat capabilities. This has manifested two significant shifts in PLA's approach in fighting an adversary: First, a departure from a 'people over weapons' approach; and second, a shift from heavy armour and land battles to electronic, cyber and spaced-based warfare. Therefore, it can be strongly stated that the "Military Strategic Guidelines" act as the fundamental guiding ideology that is inherent to the PRC's army building and military combat – thus, serving as the near equivalent of what other countries denote as 'National Military Strategy'.

Jiji Fangu in China's Military Strategy

The essence of "The Science of Military Strategy" lies in the Chinese logic of "You fight in your way, and we fight in ours", as:

> "This principle is the soul and the quintessence of strategic guidance of China and the Chinese army. It is the most precise and vivid theoretical condensation for the guiding law of the People's War and the supreme realm in guidance for war through war history. It has distinct Chinese characteristics and the spirit of the times".[94]

In this light, as already noted, strategic guidelines outline the way China plans its basis for military struggle against a strategic opponent based on the strategic assessment and identification of primary strategic direction. This then brings about the shifts in China's overall military strategy based on changes in the threat perception which then invariably changes the form of war that the PLA would fight in the future. This element of 'change' in the components makes the military strategic guidelines flexible in approach given its periodic adjustments to the strategic outlook. However, unlike the strategic guidelines, strategic ideas/concepts (*zhanlue sixiang*; 战略思) such as "people's war"[95] and "active defence" are relatively stable, whose meaning and operational implications vary only when applied in different strategic contexts. As the 2013 *Science of Military Strategy* posits, since 1949:

> "the active defensive military strategy has undergone many adjustments in its content and shape. Although the pattern has changed in different historical periods, [but] its basic spirit has always been consistent".[96]

To explain, the CMC codifies general directives based on the broad concept of 'active defence' and its applied meanings as the 'military strategic guideline' of 'active defence'. Chinese sources consistently describe these guiding principles as a subset of military strategy, frequently describing the military strategic guidelines as principles that apply the strategic concept of "active defence".[97] To argue so, one of the key components that shapes the military strategic guideline is the 'adjustment of the content of active defence'.

In view of this, it becomes imperative to understand that when describing China's military strategy, it is important to distinguish between "active defence" as a 'strategic concept' and "winning informationised local wars" as a 'strategic guideline'. What is noteworthy is that the relationship between the concept of "active defence" and the "military strategic guidelines" is so interconnected that the two appear to be indistinguishable—resulting in the ambiguous phrase "The Military Strategic Guidelines of the Active Defence", as posited by Peng Dehuai in 1956. Here, the query lies in understanding two key aspects: What is the concept of "active defence" and how is it related to "military strategic guidelines"?

I. Active Defence as the "Strategic Concept"

In March 2014, General Qian Lihua, the former director of MND's Foreign Affairs Office, in his interview on 'threats facing China', illustrated that the concept of "active defence" is "alive and well in today's PLA", by positing that:

> "In the East Asian region, the possibility of accidental clashes cannot be completely ruled out, but the extent of such possibility is not determined by us. The Chinese military will not fire the first shot, but if some people provoke us and fire the first shot, imposing conflicts and wars on us, then we will relentlessly strike back".[98]

China's current strategic guideline of "winning informationised local wars" applies the concept of "active defence" to the post-Cold War and post-Gulf War and the post-9/11 security environment. In describing China's military strategy, Peng Guangqian and Yao Youzhi in *The Science of Military Strategy* stated:

> "Strategy (or military strategy) in China's new periods is taking the national comprehensive power as its foundation, the thought of active defence as its guidance; and winning local war under high-tech conditions as its basic point to construct and exercise military strength; and carrying out the overall and whole-course operation and guidance of war preparation and war for the purpose of protecting national sovereignty and security".[99]

This definition highlights the primacy of "active defence" (*jiji fangyu*; 积极防) in China's military strategy. As Senior Colonel Zhang Yuguo of the PLA specifically posited:

> "Some countries adopt pre-emptive strategies, emphasising preventive intervention and taking the initiative in attack. Ours is totally different. Being "active" is only a kind of means and "defence" is our fundamental purpose".[100]

Furthermore, the relationship between the military strategic guideline and active defence as a strategic concept is well-captured in the 2002 Defence White Paper, which categorically states that:

> "China implements a military strategy of active defence. Strategically, China pursues a principle featuring defensive operations, self-defence and attack only after being attacked. In response to the profound changes in the world's military field and the requirements of the national development strategy, China has formulated a military strategic guideline of active defence in the new period. The guideline is based on winning local wars under modern, especially high-tech, conditions [which since 2014 is changed to 'winning informationised local wars']".[101]

This definition and conceptualisation of "active defence" as a military strategy lies at the core of a broader Chinese military doctrine, best equated as "operational doctrine"[102] in the Western sense, with "winning informationised local wars" acting as the "basic doctrine". This makes active defence an operational guideline of China's military strategy. That is, the concept establishes a set of broad strategic concepts and principles and a set of very general operational concepts for prosecuting war at the strategic level of conflict.[103] Here, the query lies in understanding: What is the significance of the concept of "active defence" in China's military strategy?

Figure 2.3: The Linkage

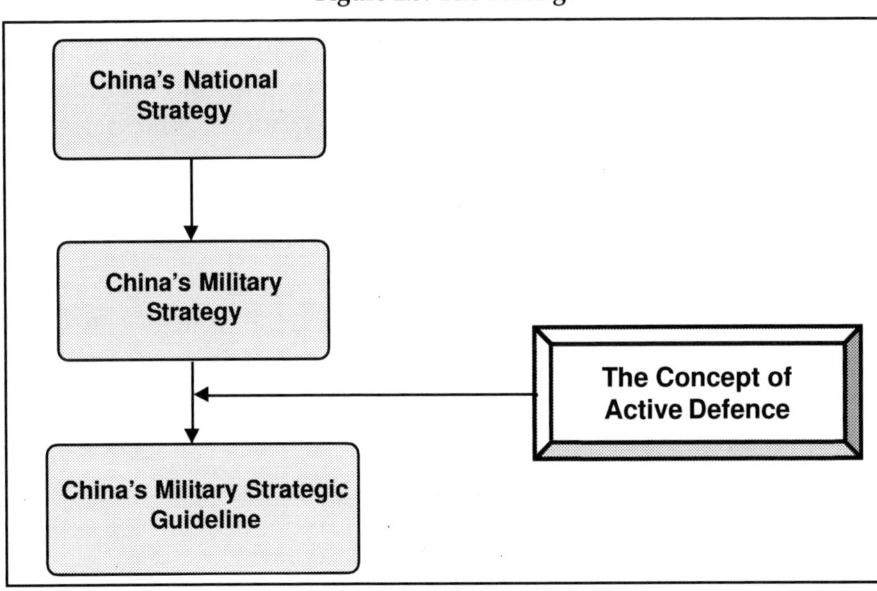

Source: Author.

It is noteworthy that in the case of China, the concepts of "people's war" and especially "active defence" have been the primary strategic ideas since 1949, informing successive generations of strategic guidelines. This very aspect has often led to the assessment of terming "active defence" as 'China's military strategy' or 'strategic guideline'. While China's strategic guidelines have experienced significant shifts since 1949 (as noted earlier), what has served as the point of continuity between China's military strategy and its predecessors is the 'strategic concept' of 'active defence'. As General Zhang Wannian notes, "active defence" is China's "foundational strategic idea" and has served as the basis for China's successive strategic guidelines since 1949.[104] Similarly, Colonel Fang Ning describes, "[t]he strategic thought of active defence is an important part of Mao Zedong's military thought and is the summation of the experience of our Party's [CPC] and our army's [PLA] long time struggle".[105]

These Chinese perceptions highlight the continuity in the use of the concept of active defence in China's military strategy, which applies till today. As noted earlier, the 2015 Defence White Paper underlined the strategic concept of "active defence" as the essence of the "CPC's military strategic thought". In view of this, the first ever official document on China's military strategy provided two key clarifications that to some extent dispel the ambiguity attached to the understanding of 'active defence'. That is: First, as 'active defence' is denoted as a "strategic concept", it clarifies that "active defence" is neither China's 'military strategy' nor is it the 'strategic guideline'; and second, the description of it as the "essence of CPC's military strategic thought", elucidates that the concept of active defence tops the systematic hierarchy of the Chinese war fighting principles. This is to suggest that active defence is the "broadest guideline for war planning and fighting within China's military doctrine".[106]

Based on these aspects, it can be argued that the strategic concept of 'active defence' holds an element of superiority, as it shapes the military strategic guideline and not otherwise. To further argue, unlike the changing nature of military strategic guidelines, the concept of active defence has been a constant in PRC's military strategy.

Figure 2.4: Active Defence in Lykke's Framework

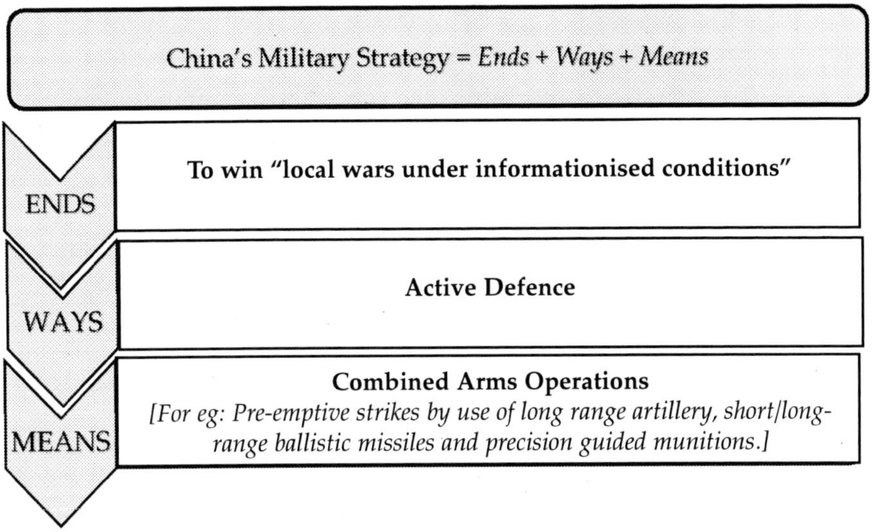

Source: Author.

II. Evolution of the Concept of Active Defence

It is apparent that China's military strategy has evolved from Mao Zedong's "people's war" to preparing to fight and win "local wars under high-tech conditions", to that of win "informationised local wars" in the current context. Here, what has remained constant is the aspect of 'active defence'. To argue so, as traditionally, the PLA acted under the key concept of "active defence" under conditions of "people's war". According to this concept, as Guoli Liu explains:

> "The best way to prevent an attack by an aggressor, or to defeat aggressive operations, once they are underway, is to undertake limited offensive operations designed to disrupt the aggressor's preparations while wearing down his strength. This should be done by creating tactical circumstances favourable to successful conduct of quick decision battles that sap the aggressor' strength, shake his confidence, and force him to restock and replenish his own force while adding to the material stockpiles of the defending forces. The opposite of active defence is passive defence, which entails merely preparing to resist an aggressors attack".[107]

This traditional PLA thinking of "active defence" finds its roots in "Mao Zedong Military Thought" (*mao zedong junshi sixiang*). It was derived from "the long-term practice of revolutionary wars",[108] Chinese Civil War and the "War of Resistance against Japanese Aggression" during World War II. In his 1936 essay on "The Problems of Strategy in China's Revolutionary War", Mao expounded the concept of fighting a strategically defensive war while at the same time engaging in offensive operations at the campaign and tactical levels of war. In Mao's definition,

> "Active defence is also known as offensive defence, or defence through decisive engagements. Passive defence is also known as purely defensive defence or pure defence. Passive defence is actually a spurious kind of defence, and the only real defence is active defence, defence for the purpose of counter-attacking and taking the offensive. [...] Militarily speaking, our warfare consists of the alternate use of the defensive and the offensive. In our case it makes no difference whether the offensive is said to follow or to precede the defensive, because the crux of the matter is to break the "encirclement and suppression". The defensive continues until an "encirclement and suppression" campaign is broken, whereupon the offensive begins, these being but two stages of the same thing; and one such enemy campaign is closely followed by another. Of the two stages, the defensive is the more complicated and the more important. It involves numerous problems of how to break the "encirclement and suppression". The basic principle here is to stand for active defence and oppose passive defence".[109]

The above statement clarifies that Mao defined "active defence" in contrast to passive defence, wherein a nation may assume a strategically defensive posture, but it must nevertheless use offensive means to achieve defensive ends. For instance, in the context of resisting Japan, Mao stated that "active defence could be named as offensive defence. It could also be called decisive campaign defence [...] which was a defence using both counterattack and attack".[110] To note, this strategic policy of active defence was well-witnessed in the Korean War to resist the USA and in the 1962 War against India under "self-defence". However, in the current context, it becomes debatable whether China is still following this form of "active defence".

Table 2.6: Active Defence under Mao Zedong

Three Major Attributes		
Strategic Defence	*Defence in Depth*	*Triadic Warfare*
Follow 'Three Stages' of Protracted War **Stage 1** Enemy's strategic offensive and our strategic defensive **Stage 2** Enemy's strategic consolidation and our preparation for the counter offensive **Stage 3** Our strategic counter offensive and the enemy's strategic retreat. **Active Defence is to be used in a war against invasion.*	Taking advantage of the "Strategic Depth"—China's large landmass and huge population **Stage 1** Strategic retreat by luring the enemy deep where the PLA enjoys geographical, combat and logistical advantage	Use of 'Triad': guerrilla warfare, mobile warfare, and positional warfare **The prioritisation of each form of warfare shifts with changes in different wars and in different stages of each war.*

Source: Annotated by the Author with reference to Huang (1994).[111]

It is worth noting that while the Chinese view of active defence bestows a defensive nature to China's military strategy, what cannot be dismissed is the fact that it is 'active' in requirements. To explain, as Colonel Wang Naiming suggests, it would require the organic integration of offence and defence, and achieving the strategic goal of defence by active offences; and when the condition is ripe, the strategic defence should be led to counterattack and offence.[112]

Based on this understanding, the line between accepting the enemy's first strike and the use of pre-emption to defend China from an immediate attack appears to be blurred. What makes it so is that Mao's understanding was guided by the perception that war is usually initiated by a powerful enemy invasion or offensive with the PLA initially on the defensive.[113] Here, the defensive stage is not static but dynamic, involving tactical manoeuvres of an active, offensive nature to gain momentum, accumulating in the stage of strategic counter-attack. It is the winning victory at this stage that leads to the stage of strategic offensive, the final stage of winning the war.[114] Owing to this logic, the concept of "active defence" is argued to be a "doctrine of the weak against the strong". Wherein, largely defensive in purpose, the doctrine seeks to take the initiative and stay on the offensive from a conflict's earliest stages in order to bring hostilities to a swift conclusion.[115] Simplistically put, in Mao's strategy of defensive posture, a big, resource-rich but weak combatant assumes to be weary and turn the tables on a stronger antagonist by making itself stronger over time and harrowing the enemy; resulting in the weaker becoming the stronger contender who seizes the offensive and finally wins, outlasting the foe through a 'protracted war' rather than hazarding a battle early on.[116]

However, in 1956, the Chinese understanding of active defence witnessed a shift, when Peng Dehuai (as already noted in the earlier section) intertwined "active defence" to the "military strategic guidelines". As Peng added a political component to the active defence strategy by citing that 'strategically, China will not attack until it is attacked' and declaring that China would adopt the 'military strategic guideline of the active defence'. Since then 'active defence' in Chinese strategic understanding refers to striking only after the opponent has struck first and a defensive posture. This Chinese logic then implies that "active defence" posits a defensive military strategy in which "China does not initiate wars or fight wars of aggression, but engages in war only to defend national sovereignty and territorial integrity".[117]

The concept of "active defence" witnessed a significant departure from Mao's conception under Deng Xiaoping's 1980 strategic idea. This called for two changes: First, Mao's idea of the strategic directive for active defence by luring the enemy in deep and the use of mobile warfare as the main form of war operations were abandoned. Second, forward defence and positional warfare under the strategic directive of "active defence" were propounded. This new construct exhibited the shift in the military doctrine from Mao's "people's war" to that of "people's war under modern conditions" under Deng Xiaoping.

From Mao to Deng, "active defence" continued to serve as the cardinal principle of China's military strategy, with 'people's war' periodically adjusted to 'modern conditions' and later to 'high-technology and informationised conditions' – with the Chinese leadership reinventing the strategy accordingly and naming it 'active defence strategy under new historical conditions'.

Table 2.7: Active Defence under Deng Xiaoping

Three Key Elements		
Initial Phase of War	*Extended Strategic Depth*	*Modernised Military Force*
No 'Three Stage War' to be pursued. Enemy to be countered in the initial phase of the conflict itself, denying him entry into Chinese territory. **Stage 1:** Strategic Defence based on Strategic retreat is replaced by "Resolute Defence". To hold key defence positions and prevent them from being occupied by the enemy. **Strategic retreat would mean giving up China's most productive areas to its enemy, resulting in the loss of the logistical ability to sustain prolonged war.*	**Aim:** To defend important industrial areas effectively and preserve the productivity needed to support a protracted war. Establish a tri-dimensional defence system of great depth and keep the battleground distant from those economic centres (at least in the initial phase of war). **Exception: Multi-layered defence lines or zones that can be extended beyond China's territorial and maritime borders when the situation warrants.* For instance, PRC changed its naval strategy from "near coasts defence" (coastal defence) to "near seas defence" (offshore defence)	**Contingency:** PLA to engage the enemy force (which employs modern C3I and equipment) decisively at the forward defence lines in the initial phase of war. Positional warfare from fixed position as the key. Retained mobile warfare but dropped guerrilla warfare To counter, China needs to modernise. **Key Reforms needed: upgrade the weaponry and equipment, improve the education and training systems, and emphasise the study of military sciences.*

Source: Annotated by the Author with reference to Huang (1994).[118]

Table 2.8: Cases of China's Use of Force Against its Opponent (1949 onwards)

Year	*Event*
1950-55	The Korean War
1954 and 1958	Artillery bombardment of Quemoy and Matzu
1962	Border War with India
1969	Border Clash with Soviet Union
1974	Seizure of western Paracel Islands from South Vietnam
1979	Border War with Vietnam
1988	Seizure of Islands in Spratly Archipelago
1996	Missile exercises in the Taiwan Straits
2020	Border Incident with India at Galwan Valley (Limited)

Source: Annotated by the Author with reference to Liu (2017).[119]

This brings into perspective that the traditional understanding of 'active defence', as outlined by Mao, has undergone gradual shifts pertaining to the changing nature of war and warfare. In this process, the concept of "active defence" has been added with new meanings under the new conditions of 'local war' that have changed from using conventional weapons to using high-tech weapons and informationised conditions resulting into significant changes in the forms of war and methods of combat. As the 2015 White Paper notes:

> "[Since 1949,] in line with the developments and changes in the national security situation, had made a number of major revisions of it. In 1993 the military strategic guideline of the new era was formulated, which took winning local wars in conditions of modern technology, particularly high technology, as the basic point in making preparation for military struggle (PMS). In 2004, the guideline was further substantiated, and the basic point for PMS was modified to winning local wars under conditions of informationization".[120]

In this context, in the present times, the war process cannot be clearly divided into the three stages of strategic defensive, strategic counter-attack and strategic offensive, due to lack of a transitional stage. What makes the difference to "active defence" in the changing times is the aspect of preparation for military struggle, which exhibits the option of first use of military force, if not achieved otherwise. These new conditions, as the Chinese argue, require to "identify an enemy attempt at an initial stage of its aggression, or at the time of restoring lost territories or protecting natural and economic resources, catching a strategic initiative swiftly through offensive operation, striking first, suppressing the enemy provocation in possibly the shortest time, setting back the enemy's aggressive attempt, and winning the war".[121] This is to suggest that the basic posture is that of 'self-defence', which then directs the military to 'strike back' but does 'not preclude pre-emptive strikes' in campaigns and combat. While the 1998 Defence White Paper defined active defence as a "self-defence" posture in which China seeks to "gain mastery by striking only after the enemy has struck".[122]

In a nutshell, over time, the strategic concept of active defence has remained relatively constant, but the content of the concept has evolved, which mainly comes down to "adherence to the unity of strategic defence and operational and tactical offence; adherence to the principles of defence, self-defence and post-emptive strike; and adherence to the stance that "We will not attack unless we are attacked, but we will surely counterattack if attacked".[123] This evolutionary trend of active defence since 1949 further signifies that it is not a static concept and has been changing in response to the emerging security environment compounded with adapting to technological advancement for the PLA to fight modern warfare. As Colonel Wang Naiming posits:

> "the strategic thinking of active defence stresses that strategic guidance should be in a planned way, have the initiative, and be flexible, and it stresses active and not passive military action, and this fully meets the requirements of modern warfare".[124]

In the current context, China's practice of "active defence" calls for a quick reaction before the enemies are ready to strike, preferably on their own territory. This action-oriented approach is premised on two key objectives:[125] First, to minimise damage to China's own infrastructure by conducting the war in the enemy's backyard. Second, to create a psychological or political shock to the enemy by upsetting the adversary's strategy and expectations, and acquiesce in a new status quo that is more favourable to China. This perspective exemplifies that China has continuously adjusted its 'active defence' policy based on its perception of the strategic balance of the international security environment and its own domestic political and economic situation.

In this regard, one of the key adjustments made is in terms of introduction of the concept of 'forward defence' or expanding the battle space beyond China's borders to increase China's strategic depth. This has been done to redefine the foundational concept of of 'active defence' in China's military strategy. As the 2013 edition of *Science of Military Strategy* states that given the new changes in the world's military development, in terms of content, the military strategy must "break through the traditional strategic thinking of simply defending the soil of the border areas", and actively and steadily pursue forward defence.[126] This calls for pushing the first line away from China's borders and coasts to ensure that combat occurs beyond China's homeland territory, not on or within it, making China's borders and coasts to be viewed as "interior lines" and not "exterior".[127]

This exemplifies the shift in the military doctrine from "people's war" under Mao to that of "people's war under modern conditions" under Deng to that of "local wars" under Jiang that continues to exist till today. Furthermore, it also highlights the departure from Mao and Deng's idea of active defence. To argue so, as in the current context, China practices 'active defence' in the form of 'forward defence'. Wherein, 'forward' is justified by China's increasing interests beyond its borders, such as the Indian Ocean. Hence, 'active defence' is a constant in China's strategic military thinking.

III. Implementation of Active Defence

On 2 June 2019, at the 18th IISS Shangri-La Dialogue, General Wei Fenghe, China's State Councillor and Minister of National Defence, categorically stated in a public forum:

> "China adopts a military strategy of active defence. China's military adheres to the principles of defence, self-defence and post-strike response. It stresses that 'We will not attack unless we are attacked, but we will surely counterattack if attacked'".[128]

Wei's remarks resonates Beijing's official position as China's MND officially posits that the PRC implements a military strategy of "active defence", wherein: "strategically, it adheres to the principle of featuring defensive operations, self-defence and striking and getting the better of the enemy only after the enemy has started an attack".[129] In addition, Beijing has consistently reiterated its adherence to "active defence", as categorically mentioned in China's Defence White Papers (noted in Table 2.9).

As the 2015 White Paper suggests, "implementing the military strategy of active defence" is "guided by national security and development strategies, and required by the situation and their [PLA's] tasks in the new historical period".[130] This perspective calls for the query: What comprises China's 'implementation of active defence'? This understanding is crucial as it brings into perspective the operational element of the concept of active defence, which in general appears to be 'less obvious', making active defence loosely interpreted to be 'passive', which China calls as 'defensive'. Here, the watchword is 'active', which holds the option of first use of military force, if the interests are not met otherwise and thus, cannot be dismissed as 'defensive'.

It is well noted that since 1949 to the present, active defence has informed every set of China's military strategic guidelines and thereby, China's national defence policy. The evidence lies in China's reference to the "military strategic guidelines" as that of "Strategic Guideline of Active Defence", as noted in the Defence White Papers. This highlights the primacy of the concept in serving as the "strategic idea/concept" that informs, defines and shapes the military strategic guidelines at any given period of time. This is to argue that without active defence, the military strategic guidelines would have no operational focus.

To say so, as under active defence, the PLA's military posture is

Table 2.9: The Element of Active Defence in China's White Papers (1998-2019)

Year	*White Paper*	*Nature of China's National Defence Policy*	*Implementing the Military Strategy of Active Defence*	*China's Defense Policy*
July 1998	*China's National Defense*	Defensive	Strategically, China pursues the defensive policy featuring self-defence and gaining mastery by striking only after the enemy has struck, and adheres to the principle: "We will not attack unless we are attacked; if we are attacked, we will certainly counter-attack".	Safeguarding the state's sovereignty, unity, territorial integrity and security.
October 2000	*China's National Defense in 2000*	Defensive	Strategically, China pursues a principle featuring defensive operations, self-defence and gaining mastery by striking only after the enemy has struck. Such defence combines efforts to deter war with preparations to win self-defence wars in time of peace, and strategic defence with operational and tactical offensive operations in time of war.	Safeguarding state sovereignty, unity, territorial integrity and security.
December 2002	*China's National Defense in 2002*	Defensive	Strategically, China pursues a principle featuring defensive operations, self-defence and attack only after being attacked. In response to the profound changes in the world's military field and the requirements of the national development strategy, China has formulated a military strategic guideline of active defence in the new period.	Safeguarding state sovereignty, unity, territorial integrity and security.
December 2004	*China's National Defense in 2004*	Defensive	China adheres to the military strategy of active defence.	To stop separation and promote reunification, guard against and resist aggression, and defends national sovereignty, territorial integrity and maritime rights and interests. *At this time, "Taiwan independence" force was perceived as the biggest immediate threat to China's national security.*

December 2006	*China's National Defense in 2006*	Defensive	China upholds the principle of counterattack in self-defence.*At this time, the reference was against a nuclear threat.*	To deter other countries from using or threatening to use nuclear weapons against China.
January 2009	*China's National Defense in 2008*	Defensive	China implements a military strategy of active defence. Strategically, it adheres to the principle of featuring defensive operations, self-defence and striking and getting the better of the enemy only after the enemy has started an attack. In response to the new trends in world military developments and the requirements of the national security and development strategy, China has formulated a military strategic guideline of active defence for the new period.	Protection of national sovereignty, security, territorial integrity
March 2011	*China's National Defense in 2010*	Defensive	Adheres to the principles of independence and self-defence by the whole nation	Defend national sovereignty and territorial integrity
April 2013	*The Diversified Employment of China's Armed Forces*	Defensive	China's armed forces unswervingly implement active defence the military strategy, [...] "We will not attack unless we are attacked; but we will surely counterattack if attacked".	Resolutely take all necessary measures to safeguard its national sovereignty and territorial integrity.
May 2015	*China's Military Strategy*	Defensive	Adherence to the unity of strategic defence and operational and tactical offence; adherence to the principles of defence, self-defence and post-emptive strike; and adherence to the stance that "We will not attack unless we are attacked, but we will surely counterattack if attacked".	Resolutely safeguard China's sovereignty, security and development interests
July 2019	*China's National Defense in the New Era*	Defensive	The military strategic guideline for a new era adheres to the principles of defence, self-defence and post-strike response, and adopts active defence. It keeps to the stance that "we will not attack unless we are attacked, but we will surely counter-attack if attacked", places emphasis on both containing and winning wars, and underscores the unity of strategic defence and offence at operational and tactical levels.	Resolutely safeguard China's national sovereignty and territorial integrity

Source: Annotated by the Author with reference to China's Defence White Papers published 1998-2019 (accessed from the website of Ministry of National Defense, PRC).[131]

guided by the following tenets:[132] (a) Overall, China's military strategy is defensive. Will attack only after being attacked. But PLA's operations are offensive. (b) Our counteroffensive will not be limited by space or time. (c) We will not put boundaries on the limits of our offensives. (d) We will wait for the time and conditions that favour our forces when we do initiate offensive operations. (e) We will focus on the opposing force's weaknesses. (f) We will use our own forces to eliminate the enemy's forces. (g) Offensive operations against the enemy and defensive operations for our own force protection will be conducted simultaneously. (h) We will maximise our advantages against the opposing forces.[133]

According to the *Science of Military Strategy*, the four pillars of active defence are:[134] First, China will not fire the first shot and will attempt to settle any disputes by peaceful means, for as long as possible. Second, China will attempt to deter war militarily or politically before it breaks out. Third, China will respond to an attack with offensive action and will seek to destroy the enemy's forces. A fourth pillar, but presented as part of pillar three, is that China would not be the first state to use or threaten to use nuclear weapons.[135] This suggests that while active defence posits a strategically defensive orientation for the PLA, it specifically instructs the PLA to engage in operationally offensive action in order to thwart an invader. As the *Science of Military Strategy* states:

> "Strategically, we would fight only after the enemy has struck. But when foreign enemies force war on us, we should be able to deal out powerful counterattack and stop the enemy's offense in predetermined areas. After gradually depriving the enemy of his strategic initiative, we would change strategic defensive to strategic offensive, so as to utterly defeat the enemy's invasion".[136]

While the concept of active defence has undergone periodic adjustments, the general principles have remained consistent. This is also posited in the 2013 *Science of Military Strategy* which suggests that despite the many adjustments, overall 'active defence' "still belongs to the national defence strategy",[137] which, in the Chinese perspective (as noted in contemporary Chinese writings), comprises the following key tenets (see Table 2.10).

Here, the query is: What circumstances call for the PLA to engage in 'offensive action'? As already noted, Mao Zedong had explicitly pointed out that the "real defence is active defence"—the PLA would respond only to an enemy's first attack but operationally the PLA should not hesitate to launch a first strike. Similarly, Deng Xiaoping stated that 'active

Table 2.10: Key Tenets of Active Defence

Tenet	*Aim*
Adhere to a position of self-defence and stay with striking back	This forms the basic principle for the use of military force under active defence. The principle suggests: "We will not attack unless we are attacked, but we will surely counterattack if attacked." Active defence may entail defensive counterattacks in response to an attack or pre-emptively striking an adversary preparing to attack.
Combine strategic defence with operational and tactical offence	This aspect offers two approaches to warfare influenced by Mao Zedong's notion of using defence and offensive in turns. First, active defence may involve offensive campaigns, operations, and tactical actions in support of the strategic defence. These may occur rapidly and along "external lines". Second, it uses strategic defence to weaken the enemy and set the conditions to transition into strategic offence in order to secure victory.
Taking the operational initiative	This aspect emphasises the effective use of offensives at the operational and tactical levels, avoiding enemy strengths, and concentrating on building asymmetric advantages against enemy weaknesses to "change what is inferior into what is superior".
Strive for the best possibilities	This calls for thorough peacetime military preparations and planning based on fighting the most challenging threat under the most complicated circumstances "in order to get the best results".This aspect stresses the importance of setting conditions in advance and suggests it is preferable to be prepared and not fight, than to fight unprepared.
The dialectical unity of restraining war and winning war	This tenet seeks to resolve the dilemma that using too little force may protract a war instead of stopping it while the unconstrained use of force may worsen a war and make it harder to stop. Calling for the "effective restraint of warfare", this tenet seeks to avoid war first through sufficient military preparations and powerful conventional and strategic forces that act in concert with political and diplomatic efforts to "subdue the enemy's troops without fighting".If war is unavoidable, however, this aspect calls for restraining war by taking the "opening move" and "using war to stop war".
Soldiers and the people are the source of victory	This integrates the concept of active defence with the concept of "people's war". People's war comprises subordinate military strategies, "guerrilla war" and "protracted war" that Mao saw as a means to harness the capacity of China's populace as a source of political legitimacy and mobilization to generate military power. Contemporary Chinese writings link people's war to national mobilisation and participation in wartime as a whole-of- nation concept of warfare.

Source: Annotated by the Author with reference to Annual Report to Congress (2020).[138]

defence is not just simple defence, it has offence in it'. The integration of defence and offence reflects the developing law of war itself, thus clarifying that active defence is 'defensive in nature' with an element of 'offence', that is, strategic defence in combination with offensive action at the operational and tactical levels. This twin dynamic can be explained in the essence of active defence that includes seizing the initiative through first strikes to achieve such defensive goals. As Zhang Wannian posits that in an operation setting, active defence "organically combines strategic defence with campaign battle offence [...] to weaken the enemy and realise strategically defensive goals through offensive operations with quickly decisive battles".[139]

The most significant aspect to note is the 'trigger aspect' which qualifies the 'offensive' and 'proactive' component in active defence. That is to suggest that while the basic tenet of this concept calls for the PLA to engage in strategic defence and 'not strike first', it also means that in active defence such a defensive posture is possible only when combined with an offensive operational posture, hence, the term "active".[140] Here, the key aspect that will qualify China's offence at any given time is the 'trigger factor'. This is to argue that China's military response need not be an opponent's military action—it can be opposed to any hostile political, economic or strategic action that China interprets as a threat, thus, justifying China's military response to an opponent's action. In this case, the Chinese leadership might justify a military response even if the PLA fires the first shot, as according to the active defence concept, the threat to China would already exist. It is noteworthy that the PLA doctrine, while strategically defensive, emphasises the offensive at the tactical and operational levels of war and allows for pre-emptive action if the enemy is perceived as poised to strike China, which Blasko explains:[141]

> "Under high-tech conditions, for the defensive side, the strategy to gain mastery by striking only after the enemy has struck does not mean waiting for the enemy's strike passively. "Striking only after the enemy has struck" in strategy is based on the "victory in advance" of comprehensive national defence construction. It is the means to win political and moral initiative [...] *"the first shot" on the plane of politics and strategy must be differentiated from the first shot on the plane of tactics [...] of any country or organisation violates the country's sovereignty and territorial integrity, the other side will have the right to "fire the first shot" on the plane of tactics.* The military counterattacks

> may be taken by the following options: to drive the invaders out of the territory; or to launch the same attacks on the enemy's homeland; or to attack the enemy's foreign military bases, targets at sea or in the air [emphasis added]".[142]

Thereby, active defence is neither a purely defensive strategy nor limited to territorial defence as it encompasses offensive and pre-emptive aspects, and that it can apply to the PRC acting externally to defend its interests,[143] highlighting the fact that the element of 'offence' is inherent in China's defensive posture. To note, in recent times, one of the key objectives for the PLA is to be able to conduct expeditionary operations and other activities to defend and secure the growing Chinese national interests overseas from "destabilising and uncertain factors".[144] This is making it imperative for the PLA to become a strong, combat-effective armed force capable of winning regional conflicts by employing integrated, real-time command and control networks.[145] For the PLA, active defence in the present context is focussed on preparation for military struggle to win digitalised local wars, and innovate basic operational doctrines, and optimise the military strategic layout.[146] Under this pretext, to implement the military strategic guideline of active defence in the new situation, the operational aspect of China's armed forces will uphold the following principles, as noted in Table 2.11.

Table 2.11: Key Principles for the PLA

Sl. No.	*Key Principles*
1	To be subordinate to and in the service of the national strategic goal, implement the holistic view of national security, strengthen PMS, prevent crises, deter and win wars.
2	To foster a strategic posture favourable to China's peaceful development, adhere to the national defence policy that is defensive in nature, persevere in close coordination of political, military, economic and diplomatic work, and positively cope with comprehensive security threats the country possibly encounters.
3	To strike a balance between rights protection and stability maintenance, and make overall planning for both, safeguard national territorial sovereignty and maritime rights and interests, and maintain security and stability along China's periphery.
4	To endeavour to seize the strategic initiative in military struggle, proactively plan for military struggle in all directions and domains, and grasp the opportunities to accelerate military building, reform and development.
5	To employ strategies and tactics featuring flexibility and mobility, give full play to the overall effectiveness of joint operations, concentrate superior forces, and make integrated use of all operational means and methods.

Sl. No.	*Key Principles*
6	To make serious preparations to cope with the most complex and difficult scenarios, uphold bottom-line thinking, and do a solid job in all aspects so as to ensure proper responses to such scenarios with ease at any time and in any circumstances.
7	To bring into full play the unique political advantages of the people's armed forces, uphold the CPC's absolute leadership over the military, accentuate the cultivation of fighting spirit, enforce strict discipline, improve the professionalism and strength of the troops, build closer relations between the government and the military as well as between the people and the military, and boost the morale of officers and men.
8	To give full play to the overall power of the concept of people's war, persist in employing it as an ace weapon to triumph over the enemy, enrich the contents, ways and means of the concept of people's war, and press forward with the shift of the focus of war mobilization from human resources to science and technology.
9	To actively expand military and security cooperation, deepen military relations with major powers, neighbouring countries and other developing countries, and promote the establishment of a regional framework for security and cooperation.

Source: Annotated by the Author with reference to the 2015 White Paper.[147]

As noted in Table 2.11, it is the 'national interest' that acts as the key to China's military strategy. According to Wang Naiming, unlike in the past, since 1993, the strategic policy of active defence in the new period contains new contents, wherein:[148] First, national interest is the highest criterion in handling the question of military strategy. As a result of which, the safeguarding of national sovereignty and national security should always come first. Second, China should win the war, but should also be able to contain the war. Here, the highest goal of China's military strategy is to create a strategic environment of long-term peace and stability to ensure the smooth construction of the country. Third, the PLA should strive to improve the ability to fight local wars of modern technology, and especially high technology.[149] This brings into perspective the 'PLA's purpose' in following China's military strategy, which the 2013 *Science of Military Strategy* states as:

> "Strictly guarding the self-defence field, adhering to the principle of post-emptive strike is China's active defence of its military strategy. The purpose is to defend national sovereignty, security and territorial integrity, and will always resist the invasion and defend it".[150]

In general terms, China's national military strategy primarily seeks to achieve three sets of national military objectives: protect the Party and safeguard stability; defend sovereignty and defeat aggression, and modernise the military and build the nation.[151] These objectives not only define what is it that the PLA must achieve as a military force, but also highlights the unique role it plays in pursuing China's national strategy. As in the "new era", the fundamental goal of China's national defence is to "resolutely safeguard China's sovereignty, security and development interests".[152] Specifically, the goal's primary objectives are: (a) to deter and resist aggression; (b) to safeguard national political security, the people's security and social stability; (c) to oppose and contain "Taiwan independence"; (d) to crack down on proponents of separatist movements such as "Tibet independence" and the creation of "East Turkistan"; (e) to safeguard national sovereignty, unity, territorial integrity and security; (f) to safeguard China's maritime rights and interests; (g) to safeguard China's security interests in outer space, electromagnetic space and cyberspace; (h) to safeguard China's overseas interests; and (i) to support the sustainable development of the country.[153]

These objectives highlight the expanding scope of the PLA's role in protecting China's evolving national security interests. Broadly, in the absence of general war (as also applicable in the current context), the PLA's strategic missions and tasks seek to provide strategic support for consolidating the leadership of the CPC and the socialist system; safeguarding national sovereignty, unity and territorial integrity; protecting China's overseas interests; and promoting world peace and development.[154]

However, more specific to military preparedness, the eight "strategic tasks" that the PLA must be ready to execute, are:[155] (a) to deal with a wide range of emergencies and military threats and effectively safeguard the sovereignty and security of China's territorial land, air and sea; (b) to resolutely safeguard the unification of the motherland; (c) to safeguard China's security and interests in new domains; (d) to safeguard the security of China's overseas interests; (e) to maintain strategic deterrence and carry out nuclear counterattack; (f) participate in regional and international security cooperation and maintain regional and world peace; (g) to strengthen efforts in operations against infiltration, separatism and terrorism so as to maintain China's political security and social stability; and (h) to perform such tasks as emergency rescue and disaster relief, rights and interests protection, guard duties, and support for national economic and social development.[156] These "missions and tasks" of the PLA appear to be forthcoming; however, the significance lies in understanding the ways in which it gets translated into the PLA's operational capabilities to deter a threat or security challenge.

Thereby, active defence provides the basic strategic posture for the PLA, its concept of operations in the early 21st century as codified by the guideline of "winning informationised local wars", which now includes new geographic areas which the PLA calls as "domains of emerging military rivalry": outer space, near space, cyber space, and under water.[157] Here, combat includes next-generation ballistic missiles, nuclear and conventional, long-range precision-strike assets such as hypersonic vehicles, offensive and defensive cyber capabilities and new classes of submarines and supported by a variety of high-tech directional rockets dropping sea mines with accurate control and guidance capacity.[158]

Besides, by applying 'forward defence', the PLA prefers to fight a military conflict as far away from China's borders and coastlines as is possible, resisting all forms of invasion by an opponent from entering into Chinese territory (including claimed territory), maritime space, air space, cyber space and others. This is also justified by China's growing expeditionary capabilities. Owing to these dynamics, the assumption is that especially the new domains of space, cyber space, electromagnetic spectrum and strategic information operations will likely enable four critical missions for the PLA, such as:[159] First, force enhancement to support combat operations and improve the effectiveness of military forces such as ISR, integrated tactical warning and attack assessment, command, control and communications, navigation and positioning, and environmental monitoring. Second, counter-space missions to protect PLA forces while denying space capabilities to the adversary. Third, information operations to direct influence on the process and outcome in areas of strategic competition. And fourth, computer network operations targeting adversary's data and networks.[160]

Owing to these dynamics, it can be rightly suggested that while strategically the PLA conforms to being defensive, China's increasing power projection and growing aggressive posture highlight the element of offence that is embedded in the concept of active defence. Thus, 'active defence' is what Mao rightly called "offensive defence".

Conclusion

Given the assessment, it can be argued that China does have a national military strategy that informs the "military strategic guidelines", which is guided by the strategic concept of "active defence" to fight under modern conditions. Here, the essence lies in understanding the difference between strategic concept and strategic guideline in China's military strategy.

The concept of "active defence" has been a key determinant since the foundation of the PRC in 1949, with changes in the meaning and operational applications over time. Earlier "active defence" was mainly functional against a perceived attack, that is, against an invasion; however, in current times, as China faces no threat of invasion, the very objective of active defence has changed to forward defence. That is to suggest, China has moved beyond the 'counter-attack' and 'no aggression' policies of active defence, as evident from China's growing military posture and power projection capabilities, which suggest otherwise. At present, the military strategic guideline aims and strives to 'win informationised local wars', wherein 'invasion' is no more the only causal factor for active defence to operate. Furthermore, the way active defence is applied is also impacted by the strategic shifts in the international security environment as perceived by China, and the 'type of war' that the PLA would have to fight in the future.

Another important aspect that makes 'active defence' significant is that, though relatively a stable component in China's military thinking, it is not static in nature. While it is interpreted to be defensive in orientation, it has an element of offence in the form of 'pre-emption' that makes it dynamic in nature. This makes active defence an 'operational concept', which calls for a quick reaction before the adversary launches a strike, calling for the PLA to be mobile, flexible and deceptive by using the element of surprise.

However, to suggest that active defence is only tactical would be an error, especially in the current strategic environment, where China faces no threat of invasion. But, the need is to watch China's military posture based on its growing military capabilities that have raised concerns over 'China Threat'. Wherein, there is a growing scepticism over a pre-emption from China based on its own 'preparedness'. Given this change in the scenario of 'threat', it can be right to posit that the context of active defence has changed and thus, its application. That is, the defining character of 'active defence' is not the much stated 'defensive posture' but the underlying 'offensive element' that does not necessitate an attack to be kinetic to warrant a countermeasure from China.

In its conceptual understanding thereby, 'active defence' should not be interpreted as China's strategic guideline or its military strategy. It should be rather conceived as the primary "strategic concept" that lies at the core of PLA's strategic thinking at any given period of time. Thus, the 'act' will be dependent on what the PLA perceives as an attack- be it political or economic, will be responded with what China calls "Active Defence".

NOTES

1. See, "Problems of Strategy in China's Revolutionary War", December 1936, *Selected Works of Mao Tse-tung*, https://www.marxists.org/reference/archive/mao/selected-works/volume-1/mswv1_12.htm, accessed online 26 October 2019.
2. See, Ministry of National Defense of the People's Republic of China (2009), "White Paper 2008", http://eng.mod.gov.cn/publications/2017-04/11/content_4778231.htm, accessed online 15 September 2019.
3. According to Sun Tzu, the five essentials of victory are: (1) He will win who knows when to fight and when not to fight. (2) He will win who knows how to handle both superior and inferior forces. (3) He will win whose army is animated by the same spirit throughout all its ranks. (4) He will win who prepared himself and waits to take the enemy unprepared. (5) He will win who has military capacity and is not interfered with by the sovereign.
4. *Sun Tzu on the Art of War: The Oldest Military Treatise in the World*, England: Allandale Online Publishing, 2000, p. 10, https://sites.ualberta.ca/~enoch/Readings/The_Art_Of_War.pdf, accessed online 30 January, 2020.
5. Ibid., p. 12.
6. Office of the Secretary of Defense (2020), "Annual Report to Congress: Military and Security Developments involving the People's Republic of China 2020", p. 27, https://media.defense.gov/2020/Sep/01/2002488689/-1/-1/1/2020-DOD-CHINA-MILITARY-POWER-REPORT-FINAL.PDF, accessed online 4 September 2020.
7. Anthony H. Cordesman et al. (2013), *Chinese Military Modernization and Force Development: A Western Perspective*, CSIS, Lanham, MD: Rowman & Littlefield, p. 53.
8. M. Taylor Fravel (2018), "Shifts in Warfare and Party Unity: Explaining China's Changes in Military Strategy", *International Security*, Vol. 42, No. 3, p. 40.
9. Ibid.
10. Ibid.
11. David M. Finkelstein (1999), "China's National Military Strategy", in James Mulvenon and Richard Yang (eds.) *The People's Liberation Army in the Information Age*, Santa Monica, CA: RAND Corporation, p. 102.
12. Ibid.
13. David M. Finkelstein (2007), "China's National Military Strategy: An Overview of the

"Military Strategic Guidelines"", in Andrew Scobell and Roy Kamphausen (eds.) *Right Sizing the People's Liberation Army: Exploring the Contours of China's Military*, Carlisle, PA: Army War College Press, pp. 79-80.

14. Ibid., p. 104.
15. Arthur F. Lykke Jr. (1993), "Toward an Understanding of Military Strategy", in Arthur F. Lykke Jr. (ed.) *Military Strategy: Theory and Application*, Carlisle Barracks: U.S. Army War College, p. 180.
16. Explained in Footnote 9 of David M. Finkelstein (1999), "China's National Military Strategy", n. 12, pp. 102-103.
17. M. Taylor Fravel (2002), "The Evolution of China's Military Strategy: Comparing the 1987 and 1999 editions of Zhanluexue", in James Mulvenon and David Finkelstein (eds.) *China's Revolution in Doctrinal Affairs: Emerging Trends in the Operational Art of the Chinese People's Liberation Army*, Washington DC: CNA Corporation, p. 82.
18. The Chief Editor is Major General Wang Wenrong (王文荣); while other members of the editorial board include Major General Ma Bao'an (马保安), Major General Zhu Chongfeng (朱崇锋), and Senior Colonel Ma Ping (马平).
19. M. Taylor Fravel (2002), "The Evolution of China's Military Strategy", n. 17, p. 83.
20. Quoted in Timothy L. Thomas (2007), *Decoding the Virtual Dragon: Critical Evolutions in the Science and Philosophy of China's Information Operations and Military Strategy*, Fort Leavenworth, KS: Foreign Military Studies Office, p. 11.
21. Quoted in M. Taylor Fravel (2018), "Shifts in Warfare and Party Unity", n. 8, p. 47.
22. Timothy R. Heath (2017), "An Overview of China's National Military Strategy", in Joe McReynolds (ed.) *China's Evolving Military Strategy*, Washington DC: The Jamestown Foundation, p. 14.
23. *The Science of Military Strategy* (China 2013) (English Translation), Beijing: Military Strategic Research Department, AMS, pp. 3-4.
24. Timothy R. Heath (2017), "An Overview of China's National Military Strategy", n. 22, p. 14.
25. David Finkelstein's proposition is founded on five key assumptions: First, China does have a national military strategy—PLA's reforms. Second assumption is that outside observers can adduce that rationale, even if imperfectly, from public domain information. Third, the PLA remains subservient to the Party and the State and therefore China's national military strategy is derived from and mutually supportive of Beijing's overarching national security strategy. Fourth, there is much that is unique about China's armed forces. There is also a good deal of universality in how defence establishments go about the business of planning at the national level. Fifth, Western models can sometimes help structure a discussion of the Chinese phenomena even to the point of using Chinese terminology comfortably within those constructs.
26. M. Taylor Fravel (2002), "The Evolution of China's Military Strategy", n. 17, p. 83.
27. David M. Finkelstein (2007), "China's National Military Strategy", n. 11, p. 74.
28. M. Taylor Fravel (2018), "Shifts in Warfare and Party Unity", n. 8, p. 47.
29. Joel Wuthnow (2020), "System Overload: Can China's Military Be Distracted in a War over Taiwan?", in Philip C. Saunders (ed.) *China Strategic Perspectives*, No. 15, Washington, D.C.: National Defense University Press, p. 5.
30. David M. Finkelstein (2007), "China's National Military Strategy", n. 11, p. 82.
31. New guidelines are usually issued in the name of the Chairman of the Central Military Commission, who historically has also served as the Communist Party Chairman and

the State President—such as, Deng Xiaoping, Jiang Zemin, or Hu Jintao. According to Chinese sources, "Military Strategic Guidelines are the core of military strategy; they are the overall plan and the overall guiding principle of the Party and the nation for guiding the preparations and implementation of warfare within a particular period of time, and they are the driving force and assume the overall responsibility for the construction of national defence and the military. As noted in Footnote 6, Eric C. Anderson and Jeffrey G. Engstrom (2009), "Capabilities of the Chinese People's Liberation Army to Carry Out Military Action in the Event of a Regional Military Conflict", *Science Applications International Corporation*, March 2009, p. 3, https://www.uscc.gov/sites/default/files/Research/CapabilitiesoftheChinesePeople's LiberationArmytoCarryOutMilitaryActionintheEventofaRegionalConflict.pdf, accessed online 20 October 2019.

32. M. Taylor Fravel (2018), "Shifts in Warfare and Party Unity", n. 8, p. 47.
33. Ibid.
34. M. Taylor Fravel (2015), "China's New Military Strategy: "Winning Informationized Local Wars"", *China Brief*, Vol. 15, Issue 13, 2 July 2015, https://jamestown.org/program/chinas-new-military-strategy-winning-informationized-local-wars/, accessed online 20 August 2019.
35. David M. Finkelstein (2007), "China's National Military Strategy", n. 11, p. 82.
36. M. Taylor Fravel (2002), "The Evolution of China's Military Strategy", n. 17, p. 84.
37. M. Taylor Fravel (2015), "China's New Military Strategy", n. 34.
38. David Shambaugh (2004), *Modernizing Chinese Military: Progress, Problems, and Prospects*, New Delhi: Bookmart Publishers, p. 58.
39. M. Taylor Fravel (2002), "The Evolution of China's Military Strategy", n. 17, p. 83.
40. David M. Finkelstein (2007), "China's National Military Strategy", n. 11, pp. 83-83.
41. Ibid., pp. 85-86.
42. Ibid., pp. 86-95.
43. Ibid., p. 87.
44. Ibid., p. 88.
45. Ibid., p. 90.
46. Ibid.
47. As a war fighting concept, the "main strategic direction" represents a decision and determination about where (geographically) and against which enemy forces operations must be conducted to achieve the strategic and/or operational results desired.
48. David M. Finkelstein (2007), "China's National Military Strategy", n. 11, pp. 91-93.
49. According to the *Chinese Military Encyclopaedia*, "strategic direction" (*zhanlue fangxiang*) refers to the operational direction with an important influence on the overall situation of the war. It directs the strategic objectives and has a defined depth and width including the ground as well as the multidimensional space of air, sea, and outer space. It is often determined on the basis of the military, political, economic, natural geographical, and demographic factors of the participating sides and other relationships as well as their strategic tasks that must be completed. Whether the strategic direction is selected correctly or not directly impacts the process and the result of the war. No matter if it is dealing with [offensive operations] or [defensive operations], the strategic direction always [distinguishes] between its main direction (*zhuyao fangxiang*) and secondary direction (*ciyao fangxiang*). Within a certain [time frame], there can only be one main strategic direction. The main strategic direction focuses on combat with the enemy, its

centre of gravity [...]. Because of this, determining the main strategic direction is the most important issue of strategic guidance [for prosecuting a particular war]. See, David M. Finkelstein (2007), "China's National Military Strategy", n. 11, pp. 91-92.

50. David M. Finkelstein (2007), "China's National Military Strategy", n. 11, p. 94.
51. See, M. Taylor Fravel (2015), "China's New Military Strategy", n. 34; M. Taylor Fravel (2018), "Shifts in Warfare and Party Unity", n. 8, p. 48.
52. Quoted in Note 15 of Joel Wuthnow (2020), "System Overload", n. 29, p. 38.
53. Dennis J. Blasko (2012), *The Chinese Army Today: Tradition and Transformation for the 21st Century* (Second Edition), New York: Routledge, p. 82.
54. Joel Wuthnow (2020), "System Overload", n. 29, p. 6.
55. Ibid., p. 11.
56. M. Taylor Fravel (2019), *Active Defense: China's Military Strategy Since 1949*, Princeton, NJ: Princeton University Press, pp. 34-35.
57. M. Taylor Fravel (2015), "China's New Military Strategy", n. 34.
58. Quoted in "White Paper outlines China's 'active defence' strategy", *China Daily*, 26 May 2015, https://usa.chinadaily.com.cn/china/2015-05/26/content_20825973.htm, accessed on 30 September 2020.
59. Elsa Kania (2016), "The PLA's Forthcoming Fifth-Generation Operational Regulations—The Latest "Revolution in Doctrinal Affairs"?", *China Brief*, Vol. 16, Issue 7, 21 April 2016, https://jamestown.org/program/the-plas-forthcoming-fifth-generation-operational-regulations-the-latest-revolution-in-doctrinal-affairs/, accessed online 30 September 2019.
60. Ibid., p. 92.
61. See, "Speeches at the National Conference of the Communist Party of China", 21 March 1955, Selected Works of Mao Tse-tung, https://www.marxists.org/ reference/ archive/mao/selected-works/volume-5/mswv5_41.htm, accessed online 27 September 2020.
62. M. Taylor Fravel (2018), "Shifts in Warfare and Party Unity", n. 8, p. 53.
63. Ibid.
64. About one-quarter of the ground forces would defend permanent fortifications, while the remainder would be manoeuvring forces to be deployed in the direction of the US attack. The ground forces would be structured to conduct combined arms operations as new equipment becomes available.
65. Operational regulations provide guidance for the PLA at the campaign (战役) and tactical (战术) levels of warfare, based on two components: campaign guidance (战役纲要) and combat regulations (战斗条令).
66. M. Taylor Fravel (2019), *Active Defense*, n. 56, p. 75.
67. Elsa Kania (2016), "The PLA's Forthcoming Fifth-Generation Operational Regulations", n. 59.
68. Ibid., p. 76.
69. The troops in artillery units increased from 20.4 to 31.8 per cent; while armoured and chemical defence units that did not exist in 1950 made up 4.7 and 1.2 per cent.
70. M. Taylor Fravel (2019), *Active Defense*, n. 56, p. 76.
71. The Advanced Military Academy aimed to train officers in the principles and techniques of modern command and operational levels of war. The other academies that were established included the Military Academy, the Political Academy and the Logistics Academy.
72. To note, in 1957, China conducted joint exercises with the Soviet Union and North

Korean forces and held a large-scale simulation of an amphibious landing in May 1959.

73. The Chinese perception was shaped by concerns over Moscow's defence treaty with Vietnam as signed in November 1978 and the Soviet invasion of Afghanistan in December 1979.
74. M. Taylor Fravel (2019), *Active Defense*, n. 56, pp. 165-173.
75. Ibid.
76. Ibid., p. 184.
77. Quoted in David M. Finkelstein (2007), "China's National Military Strategy", n. 11, pp. 102-103.
78. Quoted in Dean Cheng (2011), "Chinese Lessons from the Gulf Wars", in Andrew Scobell et al. (ed.) *Chinese Lessons from Other Peoples' Wars*, Strategic Studies Institute: US Army War College, 2011, p. 162.
79. Quoted in David M. Finkelstein (2007), "China's National Military Strategy", n. 11, p. 98.
80. See, M. Taylor Fravel (2019), *Active Defense*, n. 56, p. 184. This applied to not just the Taiwan contingency but also to Hong Kong and China's other outstanding territorial disputes. As noted, with time, Taiwan became China's "main strategic direction", resulting in a crisis in 1996 that continues till today.
81. David M. Finkelstein (2007), "China's National Military Strategy", n. 11, pp. 97-102.
82. Ibid., p. 109.
83. M. Taylor Fravel (2019), *Active Defense*, n. 56, p. 184.
84. M. Taylor Fravel (2018), "Shifts in Warfare and Party Unity", n. 8, p. 74.
85. Elsa Kania (2016), "The PLA's Forthcoming Fifth-Generation Operational Regulations", n. 59.
86. M. Taylor Fravel (2019), *Active Defense*, n. 56, p. 186.
87. As Fravel notes, for the PLA Army three headquarters were eliminated; a dozen divisions were deactivated, and another 14 light infantry divisions were transferred to the People's Armed Police (PAP). In 2003, the CMC called for further downsizing of 200,000 personnel, mainly focused on the ground forces.
88. M. Taylor Fravel (2019), *Active Defense*, n. 56, p. 186.
89. M. Taylor Fravel (2018), "Shifts in Warfare and Party Unity", n. 8, p. 74.
90. M. Taylor Fravel (2019), *Active Defense*, n. 56, p. 187.
91. Ibid.
92. Ibid.
93. Quoted in David M. Finkelstein (2007), "China's National Military Strategy", n. 11, p. 96.
94. Dennis J. Blasko (2012), *The Chinese Army Today*, n. 53, p. 124.
95. The Chinese concept of "People's War" is one in which the people actively support the military during times of warfare: this active support can be logistical, political, or operational. When describing arming the civilian population for military operations, PLA writings mostly refer to the militia, civil defence, and reserve forces.
96. *The Science of Military Strategy* (China 2013) (English Translation), n. 23, p. 48.
97. Timothy R. Heath (2017), "An Overview of China's National Military Strategy", n. 22, p. 21.
98. Quoted in Timothy R. Heath et al. (2016), *The PLA and China's rejuvenation: National Security and Military Strategies, Deterrence Concepts, and Combat Capabilities*, Santa Monica, CA: RAND Corporation, pp. 34-35.

99. Cited in Prashant Kumar Singh (2016), "Changing Contexts of Chinese Military Strategy and Doctrine", IDSA Monograph Series, No. 49, March 2016, p. 22, https://idsa.in/system/files/monograph/monograph49.pdf, accessed online 20 September 2019.
100. Quoted in Jiang Jie and Guo Yuandan (2015), "MoD unveils military strategy", *Global Times*, 27 May 2015, https://www.globaltimes.cn/content/923791.shtml, accessed online 18 May 2020.
101. Ministry of National Defence of the People's Republic of China (2002), "China's National Defense in 2002", http://eng.mod.gov.cn/Database/WhitePapers/2002.htm, accessed online 20 September 2019.
102. David Shambaugh (2004), *Modernizing Chinese Military*, n. 38, p. 58.
103. David M. Finkelstein (2007), "China's National Military Strategy", n. 11, p. 88.
104. M. Taylor Fravel (2002), "The Evolution of China's Military Strategy", n. 17, p. 86.
105. Fang Ning (1998), "Defence Policy in the New Era", in Michael Pillsbury (ed.) *Chinese Views of Future Warfare*, India Edition, New Delhi: Lancer Publishers, p. 53.
106. Anthony H. Cordesman and Martin Kleiber (2007), *Chinese Military Modernization: Force Development and Strategic Capabilities*, Washington D.C.: The CSIS Press, p. 26.
107. Guoli Liu (2017), *China Rising: Chinese Foreign Policy in a Changing World*, London, UK: Palgrave Macmillan, pp. 50-51.
108. Ministry of National Defense of the People's Republic of China (2015), "China's Military Strategy", http://eng.mod.gov.cn/Database/WhitePapers/2014.htm, accessed online 20 September 2020.
109. See, "Problems of Strategy in China's Revolutionary War", n. 1.
110. M. Taylor Fravel (2002), "The Evolution of China's Military Strategy", n. 17, p. 86.
111. Alexander Chieh-cheng Huang (1994), "The Chinese Navy's Offshore Active Defense Strategy: Conceptualization and Implications", *Naval War College Review*, Vol. 47, No. 3, p. 13.
112. Senior Colonel Wang Naiming (1998), "Adhere to Active Defense and Modern People's War" in Michael Pillsbury (ed.) *Chinese Views of Future Warfare*, India Edition, New Delhi: Lancer Publishers, p. 37.
113. Nan Li (2003), "The PLA's Evolving Warfigthing Doctrine, Strategy and Tactics, 1985-95: A Chinese Perspective" in David Shambaugh and Richard H. Yang (eds.) *China's Military in Transition*, Oxford: Clarendon Paperbacks, p. 188.
114. Ibid.
115. Guoli Liu (2017), *China Rising: Chinese Foreign Policy in a Changing World*, n. 107, p. 51.
116. James R. Holmes (2015), "The Two Words that Explain China's Assertive Naval Strategy", *Foreign Policy*, 3 June 2015, https://foreignpolicy.com/2015/06/03/the-two-words-that-explain-chinas-naval-strategy-active-defense/, accessed online 20 September 2020.
117. Guoli Liu (2017), *China Rising: Chinese Foreign Policy in a Changing World*, n. 107, p. 51.
118. Alexander Chieh-cheng Huang (1994), "The Chinese Navy's Offshore Active Defense Strategy", n. 111, p. 14.
119. Ibid., p. 50.
120. Ministry of National Defense of the People's Republic of China (2015), "China's Military Strategy", n. 108.
121. Nan Li (2003), "The PLA's Evolving Warfigthing Doctrine, Strategy and Tactics", n. 113, p. 188.
122. Ministry of National Defense of the People's Republic of China (1998), "China's National Defense in 1998", http://eng.mod.gov.cn/Database/WhitePapers/1998,

accessed online 20 September 2020.

123. Ministry of National Defense of the People's Republic of China (2015), "China's Military Strategy", n. 108.
124. Senior Colonel Wang Naiming (1998), "Adhere to Active Defence and Modern People's War", n. 112, p. 40.
125. Eric C. Anderson and Jeffrey G. Engstrom (2009), "Capabilities of the Chinese People's Liberation Army to Carry Out Military Action in the Event of a Regional Military Conflict", *Science Applications International Corporation*, March 2009, p. 5, https://www.uscc.gov/sites/default/files/Research/CapabilitiesoftheChinesePeople'sLiberationArmytoCarryOutMilitaryActionintheEventofaRegionalConflict.pdf, accessed online 20 October 2019.
126. *The Science of Military Strategy* (China 2013), n. 23, p. 104.
127. M. Taylor Fravel (2017), "China's Changing Approach to Military Strategy: The Science of Military Strategy from 2001 and 2013", in Joe McReynolds (ed.) *China's Evolving Military Strategy*, Washington DC: The Jamestown Foundation, p. 56.
128. General Wei Fenghe (2019), 18th Asia Security Summit: The IISS Shangri-La Dialogue, Fourth Plenary Session, 2 June 2019, https://webcache.googleusercontent.com/search?q=cache:81MJlBD72hMJ:https://www.iiss.org/-/media/files/shangri-la-dialog ue/2019/speeches/plenary-4—general-wei-fenghe-minister-of-national-defence-chin a-transcript.ashx+&cd=5&hl=en&ct=clnk&gl=in&client=safari, accessed online 20 November 2019.
129. Ministry of National Defense of the People's Republic of China, "Defense Policy", http://eng.mod.gov.cn/defense-policy/index.htm, accessed online 11 September 2019.
130. Ministry of National Defense of the People's Republic of China (2015), "China's Military Strategy", n. 108.
131. See, Ministry of National Defense of the People's Republic of China, "White Papers", http://eng.mod.gov.cn/Database/WhitePapers/, accessed online 26 October 2020.
132. David M. Finkelstein (2007), "China's National Military Strategy", n. 11, pp. 88-89.
133. Ibid.
134. Anthony H. Cordesman et al. (2013), *Chinese Military Modernization and Force Development*, n. 7, p. 54.
135. Ibid.
136. Ibid.
137. *The Science of Military Strategy* (China 2013), n. 23, pp. 103-104.
138. Office of the Secretary of Defense (2020), "Annual Report to Congress", n. 6, pp. 27-28.
139. Quoted in M. Taylor Fravel (2002), "The Evolution of China's Military Strategy", n. 17, p. 87.
140. Quoted in Timothy R. Heath et al. (2016), *The PLA and China's rejuvenation*, n. 98, p. 34.
141. Dennis J. Blasko (2012), *The Chinese Army Today*, n. 53, p. 123.
142. Ibid., p. 124.
143. Office of the Secretary of Defense (2020), "Annual Report to Congress", n. 6, p. 27.
144. Office of the Secretary of Defense (2018), "Annual Report to Congress: Military and Security Developments involving the People's Republic of China 2018", 16 May 2018, p. 10, https://media.defense.gov/2018/Aug/16/2001955282/-1/-1/1/2018-CHINA-MILITARY-POWER-REPORT.PDF, accessed online 27 August 2019.

145. Ibid.
146. "Ten Highlights of China's New Defense White Paper", *Xinhuanet*, 22 July 2015, http://www.xinhuanet.com//mil/2015-07/22/c_128047230.htm, accessed online 25 September 2019.
147. Ministry of National Defense of the People's Republic of China (2015), "China's Military Strategy", n. 108.
148. Senior Colonel Wang Naiming (1998), "Adhere to Active Defense and Modern People's War", n. 112, pp. 40-41.
149. Ibid.
150. *The Science of Military Strategy* (China 2013), n. 23, p. 48.
151. David M. Finkelstein (1999), "China's National Military Strategy", n. 11, p. 108.
152. Ministry of National Defense of the People's Republic of China, "Defense Policy", n. 129.
153. Ibid.
154. "Full Text: China's National Defense in the New Era", *Xinhuanet*, 24 July 2019, http://www.xinhuanet.com/english/2019-07/24/c_138253389.htm, accessed online 20 August 2019.
155. Ministry of National Defense of the People's Republic of China (2015), "China's Military Strategy", n. 108.
156. Ibid.
157. Michael Raska (2016), "PLA reforms: toward winning 'informationised local wars'", *The Interpreter*, 3 February 2016, https://www.lowyinstitute.org/the-interpreter/pla-reforms-toward-winning-informationised-local-wars, accessed online 20 August 2019.
158. Ibid.
159. Ibid.
160. Ibid.

3

Modernisation of the PLA

"China's armed forces take their dream of making the military strong as part of the Chinese Dream. Without a strong military, a country can be neither safe nor strong".

—China's Defence White Paper (2015)[1]

"A military is built to fight. Our military must regard combat capability as the criterion to meet in all its work and focus on how to win when it is called on".

—Xi Jinping (2017)[2]

"The system, structure, pattern and image of the people's military [PLA] have all been renewed".

—Xi Jinping (2019)[3]

Acting upon the 'fight and win' logic, Chinese President and Chairman of the CMC, Xi Jinping, set the resolution for the year 2019 by calling upon the People's Liberation Army to be 'battle-ready'. With future wars perceived to be 'short and limited', the PLA is no longer focused on 'luring the enemy in deep'; rather it seeks to master the ability to 'conduct high-tech mobile operations and long-range precision strikes' to 'meet the enemy away from its border', in protecting its vital economic and political centres. This shift in Chinese perception is evident from the dramatic changes in China's military modernisation (*junshi xiandaihua*), which is a central component of Xi's 'China Dream'.

The PLA, with a strength that totals approximately two million personnel in the regular forces, is ambitious of building joint operations capabilities and proficiencies across all domains of warfare – ranging from land, air, and maritime operations to that of space, counterspace, electronic warfare, and cyber operations. Here, the keywords for the PLA's transformation are 'modern' and 'strong'. With USA being the benchmark for China, the quest for the PLA lies in bridging the 'modernisation gap'. This has driven far-reaching reforms in the PLA with the goal to become a 'world-class military' by 2049. For instance, China has stepped up its shipbuilding with an aim to have six carrier battle groups operating by 2035, matching the strength of the US in the Pacific.[4]

With the bottom line being mechanisation (机械化), informatisation (信息化) and now, intelligentisation (智能化),[5] the PLA's ambition lies in sharpening its combat readiness to 'fight and win'. In Xi's words:

> "The capability to win is strategically important in safeguarding national security and strengthening that capability and combat readiness in the new era would provide strategic support to the realisation of the Chinese dream of national rejuvenation".[6]

In view of this, the four key trends that exemplify China's robust military modernisation are:[7] First, the PLA's evolving capabilities to counter an intervention by a third party along China's periphery and project power globally. Second, China's continued progress in implementing major structural reforms, fielding modern indigenous systems, building readiness, and strengthening its competency to conduct joint operations. Third, China's quest to outpace the US in several areas of military modernisation. As noted, China has achieved a "parity with, or even exceeded, the US" in areas such as shipbuilding, land-based conventional ballistic and cruise missiles, and integrated air defence systems.[8] And fourth, in recent times, China's military modernisation efforts exemplify its intention to transform its defence and logistic systems to protect its economic interests abroad, such as 'strategic assets' under the Belt and Road Initiative.

Owing to these trends, an important aspect that qualifies significant attention is that China's strategic thinking is constantly evolving with the shifts in the 'type of war' that the PLA must be prepared to fight. While "active defence" is providing the basic strategic posture for the PLA codified in the doctrine to fight and win "informationised local wars", it is also one of the key principle that is guiding China's force modernisation. As already noted in Chapter 2, one of the key components of China's military strategic guideline is the aspect of 'army building' that entails the PLA's modernisation efforts and is informed by the strategic concept of active defence. For instance, the PRC officially posits that in "building and development of China's Armed Forces", it implements the military strategic guideline of active defence, which entails that:

> "China's armed forces must closely centre around the CPC's goal of building a strong military, respond to the state's core security needs, aim at building an informationised military and winning informationised wars, deepen the reform of national defense and the armed forces in an all-round way, build a modern system of military forces with Chinese characteristics, and constantly enhance their capabilities for addressing various security threats and accomplishing diversified military tasks".[9]

This clarifies the role of 'active defence' in China's military modernisation which is in line with the strategic requirements of the changing security dimensions. To argue so, as in 1993, Jiang Zemin stated:

> "Since the founding of our country, [the PLA] has always implemented the military strategic guidelines of the active defence. Under the new historical conditions, exactly what kind of military strategic guidelines should we be carrying out? We believe that we should continue to carry out the military strategic guidelines of the active defence [...]. At the same time, along with the development and changes to the situation, we should bestow the military strategic guidelines of the active defense with the new content at this appropriate moment".[10]

Jiang's guideline has set the precedent for the PLA to work towards being ready to 'fight and win' "local wars under modern high-tech conditions", which has changed over the intervening years to "local wars under informationised conditions" under Hu Jintao; and further into "informationised local wars" under Xi Jinping. In view of this, the shifts in China's military strategic guideline impacted the PLA's modernisation efforts, from developing the 'industrial age' to that of making 'information age' based combat capabilities. This has further shifted China's focus from heavy armour and land-based warfare to that of building cyber, electronic and space-based military capabilities.

This is exemplified by China's rapid and robust military modernisation program, with defence spending growing for the 25th consecutive year in 2020, China has become the second-largest defence spender after the US. In tracing the trajectory, one can state that the phases of China's modernisation were first, doctrinal, and then organisational, followed by acquisition of equipment, and developing and deploying of new high-tech capabilities. It is to note that the PLA now ranks amongst the world's leading militaries in areas that include artificial intelligence, drones and counter-drones, and anti-ship ballistic missiles.

China's such military preparedness can be explained from a two-fold perspective:[11] First, the core objective to "win informationised local wars", acts as the basic point to call for PLA's combat readiness. Second, such advanced capabilities are aimed at increasing the PLA's ability to carry out joint operations on a modern high-tech battlefield. While military modernisation remains to be a work in progress; however, with concerted efforts, the PLA is increasingly modernising itself into a flexible and combat-ready force. In this regard, China's force modernisation, when combined with its long-standing territorial and maritime disputes, raises significant concerns over China's strategic intentions and capabilities.

Here, the crux lies in exploring two key perspectives: First, the way the PLA characterises modern warfare; and second, the PLA's ability to deploy its developing capabilities in various scenarios. In view of this, the chapter seeks to examine three key aspects: First, what explains China's rapid and robust military modernisation? Second, what are the significant reforms undertaken by the PLA? And third, what kind of operations the PLA wants to conduct in fighting future wars? Furthermore, this chapter will also draw up an assessment of the Chinese intentions as well as the implications of PLA's force modernisation.

PLA's Road to Modernisation

In the case of PRC, the PLA's force modernisation and reform programmes act as a key element in shaping China's 'comprehensive national power', clarifying the fact that military modernisation is not accomplished in isolation from other national objectives. To argue so, as a 2004 volume authored by the PLA NDU's Army Building Research Department suggests:

> "The military strategic guidelines of the new period persist with obeying and serving the development strategy of our nation. [...] Our national development strategy (*guojia fazhan zhanlue*) is a strategy of comprehensive national development that employs the strategy of economic development as the core, and is the general strategy (*zong zhanlue*) for guiding the coordinated development of our nation's economy, politics, military, diplomacy, culture, [etc]. The military strategic guidelines for the new period are a component of the national development strategy so without a doubt they should obey and serve the nation's general strategy".[12]

That is, 'military modernisation' is an indispensable element of China's national strategy of the "Chinese Dream" that envisions "building a more modern, capable, and disciplined military".[13] To note, the 2015 White Paper categorically states:

> "Subordinate to and serving the national strategic goal, China's military strategy is an overarching guidance for blueprinting and directing the building and employment of the country's armed forces".[14]

Wherein, the objective is to balance development and security in the overall national strategy. As Xi stated:

> "[d]eepening national defence and military reforms are [to be] in line with the requirements of the times to realise the Chinese dream of national rejuvenation and China's strong-military dream".[15]

This is evident from the PLA's ambitious modernisation objectives, major structural and organisational reforms, focus on combat readiness and, above all, pursuing the objectives under strict goals and timelines as announced by Xi at the 19th Party Congress. For instance, in fulfilling the national objectives, China has laid out a timeline for the PLA to achieve its modernisation goals in the "new era", as outlined in Table 3.1.

Table 3.1: Military Goals under the Chinese Dream

<table>
<tr><th>Timeline</th><th>Strategic Goals for Military Modernisation</th><th>National Development Goal</th><th>Status of the Targets</th></tr>
<tr><td>By 2020</td><td>To generally achieve mechanization with signifycantly enhanced informationisation and greatly improved strategic capabilities.</td><td>By 2021
To complete building China into a "moderately prosperous society".</td><td rowspan="3">• The 2019 Defence White Paper noted that the PLA had "yet to complete the task of mechanisation", suggesting it was also unlikely that the PLA would achieve this goal by the end of 2020.
• PLA officials have indicated that the third (and final) stage of PLA reforms would take place in 2021 or 2022.
• References to 2021 or 2022 may imply that the PLA is a year or two behind in completing its reforms.</td></tr>
<tr><td>By 2035</td><td>To comprehensively advance the modernisation of military theory, organisational structure, military personnel, and weaponry and equipment in step with the modernisation of the country and basically complete the modernisation of national defence and the military.</td><td>Beyond 2021
To realise the renewal of a "great modern socialist country".</td></tr>
<tr><td>By 2049</td><td>To fully transform the people's armed forces into world-class forces.</td><td></td></tr>
</table>

Source: Author with reference to White Paper (2019) and DoD Report (2020).[16]

Interesting to note, in October 2020, the fifth plenary session of the 19th CPC Central Committee laid out a new timeline of "ensuring the achievement by 2027 of the century-long goal of modernising the army" (确保二〇二七年实现建军百年奋斗目标), coinciding with the centenary of the formation of the PLA on 1 August 1927.[17] While this call to speed up the PLA's modernisation is not new, it would be too early to interpret; which some analysts already suggest that Beijing's goal to complete military modernisation had been brought forward by eight years—from 2035 to 2027.[18] However, such assumptions need to be validated by facts, which are yet not available in the open domain. Rather, on the contrary, one can suggest that these modernisation goals are clear signs of the PLA becoming a real combat-ready force with counter-strategic capabilities to defend China's national interests, both at home and abroad.

Furthermore, it can be rightly pointed that the PLA's force modernisation highlights two key facets:[19] First, that the PLA has come a long way from its humble origins as a foot-soldier heavy and rudimentarily equipped military in the 1940s. And second, that the challenges the PLA faces towards achieving full modernisation in 2035, while not insurmountable, are certainly not negligible. Therefore, as the PLA is still in the process of becoming a 'modern force'; to get a bigger picture, the imperative lies in tracing the trajectory of China's military modernisation in all these years.

I. The Elements and Process of Military Modernisation

While the roots of China's modern military is found in the civil wars (1927-1949) between the CPC and the Kuomintang forces, China's military modernisation process was mainly motivated by its careful observation of the changing nature of modern warfare. This led to the change from Mao's 'guerrilla-style people's war' based on mass mobilisation to that of Deng's idea of 'people's war under modern conditions', with the PLA largely preserving the old organisational structure. However, the first push for modernisation came in the 1980s and most specifically, in the 1990s when the military modernisation witnessed a high priority after a long period of relative neglect to the military budget; as under Deng, defence ranked last in the "four modernisations".[20] This led to changes in the doctrine, equipment and organisational structure in which the efforts were considered piecemeal, with limited effectiveness. More specifically, the change came in the doctrine as the defensive 'people's war' doctrine was replaced by one that was suited to fighting limited regional wars under modern conditions. However, the major shift was witnessed in the 'doctrine' under the 1993 'military strategic guideline' as discussed in Chapter 2, with the new focus in expanding the PLA's capabilities to win 'local wars under high-tech conditions'.

Essentially, the PLA's force modernisation has mainly emphasised on four key areas:[21] (a) increasing unit mobility and training in combined arms operations; (b) improving logistics, combat support, and communications, command and control systems; (c) introducing a limited number of imported modern weapon systems; and (d) developing a number of indigenously produced systems.[22] It is noteworthy that initially Chinese military modernisation comprised mainly of three facets:[23] "revolutionisation" (*geminghua*), representing political loyalty; "modernisation" (*xiandaihua*), mainly focused on updating equipment, but also on strategy and tactics; and "regularisation" (*zhengguihua*) comprising "professionalisation" (*zhuanyehua*), which emphasised on improving the quality of personnel, and "streamlining" (*xiuzheng*), which included force changes, restructuring, and standardisation of organisations and procedures.[24] Here, as one observes, the 'three-pronged process' of modernisation has modified mainly in terms of "emphasis and content" over the years, but the general outline has remained the same and so does the terminology,[25] as evident from the elements that got included in China's military modernisation (see Table 3.2).

Table 3.2: Key Elements of Military Modernisation

Sl. No.	*Elements of Modernisation*
1	Equipment acquisition
2	Changes in force structure
3	Changes in personnel system
4	Changes to the doctrine
5	Improvements in the frequency, content, and methods of military training
6	Transformation of the PLA logistics system to enable it to support "joint operations"
7	Reorganisation of the professional military education system
8	Increases in soldiers' standard of living, pay, and lifestyle
9	Reform of the structure and missions of reserves and militia
10	Modification to the PLA's interaction with society.

Source: Annotated by the Author with reference to Blasko (2012).[26]

These elements call for the query: What makes modernisation imperative for the PRC? The answer to this can be drawn from former Chinese Defence Minister Zhang Aiping's observation in 1983, that suggests:

> "The principle of war is to achieve the greatest victory at the smallest cost. To achieve this we should depend not only on political factors, but also on the correct strategy and tactics of the war's commander, the sophisticated nature of our military equipment, the quality of our personnel who use the equipment etcetera".[27]

This Chinese perspective lies at the core of the strategic issue of 'army building' (*jundui jianshe*) which acts as a key component of China's Military Strategic Guideline – encompassing PLA's modernisation efforts in terms of objectives, reforms and capabilities, to enable the armed forces' operational dynamic and enhance China's national defence at any given period of time. Simplistically put, 'army building' answers the key query: What is the PLA doing in its modernisation efforts?

To note, in 'army building', the PLA's modernisation efforts are driven by the 'strategic assessment' of the 'main strategic direction' which serves as a 'worst case scenario' – a war planning tool in peacetime for developing forces and capabilities and other preparations should conflict erupt. As the 2003 *Outline for Studying Jiang Zemin Thought on National Defence and Army Building*, produced by the PLA General Political Department, posits:

> "Planning for the national defence and modernization of army building, and planning for military combat preparations requires a prominent main strategic direction (*zhuyao zhanlue fangxiang*). While paying attention to other directions (*qita zhanlue fangxiang*), the main strategic direction is the impetus for army building (*jundui jianshe*) in other strategic directions".[28]

In view of this, the PLA's modernisation program has spanned the full range of capabilities development that includes improvements in weapon systems across the force, an increase in joint and combined arms exercise activity, doctrinal and structural changes for 'informatised' warfighting, and improvements in space and cyber capabilities with added emphasis on professionalising the force, rooting out corruption, and enhancing civil-military relations. In current times, 'army building' is heavily invested in capability development of the PLA, especially in areas such as maritime, air, space and cyber. The PLA's modernisation can be identified under "three pillars" as noted in Table 3.3.

Table 3.3: Three Pillars of China's Military Modernisation

Pillar 1	*Pillar 2*	*Pillar 3*
Objective: development, procurement, acquisition, and fielding of new weapons systems, technologies, and combat capabilities	**Objective:** institutional and systemic reforms	**Objective:** development of new war fighting doctrines for the employment of these new capabilities
Aim: To enhance combat capabilities	**Aim:** To optimise the force	**Aim:** current doctrine aims at 'joint operations' in the aerospace, maritime, and electro-magnetic battle space dimensions
Major changes comprise: (a) Enhance China's indigenous production of conventional weapons and upgrade nuclear arsenal (b) Enhance PLA's R&D to produce information-age military technologies	**Major changes comprise:** (a) Officer professional military education system (b) Force structure adjustment, downsizing of personnel and new battlefield logistics paradigms	**Major doctrinal adjustments comprise:** (a) From wars of attrition to quick decisive campaigns (b) From combined arms operations to joint operations (c) From protracted wars to short, high-intensity joint campaigns beyond China's littoral (d) From emphasis on defence to primacy on offence—static defence to mobile offence (e) From focusing on enemy's weak forces to attacking and destroying enemy's vital assets (f) From concentration on units and personnel to concentration on capabilities (g) From the need to absorb operational blows to that of executing operational-level pre-emption (h) From land warfare to multi domain warfare in land, sea, air, electro-magnetic, cyber and space dimensions (i) Towards an expeditionary force

Source: Annotated by the Author with reference to Finkelstein (2007) and Peterson Institute for International Economics.[29]

You Ji argues that China's military modernisation is dominant in three major areas:[30] (a) changing civil-military relations between the CPC and the PLA (as exemplified by the MCF strategy); (b) organisational overhaul in terms of its personnel composition and structure; and (c) force modernisation driven by doctrinal innovation, capability enhancement, and war game plans. This is evident from the successive cuts in the PLA's ground forces and increasing focus on developing ballistic and cruise missiles, naval power, air power, air defences, amphibious forces and anti-satellite (ASAT) weapons. In particular, the PLA has focused on anti-access/area denial (A2/AD)[31] capabilities and asymmetric warfare capabilities to defeat a more powerful force (USA), if armed conflict were to occur. Thereby, China's quest to build a 'strong army' is the top-most priority, as Xi notes:

> "Once a country's military lags behind, its national security will be fatally threatened. I often read historic materials about modern China, and when I see how lagging behind leaves a country vulnerable to attack, I feel deep pain in my heart!"[32]

II. Change in PLA's Thinking: From People-centric to Network- and Information-centric Warfare

At the foremost, an assessment of the PLA's modernisation demands an understanding of the Chinese perception of war and warfighting. That is, there is a significant shift in the way China perceives war in the 21st century as drawn from the assessments of modern warfare techniques. The 2019 White Paper observes, "War is evolving in form towards informationised warfare, and intelligent warfare is on the horizon",[33] in which AI and other ranges of technologies such as advanced automation and big data are driving the PLA's conduct of 'next' form of warfare. As Lieutenant General Liu Guozhi, Director of the CMC's Science and Technology Commission argues:

> "AI will accelerate the process of military transformation, ultimately leading to a profound Revolution in Military Affairs.... The combination of artificial intelligence and human intelligence can achieve the optimum, and human-machine hybrid intelligence will be the highest form of future intelligence".[34]

This suggests that future 'intelligentised' operations are expected to involve prominent employment of intelligent autonomy in weapon systems under conditions of multi-domain integration with command exercised through brain-machine integration, enabled by Cloud infrastructure,[35] thus making warfare cognitive-centric. To note, the 14th Five Year Plan (2021-2025) has called for the PLA to accelerate its transition from "mechanisation" towards "informationisation" and "intelligentisation" aiming at moving from platform modernisation towards the widespread adoption of digital and networked military systems.[36] This new Chinese thinking highlights the shift from people-centric to network-centric to information-centric warfare to that of becoming intelligence-centric.

In view of this, taking a departure from Mao Zedong's 'Protracted War', the PLA's perception of future wars mainly suggests them to be shorter, perhaps lasting only one campaign; will almost certainly not entail the occupation of China, although Chinese political, economic, and military centres are likely to be attacked; and will involve joint military operations across land, sea, air, cyberspace and outer space, and the application of advanced technology, especially information technology.[37] Hence, the query: What called for this departure?

This makes it significant to note that while the PRC has not fought an actual war since the 1979 war against Vietnam, yet in the last four decades, incremental changes have been witnessed in China's military thinking, approach and thereby, military modernisation. While 'war fighting' acts as the 'core mission' for the PLA, its own operational legacy has been mainly centred on land warfare, as noted in terms of the Korean War of 1950-53, the Sino-Indian border war of 1962, the Sino-Soviet border skirmish in 1969, and the Sino-Vietnamese border war of 1979. This demands the query: What is then driving the PLA's military modernisation? The answer lies in the fact that with no actual experience in the changing nature of war, Beijing's current strategic outlook has been primarily shaped by its discernment of the evolving information age – mainly by drawing lessons from the experiences of others to prepare itself to deal with its own national security issues. Thus, exhibiting a departure from Mao's dictum of "learn by doing" ("in war, study war").

Such a perception of China was motivated by the lessons drawn from the Gulf War, especially US Operation DESERT SHIELD/DESERT STORM in 1991. As noted in the PLA *Encyclopaedia*, China's key lessons from the First Gulf War entailed securing dominance of the electromagnetic spectrum; aerial attacks as a strategic factor; deception, coordinated operations among different services, and deep attacks in the rapid attainment of campaign objectives; fortifications and minefields; and logistical support to sustain high-technology weapons.[38] While the Gulf Wars were the most impactful, China also drew lessons from the UK's war with Argentina over the Falklands, the US involvement in the Taiwan Straits Crisis of 1996, and the US intervention in Kosovo in 1999 (especially the bombing of the Chinese Embassy in Belgrade), and the Second Gulf War of 2003 (US Operation IRAQI FREEDOM) - all red flags for the Chinese government to realise that military modernisation was indispensable. However, some analysts argue that the Taiwan Straits

Crisis of 1996 cemented the PRC's modernisation programme, as it resulted in a new urgency in the PLA since Chinese leaders became convinced that they would definitely have to contend with the USA in a cross-strait conflict.[39]

These wars heralded a new era of warfare for the PLA as US victories exemplified the use of stealth and precision-guided weaponry, and more importantly, diffused the old way of thinking by projecting that the elimination of the enemy forces on the battlefield was not a prerequisite to achieving victory. This led the PLA to perceive modern warfare under two dimensions; informatisation and mechanisation, in which the combat is system-based on precision, remoteness and networking, thus making future wars in Chinese eyes to be "unmanned, invisible, and silent".[40]

In order for the PLA to prepare for such war, Jiang Zemin set forth the 1993 "Military Strategic Guidelines for the New Period" that laid out an assessment of the new nature of modern war and how the PLA should prepare to deal with "local wars under high-tech conditions". Specific to the "Gulf War", Jiang noted that:

> "The facts of the Gulf War have shown that along with the utilization of high technology in the military arena, the enhancement of precision attack weapons and unprecedented operational intensity, the characteristics of sudden, three-dimensional, mobile, rapid, and in-depth attacks, have become more prominent, and the use of high-tech superiority has obviously taken hold of the strategic initiative to an even greater degree".[41]

Here, the key is to understand: How did the Gulf War impact China's perception? As PLA analysts note, it was perceived that "the form of joint operations appearing in it [the Gulf War], of coordination among all service arms, will undoubtedly be a key trend of future war developments"; as the "characteristics of a joint operation of all branches of the military displayed in that war [the Gulf War] gave us [China] a glimpse of things to come in the early 21st century".[42]

This perception still remains valid in China's modernisation programme. For instance, the 2003 *Outline for Studying Jiang Zemin Thought on National Defense and Army Building* (*gangyao*), which acknowledged the centrality of the Gulf War as a determinant of the need for new guidelines, mentions:

> "At the onset of the Gulf War, [Jiang Zemin] brought up the need to study the special characteristics of modern warfare through this

> conflict. He personally managed open symposiums and conferences and pointed out that "modern warfare is becoming high-tech warfare". In addition, according to our country's security situation, he promptly brought up [the need] for studying the formation of the Military Strategic Guidelines for the New Period. At the beginning of 1993, the Central Military Commission formulated the Military Strategic Guidelines for the New Period, implementing major adjustments on military strategy".[43]

Furthermore, in 2004, the PLA NDU's Army Building Research Department reiterated 'Jiang's vision' by stating:

> "[...] the CMC with Jiang Zemin as the core clearly pointed out that the focus of military combat preparations in the new period would change from fighting to win local wars under normal conditions to fighting to win local wars under modern, high-tech conditions.... Looking at these developing trends, for some time to come in the future, these different characteristics, scopes, and patterns of local wars and armed conflicts will be the main types of warfare. In the local wars our country is likely to face in the future, regardless of whether they are wars to realize the unification of the motherland *or wars to resist and counter a localized invasion by an enemy* (emphasis added), in all cases we are likely to face an enemy that possesses high-tech weapons and equipment. We can see that making the focus of military combat preparations on fighting to win local wars under modern high-tech conditions is a necessary choice based on a scientific analysis of the international strategic framework as well as our national security environment".[44]

Besides, the Second Gulf War of 2003, wherein the US Operation IRAQI FREEDOM increased the PLA's attention to the potentials of information technology. At this time, as Wang Baocun notes, the five areas that the PLA was investigating entailed: (a) command, control, communications, computers, and intelligence (C4I) modernisation; (b) network-based war-gaming; (c) training of personnel in information warfare; (d) conduct of information exercises; and (e) introduction of informationalised equipment.[45]

In view of these Chinese perceptions, it can be rightly argued that the 'Gulf Wars' provided a reality check to the Chinese leadership, mainly acquainted it with the PLA's inadequacy in fighting a modern war, making it imperative for the PLA to fill this void. As a result of which, the main areas for the PLA's modernisation and reform included: incorporation of more science and technology within the PLA; enhancing the quality of PLA personnel; improving the PLA's organisation and logistical infrastructure; and continued emphasis on ideological and political work.

As noted, since 2004, the strategic goal of Chinese military modernisation has been officially defined as "building informationised armed forces" (*jianshexinxihuajundui*) that are capable of 'winning informationised wars'. Besides, the changes in the PLA's strategic guidance, operational regulations, force structure, and defence programmes clearly highlight the fundamental shifts in the Chinese perception of the 'nature of warfare' caused by the advent of information technology and the 'revolution in military affairs' (RMA). These major changes have been catalysed by China's acute sense of vulnerability in the maritime, electromagnetic, space, and cyberspace domains, which are the new domains of modern warfare. This led to the development of the aspect of "informationisation" (*xinxihua*) in the PLA's thinking, making it the defining factor of the ongoing RMA and the key goal of PLA's modernisation. As the 2015 White Paper notes:

> "The world revolution in military affairs (RMA) is proceeding to a new stage. Long-range, precise, smart, stealthy and unmanned weapons and equipment are becoming increasingly sophisticated. Outer space and cyber space have become new commanding heights in strategic competition among all parties. The form of war is accelerating its evolution to informationization".[46]

What makes information a central feature of 21st century warfare are two factors:[47] First, at the tactical level are the intelligence, surveillance and reconnaissance (ISR) capabilities on which the precision-centric operations are critically dependent as without accurate target locations, precision-guided munitions would lack efficacy. Second, the advantages of information are more significant than sensors and ISR systems, irrespective of being on manned aircraft, unmanned aerial vehicles or satellites. Battle networks that provide command, control, communications and computers (C4) then help to exploit the ISR before and during operations.[48] This is echoed in the Chinese perception, as Peng Guangqian and Yao Youzhi argue that information superiority has not only "become a pre-requisite of supremacy in the air, on the ground and at sea," but has "become the priority mission of modern warfare".[49] Wherein, degrading the opponent's information resources acts as a decisive factor in the fighting power of modern weapons and equipment.

In China, the shift towards network centricity is driven by the perception that "the form of war is accelerating its evolution to informationization".[50] This has made it essential for the PLA to secure 'information dominance' (*zhixinxiquan*; 制信息权), which encompasses not only information systems but also the cognitive and decision-making aspects of military and political command. As the 2015 White Paper notes:

> "[To persevere] in information dominance [...] China's armed forces will speed up to upgrade weaponry and equipment, and work to develop a weaponry and equipment system which can effectively respond to informationized warfare and help fulfil the missions and tasks".[51]

In view of this, PLA's 'military missions and tasks' would involve joint military operations across land, sea, air, cyberspace and outer space, and the application of advanced technology, especially information technology. In this regard, military modernisation would require the PLA to have achieved a networked system-based C4ISR and counter-C4ISR capabilities to kinetically or non-kinetically defeat or paralyse the enemy's operational system, waging a "system destruction warfare" (体系破击战).[52]

In aiming for transformation towards informatisation, China seeks to enhance its capabilities for system-vs-system operations based on information systems, which entails more efficient utilisation of information resources, strengthening the building of the systems of reconnaissance, early-warning and command and control, develop medium and long-range precision strike capabilities, and improve comprehensive support systems.[53] As a result, the key technologies that China is targeting to excel includes quantum computing, big data, semiconductors, 5G, advanced nuclear technology, aerospace technology, and AI – with the ultimate aim to exploit the inherent 'dual-use' nature of many of these technologies, which have both military and civilian applications. As the Chinese argue, it entails expertising "combat operations in a high-tech battlefield environment" in which "both sides use information-technology means, equipment, or systems in a rivalry over the power to obtain, control and use information".[54] Here, the crux lies in achieving information superiority, which is seen as a precondition for achieving and maintaining battlefield supremacy.

PLA's Road to Reform under Xi

In 2017, at the 19th National Congress of the CPC, Xi Jinping noted that China has "initiated a new stage in strengthening and revitalising the armed forces".[55] Xi categorically stated that:

> "Historic breakthroughs have been made in reforming national defence and the armed forces: a new military structure has been established with the Central Military Commission exercising overall leadership, the theatre commands responsible for military operations, and the services focusing on developing capabilities. This represents a revolutionary restructuring of the organization and the services of the people's armed forces".[56]

The above statement by Xi reflects China's resolve to adapt the military for the new era under new conditions by making structural, organisational and other adjustments to China's armed forces. While China perceives that in "the foreseeable future, a world war is unlikely, and that the international situation is expected to remain generally peaceful", but what calls for China's anxiety in the current times are the "new threats from hegemonism, power politics and neo-interventionism", whereby, "the world still faces both immediate and potential threats of local wars".[57]

In this perspective, China's contingencies are mainly three-fold:[58] First, the Taiwan Challenge—this factor bears heavily on China's reunification and long-term development calculus. The PLA aims to deter and, if necessary, compel Taiwan to abandon moves towards independence, as the 2015 White Paper categorically mentions that the root cause of instability in the cross-Straits relations is the "Taiwan independence" separatist forces and their activities that act as the "biggest threat to the peaceful development of cross-Straits relations". In view of this, the PLA's combat readiness seeks to prepare itself for a contingency to unify Taiwan with China by force, while simultaneously deterring, delaying or denying any third-party intervention on Taiwan's behalf.[59]

Second, the challenge of securing China's sovereignty, as the 2015 White Paper emphasises:

> "China's offshore neighbours take provocative actions and reinforce their military presence on China's reefs and islands that they have illegally occupied. Some countries are also busy meddling in South China Sea affairs; a tiny few maintain constant close-in air and sea surveillance and reconnaissance against China. It is thus a long-

> standing task for China to safeguard its maritime rights and interests. Certain disputes over land territory are still smouldering".[60]

In view of this, China's imminent contingencies include the ongoing territorial and maritime disputes in the South China Sea, the East China Sea, and the unresolved boundary dispute with India. These three factors challenge China's security and stability along its periphery and strongly affect its quest for regional dominance.

Third, the challenge of 'separatist and extremist forces', that pose a severe threat to China's national security and social stability. For China, separatist forces such as the "East Turkistan independence" in Xinjiang and "Tibet independence" forces have become a serious challenge to its internal security. There is increased concern over escalating violent terrorist activities, especially by "East Turkistan independence" forces. In addition, China also faces challenges of a "Colour Revolution" from the anti-China forces within the country. To say so, forces hostile to the Chinese government are seen to turn Hong Kong into a "bridgehead for political subversion and infiltration into the Chinese mainland". In view of this, the 2014 "Occupy Central" movement in Hong Kong is perceived by the Chinese government as a "Colour Revolution", which was "deliberately plotted by some extremist groups" in Hong Kong. [61]

These contingencies make it a formidable task for the PLA to maintain the PRC's political security and social stability. In this security matrix, China is determined to maintain a non-compromising attitude in defending its sovereignty, as Xi pointedly stated that "no one should expect us [China] to swallow bitter fruit that is harmful to our sovereignty, security or development interests".[62] The 2017 White Paper on "China's Policies on Asia-Pacific Security Cooperation" mentions:

> "Building strong national defence and armed forces that are commensurate with China's international standing and its security and development interests is a "strategic task" in China's modernization drive, and provides a strong guarantee for its peaceful development".[63]

With threats becoming increasingly diverse and less likely to be local or short term, China's strategy lies in building a strong military force with capabilities pertaining to long-range, precision-strike, stealth and unmanned weapons and weapon systems as well as in outer space, cyberspace and electromagnetic spectrum. Under this dictum of 'building a strong national defence and military', China has witnessed the most extensive restructuring of its national defence establishment driven by the quest to make the PLA an effective combat force operating under an 'integrated joint command and control structure' (a lesson learnt from the Gulf War), to prepare for the "threat of war" and make "preparations to contain ... [or win] war".[64] As the 2013 *Science of Military Strategy* notes, the types of warfare that China is likely to face in the future are four-fold: (a) a "relatively large-scale high-intensity anti-separatist war" that would centre on Taiwan; (b) a "medium-scale, low- to medium-intensity self-defence and counterattack operation" along the periphery that could involve encroachments or threats to PRC maritime claims; (c) a "small-scale, low-intensity anti-terrorist, stability maintenance" operation to protect internal stability and Chinese citizens in China and abroad; and (d) a large-scale ground invasion, which is seen to be a remote possibility.[65]

On 1 August 2017, on the occasion of the 90th anniversary of the PLA, Xi categorically stated that China must step up transforming its armed forces into a world-class military that is "ready to fight and win wars" as the country "will never compromise on defending sovereignty"[66] and that "no one should expect us [to do so]".[67] These statements exemplify the imperative need for the PLA to be 'combat-ready'. In the first ever mobilisation meeting of the CMC, Xi urged the PLA to enhance military training oriented at combat readiness and put military training in a strategic position and as the central work with effective results.[68] The outcome calls for the PLA to:

> "[B]e brave to overcome difficulties and surpass opponents, and create an elite and powerful force that is always ready for the fight, capable of combat and sure to win in order to fulfil the tasks bestowed by the Party and the people in the new era".[69]

In this regard, PRC's military modernisation aims at building a strong, combat-effective force, as in the Chinese view, the only option for China is to win in all circumstances. This is embedded in China's national strategy of fulfilling the 'Chinese Dream' that is focused on the PLA becoming 'an army that not only can fight, but also win wars, restoring China to greatness by "building a more modern, capable, and disciplined military".[70] Owing to which, the road to PLA's latest reforms was laid in November 2013, at the Third Plenum of the 18th Central Committee of the CPC that called for "deepening national defence and military reform", as the communiqué notes:

"objective of building a line of strong armies for this Party under new circumstances, [...] build a modern military force system with Chinese characteristics. We must deepen military structural and personnel allocation adjustment and reform, move adjustment and reform of military policies and institutions forward, and promote the integrated and deep development of the military and the people".[71]

Regarded as one of the "biggest military reforms" in modern China, the decision to deepen the reform mainly aims at breaking down systematic, structural, and policy barriers, modernising the organization of the military and improving combat capacity.[72] In this process, China's military transformation is defined by roadmaps to guide the policy formulation and force modernisation with objectives, as listed in Table 3.4. In view of this, the key reforms undertaken by Xi are noted in Figure 3.1.

Table 3.4: Key Objectives of Military Modernisation

Sl. No.	*Objective*
1	To change the PLA from a military of quantity to one of quality.
2	To change the PLA's posture from being defensive-offence to one that is capable of offensive-defence—*from homeland to sustained operations of long-range power projection in "far seas" areas.*
3	To change the PLA's force structure from being army-centric to one that suits joint operations with Special Services. The PLAAF and PLAN are to play a primary role in future warfare.
4	To change the PLA's operational command structure from five-layers and vertically distributed to one that is horizontally arranged in a three-level system of CMC joint operational headquarters, forward war-zone commandant and campaign units.
5	To change the PLA's force building from focusing on mechanisation (platform-centric warfare) to one paralleling mechanisation and informationisation (network-centric warfare).
6	To change the PLA's weapons R& D and equipment priority from high-tech hardware modernisation to one that combines both platform upgrade and IT-software advancement for future network-centric warfare.

Source: Annotated by the Author with reference to You (2016).[73]

Figure 3.1: Key Military Reforms under Xi Jinping (2013-2020)

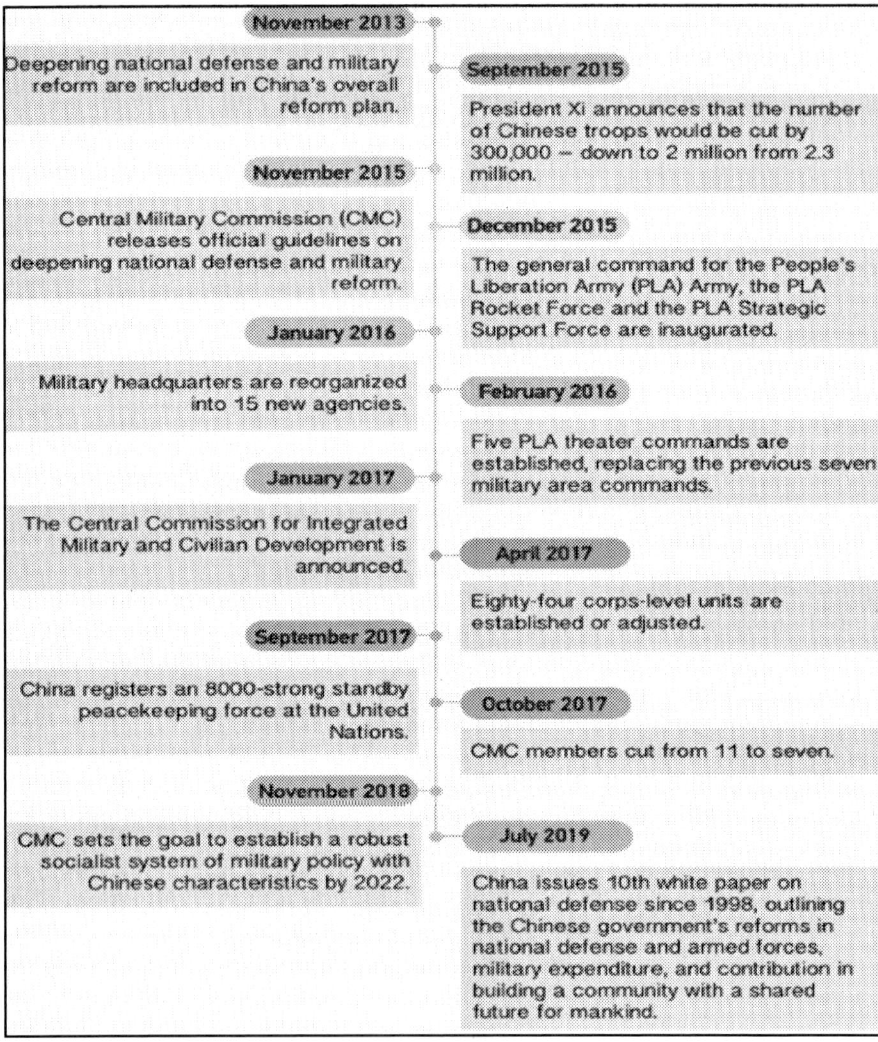

Source: Adapted from *CGTN* (2020).[74]

It is also significant to note that this was the first time in PRC's history that a CPC plenary session had adopted "independent" defence and military reforms[75] by proposing: "That joint operation command authority under the (Central Military Commission), and theatre joint operation command system, will be improved" and decided to "optimise the size and structure of the army, adjust and improve the proportion between various troops, and reduce non-combat institutions and personnel".[76] This highlights the need felt by the PRC to create a more modern joint operation command system structure for the PLA.

China's such drastic reforms can also be attributed to the "self-assessments" of the military modernisation provided by the PLA media via a number of slogans or formulas. These mainly refer to the 'internal shortcomings' of the PLA, as noted in Table 3.5.

Table 3.5: "Self-Assessment of the PLA" by PLA Media

Slogans/Formulas	*Implications*
"Two Incompatibles" or "Principle Contradiction"	The PLA's level of modernisation (1) does not meet the requirements of winning local wars under informa-tionised conditions; and (2) its military capability does not meet the requirements of carrying out its historic missions at the new stage of the new century.
"Two Big Gaps"	(1) Currently, there are big gaps between the level of our military modernisation compared to the requirements for national security; and (2) the level of the world's advanced militaries.
"Three Whethers"	(1) Whether our armed forces can constantly maintain the party's absolute leadership; (2) whether they can fight victoriously when needed by the party and the people; and (3) whether commanders at all levels are competent to lead forces and command in war.
"Two Inabilities"	The PLA's ability: (1) to fight a modern war is not sufficient:, (2) the ability of our cadres at all levels to command modern war is insufficient.
"Five Incapables"	Some cadres cannot: (1) judge the situation; (2) understand the intention of higher authorities; (3) make operational decisions; (4) deploy troops; and (5) deal with unexpected situations.

Source: Annotated by the Author with reference to Blasko (2019).[77]

In November 2015, at the CMC's Reform Work Conference, Xi Jinping expressed the intent to resolutely implement national defence and military reform as part of a comprehensive strategy to build a strong army and to unswervingly follow the path of building a strong military with Chinese characteristics.[78] Xi outlined the targets as: to make breakthroughs in military administration and joint operational command; to optimise the military structure, enhance policy systems and civilian-military integration; to build a modern military with Chinese characteristics that can win digital wars and effectively fulfil its duties; and to perfect the military system with Chinese characteristics.[79]

Reaffirming to this commitment, on 12 March 2019, at the plenary meeting of the delegation of the PLA and the PAP at the second session of the 13th NPC, Xi emphasised on "fulfilling the set targets and tasks of national defence and military development as scheduled",[80] with no space for any kind of delay in the missions. Xi also noted that the military should primarily focus on issues concerning urgent necessities for military preparedness, crucial support for combat systems, and coordinated projects for the reform of national defence and armed force. In doing so, Xi's four-point agenda for military reform called for: adjustment of China's military leadership and command system, optimising structure and function, reforming policies and systems and promoting deeper civil-military integration.[81]

With 'active defence' as the essence of China's military strategic thought, the PLA's agenda entails optimising its power structure and troop formation and speeding up the Army's transformation from the "regional defensive type to the full-spectrum combat type";[82] in which "implementing active defence" to the new security situation, China's armed forces will seek to adhere to the principles of "flexibility, mobility and self-dependence",[83] an understanding that defines Xi's 'fight and win' theorem. These perspectives highlight the application of the concept of active defence in China's military modernisation. The outcome of this is witnessed in the most extensive restructuring of China's national defence establishment in which the watchword is 'jointness', transforming the PLA into an effective combat force operating under an integrated joint command and control structure.

Here, the priority lies in modernising the PLA's command, control, communications, computers, intelligence, surveillance, and reconnaissance (C4ISR) system as a response to trends in modern warfare with the emphasis on "importance of rapid decision-making and information sharing and processing".[84] That is, with 'integrated joint operations' (一体化联合作战) as the key benchmark, the mission of the Chinese military is at the foremost, to deter many types of threats to China's sovereignty and territory, and, if deterrence fails, to win informationised local wars, which is considered to be the most likely form of combat the PLA will face in the future.[85] In addition to its core task of preparing to conduct combat operations, the Chinese military doctrine contends that the PLA may also be required to perform non-traditional security tasks, known as "military operations other than war" (MOOTW).[86]

Thereby, the perceived challenges of the future and China's own 'self-assessment' has prompted the PLA's commitment towards military preparedness to tackle contingencies in multiple theatres – justifying the reforms in the PLA's force structure, development and operational command and control structure.

I. Structural Reforms in Force Structure and Development: PLA be Combat Ready

In December 2012, in his three-day inspection visit to the PLA's Guangzhou military theatre of operations, Xi Jinping, as the new General Secretary of the CPC and the Chairman of the CMC, ordered the PLA to intensify its "real combat" awareness in order to sustain military readiness by stating:

> "[...] it is the top priority for the military to be able to combat and win battles, and it is fundamental that the military consolidate itself through governing the troops lawfully and austerely, so as to reinforce its development featuring loyalty to the Party, modernization and standardization".[87]

In the Chinese perspective, to quell the growing risks, the key is to build the PLA's combat capabilities in both traditional and new security fields. This factor further justifies the cut in the non-combatant units as opposed to the combat units. The query is: What does the PLA seeks to achieve?

In outlining the expectations for the PLA, Xi in his 19th Party Congress report, categorically stated:

> "A military is built to fight. Our [the PLA] military must regard combat capability as the criterion to meet in all its work and focus on how to win when it is called on. We will take solid steps to ensure military preparedness for all strategic directions, and make progress in combat readiness in both traditional and new security fields. We will develop new combat forces and support forces, conduct military training under combat conditions, strengthen the application of military strength, speed up development of intelligent military, and

> improve combat capabilities for joint operations based on the network information system and the ability to fight under multi-dimensional conditions. This will enable us to effectively shape our military posture, manage crises, and deter and win wars".[88]

This mandate points at the need for the PLA to prepare to fight and win informationised local wars. In doing so, the key trends that define China's military modernisation are listed below.

Table 3.6: Key Trends in PLA's Capabilities and Force Structure

Sl. No.	*PLA's Capabilities and Force Structure*
1	Testing and Deployment of New High-Technology Platforms such as unmanned aerial vehicles (UAV) and unmanned combat aerial vehicles (UCAV); hypersonic glide vehicles (HGV); and stealth fighters
2	Continued development of power projection capabilities: amphibious warfare ships; aircraft carriers, long-range strikes
3	Investment in C4ISR, counter-C4ISR, and Space-Based Capabilities: Situational awareness and over-the-horizon targeting (OTH-T), counter-C4ISR, cyber warfare and cyber espionage
4	Efforts to improve the capabilities of Military Personnel
5	PLA reform and reorganisation

Source: Annotated by the Author with reference to Heath et al. (2016).[89]

In this process, undertaking the "largest scale military reform since the 1950s", the key characteristic has been streamlining the PLA's structure and functioning under the authority of the CMC[90] to achieve unification of the PLA's operational and administrative command under the CMC.[91]

In view of this, China has streamlined the command structure with the primary aim to prevent bottlenecks in communication and for greater centralisation of the military authority, as noted in Figure 3.2.

Figure 3.2: China's Military Leadership: Chain of Command and Control

Source: Adapted from DoD Report (2020).[92]

Streamlining of the PLA

In 2015, Xi Jinping announced that the PLA will reduce its forces by 300,000 troops. This announcement was followed by downsizing of the ground forces in 2019, with the army accounting for less than 50 per cent of the armed forces. This move is seen as part of the larger plan of restructuring the PLA, as part of the modernisation of China's armed forces. It is important to note that this reduction fits in the long line of streamlining made since the 1980s, as outlined in Table 3.7.

Table 3.7: Streamlining of the PLA (1980-2020)

Year	*1980*	*1985*	*1990*	*1995*	*2000*	*2005*	*2010*	*2015*	*2020*
PLAA	3.6	3.16	2.3	2.2	1.7	1.6	1.6	1.6	2.035
PLAN	0.63	0.35	0.26	0.26	0.22	0.255	0.255	0.235	*(Combined*
PLAAF	0.4	0.49	0.47	0.47	0.42	0.4	0.33	0.398	*Active*
Strat Forces/ Coast Guard	0	0	0.09	0.09	0.1	0.1	0.1	0.1	*Armed Forces)*
Reserves	0	5	4	1.2	0.55	0.8	0.51	0.51	0.51
Paramilitary	7	4.3	12	1.2	1.1	1.5	0.66	0.66	0.66
Total No. of PLA Personnel	11.63	13.3	16.32	5.42	4.49	4.665	3.455	3.503	3.205

Source: Adapted from Bommakanti and Mann (2020).[93]

While the reductions in the 1980s were mainly aimed at justifying China's "determination to actively promote arms control and disarmament"; in the 1990s, it aimed to dispel the China threat syndrome; however, in the current times, neither of this logic validates China's such a strategic move.[94] As the current reduction does not entail the downsizing of the PLA's 'combat force', but the 'non-combatant' units, as noted by *Xinhua* that "almost half of our [PLA's] non-combatant units have been made redundant, and the number of officers in the PLA has been reduced by 30 per cent".[95]

This explains that the 'reduction' of the ground forces is aimed at strengthening the other services of the PLA, which has two key objectives:[96] First, to rebalance the distribution of forces within the PLA to make it more capable of executing joint campaigns beyond China's borders. Second, to downplay the long-held superiority of the PLA Army to break the "Big Army" thinking which has hindered PLA's joint operational capabilities especially in the maritime, air, space/cyber domains.[97] This shift of focus from the Ground Forces to the other services is driven by what the White Paper of 2019 describes as the new "RMA with Chinese characteristics", which is aimed at completing the task of "mechanisation" compounded with the urgent need for improving "informationisation", given the risks from technology surprise and growing technological gap.[98] What calls for this new RMA with Chinese characteristics? The answer to the query, as the 2019 White Paper explains:

> "[...] the application of cutting-edge technologies such as artificial intelligence (AI), quantum information, big data, cloud computing and the Internet of Things is gathering pace in the military field. International military competition is undergoing historic changes. New and high-tech military technologies based on IT are developing

rapidly. There is a prevailing trend to develop long-range precision, intelligent, stealthy or unmanned weaponry and equipment. War is evolving in form towards informationized warfare, and intelligent warfare is on the horizon".[99]

Owing to this, the troop cuts are part of the long-mooted reforms to simplify and further professionalise the Chinese military, especially command and leadership structures that are still largely run along Soviet lines.[100]

Reorganisation of PLA's Force Structure

With the core objective to "integrate the administrative system and the joint battle command system", in 2015 the CMC undertook certain key 'above the neck reforms'.

Figure 3.3: Structural Reforms in CMC General Departments

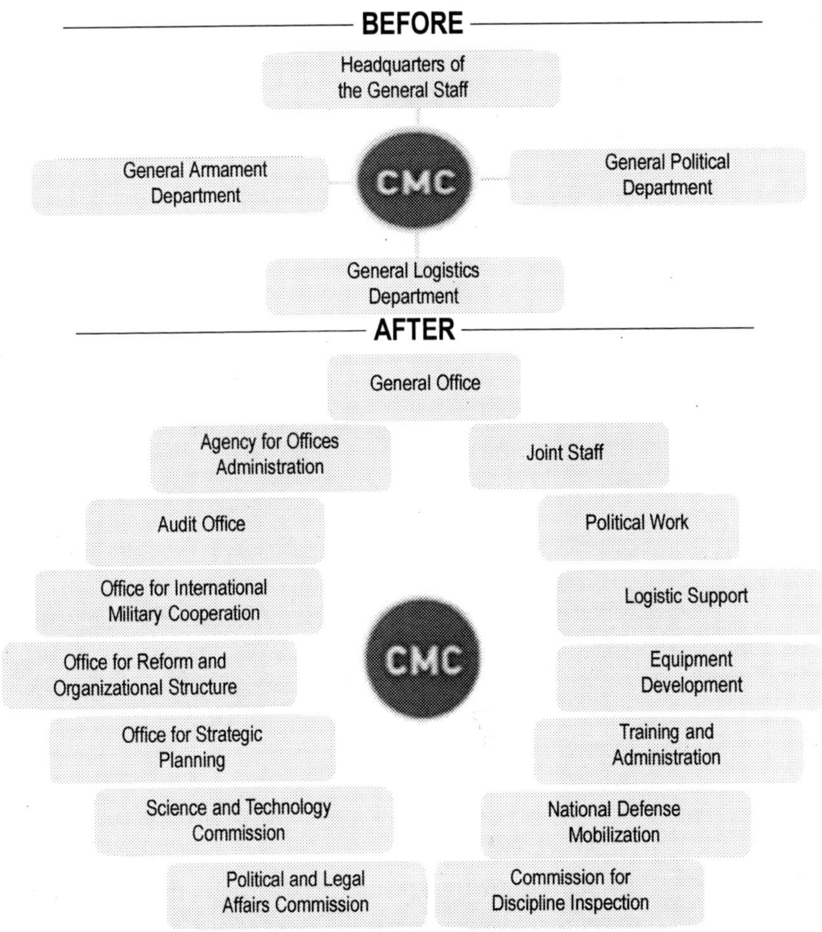

Source: Adapted from *CGTN* (2019).[101]

At the foremost, the CMC established a new Army Headquarters in Beijing; the former Second Artillery Force was upgraded to a full-fledged service and renamed as the PLA Rocket Force; and a new Strategic Support Force was created. Following this, the four General Departments were abolished and a new, expanded CMC organisation set up consisting of 15 functional departments, commissions and offices was established, as noted in Figure 3.3. Thereafter, the Army-centric seven Military Regions were replaced by five Theatre Commands and later, the Joint Logistics Support Force (JLSF) was established to streamline the logistics structures of different military services and place it under the new force. The JLSF is responsible for coordinating logistics operations for overseas deployments alongside service-level logistics support - so far, JLSF has conducted 50 cross-theatre exercises involving different military services.[102] This restructuring is made to establish a three-tier "CMC—battle zone commands—troops" command system and an administration system that runs from the CMC through various services to the troops.[103]

Figure 3.4: PLA Structural Reform (From 3 to 6 Services)

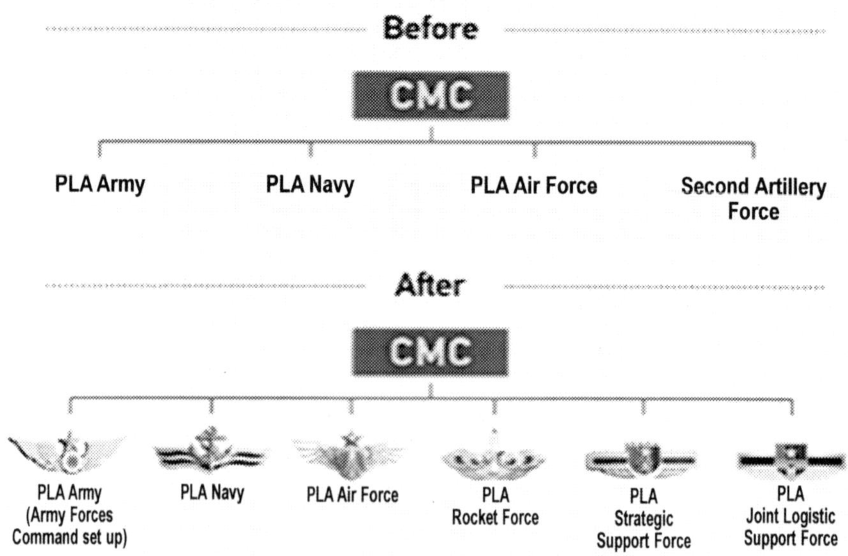

Source: Adapted from *CGTN* (2019).[104]

Apart from the structural reorganisation, the reforms in the operational units are meant to increase its combat effectiveness to contribute to the PLA's joint operations capabilities and to expand the percentage of "new-type combat forces"[105] (see Table 3.8).

Table 3.8: Strategic Needs of the Services of the PLA and the PAP

Service	*Strategic Requirement*	*Strategic Aim*	*To develop capabilities*	*Training/Exercises Conducted*
PLAA	Mobile operations and multi-dimensional offence and defence.	Continue to reorient from theatre defence to trans-theatre mobility.	Capabilities for precise, multi-dimensional, trans-theatre, multi-functional and sustainable operations.	Conducted live exercises codenamed *Stride* and *Firepower*.
PLAN	Offshore waters defence and open seas protection.	Shift its focus from "offshore waters defence" to the combination of "offshore waters defence" with "open seas protection", and build a combined, multi-functional and efficient marine combat force structure.	Capabilities for strategic deterrence and counterattack, maritime manoeuvres, joint operations at sea, comprehensive defence and comprehensive support.	Extended training to the far seas and deployed the aircraft carrier task group for its first far seas combat exercise in the West Pacific.It has organised naval parades in the South China Sea and the waters and airspace near Qingdao, and conducted a series of live force-on-force exercises codenamed *Mobility* and systematic all-elements exercises.
PLAAF	Building air-space capabilities and conducting offensive and defensive operations.	Shift its focus from territorial air defence to both defence and offense, and build an air-space defence force structure that can meet the requirements of informationised operations.	Capabilities for strategic early warning, air strike, air and missile defence, information countermeasures, airborne operations, strategic projection and comprehensive support.	Strengthened systematic and all-airspace training based on operational plans. Conducted combat patrols in the South China Sea and security patrols in the East China Sea, and operated in the West Pacific. Completed a series of regular system vs. system exercises such as *Red Sword*.
PLARF	Being lean and effective and possessing both nuclear and conventional missiles.	Strive to transform itself in the direction of informationisation, press forward with independent innovations in weaponry and equipment by reliance on science and technology, enhance the safety, reliability and effectiveness of missile systems, and improve the force structure featuring a combination of both nuclear and conventional capabilities.	Capabilities for strategic deterrence and nuclear counterattack, and medium and long-range precision strikes.	Organised force-on-force evaluation-oriented training and training based on operational plans at brigade and regiment levels, strengthened training for joint strikes, and completed regular exercises such as *Heavenly Sword*.

PLASSF	Integrating existing systems and aligning civil and military endeavours.	To achieve big development strides in key areas and accelerate the integrated development of new-type combat forces.	Capabilities to build a strong and modernised strategic support force.	Made active efforts to integrate into the joint operations systems. Carried out confrontational training in new domains and trained for emergencies and combats.
PLAJLSF	Providing joint support for joint operations and joint training.	To integrate into the joint operations system.	Capabilities of integrated joint logistics, so as to build a strong and modernised joint logistic support force.	Has striven to align itself with the joint operations systems, and conducted exercises such as *Joint Logistics Mission 2018*.
PAP	Performing multiple functions and effectively maintaining social stability.	To build a strong and modernised armed police force.	Capacity in guard duties, emergency response, counter-terrorism, maritime rights protection, administrative enforcement and disaster relief.	Has developed to meet the requirements of nationwide coverage, effective connectivity, all-area response and integrated functions, and conducted a series of exercises including *Guard*.

Source: Annotated by the Author with reference to China's White Papers (2015 and 2019) and Ministry of National Defense, PRC.

What makes the reforms under Xi significant is that the past reforms were mainly witnessed in terms of revision of the military region system in 1985, creation of a new general department in 1998, and addition of an independent branch, the Second Artillery Force in 1966. However, the PLA largely remained centred on the ground forces. This one-way Chinese approach therefore, called for a significant weakness in terms of "an outdated command and control (C2) structure in which the services, rather than theatre commanders, possessed operational authority during peacetime".[106] In view of this, the current centralisation is intended to guarantee the Party's absolute leadership of the military and the CMC's centralised leadership, enable CMC organs[s] to perform their duties of strategic planning and macro management, and enhance the oversight and supervision of the exercise of power.[107]

Given this perspective, it is important to note that the structural changes announced in late 2015 and 2016 represent only the initial phase of a five-year reform agenda, in which the key decisive factor that will determine the success of China's military modernisation is the 'timeline' outlined by the *CMC Opinions on Deepening National Defense and Military Reforms*, as summarised in Table 3.9.

Table 3.9: PLA Reform Agenda Through 2020

Reform Area (English)	*Reform Area (Chinese)*	*Topics*	*Target Completion*
Leadership Management System	领导管理体制	Reforms to CMC departments, military services. Logistics system, equipment development system	2015
Joint C2 System	联合作战指挥体制	Establish two-level joint command system, reform joint training, establish theater com mand s	2015
Military Scale Structure	军队规模结构	Reduce force size by 300,000, reduce noncombat personnel, reduce officer billets, phase out old equipment	2016
Force Composition	部队编成	Adjust force structure, optimize reserve force, reduce militias	2016
Cultivating New-Type Military Talent	新型军事人才培养	Enhance PME	2016
People's Armed Police Command and Control System (C2) and Force Composition	武装警察部队指挥管理体制和力量结构	Adjust PAP C2 and force structure	2016

Reform Area (English)	*Reform Area (Chinese)*	*Topics*	*Target Completion*
Policy System	政策制度	Reform personnel system, budget management, procurement system, salary and welfare system	2017-2020
Developing Civil-Military Integration	军民融合发展	Enhance management of civilian-military integration	2017-2020
Military Legal System	军事法治体系	Reform military regulations and the military justice system	No date provided

Source: Adapted from Wuthnow and Saunders (2017).[108]

With reforms enforced, it is also imperative to assess the factors that hinder China's military modernisation. For instance, in the Chinese view, the PLA "still lags far behind the world's leading militaries" making the Chinese government believe that it must invest more in new technologies and improve logistics.[109] While some analysts see the aspect of 'personnel' to be crucial, given the struggles to recruit, train, and retain a professional fighting force. In addition, Beijing also faces the challenge from 'corruption' which in the Chinese perspective is 'weakening the PLA's loyalty to the Party'.[110]

II. Theatre Commands – Key to PLA's Operational Command and Control

The cornerstone of the PLA's ability to undertake joint operational missions is the command and control structure. In doing so, the reform's main target is to be capable of winning wars, essentially removing barriers and obstacles that have restrained the combat capacity.[111] To fill this gap, by establishing the "CMC-battle zone command-troops command system", the Chinese armed forces have taken a key step forward towards a joint command system[112] in which it is not just a key reform on national defence and military, but as Xi notes, is also a "key measure to strengthen the CMC's function of strategic command".[113] In this process of reform, on 1 February 2016, China abolished the existing seven military regions (Shenyang, Beijing, Jinan, Nanjing, Guangzhou, Chengdu, and Lanzhou) and replaced it with five newly-created Theatre Commands (战区)—Eastern, Southern, Western, Northern and Central, as outlined in Figure 3.5.

The creation of TCs led to the change in the force structure at the division level—the division-sized forces gave way to brigades with combined arms capabilities, with each brigade being assigned artillery units, along with air defence and combat support, and infantry units.[114] To ensure that there are no problems in supporting this change in organisation on the ground, the PLA has also made improvements to the Teeth-To-Tail Ratio (TTR).[115]

Figure 3.5: PLA's Operational Command Structure (7MRs to 5TCs)

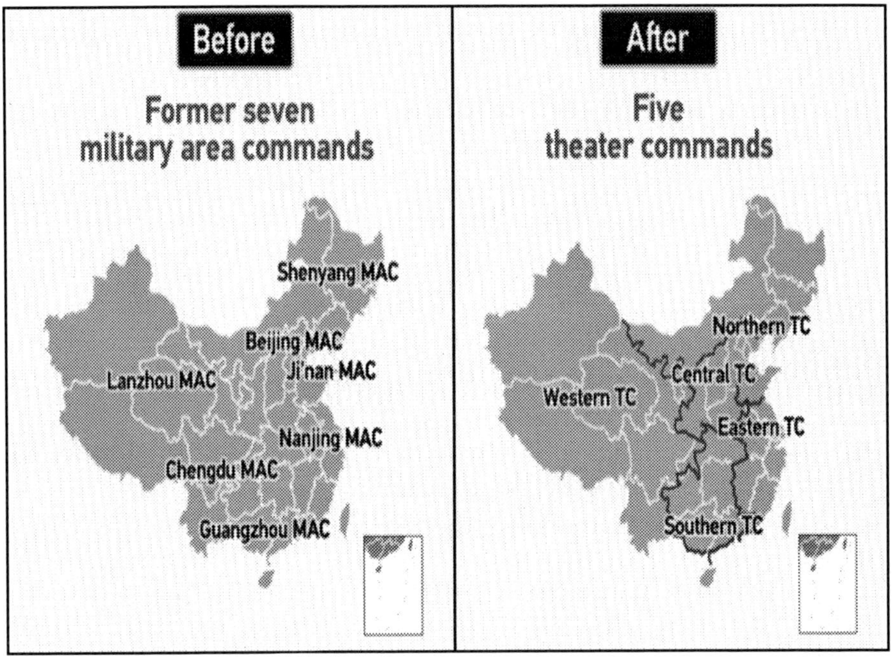

Source: Adapted from *CGTN* (2019).[116]

The key objective behind the creation of the TCs are two-fold: First, to centralise the PLA's decision-making in the hands of the CMC. And second, to build a joint battle system and strong joint command structure in which the CMC and its subsidiary departments will provide overall management, while the theatres will focus on operations, and the services will manage force building (军委管总、战区主战、军种主建).[117] Under this new operational (warfighting) formula, the chain of command runs from the CMC to the TCs down to the units, while the administrative chain runs from the CMC to the service headquarters and then to the units.[118] This distribution of order separates the combat commanding function from the construction and management functions by putting the focus of joint operational command on the TCs, and making the Services responsible for troop construction and management.[119]

These benchmarks thereby, point at the continuum of change that the PLA has been witnessing under China's quest to implement the 13th Five-Year Plan (2016-2020) to ensure that the set targets and tasks are fulfilled as scheduled. More importantly, the success of these will pave the path for the 14th Five-Year Plan for military development.

Taking a departure from the old structure, this new framework has replaced the pre-existing "CMC-four general departments—military region/branch—troops" four-layer structure with a "CMC-Theatre Commands-Troops" three-layer structure in order to strengthen powers of the five TCs.[120] Wherein, the CMC would provide "general management", the TCs would focus on "operation", and the military services would manage "force building".[121]

In view of this, against the erstwhile MR, the TCs function as a joint operational command, with the ability to quickly shift to command status in wartime without setting up a temporary command system as that of the MRs. Besides, as noted, each TC has Army and Air Force components and three coastal commands have Navy components. And unlike the MRs, the theatres have subordinate units drawn from the individual services.[122] More specifically, each TC has key focus areas as outlined in the order of protocol in Table 3.10 below.

Table 3.10: Operational Focus and Structure of Theatre Commands

Theatre Command/ Former Military Region	*TC Army Headquarters Location*	*Focus Areas*
Eastern TC/Nanjing MR	Fuzhou	Preventing Taiwan independence Compelling Taiwan unification Countering any foreign intervention during a Taiwan conflict Defending maritime sovereignty claims in the East China Sea
Southern TC/ Guangzhou MR	Nanning	Defending maritime sovereignty claims and China's sea lines of control in the South China Sea Defence along the border with Vietnam
Western TC/ Chengdu and Lanzhou MRs	Lanzhou	Combating domestic extremism and terrorism in Xinjiang Uyghur Autonomous Region and Tibet Autonomous Region Addressing an Indian border dispute contingency Guard against infiltration by Central Asian extremist and terrorist groups

Northern TC/Shenyang MR plus Inner Mongolia and Shandong provinces	Jinan	Stabilising the Korean Peninsula and conducting border stability operations associated with a North Korean contingency May share responsibility for contingencies involving Japan with the Eastern theatre Likely be responsible for northern border contingencies involving Mongolia and Russia
Central TC/Beijing and Jinan MRs	Shijiazhuang	Conducting capital defence operations during any contingency involving another theatre's area of responsibility Responsible for responding to domestic emergencies

Source: Annotated by the Author with reference to USCC 2016 Annual Report[123] and Ministry of National Defense, PRC.[124]

As Table 3.10 suggests, the very distribution of the command structure exemplifies that China's vision of reorganisation is not just guided by geography but most importantly, by the threats and challenges it encounters in each quarter, both internal and external.[125] Furthermore, the distinction of each theatre is also witnessed in their combat capabilities, as noted in Table 3.11.

Table 3.11: Combat Capability Distribution Across Theatre Commands

	Eastern	*Southern*	*Central*	*Northern*	*Western*
PLA Army					
Croup Armies	3			3	2 (+ Xinjiang and Tibet Military Districts)
PLA Navy					
Nuclear attack submarines	0	2	N/A	4	N/A
Diesel submarines	16	16	N/A	18	N/A
Destroyers	9	1 1	N/A	8	N/A
Frigates	20	19	N/A	12	N/A
Marine brigades	0	2	N/A	1	N/A
PLA Air Force					
Attack units	2 reg. 1 bd	0	0	2 reg. 3 bd	1 bd
Fighter ground attack brigades	6	8	3	7	0
Fighter units	1 reg. 3 bd	3 reg.	4 reg. 2 bd	4 reg. 2 bd	3 reg. 4 bd
Bomber regiments	3	3	0	0	3
Airborne brigades	0	0	6	0	0
PLA Rocket Force					
Conventional SRBM brigades	6	4	0	0	0

*Key: bd = brigade; reg = regiment; SRBM = short-range ballistic missile
Source: Adapted from Wuthnow (2020).[126]

What lies at the core of the TC system is the concept of 'jointness,' which according to the US military doctrine, implies a "cross-Service combination wherein the capability of the joint force is understood to be synergistic, with the sum greater than its parts (the capability of individual components)".[127] The applicability of it lies in a theatre command which acts as the organisational structure that coordinates and controls the jointness of all military assets in a theatre of war, wherein the primary focus of the theatre commands lies in 'combat'.

In the Chinese perspective, "integrated joint operations" (一体化联合作战) is the key concept that forms the foundation of PLA's thinking on joint operations.[128] The PLA textbook *Science of Campaigns* defines 'integrated joint operations' as "using integrated methods and information technology, blending an operational system from all services and arms and other types of armed strengths with operational units to form an integrated whole".[129] In doing so, the ultimate objective is to seize control of the "three superiorities" (information, air and sea superiority), controlling the battlefield, and destroying the enemy's operational system.[130] The PLA's evolving framework for integrated joint operations is the key driving force behind two key concepts—non-contact warfare (非接触作战) and target-centric warfare (标中心战)[131]—driven by the guiding ideology of 'comprehensive supremacy, precision strike, and destruction of systems'. The two key ideas that drive the PLA's modernisation objectives are "informatisation" (信息化) and "system-of-systems operations" (体系作战).[132] Here, the "system-of-systems" concept is based on linking command automation; ISR; precision strike; and rapid mobility in order to rapidly and efficiently strike an enemy's systems composed of vital sites and key nodes.[133]

Owing to this conceptual framework of seeking jointness, Xi has called for building a "joint battle command system with Chinese characteristics"—a system that is "absolutely loyal, resourceful in fighting, efficient in commanding and courageous and capable of winning wars" and be "efficient and active in both peace and war".[134] Such military primacy lies in enhancing the training of joint operations and command in order to win the initiative in future wars, more specifically, to "meet the needs of fighting and winning an informationised war".[135] This refers to the evolving nature of modern warfare featuring greater emphasis on cyber and space operations, and on long-range precision-strike systems, which would need China to improve its ability to conduct high-end joint operations in multiple domains, including establishing a permanent joint command and control mechanism.[136] To note, in the aftermath of the US operations in former Yugoslavia, the PLA's training for future wars was based on the notion of "three attacks, three defences" (三打三防), which called for attacking with precision-guided munitions, cruise missiles, and attack helicopters while defending against electronic warfare, stealth aircraft, and ISR.[137]

Furthermore, the quest towards expertising 'integrated joint operations' is also significantly driven by the recognition that PLA has no combat experience in modern high-technology joint warfare. What the PLA seeks to achieve is the capability to employ "combat systems" that optimise operational strengths and the efficiency of critical weapons and capabilities from across PLA's services based on specific operational purposes, usually defined in the context of joint or combined campaigns.[138] This is well-witnessed in the way China perceives the modern campaigns, as noted in *The Campaign Theory Study Guide*, an old PLA textbook that explains the connection between campaigns and combat systems as:

> "Paralyzing the enemy's combat system has become an important means of winning a war. [...] Once there are problems in key links of the system, the entire weapon system and combat system will lose its combat effectiveness, or will even become paralyzed. This illustrates that modern campaigns are the confrontation between combat systems. Advanced weapons and equipment and good strategy and planning both depend upon the integrity and coordination of combat systems. Therefore, in modern campaigns, attacking and paralyzing key nodes in the enemy's combat system while ensuring the integrity and coordination of one's own combat systems has become an important way of winning".[139]

From the above statement, two significant imperatives can be drawn: First, the need for the PLA to build and protect its own combat system; and second, the ability to simultaneously identify and attack an adversary's critical weaknesses,[140] central to the PLA's thinking of building an integrated joint operations system.

In view of this, the transition from MR to TC framework system is embedded in China's quest to achieve jointness for the PLA. For, unlike the MRs, each theatre has a Joint Operations Command Center (JOCC) to exercise operational C2 of its forces. This is complemented by the

CMC's JOCC (in its Joint Staff Department) to exercise joint C2 at the supreme command level, providing a full-time joint planning staff in strategic directions along China's periphery.[141] To note, the functions of the Joint Staff Department are defined as "executing support for operation planning, command and control, and operation command", "conducting evaluation of operation capabilities," and "organizing joint operations training and building preparation for war".[142] The JOCC structure provides the PLA substantial capabilities to muster resources of the PLAAF and coordination of the employment of the PLARF. This makes the JOCC an important part in deepening of national defence and military reform and an important measure in strengthening the strategic command function of the CMC.

The significance of this lies in the fact that the TC system provides the PLA with an opportunity to achieve a more effective C2 to integrate joint C4ISR capabilities and plan for multi-region campaigns that require subordination of one command to another.[143] This JOCC structure at each theatre has provided Beijing with the ability, both for managing crises and conflict on the periphery, as well as potentially for overseas deployments in the future based on the CMC's expectation of "unprecedented global change".[144]

Role of Theatre Commands: Be Combat Ready

In December 2015, following Xi's announcement of the military reforms, China's MND spokesman stated that, overall, the reforms sought to improve "leadership administration and command of joint operations" so that the PLA would have a force structure able to fight and win modern conflicts.[145] For this, the targets and tasks of the newly-established theatre commands, as the MND notes, are mainly: to be responsible for dealing with security threats in their respective strategic scopes, maintaining peace, containing wars and winning wars, noting their pivotal role in safeguarding the country's overall national security and military strategies.[146] However, the exact extent of the areas of responsibilities for each of the five theatre commands has not been announced officially by the PLA. But, with these objectives, the current security situation of China requires the joint battle command to be highly strategic, coordinated, timely, professional and accurate. This is guided by the key principle of 'fight and win' which calls for "flexibility, mobility and self-dependence".[147]

What explains China's such a combat-ready attitude are its growing concerns over the PLA's "peace disease" (*hépíngbìng*), "peacetime habits" (*hépíngjìxí*) and "peace problems" (*hépíngjìbì*), and the lack of ability to fight and win a modern campaign. Highlighting this issue, the *People's Liberation Army Daily* in an editorial stated:

> "Peace disease has been a common symptom in our military for decades" [...] "If we do not make up our mind to eliminate those evils, we must pay a heavy cost in the event of a war" and that "we can only stop a war if we are able to fight".[148]

This very statement reflects China's current dilemma. What caused this 'peace disease' is China's long-standing inexperience in warfighting given the last war it fought was in 1979 against Vietnam.[149] This 'gap', therefore, has necessitated the need for the PLA to become combat-ready to fight modern warfare. Calling this shortcoming as PLA's "Five Incapables", Xi identifies them as: the inability of some PLA leaders to effectively judge the military situation and understand their orders, make operational decisions, direct troops in combat, and handle unforeseen battlefield developments.[150]

In addition, this aspiration is also fuelled by the need to defend China's status of being a major world power given its recognition as the world's number two economy. For China under Xi aspires to 'build a security maximising state,' which aims at building its military means to meet the end of becoming a strong national security state.[151] In building a joint command system, the central aim is to enhance the PLA's "combat readiness" and make it a "powerful force that is always ready for the fight, capable of combat and sure to win,"[152] —as in Xi's view, "combat capability is the criterion to meet [for the PLA] in all its work and focus on how to win when it is called on".[153]

In this regard, China has upscaled its training to prepare PLA troops for the future, as witnessed in the PLA's focus toward combined arms and joint training, as noted in the Zhurihe Combined Tactics Training Base in Inner Mongolia, the PLA's largest and most advanced training base that involves two units—red and blue units.[154] To note, China's Zhurihe Training Base is comparable to the US military's National Training Center at Fort Irwin, California, with a large amount of manoeuvre space, a dedicated opposing force, and an urban terrain training area.[155] Of the two units of the PLA, the red unit is composed of PLA troops from different regions, while the blue force, also called the

195th Mechanised Infantry Brigade, is China's first professional simulation opposition force brigade, which came into being in 2014.[156] Adapting it to the PLA's new command structure, in July 2016, at Zhurihe, troops from the five TCs conducted a large-scale drill with an aim to boost their "trans-regional" capabilities,[157] further adding to the combat mission of the TCs.

More importantly, this restructuring towards 'jointness' further clarifies China's significant departure from Deng Xiaoping's dictum of "Keeping a low profile". The TCs exemplify China's confidence and military preparedness towards fighting future wars; however, though it is in its evolutionary phase, it is still necessary to watch how it qualifies for the PLA's effectiveness in fighting future wars. Besides, at the moment, the TCs have a territorial outlook; but will it remain so in the long-term is another area to watch. To intervene, given that China faces no threat of invasion, one can assume that the TCs are then likely to play a significant role in advancing China's power projections with a focused approach.

Given the current pace and scale of the PLA's military modernisation, China's military intentions call for scrutiny. Xi's reforms are mainly aimed at making the PLA a modern military force with an advanced degree of readiness on land, sea and air; and in the new domains such as space, cyber and others. In this, one of the key aspects of PLA's modernisation is witnessed in its increasing footprints beyond China's periphery. However, some analysts argue that China's future combat capability may be 'overstated' as evitable from its inability to deter the US from sending reconnaissance flights close to the Chinese mainland. In view of this, Taipei-based military expert Chi Le-yi argues that: "If the PLA can't strengthen its joint and systematic operations like their American counterparts by projecting troops and weapons 1,500 kilometres outside the mainland, they will definitely fail".[158] Adding further, it is also argued that, in Beijing's view, making the PLA 'combat-ready' refers to:

> "Building a fully modern military will mean more than just building and deploying the "heavy metal"—ships, aircraft, modern artillery, and missiles. It has just as much to do with "heart ware", which in some ways can be much more complicated: recruiting and retaining talented personnel, educating them in new doctrine and modern warfare, and training troops in realistic conditions to achieve combat-readiness".[159]

While China's military capabilities are expanding, but one cannot dismiss the fact that China's growing military muscle does not guarantee it an absolute win. Thus, with the stakes raised higher than ever, China has no other alternative but for the PLA to excel its 'combat readiness'.

III. China's Military-Civil Fusion Strategy: Building a Strong Country with a Strong Military

Apart from restructuring, Xi's reform agenda also called for promoting deeper civil-military integration. Highlighting the 'significance', Xi stated:

> "Implementing the strategy of military-civilian integration is a prerequisite for building integrated national strategies and strategic capabilities and for realising the Party's goal of building a strong military in the new era".[160]

Xi's addition of "military-civil integration" to the reform agenda has confirmed its significant role in the PLA's overall military modernisation and China's larger national security imperative. The 19th CPC Central Committee, in laying out the 14th Five Year Plan, set the key target to "make major strides in the modernisation of national defence and the armed forces",[161] as the communique stated:

> "We [China] must improve the quality and efficiency of national defence and military modernisation; promote simultaneous improvements in national defence and economic strength; build an integrated national strategic system and capabilities; promote the co-ordinated development of key areas and emerging fields; optimise the layout of defence technologies and industry; and consolidate military, political, and military-civilian unity".[162]

The references in the above statement to integrated systems, emerging fields, and military-civilian unity highlight China's push for military-civil fusion (MCF), a key factor that is driving China's military modernisation.

The foundation for the MCF was laid in March 2015, when Xi[163] called for the elevation of "Military-Civil Fusion"[164] development into a national strategy (军民融合发展作为一项国家战略), transitioning it from "early-state fusion" to "deep fusion"—a "move to rejuvenate the nation and a strategy to strengthen the armed forces" (关乎国家安全和发展全局, 既是兴国之举, 又是强军之策).[165] Here, one needs to note that the reforms have been a result of PRC's concerns over lack of resources and the need for defence modernisation, as a result of which, Xi's MCF strategy is driven by the need to coordinate building of China's economy and defence capabilities simultaneously. To implement the strategy, in January 2017, the Central Commission for Integrated Military and Civilian Development[166] (*zhongyangjunminronghefazhanweiyuanhui*; 中央军民融合发展委员) was set up, with Xi Jinping as the head. Thereafter, on 20 June 2017, Xi articulated MCF by stating that:

> "We must accelerate the formation of a full-element, multi-domain, and high-return military-civil fusion deep development pattern, and gradually build up China's unified military-civil system of strategies and strategic capability".[167]

What is noteworthy is that the MCF is the Chinese equivalent of the American notion of "Civil-Military Integration". Though phrased differently, the essence remains the same. Under the MCF, the aim is to achieve a state of "deep fusion" through the integration of the two essential building blocks: the military, and the civil. Here, 'military' includes every aspect of national defence and force building endeavour; while 'civil' refers to fields in the economic and social system that are closely related to national defence and force-building.[168]

What explains Xi's push towards MCF is the imminent need to modernise China's defence science, technology, and industrial base given the growing complexity in the security environment and the need for the PLA to match the technological demands to fight and win informationised local wars. As the 2019 White Paper stated:

> "Building a fortified national defence and a strong military commensurate with the country's international standing and its security and development interests is *a strategic task for China's socialist modernization*" [emphasis added].[169]

This is motivated by the desire to make the PLA well-versed in modern technology-driven warfare, as the lessons learnt by the Chinese from the Gulf Wars and the Kosovo crisis emphasised on the need to upgrade defence technology to match the pace of technological innovation. As failing to do so will result in dire effects on a country's national security. To add further, Xi's move came in response to his concerns over "problematic mindsets, *tizhi*[170] barriers, and vested interests" that have restricted the development of MCF in all these years – as "integration is a problem that has yet to be resolved".[171]

In assessing the MCF strategy, the PLA's NDU researchers interpret Xi's vision to be representing the basic (near-term) and ultimate (long-term) goals of the strategy. The 'near-term' goal of the strategy is to form a "military-civil fusion deep development pattern", which comprises three core components: full-element, multi-domain and high-return (see Figure 3.6).[172]

Figure 3.6: Military-Civil Fusion Deep Development Pattern

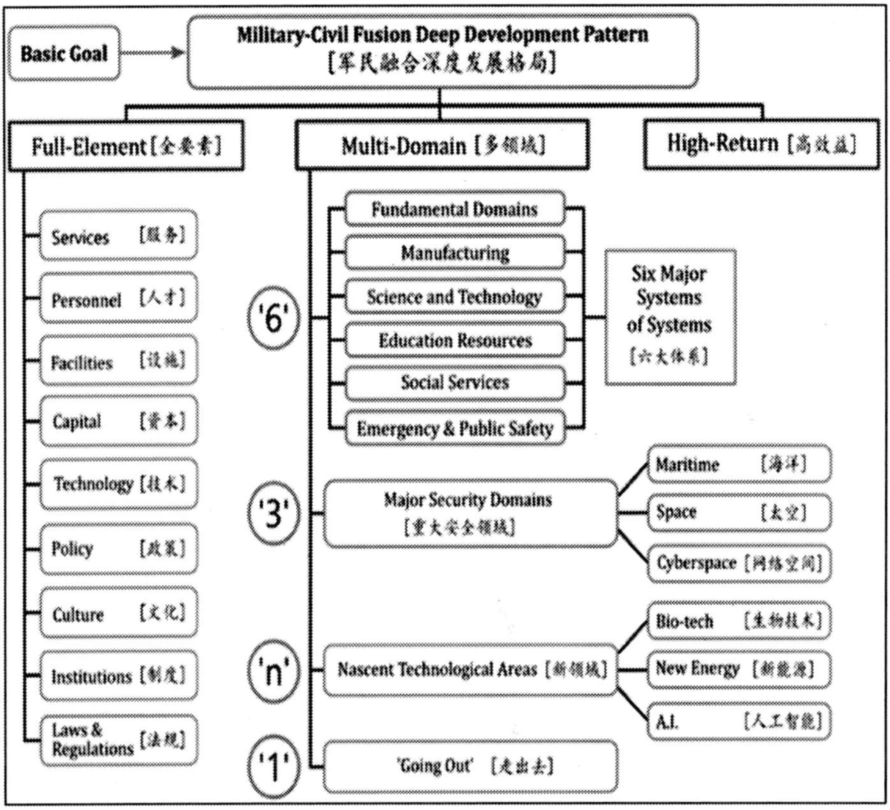

Source: Adapted from Stone and Wood (2020).[173]

The MCF encompasses six inter-related efforts :[174] (1) fusing China's defence industrial base and its civilian technology and industrial base; (2) integrating and leveraging science and technology innovations across military and civilian sectors; (3) cultivating talent and blending military and civilian expertise and knowledge; (4) building military requirements into civilian infrastructure and leveraging civilian construction for military purposes; (5) leveraging civilian service and logistics capabilities for military purposes; and (6) expanding and deepening China's national defence mobilisation system to include all relevant aspects of its society and economy for use in competition and war. This suggests that the aim of MCF is to harness the capability of the civilian sectors including science and technology to advance China's military, economic, and technological prowess, making it an all-encompassing approach.

Table 3.12: Domains Prioritised under Xi's MCF Strategy

Six Traditional Domains	*Six System of Systems (SoS)*	*Three Major Security Domains*	*"n" Nascent Technological Areas*
1. Fundamental (Infrastructure)	1. Fundamental Domain Resource Sharing SoS	1. Maritime	1. Biotechnology
2. Manufacturing	2. Advanced Defence STI SoS with Chinese characteristics	2. Space	2. New Energy
3. Science and Technology	3. Military-Civil Coordinated Technological Innovation SoS	3. Cyberspace Security and Informatization	3. Artificial Intelligence
4. Education	4. Military Personnel Training SoS		
5. Social Services	5. Socialised Support and Sustainment for the PLA SoS		
6. Emergency and Public Safety	6. National Defence Mobilisation SoS		

Note: The six SoS are related to the six "traditional domains" that are meant to gradually take shape through the promotion of MCF in these domains.

Source: Annotated by the Author with reference to Stone and Wood (2020).[175]

The six SoS as noted above are formed by fusing civilian and defence ecosystems that possess high levels of commonality, which were previously operating in silos. The domains as listed in Table 3.12 and the six SoS form the backbone of Xi's MCF strategy, as noted in Table 3.13 below.

Table 3.13: Military-Civil Fusion and the Creation of the Six SoS

Defense Infrastructure	+	Civilian Infrastructure	=	Fundamental Domain Resource Sharing SoS
Defense Technology Industrial Base	+	Civilian Technology Industrial Base	=	Advanced Defense Technology Industrial SoS
Defense Innovation System	+	Civilian Innovation System	=	Military-Civil Coordinated Technology Innovation SoS
Military Personnel Cultivation System	+	National Education System	=	Military Personnel Cultivation SoS
Military Logistics System	+	State Social Service System	=	Socialized Support and Sustainment for the PLA SoS
National Defense Mobilization System	+	State Emergency Management System	=	National Defense Mobilization SoS

Source: Adapted from Stone and Wood (2020).[176]

Under MCF, the "ultimate goal" is to build a "unified military-civil system of strategies and strategic capability" and weave the components of the MCF strategy into other national strategic priorities to achieve an organic, powerful, and comprehensive national system of strategies (see Figure 3.7).[177]

Figure 3.7: Unified Military-Civil System of Strategies and Strategic Capability

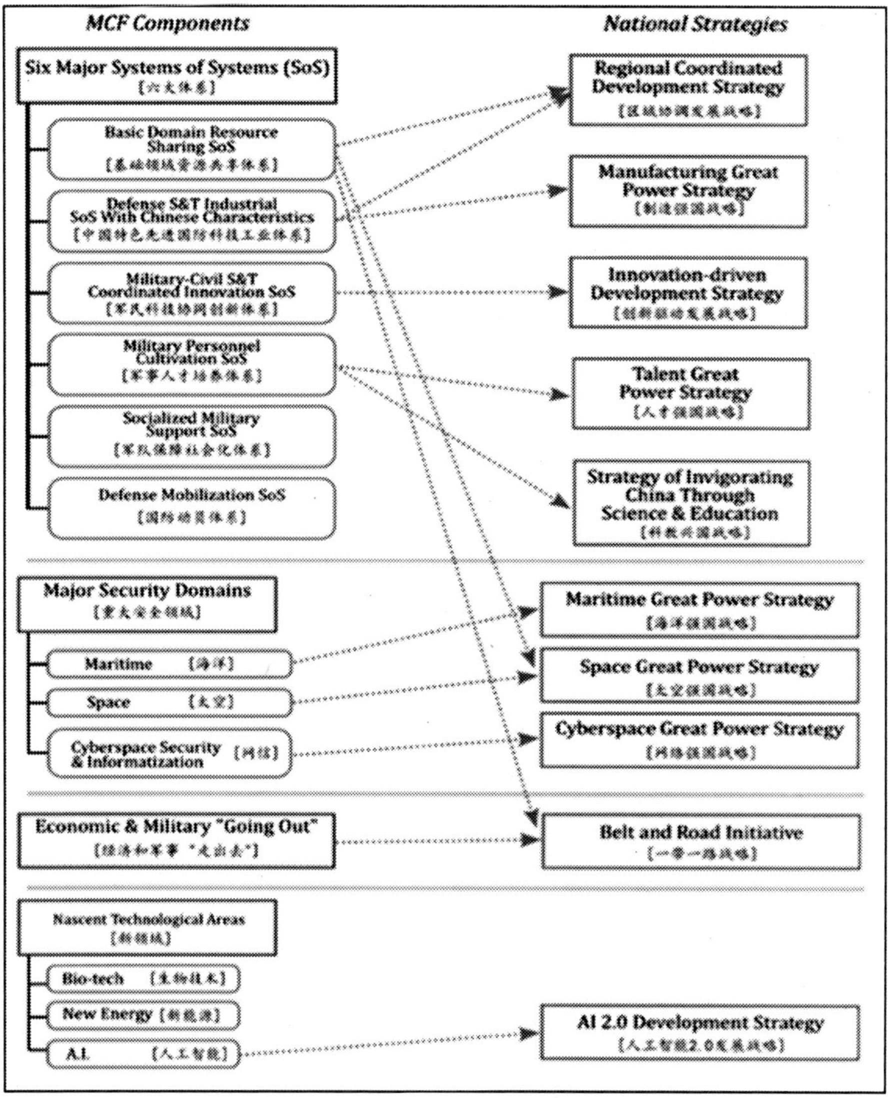

Source: Adapted from Stone and Wood (2020).[178]

Owing to these goals, it can be rightly argued that the MCF is the lynchpin of China's 'world class military' ambition. Xi has also expanded the scope of the military-civil fusion by adding new areas, such as:[179] infrastructure, national defence-related sci-tech industry, weapons and equipment procurement, talent cultivation, socialisation of the support system for the military, as well as the mobilisation for national defence for the integration of military and civilian industries. With AI and other ranges of technologies such as autonomous systems driving the next RMA, the MCF aims to pave the way for the PLA to conduct 'intelligentised warfare'. Fundamentally, the MCF offers to ease the PLA's competition for resources by broadening and strengthening China's defence industrial base by "leveraging of dual-use technologies, policies, and organisations for military benefit".[180] With technology becoming increasingly 'dual-use', thus blurring the distinction between civil and military, it has become imperative for China to promote MCF to safeguard its national interest.

In this regard, MCF being a key strategy behind China's military modernisation is broader than simply being a public-private partnership. The very fact that China puts 'military' before 'civil' in its priority of order calls for significant attention. As a result of which, one cannot ignore the risks posed by the MCF strategy as it is embedded in China's geopolitical ambitions, both to protect and advance Chinese interests. As noted by the Pentagon, some of China's leading e-commerce companies are directly supporting the PLA by providing them with drones for logistics; while some Chinese shipping companies are contributing to cross-sea transport drills, providing capabilities that could be leveraged for an amphibious landing on Taiwan or in the South China Sea[181]—thus raising concerns over China's intentions behind its MCF strategy.

China's Quest for Power Projection and Expeditionary Capabilities

Harold Brown suggests that the "modernisation and the rise of China" is "the major new force in international relations in the first half of the 21st century", which for many, pose a threat, while some view it as an opportunity.[182] This perception calls for a key query: What are China's intentions? More importantly, as China today, is not faced with any direct threat of invasion, then it makes it further essential to ponder: What explains China's military modernisation and robust reforms? Or, what does the PLA wants to achieve?

The answer to these queries lies in China's own insecurities which, as the 2015 White Paper explains:

> "With the growth of China's national interests, its national security is more vulnerable to international and regional turmoil, terrorism, piracy, serious natural disasters and epidemics, and the security of overseas interests concerning energy and resources, strategic sea lines of communication (SLOCs), as well as institutions, personnel and assets abroad, has become an imminent issue".[183]

> "It is necessary for China to develop a modern maritime military force structure commensurate with its national security and development interests, safeguard its national sovereignty and maritime rights and interests, protect the security of strategic SLOCs and overseas interests, and participate in international maritime cooperation, so as to provide strategic support for building itself into a maritime power".[184]

This perception is aided by the fact that in the current situation China's ability to project conventional military power beyond its periphery remains limited. In view of this, China's military build-up can be explained in a four-fold framework: First, concerns over Taiwan, the biggest challenge to CPC's legitimacy. As Jia Qingguo notes, "acquiring the military power to conquer Taiwan is an important piece of China's Taiwan strategy".[185] Second, some analysts see it as China's quest for respect to restore its past glory and to be seen as the most influential state in Asia. As Ming Yen Tsai asserts, China seeks to "challenge U.S.-centred regional security arrangements" and "U.S. predominance".[186] Third, to project power, as evident from the PLA's quest towards "trans-regional mobility"; PLAN's focus on "offshore defensive operations"; PLAAF's transitioning to "offensive and defensive operations"—all aimed at China's desire to penetrate the first and second island chain and expand China's strategic survival space.[187] And fourth, possible conflicts in the South China Sea, East China Sea, at the India-China border and others, as analysts argue that "China must keep up not with one country, but a host of powerful neighbours".[188]

In broad terms, PRC's overall goal is to achieve significant progress in joint operational command, optimising force structure, enhancing policy systems and civil-military integration, and building a modern world-class military with Chinese characteristics to win informationised local wars. In addition to immediate territorial concerns, the PLA is also modernising its military capabilities to include MOOTW missions such as HADR, counter-piracy, peacekeeping and regional military operation, that help strengthen overseas operational capabilities. Here, the bottom line is China's quest for 'power projection and expeditionary capabilities'.[189] However, the query is: Does China has such capabilities? If so, then the defensive nature of "active defence" calls for severe scrutiny.

Simplistically put, China's military modernisation primarily aims at four key objectives: internal security; securing of continental borders and regaining lost territories; developing far sea defence and expeditionary capabilities; and building deterrence capabilities against all domain threats. Of these, building power projection and expeditionary capabilities is gaining momentum in Beijing's strategic calculus. The rationale is embedded in China's longstanding ambition to match and ultimately surpass the USA as the world's most powerful nation. Wherein, the key objective is to build a modern force that has the ability to access as well as sustain and gain superiority in all domains. As noted, the 2013 edition of *Science of Military Strategy*, called on the PLA to "push the strategic forward edge from the home territory to the periphery, from land to sea, from air to space, and from tangible spaces to intangible spaces".[190]

The intention is to transform the PLA into a force capable of robust overseas military operations based on a timeline. In suggesting so, in February 2019, CMC's Transport and Projection Bureau Chief of Staff, Liu Jiasheng, in a PLA journal article stated that China's power projection would occur in short-, medium-, and long- term phases.[191] Wherein, in the short-term, the PLA must be ready to fight a limited war in the maritime domain around China's periphery requiring robust sea and air lift forces. The medium-term requires the PLA to be able to fight a limited war overseas to protect its interests in countries participating in BRI. And in the long-term, the PLA must focus on "global projection," making use of China's overseas bases as well as air and space assets to be prepared to be rapidly deployed anywhere around the globe.[192]

While China has gained some foothold in East and South East Asia in projecting its power as evident from the artificial islands and fortifications in the South China Sea; it is aiming towards building power projection and expeditionary capabilities in the Indian Ocean Region (IOR), Africa, Latin America, Caribbean and the Arctic. In this process, China's BRI and MCF strategy are playing key roles in enhancing Beijing's such capabilities. China's infrastructure and port activities in BRI-financed countries such as Pakistan, Bangladesh, Sri Lanka, Myanmar and others are creating the basis for military access for the PLA into the IOR. China's first overseas military base in Djibouti significantly confirms the speculation that suggests China could turn its maritime infrastructure into military bases, making provisions to project power in distant regions, to respond to contingencies, and to create its sphere of influence. Of which, one of the most evitable outcomes to anticipate is the transformation of Pakistan's Gwadar port into a Chinese military base.

In this regard, what makes building power projection and expeditionary capabilities significant is that they serve China's "strategic requirements", such as:[193] First, the requirement to resolve outstanding territorial disputes in its favour; second, to deny US forces access to or delay their arrival in a potential East Asian contingency; and third, to defend its overseas economic interests that includes security of Chinese assets and people abroad as well as access to foreign markets, natural resources, and advanced technologies. In this quest, a decisive role is played by factors such as stability in China-US relations; and China's regional neighbourhood such as North Korea, Japan, Taiwan, Vietnam, the Philippines and India.

Thus, both domestic and external factors are increasingly influencing the PLA's need to act globally. If the PLA is able to build a global expeditionary force to meet the timeline 2025-2030, then three possible scenarios can be anticipated, that include:[194] First, the PLA could be able to project limited power in a limited area for a short duration anywhere in the world. Second, China could develop capabilities such as expeditionary strike groups and special operations to conduct raids, non-combatant evacuation operations (NEOs), security operations, counter-blockades, strikes and amphibious exercises. And third, the PLA could modernise and operate beyond the first and second island chains, with the majority of the efforts undertaken by PLAN and PLAAF. Therefore, for the PLA to become a global expeditionary force or a 'world-class military', China needs to build capabilities such as: long-range amphibious assault capabilities, air and missile capabilities, precision strike capabilities, joint logistics capabilities, and space-based and cyber capabilities. However, in assessing China's expeditionary capabilities by 2030, a *Jane's* report suggests that:

> "The PLA's actual fixed overseas footprint may continue to remain light until approximately 2030 because it can still rely on civilian infrastructure and platforms to support its expeditionary operations. However, after 2030, the PLA will likely pursue more dedicated military bases beyond its existing Djibouti Logistics Support Base. PLAN and PLAAF's capabilities in 2035 would theoretically allow the PLA to perform higher-level overseas combat operations, but operations in contested environments will almost assuredly require overseas military facilities or, at the least, preferred access to both ports and airfields in friendly countries. Further, the PLA will still likely have limited capability to conduct operations in hostile countries with integrated air defence systems without support from future PLAN aircraft carriers. This may be difficult for the PLA given (the) slowing (down of) economic growth and defence budgets".[195]

It can be rightly stated that one of the aims behind China's military modernisation and structural reforms is to aid its power projection and expeditionary capabilities by building combat strengths in informatised, system-of systems and multi-domain operations. Guided by the essence of 'active defence', the aim is to build a "powerful, modern and new-type of Army" by optimising the PLA's power structure and troop formation and speeding up the Army's transformation from the "regional defensive type to the full-spectrum combat type".[196] To which, in implementing active defence to the new security situation, China's armed forces will have to adhere to the principles of "flexibility, mobility and self-dependence".[197] These perspectives highlight the application of the concept of active defence in China's military thinking and further justifies that China's modernisation is meant to ensure that the PLA is 'battle-ready' at all times. And, most importantly, it implies that 'hard military power' is the central component towards fulfilling the Chinese Dream – thereby, raising significant concerns over China's intentions.

Conclusion

While the rapid developments in China's military modernisation have spurred much debate and comparison about China's military capability in terms of warfighting and deterrence capabilities, it also clarifies that the PRC does have a national military strategy that is based on the concept of active defence. As it is, one cannot ignore that modernisation aims at building military capabilities meant for both offence and defence. Due to which, there remains little doubt to suggest that China's growing military capabilities holds severe implications for the globe at large and

China's adversaries in particluar. This is augmented by the PLA's reforms which are centred on joint operations, with operational and strategic preparedness in all domains of threat.

Beijing's military calculus aims at making China a security maximising state by building its military means to meet the goal of becoming a strong national security state. In this regard, Xi Jinping's vision of a 'world-class military' is driven by the logic of elevating the PLA's role in shaping the country's future, given China's forceful quest in securing its strategic space, both regionally and globally. To pursue such a goal, the quest lies in transforming the PLA into a more professional and modern fighting force, making it combat-ready to quell the risks of contingencies.

Furthermore, PRC's efforts to strengthen its armed forces by its 'ambitious' military modernisation have led to the reinforcement of the CPC's authority over the military, improvement in the PLA's ability to conduct joint operations, increase in the PLA's focus on combat effectiveness, and the quest towards expertising fighting multi-domain warfare by downplaying the institutional primacy of the army over the other services. More importantly, as the reforms take effect, the PLA will advance towards becoming a modern military force and better positioned to impose costs on its adversaries to achieve its strategic aims.

With its rapid pace and enlarged scope, China's military modernisation efforts has created a favourable asymmetry in military strength by which China can pose a serious challenge to its adversaries and aim at potential targets for pre-emption and disruption. This further confirms that active defence is rooted in China's military modernisation, wherein China's efforts are not just defensive in posture, but have an embedded element of offence, calling for the PLA to be 'battle-ready' at all times.

NOTES

1. Ministry of National Defense of the People's Republic of China (2015), "China's Military Strategy", http://eng.mod.gov.cn/Database/WhitePapers/2014.htm, accessed online 20 September 2020.
2. Xi Jinping (2017), "Secure a Decisive Victory in Building a Moderately Prosperous Society in All Respects and Strive for the Great Success of Socialism with Chinese Characteristics for a New Era", Speech at the 19th National Congress of the Communist Party of China, 18 October 2017, http://www.xinhuanet.com/english/ download/ Xi_Jinping's_report_at_19th_CPC_National_Congress.pdf, accessed online 20 November 2019.

3. "China Focus: "Be ready to win wars, China's Xi orders reshaped PLA", *Xinhuanet*, 1 August 2017, http://www.xinhuanet.com//english/2017-08/01/c_136491455.htm, accessed online 15 November 2020.
4. Minnie Chan and William Zheng (2020), "Why Taiwan may be a key factor in China's military modernisation plan", *South China Morning Post*, 30 October 2020, https://www.scmp.com/news/china/military/article/3107867/why-taiwan-may-be-key-factor-chinas-military-modernisation-plan, accessed online 2 November 2020.
5. The term 'mechanisation' refers broadly to ambitions to modernise and replace the PLA's legacy equipment across all services and branches, though with significant focus on the ground forces. It is also understood to be closely linked to the reorganisation of the PLA Army from 18 to 13 group armies, which was intended to improve quality and military efficiency. The term 'informatisation' can be understood as a force's ability to use advanced IT and communications systems to gain operational advantage over an adversary', while 'intelligentisation' is a new concept that is understood to be based on the premise that military systems will be enhanced by the integration of advanced automation, big data and AI. For details see, "Chapter One: Defence and military analysis", *The Military Balance*, 120:1, February 2020, p. 10.
6. "Xi instructs army to improve its combat readiness", *Xinhuanet*, 4 November 2017, http://www.xinhuanet.com//english/2017-11/04/c_136726863.htm, accessed online 17 January 2020.
7. Office of the Secretary of Defense (2020), "Annual Report to Congress: Military and Security Developments involving the People's Republic of China 2020", p. 38, https://media.defense.gov/2020/Sep/01/2002488689/-1/-1/1/2020-DOD-CHINA-MILITARY-POWER-REPORT-FINAL.PDF, accessed online 4 September 2020.
8. Ibid.
9. Ministry of National Defense of the People's Republic of China (2015), "China's Military Strategy", n. 1.
10. Quoted in David M. Finkelstein (2007), "China's National Military Strategy: An Overview of the "Military Strategic Guidelines"," in Andrew Scobell and Roy Kamphausen (eds.) *Right Sizing the People's Liberation Army: Exploring the Contours of China's Military*, Carlisle, PA: Army War College Press, p. 104.
11. Amrita Jash (2018), "Xi Jinping's Theorem of Fight and Win", CLAWS Focus No. 1940, 3 October 2018, https://archive.claws.in/1940/xi-jinping's-theorem-of-"fight-and-win"-dr-amrita-jash.html, accessed online 15 January 2020.
12. Quoted in David M. Finkelstein (2007), "China's National Military Strategy", n. 10, p. 101.
13. Joel Wuthnow and Philip C. Saunders (2019), "Chairman Xi Remakes the PLA" in Philip C. Saunders, et al. (eds.) *Chairman Xi Remakes the PLA: Assessing Chinese Military Reforms*, Washington, D.C.: National Defence University Press, p. 1.
14. Ministry of National Defense of the People's Republic of China (2015), "China's Military Strategy", n. 1.
15. Xi Jinping (2017), "Secure a Decisive Victory", n. 2.
16. Ibid., also see, Office of the Secretary of Defense (2020), "Annual Report to Congress", n. 7, p. 160.
17. Quoted in David Bandurski (2020), "Insights from the Fifth Plenum", China Media Project, 29 October 2020, https://chinamediaproject.org/2020/10/29/insights-from-the-fifth-plenum/, accessed online 5 November 2020.

18. Meia Nouwens (2020), "Is China speeding up military modernisation? It may, but not yet", The Interpreter, 4 November 2020, https://www.lowy institute.org/the-interpreter/is-china-speeding-up-military-modernisation-it-may-but-its-not-yet, accessed online 10 November 2020.
19. Ibid.
20. In 1975, China adopted the policy of the "four modernisations" as the way to ensure long-range comprehensive security. China's plan was to modernise its agriculture, industry, science and technology, and defence. Until 1989, when China began devoting more resources to its military, economic development through the modernization of agriculture, industry, and science and technology clearly preceded defence modernisation.
21. United States General Accounting Office (1995), "National Security: Impact of China's Military Modernization in the Pacific Region", GAO/NSIAD-95-84, 6 June 1995, p. 19, https://www.gao.gov/assets/160/155059.pdf, accessed online 20 August 2020.
22. Ibid.
23. Dennis J. Blasko (2012), *The Chinese Army Today: Tradition and Transformation for the 21st Century* (Second Edition), New York: Routledge, p. 7.
24. Ibid.
25. Ibid.
26. Ibid.
27. Quoted in Kartik Bommakanti and Anant Singh Mann (2020), "China's Military Modernisation: Recent Trends", ORF Issue Brief, Observer Research Foundation, 14 July 2020, https://www.orfonline.org/research/chinas-military-modernisation-recent-trends/#_ftn1, accessed online 18 August 2020.
28. Quoted in David M. Finkelstein (2007), "China's National Military Strategy", n. 10, p. 92.
29. Ibid., pp. 70-72. Also see, "China's Military Modernization," in *China Rise*, Peterson Institute for International Economics, pp. 194-196, https://www.piie.com/publications/chapters_preview/4174/09iie4174.pdf, accessed online 20 July 2020.
30. You Ji (2016), *China's Military Transformation: Politics and War Preparation*, Cambridge, UK: Polity Press, p. 1.
31. Anti-access actions are intended to slow the deployment of an adversary's forces into a theatre or cause them to operate at distances farther from the conflict than they would prefer. Area denial actions affect manoeuvres within a theatre and are intended to impede an adversary's operations in key areas. For details, see *2020 Report to Congress of the U.S.-China Economic and Security Review Commission*, Washington: U.S. Government Publishing Office, 1 December 2020, p. 389, https://www.uscc.gov/sites/default/files/2020-12/2020_Annual_Report_to_Congress.pdf, accessed on 10 December 2020.
32. Quoted in "Building a strong army through reform", *Xinhuanet*, 16 March 2016, http://www.xinhuanet.com//mil/2016-03/16/c_128804009.htm, accessed on 2 May 2020.
33. "Full Text: China's National Defense in the New Era", *Xinhuanet*, 24 July 2019, http://www.xinhuanet.com/english/2019-07/24/c_138253389.htm, accessed online 20 October 2019.
34. Quoted in Elsa B. Kania (2020), "Minds at War: China's Pursuit of Military Advantage through Cognitive Science and Biotechnology", *PRISM*, Vol. 8, No. 3, p. 84, https://ndupress.ndu.edu/Portals/68/Documents/prism/prism_8-3/prism_8-3.pdf, accessed online 20 July 2020.

35. Ibid.
36. John Grevatt (2020), "China to deepen 'civil-military fusion' in 14th Five Year Plan", *Jane*'s, 2 November 2020, https://www.janes.com/defence-news/news-detail/china-to-deepen-civil-military-fusion-in-14th-five-year-plan, accessed online 10 November 2020.
37. Dean Cheng (2011), "China's Active Defence Strategy and Its Regional Impact", *The Heritage Foundation*, 1 February 2011, https://www.heritage.org/testimony/chinas-active-defense-strategy-and-its-regional-impact, accessed online 18 January 2020.
38. Cited in Dean Cheng (2011), "Chinese Lessons from the Gulf Wars", in Andrew Scobell et al. (eds.) *Chinese Lessons from Other Peoples' Wars*, Carlisle, PA: Strategic Studies Institute, US Army War College, pp. 156-157.
39. Zenel Garcia (2019), *China's Military Modernization, Japan's Normalization and the South China Sea Territorial Disputes*, Switzerland: Palgrave Macmillan, p. 47.
40. *The Science of Military Strategy* (China 2013) (English Translation), Beijing: Military Strategic Research Department, AMS, pp. 93-98.
41. Quoted in David M. Finkelstein (2007), "China's National Military Strategy", n. 10, p. 102.
42. Quoted in Dean Cheng (2011), "Chinese Lessons from the Gulf Wars", n. 38, pp. 161-162.
43. Quoted in David M. Finkelstein (2007), "China's National Military Strategy", n. 10, p. 103.
44. Ibid., p. 105.
45. Cited in Dean Cheng (2011), "Chinese Lessons from the Gulf Wars", n. 38, p. 165.
46. Ministry of National Defence of the People's Republic of China (2015), "China's Military Strategy", n. 1.
47. Amrita Jash (2019), "China seeks to 'Informationisation' to Fight Modern Warfare", Centre for Land Warfare Studies, 7 May 2019, https://www.claws.in/china-seeks-to-informationisation-to-fight-modern-warfare/, accessed online 20 June 2020.
48. Ibid.
49. Quoted in "Countering Enemy "Informationized Operations in War and Peace", Centre for Strategic and Budgetary Assessments, 2013, p. 34.
50. Ministry of National Defense of the People's Republic of China (2015), "China's Military Strategy", n. 1.
51. Ibid.
52. For details, see Jeffrey Engstrom (2018), *Systems Confrontation and System Destruction Warfare: How the Chinese People's Liberation Army Seeks to Wage Modern Warfare*, Santa Monica, CA: RAND Corporation.
53. Ministry of National Defense of the People's Republic of China (2015), "China's Military Strategy", n. 1.
54. Senior Colonel Wang Baocun and Li Fei (1998), "Information Warfare", in Michael Pillsbury (ed.) *Chinese Views of Future Warfare*, New Delhi: Lancer Publishers, p. 328.
55. Xi Jinping (2017), "Secure a Decisive Victory", n. 2, p. 5.
56. Ibid.
57. Ministry of National Defense of the People's Republic of China (2015), "China's Military Strategy", n. 1.
58. Amrita Jash (2019), "Xi Jinping's World-Class Military: Not Only Fights, But Also Wins Wars," *Indian Defence Review*, Vol. 34, Issue 1, pp. 48-49.
59. Office of the Secretary of Defense (2018), "Annual Report to Congress: Military and Security Developments involving the People's Republic of China 2018", 16 May 2018,

p. 10, https://media.defense.gov/2018/Aug/16/2001955282/-1/-1/1/2018-CHINA-MILITARY-POWER-REPORT.PDF, accessed online 27 May 2019.

60. Ministry of National Defense of the People's Republic of China (2015), "China's Military Strategy", n. 1.
61. Amrita Jash (2019), "Xi Jinping's World-Class Military", n. 58, pp. 49.
62. "China Focus: "Be ready to win wars, China's Xi orders reshaped PLA", *Xinhuanet*, 1 August 2017, http://www.xinhuanet.com/english/2017-08/01/c_136491455.htm, accessed online 26 November 2019.
63. The State Council of the People's Republic of China (2017), "Full text: China's Policies on Asia-Pacific Security Cooperation", 11 January 2017, http://english.gov.cn/archive/white_paper/2017/01/11/content_281475539078636.htm, accessed online 3 June 2020.
64. *2018 Report to Congress of the U.S.-China Economic and Security Review Commission*, Washington: U.S. Government Publishing Office, p. 210, https://insidecybersecurity.com/sites/insidecybersecurity.com/files/documents/2018/nov/cs2018_0480.pdf, accessed online 3 June 2020.
65. Cited in Mark R. Cozad (2017), *Chinese Contingency Planning for Regional Hotspot*, Santa Monica, CA: RAND Corporation, p. 10.
66. Ibid.
67. Ibid.
68. "Xi stressed real combat training", *Xinhuanet*, 3 January 2018, http://www.xinhuanet.com/english/2018-01/03/c_136870001.htm, accessed online 15 January 2020.
69. Ibid.
70. Joel Wuthnow and Philip C. Saunders (2019), "Chairman Xi Remakes the PLA", n. 13, p. 1.
71. "Communiqué of the Third Plenary Session of the 18th Central Committee of the Communist Party of China", China.org.cn, 15 January 2014, http://www.china.org.cn/china/third_plenary_session/2014-01/15/content_31203056.htm, accessed online 4 May 2020.
72. Liu Hui (2019), "Graphics: Reform in China's national defence and armed forces", *CGTN*, 25 December 2019, https://news.cgtn.com/news/2019-12-25/Graphics-Reform-in-China-s-national-defense-and-armed-forces-MGRXIeWBZm/index.html, accessed online 20 June 2020.
73. You Ji (2016), *China's Military Transformation*, n. 30, p. 15.
74. See, "Graphics: China's military reform in past 5 years", *CGTN*, 1 August 2020, https://news.cgtn.com/news/2020-08-01/Graphics-China-s-military-reform-in-past-5-years—SceNvpfC92/index.html, accessed online 14 August 2020.
75. "Building a strong army through reform", *Xinhuanet*, n. 32.
76. Quoted in Dennis J. Blasko (2016), "Integrating the Services and Harnessing the Military Area Commands", *Journal of Strategic Studies*, Vol. 39, Issue 5-6, p. 686.
77. "Building a strong army through reform", *Xinhuanet*, n. 32.
78. The fundamental guidelines for deepening reform were stated explicitly: to use the scientific theory of the CPC as its pointer; to use the goal of building a strong army as its guide; to use military strategies and policies under new circumstances as its overall direction; to remove systematic, structural and policy barriers as well as policy problems as its focus; to adopt the modernization of the military as its orientation; and to unleash the combat capacity and vigour of the military as its aim. See "Building a strong army through reform", *Xinhuanet*, n. 32.

79. "Building a strong army through reform", *Xinhuanet*, n. 32.
80. Chen Zhuo (2019), "Xi Stresses timely completion of military development goals", *China Military Online*, 12 March 2019, http://eng.chinamil.com.cn/2019special/2019-03/12/content_9448180.htm, accessed online 5 May 2020.
81. Guoli Liu (2017), *China's Foreign Policy in a Changing World*, London: Palgrave Macmillan, p. 59.
82. Ministry of National Defense of the People's Republic of China (2016), "China establishes Rocket Force and Strategic Support Force", 1 January 2016, http://eng.mod.gov.cn/DefenseNews/2016-01/01/content_4634924.htm, accessed online 15 January 2020.
83. Ministry of National Defense of the People's Republic of China (2015), "China's Military Strategy", n. 1.
84. Defense Intelligence Agency (2019), "China Military Power: Modernizing a Force to Fight and Win", https://www.dia.mil/Portals/27/Documents/ News/Military%20 Power%20Publications/China_Military_Power_FINAL_5MB_20190103.pdf, accessed online 7 June 2020.
85. Dennis J. Blasko (2016), "Integrating the Services and Harnessing", n. 76, p. 687.
86. Ibid.
87. "Xi Jinping orders PLA to intensify combat awareness", *Xinhua*, 13 December 2012, http://en.people.cn/90786/8056563.html, accessed online 10 May 2020.
88. Xi Jinping (2017), "Secure a Decisive Victory", n. 2, pp. 48-49.
89. Timothy R. Heath et al. (2016), *The PLA and China's Rejuvenation: National Security and Military Strategies, Deterrence Concepts, and Combat Capabilities*, Santa Monica, CA: RAND Corporation, pp. 37-43.
90. Xi Jinping (2017), "Secure a Decisive Victory", n. 2, p. 48.
91. You Ji (2018), "Xi Jinping and PLA Transformation through Reforms", RSIS Working Paper No. 313, 21 May 2018, p. 2, https://www.rsis.edu.sg/wp-content/uploads/ 2018/ 05/WP313.pdf, accessed online 5 May 2020.
92. Office of the Secretary of Defense (2020), "Annual Report to Congress", n. 7, p. 34.
93. Kartik Bommakanti and Anant Singh Mann (2020), "China's Military Modernisation", n. 27.
94. Amrita Jash (2019), "China Streamlines the PLA, But with Strings Attached", Centre for Land Warfare Studies, 30 January 2019, https://archive.claws.in/1974/china-streamlines-the-pla-but-with-strings-attached-dr-amrita-jash.html, accessed online 30 June 2020.
95. "Chinese army now makes up less than half of PLA's strength as military aims to transform itself into modern fighting force", *South China Morning Post*, 21 January 2019, https://www.scmp.com/news/china/military/article/2183050/chinese-army-now-makes-less-half-plas-strength-military-aims, accessed online 25 January 2020.
96. Dennis J. Blasko (2019), "The PLA army after 'below the neck' reforms: contributing to China's joint war fighting, deterrence and MOOTW posture", *Journal of Strategic Studies*, p. 6.
97. Ibid.
98. "Full Text: China's National Defense in the New Era", *Xinhuanet*, n. 33.
99. Ibid.
100. "China's Xi says to shake up military structure in reform push", *Reuters*, 26 November 2015, https://www.reuters.com/article/us-china-defence/chinas-xi-says-to-shake-

up-military-structure-in-reform-push-idUSKBN0TF13T20151126, accessed online 20 June 2020.

101. Liu Hui (2019), "Graphics", n. 72.
102. 2020 *Report to Congress of the U.S.-China Economic and Security Review Commission*, n. 31, pp. 400-401.
103. "Xi urges breakthroughs in military structural reform", *China Military Online*, 26 November 2015, http://english.chinamil.com.cn/news-channels/china-military-news/2015-11/26/content_6787704.htm, accessed online 20 March 2020.
104. Ibid.
105. Dennis J. Blasko (2019), "The PLA army after 'below the neck' reforms", n. 96, p. 7.
106. Phillip C. Saunders and Joel Wuthnow (2016), "China's Goldwater-Nichols? Assessing PLA Organizational Reforms", Strategic Forum: National Defense University, April 2016, p. 2, https://inss.ndu.edu/Portals/68/Documents/stratforum /SF-294.pdf, accessed online 26 May 2020.
107. Dennis J. Blasko (2019), "The PLA army after 'below the neck' reforms", n. 96, p. 6.
108. Joel Wuthnow and Phillip C. Saunders (2017), *Chinese Military Reform in the Age of Xi Jinping: Drivers, Challenges, and Implications*, Washington, D.C.: National Defense University Press, p. 50.
109. Lindsay Maizland (2020), "China's Military Modernization", Council on Foreign Relations, 5 February 2020, https://www.cfr.org/backgrounder/chinas-modernizing-military, accessed online 28 March 2020.
110. Ibid.
111. "Building a strong army through reform", *Xinhuanet*, n. 32.
112. Ibid.
113. Ministry of National Defense of the People's Republic of China (2016), "Xi stresses joint battle command for military reform", 20 April 2016, http://eng.mod.gov.cn/DefenseNews/2016-04/20/content_4650177.htm, accessed online 26 May 2020.
114. Kartik Bommakanti and Anant Singh Mann (2020), "China's Military Modernisation", n. 27.
115. Teeth-To-Tail Ratio (TTR) is a military term that refers to the amount of personnel it takes to supply and support each combat soldier. Ibid.
116. Liu Hui (2019), "Graphics", n. 72.
117. Phillip C. Saunders and Joel Wuthnow (2016), "China's Goldwater-Nichols?", n. 106, p. 3.
118. Dennis J. Blasko (2016), "Integrating the Services and Harnessing", n. 76, p. 688.
119. Zhang Tao (2016), "Army adjustment and establishment completed in five Theatre Commands," *China Military Online*, 4 February 2016, http://english.chinamil.com.cn/news-channels/china-military-news/2016-02/04/content_6890499.htm, accessed online 5 May 2020.
120. Yasuyuki Suigura (2017), "The Joint Operation Structure of the Chinese People's Liberation Army with Focus on the Reorganization of the Chain of Command and Control under the Xi Jinping Administration", *NIDS Journal of Defense and Security*, Vol. 18, p. 17.
121. Ibid., p. 16.
122. Phillip C. Saunders and Joel Wuthnow (2016), "China's Goldwater-Nichols"? n. 106, p. 3.
123. *2016 Report to Congress of the U.S.-China Economic and Security Review Commission*,

Washington: U.S. Government Publishing Office, 2016, p. 206, https://www.uscc.gov/sites/default/files/annual_reports/2016%20Annual%20Report%20to%20 Congress.pdf, accessed online 4 June 2020.

124. Ministry of National Defense of the People's Republic of China, "Theatre Commands", http://eng.mod.gov.cn/theater-commands/index.htm, accessed online 4 June 2020.
125. Amrita Jash (2019), "Tibet Military Command: People's Liberation Army's Combat Role in High-Altitude", Issue Brief, no. 181, Centre for Land Warfare Studies, May 2019, p. 2, https://www.claws.in/publication/tibet-military-command-peoples-liberation-armys-combat-role-in-high-altitude/, accessed online 4 June 2020.
126. Joel Wuthnow (2020), "System Overload: Can China's Military Be Distracted in a War over Taiwan"? in Philip C. Saunders (ed.) *China Strategic Perspectives*, no. 15, Washington, D.C.: National Defense University Press, p. 18. For greater details of China's military capabilities across all services, see "Chapter Six: Asia", in *The Military Balance 2020*, Vol. 120, No. 1, pp. 259-268.
127. Quoted in "Large-Scale Combat Operations" in FM 3-0 Operations, Washington DC: Headquarters, Department of the Army, 6 October 2017, p. 5-1, https://fas.org/irp/doddir/army/fm3-0.pdf, accessed on 8 June 2020.
128. Edmund J. Burke et al. (2016), *Assessing the Training and Operational Proficiency of China's Aerospace Forces: Selections from the Inaugural Conference of the China Aerospace Studies Institute (CASI)*, Santa Monica, CA: RAND Corporation, p. 37.
129. Ibid.
130. Ibid.
131. Ibid, pp. 36-37.
132. Ibid., p. 37.
133. Mark R. Cozad (2016), *PLA Joint Training and Implications for Future Expeditionary Capabilities*, Santa Monica, CA: RAND Corporation, p. 3.
134. *2016 Report to Congress of the U.S.-China Economic*, n. 123.
135. Ibid.
136. Phillip C. Saunders and Joel Wuthnow (2016), "China's Goldwater-Nichols?", n. 106, p. 7.
137. Edmund J. Burke et al. (2016), *Assessing the Training and Operational Proficiency of China's Aerospace Forces*, n. 127, p. 35.
138. Mark R. Cozad (2016), *PLA Joint Training and Implications*, n. 133, p. 3.
139. Quoted in Mark R. Cozad (2019), "Toward a more Joint, Combat-Ready PLA?", in Phillip C. Saunders et al. (eds.), *Chairman Xi Remakes the PLA: Assessing Chinese Military Reforms*, Washington, D.C.: National Defense University Press, p. 209.
140. Ibid.
141. That is, assigning responsibility for joint planning and C2 at theatre echelon is in part justified by the need to push C2 closer to the operational space, particularly considering the requirement to operate outside the traditional confines of China's borders. See Cortez A. Cooper III (2018), *PLA Military Modernization: Drivers, Force Restructuring, and Implications*, Santa Monica, CA: RAND Corporation, p. 10.
142. Yasuyuki Suigura (2017), "The Joint Operation Structure of the Chinese People's Liberation Army", n. 120, p. 15.
143. Ibid.
144. Ibid.
145. Quoted in Anthony H. Cordesman and Joseph Kendall (2017), "Chinese Strategy and

Military Modernization: A Comparative Analysis", Centre for Strategic and International Studies, 12 January 2017, https://csis-prod.s3.amazonaws.com/s3fs public/publication/170112_Chinese_Strategy_and_Military_Modernization%28 reduced%29.pdf, accessed online 20 April 2020.

146. Ouyang (2016), "Defense Ministry introduces aims of the theatre commands", *China Military Online,* 2 February 2016, http://eng.chinamil.com.cn/view/2016-02/02/content_7160676.htm, accessed online 5 April 2020.
147. Ministry of National Defense of the People's Republic of China (2015), "China's Military Strategy", n. 1.
148. Quoted in Minnie Chan (2018), "China's army infiltrated by 'peace disease' after years without a war, says its official newspaper", *South China Morning Post,* 3 July 2018, https://www.scmp.com/news/china/diplomacy-defence/article/2153579/chinas-army-infiltrated-peace-disease-after-years, accessed online 20 June 2020.
149. Till now, China has fought only on four episodes: in 1950-53 against the USA and UN forces in the Korean War, in 1962 against India, in 1969 against the Soviet Union and in 1979 against Vietnam.
150. *2018 Report to Congress of the U.S.-China Economic and Security Review Commission,* n. 64, p. 209.
151. Amrita Jash (2019), "Xi Jinping's Theorem" of "Fight and Win"," Centre for Land Warfare Studies, 3 October 2018, https://archive.claws.in/1940/xi-jinping's-theorem-of-"fight-and-win"-dr-amrita-jash.html, accessed online 26 May 2020.
152. Amrita Jash (2019), "Xi Jinping's World-Class Military", n. 58.
153. Xi Jinping (2017), "Secure a Decisive Victory", n. 2, p. 48.
154. Amrita Jash (2018), "Can't be Called a 'Paper Tiger', China Gears its 'Combat Readiness'," Centre for Land Warfare Studies, 19 December 2018, http://www.claws.in/1957/can%E2%80%99t-be-called-a-%E2%80%98paper-tiger%E2%80%99-china-gear s-its-%E2%80%98combat-readiness%E2%80%99-dr-amrita-jash.html, accessed online 4 June 2020.
155. Office of the Secretary of Defense (2020), "Annual Report to Congress", n. 7, p. 48.
156. Ibid.
157. Yao Jianing (2016), "Chinese army begins large-scale drill", *China Military Online,* 16 July 2016, http://eng.chinamil.com.cn/view/2016-07/16/content_7176139.htm, accessed online 5 June 2020.
158. Quoted in Minnie Chan and William Zheng (2020), "Why Taiwan may be a key factor in China's military modernisation plan", n. 4.
159. Meia Nouwens (2020), "Is China speeding up militarymodernisation? It may, but not yet", n. 18.
160. Quoted in "Xi calls for deepened military-civil fusion," NPC and CPPCC Annual Sessions 2018, *Xinhuanet,* 12 March 2018, http://www.xinhuanet. com/english/2018-03/12/c_137034168_2.htm, accessed online 10 September 2020.
161. Quoted in John Grevatt (2020), "China to deepen 'civil-military fusion'", n. 36.
162. Ibid.
163. It is to note that it was former Chinese President Hu Jintao in 2007, who was the first to lay the foundation of the MCF in Chinese strategic thinking; wherein at the 17th Party Congress, Hu urged the country to "take a path of military-civilian fusion with Chinese characteristics", which was intensely pushed further by Xi Jinping.
164. The language used to describe the MCF has evolved significantly between different

Chinese administrations. The following terms have been used: "military and civilian dual use" [军民两用], "military-civilian integration" [军民结合], combining peacetime and wartime preparations [平战结合], "nestling the military within the civilian" [寓军于民], "military-civilian fusion-style develop path" [军民融合式发展路子], among others. On 21 July 2016, the *Opinion on the Integrated Development of Economic Construction and National Defense Construction (2016 Opinion)* [关于经济建设和国防建设融合发展的意见] was released by the CPC Central Committee, the State Council, and the Central Military Commission. As of writing, the *2016 Opinion* is believed to be the only public (partial summary) authoritative document on MCF development to date. Since then, the MCF has come to the forefront and entered a stage of rapid development.

165. Alex Stone and Peter Wood (2020), *China's Military-Civil Fusion Strategy: A View from Chinese Strategists*, Montgomery, AL: China Aerospace Studies Institute, Air University, p. 23, https://www.airuniversity.af.edu/Portals/10/CASI/documents/Research/Other%20topics/CASI%20China's%20Military%20Civil%20Fusion%20Strategy-%20Full%20final.pdf?ver=2020-06-15-152810-733, accessed online 25 July 2020.
166. The Commission acts as the highest level "decision-making and coordination mechanism" for MCF development, and is instrumental in breaking down institutional barriers across government, military, and industry that have hindered MCF implementation. The first plenary meeting of the Commission was held in 2017 and the second was held in 2018. For details, see Greg Levesque (2019), "Military-Civil Fusion: Beijing's "Guns AND Butter" Strategy to Become a Technological Superpower", *China Brief*, Vol. 19, No. 8, The Jamestown Foundation, https://jamestown.org/program/military-civil-fusion-beijings-guns-and-butter-strategy-to-become-a-technological-superpower/, accessed online 15 September 2020.
167. Ibid., p. 25.
168. The military component includes the armed forces, national defence technology, industry, facilities, mobilisation, education, resources, as well as the major operational domains, while the civil component includes national science and technology and industrial system, the national talent education and training system, the national social services system, the national emergency management system, as well as emerging domains and nascent technological areas such as maritime, space, cyberspace, and artificial intelligence that are closely linked to the generation of "New Type Combat Capabilities". For details, see Jiang Luming [姜鲁鸣], Wang Weihai [王伟海] and Liu Zuchen [刘祖辰], *Initial Discussion on the Military-Civil Fusion Strategy* [军民融合发展战略探论], Beijing: People's Press, p. 15.
169. "Full Text: China's National Defense in the New Era", *Xinhuanet*, n. 33.
170. *Tizhi* is a general term for the systems, institutions, methods, forms, etc., involved in matters related to the institutional setup, leadership affiliation, and management authority of state organs, political party organisations, enterprises, and public institutions.
171. Alex Stone and Peter Wood (2020), *China's Military-Civil Fusion Strategy*, n. 165, p. 23.
172. The "full-element" attribute defines the types of resources shared between the military and civilian sectors; the "multi-domain" attribute identifies the domains prioritised for MCF development. Taken together, they provide a roadmap for MCF development, explaining how China plans to achieve the deep fusion pattern. While subject to modifications, these areas, serve as the "backbone" of the MCF strategy. The last

attribute—"high return"—describes the effect Chinese leaders and MCF strategists hope to derive from MCF development. For details, see Alex Stone and Peter Wood (2020), *China's Military-Civil Fusion* Strategy, n. 165, pp. 28-35.

173. Alex Stone and Peter Wood (2020), *China's Military-Civil Fusion Strategy*, n. 165, p. 28.
174. Office of the Secretary of Defense (2020), "Annual Report to Congress", n. 7, p. vi.
175. Ibid., p. 30.
176. Ibid., p. 31.
177. Ibid., pp. 36-38.
178. Ibid., p. 38.
179. "China names key areas of military-civil integration," *CGTN*, 21 June 2017, https://news.cgtn.com/news/7741444d30517a6333566d54/index.html, accessed on 10 September 2020.
180. Brian Lafferty (2019), "Civil-Military Integration and PLA Reforms," in Phillip C. Saunders et al. (eds.) *Chairman Xi Remakes the PLA: Assessing Chinese Military Reforms*, Washington DC: National Defense University Press, p. 632.
181. Elsa B. Kania (2019), "In Military-Civil Fusion, China Is Learning Lessons From the United States and Starting to Innovate," *Real Clear Defense*, 27 August 2019, https://www.realcleardefense.com/articles/2019/08/27/in_military-civil_fusion_china_is_learning_lessons_from_the_united_states_and_starting_to_innovate_114699.html, accessed on 19 September 2020.
182. Quoted in Major Donna L. I. Welch (2011), *China's Expeditionary Progression*, Fort Leavenworth, Kansas: School of Advanced Military Studies, US Army Command and General Staff College, p. 14, https://www.hsdl.org/?view&did=704586, accessed online 20 July 2020.
183. Ministry of National Defense of the People's Republic of China (2015), "China's Military Strategy", n. 1.
184. Ibid.
185. Paul J. Bolt and Adam J. Gray (2007), *China's National Security Strategy*, Colorado Springs, CO: Institute for National Security Studies, p. 8.
186. Ibid.
187. Ibid.
188. Ibid., p. 9.
189. The U.S. Department of Defense defines power projection as "the ability of a nation [...] to rapidly and effectively deploy and sustain forces in and from multiple dispersed locations to respond to crises, to contribute to deterrence, and to enhance regional stability." An important subset of power projection is expeditionary warfare, which DOD defines as "military operations conducted by an armed force to accomplish a specific objective in a foreign country". Quoted in *2020 Report to Congress of the U.S.-China Economic and Security Review Commission*, n. 31, p. 322.
190. Quoted in *2020 Report to Congress of the U.S.-China Economic and Security Review Commission*, n. 31, p. 389.
191. Ibid., pp. 391-392.
192. Ibid.
193. Ibid., pp. 388-390.
194. Oriana Skylar Mastro (2015), "A Global Expeditionary People's Liberation Army: 2025-30", in Roy Kamphausen and David Lai (eds.) *The Chinese People's Liberation Army in 2025*, Carlisle, PA: Strategic Studies Institute and U.S. Army War College Press, pp. 209-210.

195. Chad Peltier, Tate Nurkin and Sean O'Connor (2020), "China's Logistics Capabilities for Expeditionary Operations", *Jane's*, p. 6, https://www.uscc.gov/sites/default/files/2020-04/China%20Expeditionary%20Logistics%20Capabilities%20Report.pdf, accessed online 20 November 2020.
196. Ministry of National Defense of the People's Republic of China (2016), "China establishes Rocket Force and Strategic Support Force", 1 January 2016, http://eng.mod.gov.cn/DefenseNews/2016-01/01/content_4634924.htm, accessed online 15 January 2020.
197. Ministry of National Defense of the People's Republic of China (2015), "China's Military Strategy", n. 1.

4

Defence Budget, Industry & Weapons

"Once a country's military lags behind, its national security will be fatally threatened. I often read historic materials about modern China, and when I see how lagging behind leaves a country vulnerable to attack, I feel deep pain in my heart!"

—Xi Jinping (2016)[1]

"The fact that China's defense expenditure ranks second in the world is determined by the demands of its national defense, the size of its economy, and the defensive nature of its national defense policy".

—China's Defence White Paper (2019)[2]

"No force can stop the Chinese people and the Chinese nation forging ahead".

—Xi Jinping (2019)[3]

China's rapid economic growth has demonstrated a robust military modernisation, exemplified by extensive structural reforms and streamlining of command structures to build and sustain a modern armed force. The U.S. Defense Intelligence Agency's (DIA) 2019 report concludes that Chinese military modernisation was not undertaken with a major global war in mind, but rather in preparation for further challenges to its regional efforts, potentially leading to a local war,[4] as the PLA's doctrine calls for "winning informationised local wars". This is qualified by

China's growing capabilities of power projection, as noted in the Chinese military's 'active' presence everywhere, highlighting the 'offensive defence' aspect of China's "active defence". This is to argue that Beijing's power projection ability is improving, and that the relative balance in areas more distant from China is also shifting, suggesting that China's military rise is 'well-planned' with serious global and regional implications.

In this context, active defence as understood in terms of the PLA's military capability can be assessed from China's overall military readiness, which is quantified by factors such as:[5] PLAA is the world's largest standing ground force, with 13 group armies; PLAN is now the world's largest navy with an aircraft carrier and a credible fleet of about 350 ships and submarines (both diesel and nuclear); PLAAF is one of the largest air forces in the world; and PLARF has an inventory of over 1,250 ground-launched ballistic and cruise missiles, of which, the DF-26 holds a capability to switch between conventional and nuclear warheads. In addition, China is making significant progress towards building a nuclear triad deterrent to absorb a potential pre-emptive strike in order to retaliate. In its new warfighting methods, China seeks to employ advanced cruise missiles, sea mines, submarines, imaging satellites, anti-satellite weapons, and other advanced and specialised weaponry – to exploit the opponent's vulnerabilities in fighting 'high-tech local wars'. In assessment of these trends, the 2020 DoD report categorically suggests that "China is already ahead of the USA in certain areas",[6] which includes ship-building, as well as the number of ballistic, cruise and anti-aircraft missile systems. Furthermore, as per the 2020 Stockholm International Peace Research Institute (SIPRI) data on "global military expenditure", China is second only to the USA in its defence spending.[7] Furthermore, as per SIPRI's 2020 estimates, China is also the world's second largest arms industry, behind the USA and ahead of Russia,[8] making it a major arms exporter.

Such trends call for significant worry as China's capabilities are not just at near par to US capabilities, but in some cases, China seems to or has already surpassed America. For instance, China now leads especially in areas of hypersonic weaponry, precision-strike capabilities, mainly with medium-range and intermediate-range ballistic missiles; and in development of anti-satellite capabilities. With China's military capabilities on the rise, it is important to note that more than military hard power, what is more worrying is the 'critical point of confidence', that when China feels it can strike an opponent in safeguarding its interests. This then makes the Chinese 'use of military force' for regional conflict more imminent than ever.

In this regard, to argue that China's military build-up is a natural outcome of its ascension to great power status will be a linear assessment, thus, calling for an oversight of critical aspects. To avoid a faulty assessment, at the foremost, it is essential to have a clear understanding of the PRC's military spending. This is crucial given the uncertainties surrounding Beijing's official numbers, as China's increasing military capabilities run contrary to its modest figures and justifications of the same. Therefore, as China's military capabilities are on the rise, the need lies in enquiring into three key questions: First, What explains China's military spending? Second, What is the scope and size of China's defence industry? And third, What comprises China's weapons inventory?

These queries are of significance given that a clear picture of each of these aspects provides greater transparency to the understanding of the PLA's doctrine, the force structure, and the threat perception – an assessment of which is essential for tracking China's military intentions and strategic behaviour. In view of this, the chapter will examine two key perspectives: the increasing trend of China's defence expenditure and the exponential growth of China's defence industry. The crux of this chapter lies in providing a greater context and perspective for Chinese and Western discussions on three key fundamental aspects: First, the ambiguity over China's official defence budget; second, the status of China's military-industrial complex (MIC); and third, the capabilities of China's 'new age' weapons and weapon systems that make a critical difference to China's military capabilities.

China's Military Spending

In general, Beijing announces a single overall figure for its official defence budget for the year during the annual March session of the NPC and CPPCC. However, the proposed figure gets revised during the course of the year, thus highlighting the ambiguity attached to China's actual defence spending.

In May 2020, at the annual session of the NPC and CPPCC, the Chinese government proposed an official defence budget of 1.27 trillion yuan (about 179 billion USD), with an increase of 6.6 per cent from 2019;

but the lowest since 1988 - wherein a 3.81 per cent increase in the defence budget was proposed.[9] China raised the defence budget by about 7.5 per cent year-on-year, setting military expenditure at nearly 1.19 trillion yuan in 2019, with an increase of 6.6 per cent.[10] To note, this single-digit growth rate was consecutively fifth in a row, with previous estimates being 7.6 per cent in 2016, 7 per cent in 2017, 8.1 per cent in 2018 and 7.5 per cent in 2019 against 10.1 per cent in 2015.[11] Here, the query is: Does a slow growth rate call for a limitation in China's military ambitions?

Figure 4.1: China's Defence Budget (2011-2020)

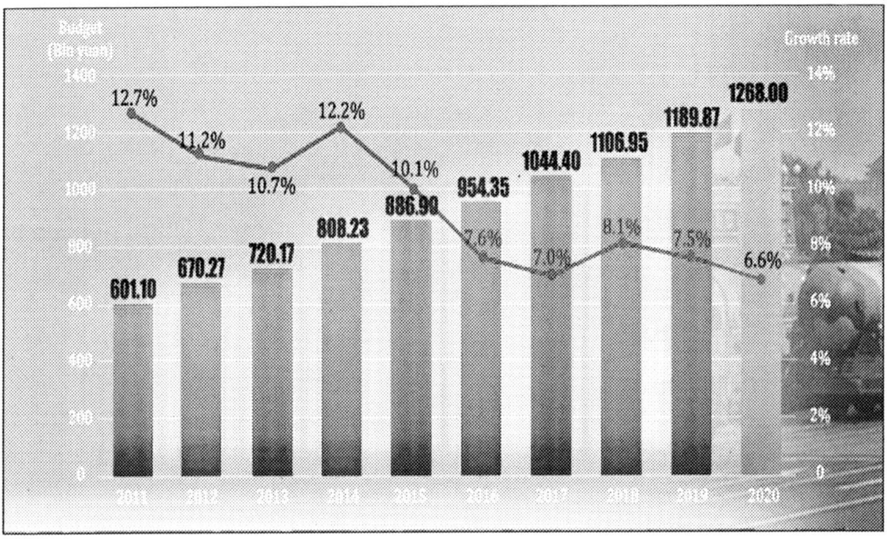

Note: Here it is important to note that in 2010, China became the second largest world economy.
Source: Adapted from *Global Times* (2020).[12]

Unlike the past increases, the 2020 military budget holds greater significance given it comes at a time of China's worst economic downturn caused by the COVID-19 pandemic. Moreover, while other areas witnessed a cut, defence spending remained uncompromised. This clarifies two things: First, China's commitment towards military modernisation at all cost as exemplified by Li Keqiang's 13th Work Report, that categorically states:

> "We will advance military training and war preparedness to the best of our ability and firmly safeguard China's sovereignty, security, and development interests. We will complete the crucial tasks laid down in the 13th five-year plan for the development of the armed

> forces and draw up the 14th five-year plan. We will deepen reforms in national defense and the military, increase our logistic and equipment support capacity, and promote innovative development of defense-related science and technology. We will improve the system of national defense mobilization and ensure that the unity between the military and the government and between the military and the people remains rock solid".[13]

As Wei Dongxu posits, the increased defence budget is significant as it ensures that the "Chinese military's major programs and key spending fields are not affected by the pandemic and will remain on schedule".[14] This highlights China's undeterred commitment towards fulfilling the strategic goals of military modernisation, which is a crucial factor in the military budget.

Second, the increased defence spending amidst the pandemic has only made Beijing's intentions clear. To which, one can argue that this highlights PRC's sensing of an increasing security threat and thereby giving the PLA the military muscle to deal with it. This intention is well-witnessed in Xi's pointed instructions to the PLA that the military should: think about worst-case scenarios, scale up training and battle preparedness, promptly and effectively deal with all sorts of complex situations, and resolutely safeguard national sovereignty, security and development interests.[15]

What is noteworthy is that, in the Chinese perspective, Beijing's defence spending is argued to be "reasonable and appropriate".[16] For instance, Song Zhongping argues that compared to the scope of the threats that China faces (both traditional and non-traditional security fields), the 2020 budget is "far from enough" and suggests that a growth rate of 6.6 is "not a high figure" even under the pandemic.[17] However, in a counter, Andrew Erickson argues that while it is reportedly China's lowest such increase since 1988, it is still by far the largest planned increase for any major nation.[18] This makes China's defence spending an exception, especially at a time when every other nation would struggle to do so due to the economic slowdown caused by the pandemic.

In this regard, it is imperative to understand the pattern of China's defence spending, which acts as one of the key indicators of the modernisation of the PLA – thus, exemplifying Beijing's intentions. As the 2019 White Paper notes:

> "In the new era, to keep pace with the country's modernization, China is focusing on building a fortified national defence and a strong military commensurate with the country's international standing, and its national security and development interests. China is striving to narrow the gap between its military and the world's leading militaries, and make up the deficiencies in the military's capabilities in modern warfare. Defense expenditure is growing steadily and the breakdown of spending is being continuously optimized".[19]

In this context, the query over China's military expenditure is significant given the fact that Beijing's defence spending has often been accused of 'not being transparent'. To cite an example, in June 2005, at the Shangri-La Dialogue, then-U.S. Secretary of Defense, Donald Rumsfeld stated:

> "Since no nation threatens China, one must wonder: Why this growing investment [defence spending]? Why these continuing large and expanded arms purchases? Why these continued deployments?"[20]

Rumsfeld's queries remain relevant even today. For if there is no perceived threat, then what ensures an increasing defence spending. This budgetary opacity is often simplistically linked to China's rise and its 'not so benign' long-term strategic intentions. In that case, can transparency help dispel the distrust over China's intentions – becomes a crucial point of assessment.

In response to the international calls for greater openness, a Chinese military official countered by stating that "transparency is a tool of the strong to be used against the weak".[21] Interestingly, if one applies this Chinese logic, does it suggest that China considers itself as 'weak' against its 'transparent strong' Western counterparts. However, China officially justifies its spending by negating the "hidden military spending" theory on the grounds that it has been submitting reports on its military expenditure to the United Nations every year since 2007 (as noted in Table 4.1). To note, China submits the "Simplified Reporting Form" on military expenditures annually. Upholding the view that China is 'transparent' about its military spending, Zhang Yesui, spokesperson for the third session of the 13th NPC, categorically stated: "[f]rom where the money comes, to how the money is used, everything is accounted for".[22] While China perceives the form submission as providing transparency, but it makes no real difference. The "Simplified" form contains much less information than the "Standard Reporting Form" submitted by most advanced industrial democracies, as it includes no "breakdown" to include even branches and services.[23]

Table 4.1: Breakdown of China's Defence Expenditure (2010-2017)

(in RMB billion yuan)

Item → ↓	Personnel Expense		Training and Sustainment Expense		Equipment Expense		Total
Year	Amt.	Percentage (%)	Amt.	Percentage (%)	Amt.	Percentage (%)	
2010	185.931	34.9	170.047	31.9	177.359	33.2	533.337
2011	206.506	34.3	189.943	31.5	206.342	34.2	602.791
2012	195.572	29.2	232.994	34.8	240.626	36.0	669.192
2013	200.231	27.0	269.971	36.4	270.860	36.6	741.062
2014	237.234	28.6	267.982	32.3	323.738	39.1	828.954
2015	281.863	31.0	261.538	28.8	365.383	40.2	908.784
2016	306.001	31.3	266.994	27.4	403.589	41.3	976.584
2017	321.052	30.8	293.350	28.1	428.835	41.1	1043.237

Source: Adapted from China's Defence White Paper (2019).[24]

This lack of transparency has often raised alarms over China's military spending, calling for the China threat theory. Moreover, amidst COVID-19, the increase only added to the speculations over Chinese intentions. However, in its defence, Beijing maintains that it is committed to 'peaceful development' and denounces the hype over the 'China threat'. As the official news portal *China Military Online* wrote in a 2019 commentary: "China does not export revolution, hunger or poverty and does not interfere in other countries' internal affairs. So where does this threat thing come from?"[25] While Chinese officials suggest that:

> "Whether a country poses a military threat to others or not is decided by its diplomatic and national defense policies and not by how much it increases its defence budget. [Adding further that] China has only a limited defence budget, and it is used for safeguarding the country's sovereignty, security, and territorial integrity. This will not pose a threat to other countries".[26]

But despite the official balance sheet provided by China, the debate still prevails: How much does the PRC actually spend on its military? This only highlights the 'uncertainty' attached to the figures put forward by the Chinese authorities. Besides, one cannot ignore that Beijing's military expenditure holds significant regional and global implications.

I. Major Trend: China's Increasing Military Expenditure

Since the reform and opening up in 1978, China's defence spending has consistently increased within a certain range of China's economic growth and fiscal spending – levelling up from mere sustainability to that of moderate growth. Most notably, China's heavy military spending has been in alignment with the broader upward trend in global defence spending.

Figure 4.2: China's Defence Spending 1978-2017

(in 100 million yuan)

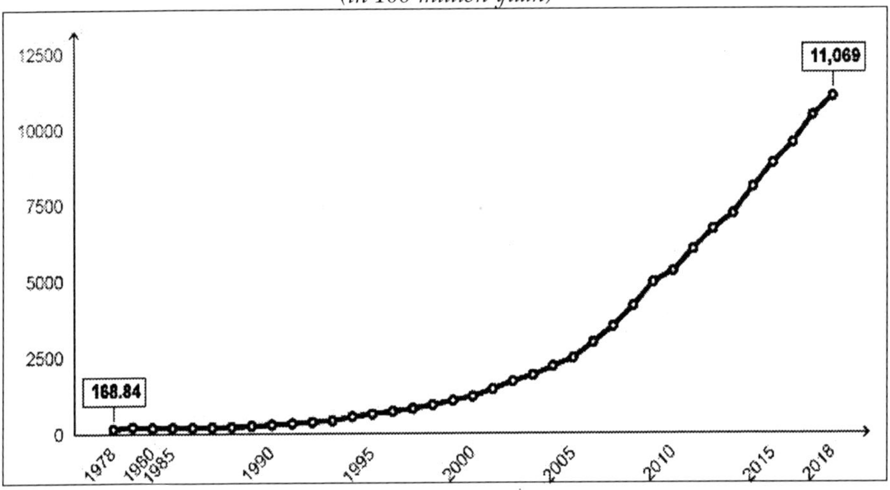

Source: Adapted from *DW* (2018).[27]

China's economic growth is a critical underlying factor in assessing PRC's military power. That is, the increasing trend in Chinese military spending is tied to its rising GDP. China contends that its military spending remains proportional to the country's rapid economic development, as the 2019 White Paper suggests:

> "China attends to both development and security. It is making an integrated effort to build a prosperous country and a strong military, and striving for the coordinated development of national defense and the economy. Following the principle of building the armed forces through diligence and thrift, China takes into consideration the development of the economy and the demands of national defense, decides on the appropriate scale and composition of defense expenditure, and manages and applies these funds in accordance with law".[28]

Table 4.2: China's Defence Expenditure Since 2012

Year	*GDP (RMB billion)*	*Total Defence Expenditure (RMB billion)*	*CPI (Previous Year = 100)*	*Growth Rate of Govt Expenditure (%)*	*Growth Rate of Defence Expenditure (%)*	*Defence Expenditure to GDP (%)*	*Defence Expenditure to Govt Expenditure (%)*	*Real Defence Expenditure Growth Rate (Inflation-adjusted) (%)*
2012	54036.74	669.192	102.6	15.29	11.02	1.24	5.31	8.42
2013	59524.44	741.062	102.6	11.32	10.74	1.24	5.29	8.14
2014	64397.4	828.954	102.0	8.25	11.86	1.29	5.46	9.86
2015	68905.21	908.784	101.4	15.87	9.63	1.32	5.17	8.23
2016	74358.55	976.584	102.0	6.75	7.46	1.31	5.20	5.46
2017	82712.17	1043.237	101.6	8.17	6.83	1.26	5.14	5.23

Source: Adapted from China's Defence White Paper (2019).[29]

Table 4.2 suggests that China's defence expenditure has grown in tandem with the growth of the national economy and government expenditure. What is noteworthy is that the expenditure as a percentage of GDP has fallen from a peak of 5.43 per cent in 1979 to 1.26 per cent in 2017, and remained below 2 per cent for the past three decades (Figure 4.3). While defence expenditure as a percentage of government expenditure was 17.37 per cent in 1979 and 5.14 per cent in 2017, a drop of more than 12 percentage points (Figure 4.4).

Figure 4.3: China's Defence Expenditure as a Percentage of its GDP (1979-2017) (%)

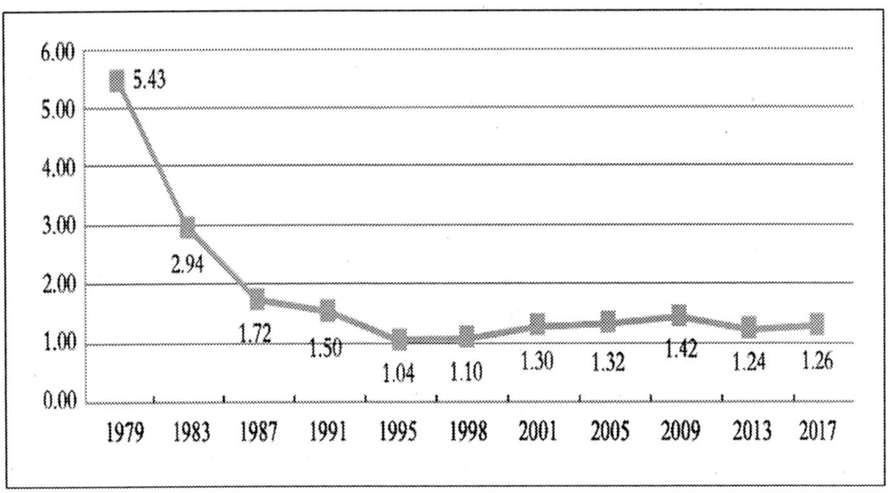

Source: Adapted from China's Defence White Paper (2019).[30]

Figure 4.4: China's Defence Expenditure as a Percentage of its Government Expenditure (1979-2017)
(%)

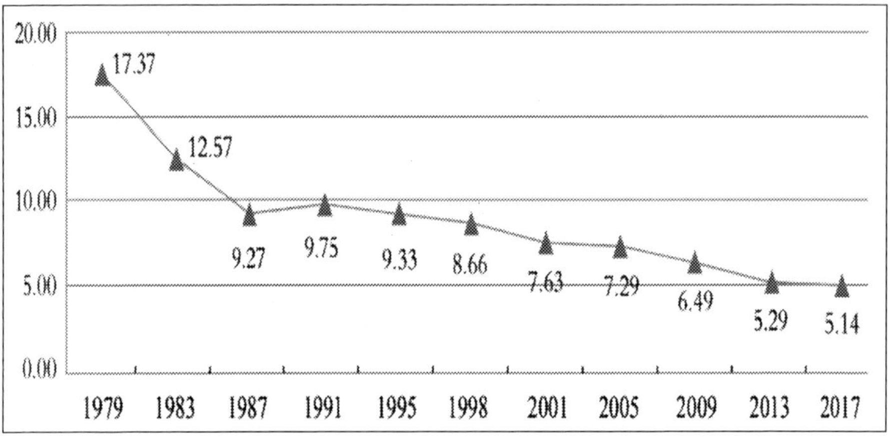

Source: Adapted from China's Defence White Paper (2019).[31]

In analysing the overall trends in China's defence spending, one cannot discount the fact that inflation does play a role, as noted from the 'downturns' in the expenditure. Here, two key observations can be made: First, while China's defence spending has certainly increased in absolute terms; in the long-term, the growth rate is experiencing a downward trend, as exemplified by Figures 4.3 and 4.4. Second, while the growth rate has slowed, China's defence spending has witnessed an upward trajectory. To note, China's military spending has surpassed its economic growth, which projects a significant shift in China's own policy. That is, there is a reversal of China's 2015 policy that emphasised on the need to closely match spending on the armed forces with a slower growth rate; but China has failed to bridge the gap. This clarifies that Chinese military spending will continue to grow despite even if the GDP growth slows down, as exemplified by Beijing's 2020 budget under the pandemic.

In this perspective, to suggest that a lower growth rate is directly proportional to China's military ambitions will be a faulty assessment. Besides, in the global chart, China currently spends more on defence than Japan, South Korea, the Philippines, and Vietnam combined; and China's military spending is second only to the USA (Figure 4.5). These trends make it imperative to understand the rationale behind China's increasing numbers despite the slow economic growth.

Figure 4.5: Top 15 Countries with the Highest Spending in 2019

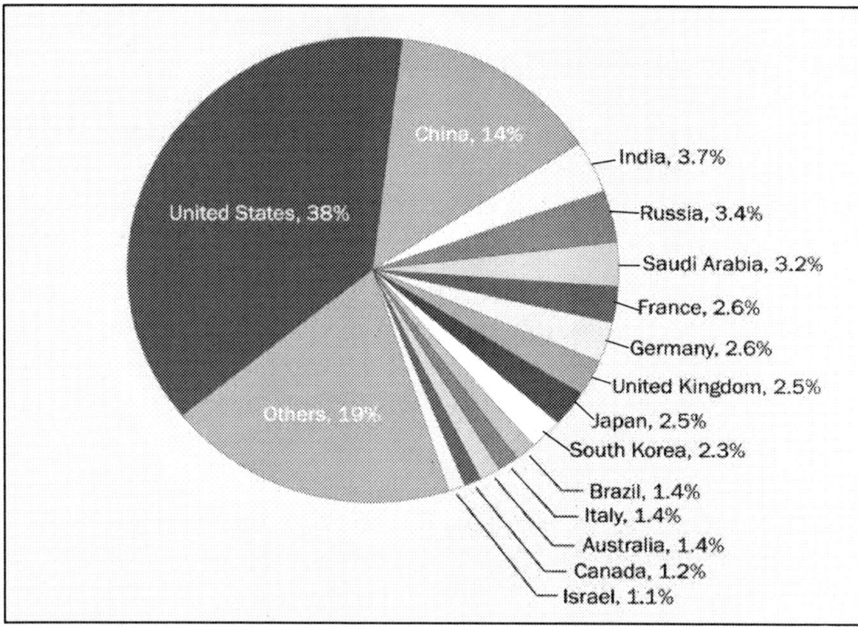

Source: Adapted from SIPRI (2020).[32]

Here, PRC's intentions behind the military spending can be argued under four perspectives:[33] First, it clarifies China's determination to fulfil its three strategic goals of mechanisation, modernisation and a 'World Class Military'. Second, it exemplifies China's growing military ambitions, as demonstrated in its power projections in the South China Sea, the East China Sea, the 21st Century Maritime Silk Road, at the Himalayan border with India and in the Indian Ocean Region. Third, it highlights Beijing's aspirations to become a security maximiser by use of high-end technology, as the 19th Party Congress report posits: "We [China] must keep it firm in our minds that technology is the core combat capability, encourage innovations in major technologies, and conduct innovations independently". Fourth, to pursue PLA's military preparedness to conduct joint military operations across land, sea, air, cyberspace and outer space and the application of advanced technology, especially information technology, a prerequisite for 'winning informationised local wars'.

China's such intentions are further clarified by the 2019 White Paper that specifically mentions that since 2012, the increase in defence expenditure has been primarily spent for:[34] First, in increasing input in weaponry and equipment development, phasing out the outdated, upgrading the old, and developing and procuring the new, such as aircraft carriers, fighters, missiles and main battle tanks, to steadily modernise weaponry and equipment. Second, to support training in real combat conditions, enhancing strategic-level training, joint training at TC level and training of services and arms, and improving the conditions for simulated, networked and force-on-force training.[35]

China justifies its 'defensive posture' by posing a counter argument that despite the increase, PRC's defence spending accounts for only 1.3 per cent of its GDP, which is significantly lower than the world average of 2.6 per cent while the USA and Russia account for around 4 per cent.[36] As the 2019 White Paper argues:

> "All in all, China's defence expenditure is open and transparent, and its spending is reasonable and appropriate. Compared to other major countries, the ratios of China's defense expenditure to GDP and to government expenditure, as well as the per capita defense expenditure of the country, remain at a relatively low level".[37]

However, although China publishes its official defence budget and provides justifications for the increase in its military spending, the scepticism fails to fade, thus raising serious concerns over China's military modernisation. What causes worry is the anticipation that if China's per capita GDP reaches US$ 30,000, there is the possibility that it will come close to or surpass the USA in terms of military spending and military technology development, causing the PLA to reach the third stage of the strategic goal to build a strong military.[38]

According to *Next Big Future*, China is expected to increase its military hardware spending by about 5 per cent per year and the USA by about 1-2 per cent per year; and by 2025, China will grow from double Russia's military hardware spending to triple. The projections of the top 10 countries by 2030 are highlighted below (see Figure 4.6). Here, it is to note, that in all likelihood, the projected figures will vary, given the economic slowdown under the pandemic.

Figure 4.6: Projected Military Expenditure of Top 10 Countries by 2030

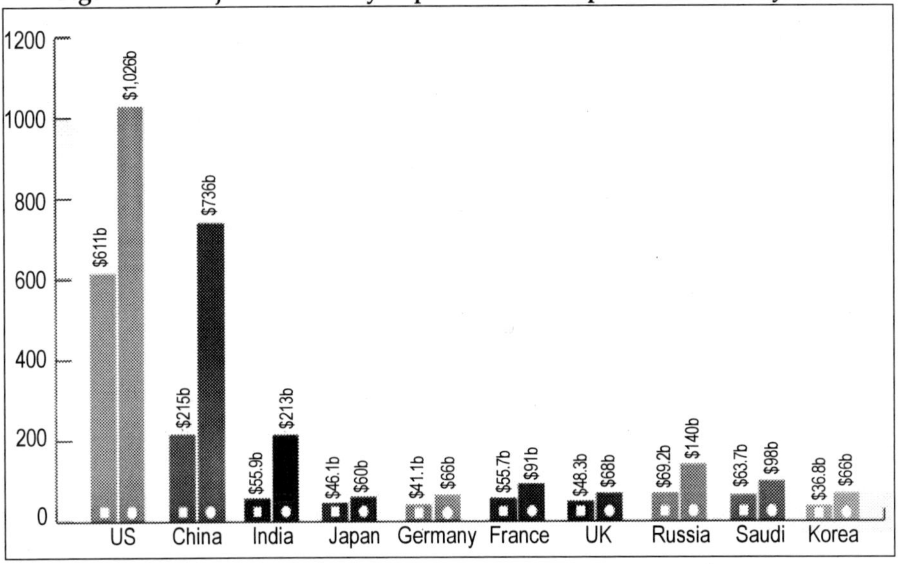

Note: □ 2016 Spending ○ 2030 Projected Spending
Source: Adapted from Wang (2018).[39]

In assessing the broader regional trends, it is found that East Asia spends close to the same amount as Western and Eastern Europe combined. East Asian spending has increased from US$ 92.8 billion in 1990 to US$ 363 billion in 2019, mainly driven by China, which in 1990 constituted 23.6 per cent and in the same year accounted for 70.5 per cent of the total East Asian expenditure.[40] Furthermore, in terms of the broader regional context, the Chinese military budget constitutes 52.2 per cent of the total cumulative spending across all of Asia (including those in the Middle East).[41]

With these trends at play, one can rightly argue that China's military reforms, mechanisation, informationisation, and modernisation will get a further boost in upgrading the PLA. Much of the funding will aim at R&D in terms of aircraft carriers, nuclear-powered submarines, stealth fighters, ballistic missiles, quantum communications and artificial intelligence amongst others – a potent cause of 'worry' for global and regional powers.

II. Scepticism over the Numbers: The Element of Discrepancy in China's Official Figures

Defence expenditure acts as a potent factor in determining China's strategic trajectory, and therefore, policy responses to it. However, the actual amount that China spends on its military still remains widely debated. This is due to the lack of transparency given that China remains opaque and there is limited information available on its defence spending. The exact figures of China's annual military spending have been a point of contention. As a result of which, most analysts claim that China intentionally underreports its actual defence spending.

Interesting to note is the 'discrepancy in numbers' that exists between China's official estimates and figures estimated by organisations such as the SIPRI, the DoD, and the International Institute for Strategic Studies (IISS). To cite an example, in 2017 the Chinese government officially estimated the defence budget at 1.044 trillion yuan (US$ 151.4 billion) and its 2016 defence budget at 955 billion yuan (US$ 143.7 billion). To which, SIPRI estimated the overall 2017 figure at US$ 228 billion and the 2016 budget at US$ 216 billion; while the DoD estimated the 2016 defence budget at more than US$ 180 billion, and the IISS estimated it at US$ 197 billion.[42]

Table 4.3: Variations in the Estimates of Chinese Defence Spending
(Nominal USD)

Year	*Official Chinese Defence Budget*	*SIPRI Estimate*	*IISS Estimate*
2010	76.5	115.7	111.3
2011	90.3	138.0	136.7
2012	103.1	157.4	146.3
2013	116.3	179.9	162.2
2014	131.1	200.8	180.1
2015	142.4	214.4	193.0
2016	143.7	216.7	197.0
2017	151.5	228.8	209.3
2018	167.4	253.6	225.0
2019	172.3	261.1	—
2020	178.6	—	—

Source: Annotated by the Author with reference to CSIS.[43]

Table 4.3 clearly highlights the 'existing discrepancy' in the various estimates. Vast differences are noticed between China's official figures and that of the estimates from outside observers. In view of this, it can be stated that while there is no consensus on the 'exact figures' among outside observers; however, there is an understanding amongst all that China's military spending is 'underreported' by the Chinese government. Besides, it is also important to note that there is an inconsistency in China's own reported figures, as highlighted in Table 4.4 below.

Table 4.4: Comparison of China's Official Spending Figures
Billions of RMB (Billions of USD)

Year	*Ministry of Finance of the PRC*	*2019 Defence White Paper*
2017	¥1023.7 ($151.5)	¥1043.2 ($154.4)
2016	¥954.6 ($143.7)	¥976.6 ($147.0)
2015	¥886.9 ($142.4)	¥908.8 ($145.9)
2014	¥805.5 ($131.1)	¥829.0 ($134.9)
2013	¥720.2 ($116.3)	¥741.1 ($119.6)
2012	¥650.6 ($103.1)	¥669.2 ($106.0)
2011	¥583.0 ($90.2)	¥602.8 ($93.3)
2010	¥518.2 ($76.5)	¥533.3 ($78.8)

Source: Adapted from CSIS.[44]

In assessing the various recent estimates, two observations can be made: First, as compared to the past, the gap between China's official figures and outside estimates is sharply decreasing. Second, notwithstanding the differences, it can be suggested that Beijing's official figures may now more accurately represent defence expenditures than in the past. To say so, as in 2002, the DoD reported that China's actual defence spending may have been upwards of four times larger than its officially announced budget; which when compared to the 2019 estimates shows that SIPRI suggested China's nominal defence spending at US$ 261 billion—1.5 times more than the official figure.[45] Here the query remains: What calls for the discrepancy in the various estimates?

At the foremost, the discrepancy between the various calculations can be attributed to the military-related outlays—what spending lines are included or excluded in the budget. Besides, the data on China's official spending often employs inconsistent terms and definitions. As per PRC's Defence White Papers, Beijing's defence expenditure is categorised by application of, namely - personnel expenses, training and sustainment, and equipment spending. The details of the distribution are listed in Table 4.5.

Table 4.5: Distribution of China's Military Spending

Category of Expenses	*Key Components*
Personnel *(shenghuofei)*	Covers the salaries, allowances, food, bedding, clothing, insurance, subsidies and pensions for officers, non-ranking officers, soldiers and contracted civilians, as well as retirees supported from the defence budget.
Training and Sustainment *(shiye he gongwufei)*	Covers training of the troops, institutional education, construction and maintenance of installations and facilities, and other expenditure on routine consumables.
Equipment *(zhuangbeifei)*	Covers R&D, testing, procurement, repairs, maintenance, transport and the storage of weaponry and equipment.

Source: Annotated by the Author with reference to China's Defence White Paper (2019).[46]

Of the three categories cited in the White Papers, it is noted by some US experts that China is most transparent about the first category and least transparent about the third category of defence spending.[47] To say so, as very little is known about the cost of weapons and equipment produced by the Chinese defence industry or the amount of money allocated to weapons search and development.[48] This brings into perspective the aspect of 'exclusions' in China's defence spending, in which one of the key exclusions is that of the budget of the PAP—a major security agency. This is crucial given that the role of the PAP in safeguarding China's security with primary focus on domestic includes responsibilities, such as: routine guard duties, fire-fighting, public emergency response (e.g., natural disaster relief), counter-terrorism and border security. While, the PAP's secondary mission is to support the PLA in local defence.[49]

With reference to internal Chinese military sources, a 2005 RAND report suggests that the key components of the overall PLA budget, which can be divided into 15 functional categories, includes:[50] (1) living expenses (*shenghuo fei*), (2) official expenses (*gongwu fei*), (3) operating expenses (*shiye fei*), (4) education and training expenses (*jiaoyu xunlian fei*), (5) equipment procurement expenses (*zhuangbei gouzhi fei*), (6) logistics procurement and maintenance expenses (*houqin zhuangbeu gouzi weixu fei*), (7) weapons maintenance management expenses (*zhuangbei weichi guanli fei*), (8) scientific research expenses (*kexue yanjiu fei*), (9) militia expenses (*minbing fei*), (10) fuel expenses (*youliao fei*), (11) war preparation and combat expenses (*zhanbei zuozhan fei*), (12) miscellaneous and flexible expenses (*qita he jidong jing fei*), (13) CMC reserve funds (*Junwei dingwu fei*), (14) basic construction expenses (*jiben jianshe fei*), and (15) People's Air Defence expenses (*renmin fankong fei*).[51] This clarifies that these functional categories are not the same as the contents of the "official" Chinese defence budget. It is also to note that these excluded budget items are included in other parts of the state budget, as the 2002 Defence White Paper categorically mentions that "the entire defence expenditure comes from the state financial budget".[52]

As already noted, the other area that remains unlisted is information on the specific costs of procuring weapons and equipment built by the domestic defence industry as well as defence-related R&D funds that are allocated to PLA armament research institutes and civilian defence contractors. This makes a big subtraction in PLA's official spending. For instance, most of China's advanced weapons technology and weapons platforms are acquired from overseas, such as: Kilo-class submarines and Sovremenny-class destroyers from Russia; *Jian*-11B fighters based on Russia's Su-27and *Jian*-15 based on Russia's Su-33 and others. In view of this, it is largely argued that China excludes a wide range of military accounting items typically included in the defence budgets of Western nations. As a RAND report specifically notes, the official Chinese military budget excludes the following categories, such as:[53] procurement of weapons from abroad (see Table 4.6), expenses for paramilitaries, nuclear weapons and strategic rocket programs, state subsidies for the military-industrial complex, some military-related research and development, and extra-budget revenue,[54] which account for 1.5-1.8 times the defence budget announced by the Chinese government.[55] Besides, China ranks fifth in the global share of 10 largest arms importers, accounting for 4.3 per cent, as noted in Figure 4.7.

Figure 4.7: Ten Largest Arms Importers (2015-2019)

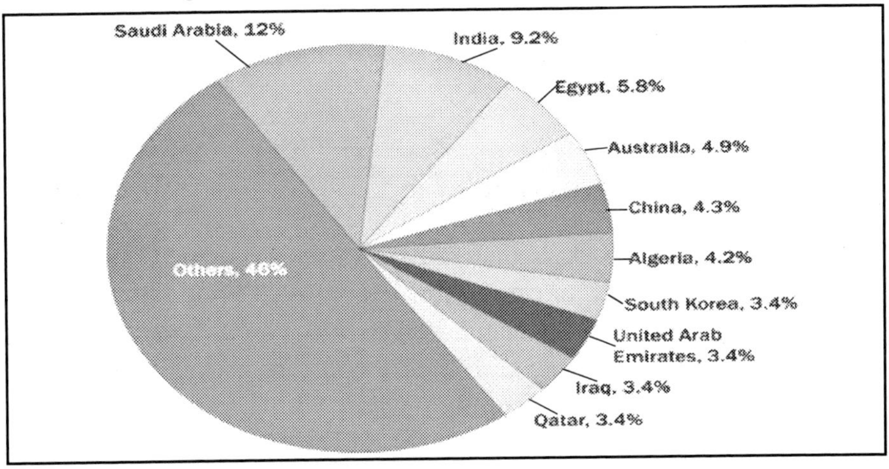

Source: Adapted from SIPRI (2020).[56]

Table 4.6: China's Arms Imports (2012-2016)

Country	*Share of China's Arms Imports (%)*
Russia	57.31
Ukraine	16.16
France	14.73
Switzerland	4.07
United Kingdom	2.82
Belarus	2.66
Uzbekistan	1.60
Germany	0.64

Source: Annotated by the Author with reference to SIPRI (2017).[57]

As per the SIPRI 2020 report (also noted in Table 4.6), China's major suppliers are mainly Russia, France and Ukraine,[58] with imports amounting to 76 per cent, 8.8 per cent and 6.9 per cent, respectively from 2015-2019.[59] Besides, in the regional index, with East Asia's arms imports increased by 3.0 per cent between 2010–14 and 2015–19, China ranks as the largest importer in the sub-region, with a share of 4.3 per cent.[60] To note, Chinese imports from Russia mainly comprise of specific components pertaining to air defence systems, combat aircraft and engines for combat aircraft that can be outfitted on its domestically designed and built platforms (noted in Table 4.7). Thereby, the share of imports acts as a major determinant of China's defence expenditure.

Table 4.7: China's Aircraft and Engine Imports from Russia (1987-2016)

Years	*Combat Aircraft*	*Aircraft Engines*
2012-2016	4	424
2007-2011	11	202
2002-2006	145	70
1997-2001	79	4
1992-1996	45	-
1987-1991	3	-

Source: Adapted from China Power (2016).[61]

While the other sectors that remain unaccounted are:[62] provincial spending on military affairs; government subsidies to military-industrial enterprises and funding of defence R&D, which amounts to an estimated US$ 3-4 billion annually, and additional income from arms exports which accounts for extra-budget revenue – where China accounts for 5.5 per cent of the global arms exports.[63] To note, R&D is an important component of Beijing's expenditure given that China spends more on R&D than Japan, Germany and South Korea combined, and only trails the USA in terms of gross expenditure. China's R&D has experienced a 30-fold increase from 1991 to 2016—from US$ 13 billion to US$ 410 billion; and estimates suggested that China will overtake the USA as the top R&D spender by 2020.[64] Under Xi, R&D got a further boost given the emphasis to "strengthen basic research, and make major breakthroughs in pioneering basic research and groundbreaking [...] innovations", as stated at the 19th Party Congress.[65]

These 'exceptions' in Chinese calculus explain the causal disparity between the official Chinese budget and the other external estimates, thus, furthering the 'lack of transparency' debate. However, in its defence, China responds to the criticisms by arguing in one of the three ways:[66] (1) emphasise that there is no universal standard for military transparency; (2) compare the current level of transparency favourably to even greater opacity previously; or (3) contend that "the most fundamental and most important form of transparency" is the transparency of China's strategic intentions, as opposed to the transparency of military capabilities or doctrine.[67] While the first two claims do hold some relevance, the third claim is controversial. As most analysts would argue, 'intentions' are difficult to quantify and are susceptible to change, particularly in the event of a domestic or international crisis.

While on the increase in the 'pace and scale' of the defence budget over time, China's justifications can be explained under six notional categories, such as:[68] First, *catch up arguments* compensating for the limited investments in military modernisation during the first two decades of China's post-1978 "reform and opening up". Second, *inflation-adjustment arguments* attributed to surging fuel, water, commodity, electricity and personnel costs (such as the PLA's education, training, social security and salaries) as well as inflation, interest rates and exchange rates as major drivers of the defence budget increases. Third, the *economic-growth-as-priority argument*, which aims to dissuade outsider observations by stating that China's defence budget increase is proportional to China's GDP growth rate. This is also justified by the argument that for China, economic development remains a higher priority than military development. Fourth, the *palliative comparison approach,* which claims that

China's defence spending is still low as compared to other militaries by some metrics. Fifth, the *strategic insecurity arguments* contend that China's territorial size, geopolitical environment and international status necessitate greater defence spending than that of many other nations. And sixth, the *"new historic missions" argument,* which claims that the PLA's growing contribution to disaster relief, particularly given China's disproportionate, rising incidence of extreme weather and other non-traditional security missions, as well as international joint military exercises.[69]

Of the six notional justifications, the most prominent key driver of China's defence spending increases qualifies to be the strategic environment, wherein to contextualise Rumsfeld's query (as cited earlier), it can be rightly pointed out that China's rapid economic and most importantly, its military rise does not make it immune from threats and challenges. To argue so, as China's anxiety is driven by its perceived threats, that include its core interests attributed to: First, protecting national sovereignty, territorial integrity, and national unification with respect to Tibet, Xinjiang, Inner Mongolia and Taiwan. Second, concerns over territorial integrity and sovereignty issues over 'unstable periphery', as China has land borders with 14 nations that include four nuclear-weapons states and two unresolved borders (India and Bhutan); while China exhibits maritime disputes with most of its maritime neighbours, as noted in the South China Sea and East China Sea. And finally, the US factor, wherein tense relations with America affect the overall security gambit of China, both domestic and international.

Owing to this 'strategic context', the 'discrepancy' in Beijing's official defence spending calls for suspicion. It rather justifies the scepticism that the Chinese government is actively focusing on strengthening its military power by utilising expenses that are not captured by the official defence budget.[70] China evades such scepticism by suggesting its 'peaceful rise stance' that "it poses no threat to any other country".[71] However, China's actions exemplify its expanding military capabilities such as its missile forces with the ability to reach targets both within the region as well as beyond its periphery. This is added with China's quest to improve its ability to project power, highlighting expeditionary capabilities and its continuous development of advanced systems of military technology. Beijing's such actions further add to the doubt over its military spending, exemplifying that PRC's budget comes with strings attached.

Thereby, it remains indisputable that 'numbers matter'. As projections in Figure 4.6 suggest that Chinese military spending will be US$ 736 billion in 2030, equal to about 71 per cent of anticipated US spending (US$ 1.026 trillion), the increasing numbers thereby call for significant worry. While Washington still outpaces Beijing in defence spending, but one cannot ignore the Chinese intention to close the gap as evident from the increasing defence spending as well as the fact that despite the economic slowdown, Beijing still maintains its budgeting position. Thereby, if the PRC catches up with the USA, there remains little doubt to suggest that the strength of the PLA and its power projection will begin to spread beyond Asia to the rest of the world, in both scope and range. Most importantly, in its active pursuit of military modernisation, especially with military-civil fusion, the actual defence spending that China officially fails to cite will only increase in the future. Thus, the uncertainties attached to China's military preparedness and modernisation make it imperative for countries to think 'how to respond to China's growing military', thus, fuelling anxiety among countries and bolstering their defences in response.

China's Defence Industry

One of the key factors that explains China's ascending military expenditure is its growing defence industry. An upward swing in China's defence expenditure is indicative of its increasing military capabilities and undeterred military intentions as exemplified by the change in China's status from being an arms importer to that of being ranked as a top global arms exporter. This shift clarifies that much of the PLA's weapons and equipment are now built domestically. The impetus to this shift came with the 1998 reforms of China's defence industries. In addition to the creation of the GAD, established to oversee the entire military-industrial establishment, the COSTIND was also redesigned; wherein the existing five ministerial-level corporations were expanded into ten new corporate bodies (*gongsi*) and an enterprise conglomerate (*jituan*), as shown in Table 4.8. To note, in March 2008, COSTIND was merged with a new super bureaucracy called the Ministry of Industry and Information Technology (MIIT) and renamed as the State Administration for Science, Technology and Industry for National Defense (SASTIND).[72]

Table 4.8: China's Defence Industries in 2000

Corporation	*Production Line*
China First Aviation Corporation	Fighter aircraft, bombers, transports, advanced training jets, commercial airliners
China Second Aviation Corporation	Helicopters, light trainers, unmanned aerial vehicles (UAVs)
China Aerospace Science Technology Corporation	Space launch vehicles, satellites
China Aerospace Machinery Electronics Corporation	Missiles, electronics, other ballistics
China North Industries Group Corporation	Tanks, armoured vehicles, artillery, ordnance
China South Industries Group Corporation	Miscellaneous ordnance, trucks, automobiles, motorcycles
China State Shipbuilding Corporation (Northern Shipyards in Dalian)	Destroyers, submarines, large container and commercial vessels
China State Shipbuilding Corporation (Southern Shipyards in Shanghai and Wuhan)	Frigates and smaller surface combatants, submarines, merchant ships
China National Nuclear Corporation	Nuclear fuel, energy, and weapons
China Nuclear Engineering and Construction Corporation	Nuclear power plants

Source: Adapted from Shambaugh (2004).[73]

As stated earlier, China now is the second-largest arms producer in the world. More importantly, as SIPRI's estimates suggest, of the 20 largest companies in the SIPRI Top 100 (Figure 4.8) that accounted for US$ 284.1 of total arms sales, 11 were based in the USA, six in Western Europe, three in Russia and the four Chinese arms companies as noted had a combined estimated arms sales of US$ 54.1 billion, wherein three can be ranked in the top 10.[74] This is a significant development that needs to be monitored. To argue so, as for long, due to lack of transparency, the growth of China's arms industry has been either unknown or was difficult to estimate reliably.

Here, it is important to note that in 2010, Chinese companies did not even figure in the SIPRI Top 100 arms-producing and military companies.[75] The Top 20 comprised of mainly the following, as listed in Table 4.9. The SIPRI ranking is a significant tool of assessment given that companies in the Top 100 account for the majority of the global financial value of sales of military goods and services, in particular, high-technology systems and services. Hence, the significant 'jump' in China's position is exemplified by the comparison noted in Table 4.9 and Figure

4.8—which in itself provides a testimony to the exponential growth of China's defence industry in a span of 10 years.

Table 4.9: Top 20 Largest Arms-Producing Companies (2010)

Rank	*Company*	*Country/Region*	*Arms Sales (US$ m.)*	*Profit (US$ m.)*
1	Lockheed Martin	USA	35,730	2,926
2	BAE Systems	UK	32,880	-1,671
3	Boeing	USA	31,360	3,307
4	Northrop Grumman	USA	28,150	2,053
5	General Dynamics	USA	23,940	2,624
6	Raytheon	USA	22,980	1,879
7	EADS	trans-Europe	16,360	732
8	Finmeccanica	Italy	14,410	738
9	L-3 Communications	USA	13,070	955
10	United Technologies	USA	11,410	4,711
11	Thales	France	9,950	60
12	SAIC	USA	8,230	618
13	Oshkosh Truck	USA	7,080	790
14	Computer Sciences Corp.	USA	5,940	759
15	Honeywell	USA	5,400	2,022
16	Safran	France	4,800	673
17	Rolls-Royce	UK	4,330	839
18	General Electric	USA	4,330	11,644
19	ITT Corp.	USA	4,000	654
20	Almaz-Antei	Russia	3,950	24

Source: Annotated by the Author with reference to SIPRI Year Book (2012).[76]

Figure 4.8: Top 20 Arms Companies in the World (2020)

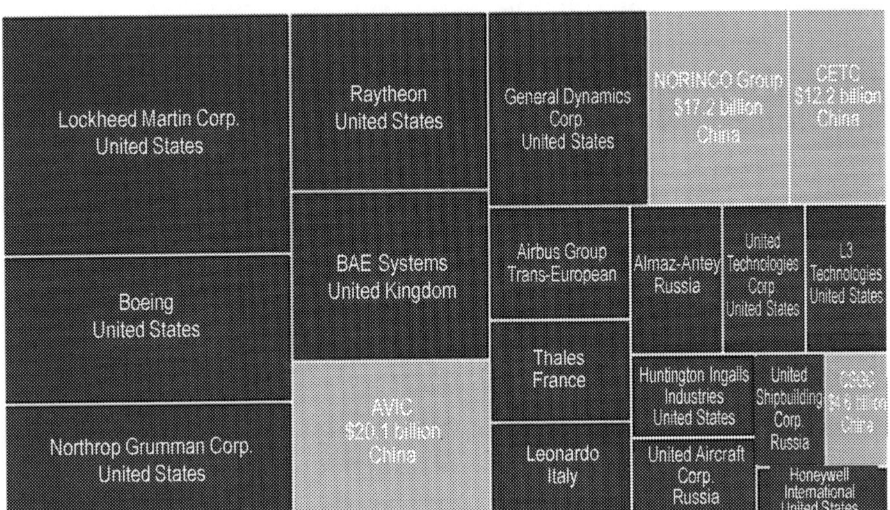

Note: Light grey are Chinese arms companies.
Source: Adapted from SIPRI (2020).[77]

Of the four Chinese companies (as highlighted in Figure 4.8), the largest is the Aviation Industry Corporation of China (AVIC), with arms sales totalling US$ 20.1 billion and would rank as the sixth largest in the world; while China's North Industries Group Corporation (NORINCO) would rank eighth in the Top 100 with sales of US$ 17.2 billion, ranking as the world's largest producer of land systems.[78]

Owing to the current trends, it is suggested that China's defence industry is driven by the core objective of making China a security maximiser by:[79] First, building a strong national security state, especially prioritising the development of military, internal security, and information control capabilities across a wide array of domains, of which cyber is of central importance. Second, building an advanced defence science, technological and industrial base. And third, forging a dual-use civil-military economy.[80] These aspects make it imperative to understand the growing size and scope of China's defence industry from two key perspectives: military-industrial complex and arms transfer.

I. China's Military-Industrial Complex: Calling-off Technological Backwardness

Since the founding of the PRC, China's quest for 'self-reliance' in development and production of armaments led it to create the largest MIC in Asia, with the defence industry comprising of state-owned enterprises (SOEs). What makes China's MIC an exception is that the PRC is one of the few countries in the world to produce a full range of military equipment - from small arms to armoured vehicles to fighter aircraft to warships and submarines, in addition to nuclear weapons and intercontinental ballistic missiles.[81] But despite its size and scope, China's MIC failed to stand out due to its technological backwardness, with weapon systems at least 15 to 20 years behind that of the West. This resulted in Beijing's heavy reliance on foreign imports, particularly from Russia, to equip the PLA with the most advanced weaponry. However, this 'redundancy' in the Chinese defence industry is witnessing a significant shift as exemplified by China's sincere efforts to replace the PLA's antiquated and outmoded inventory with new age weapons.

For instance, in November 2018, China hosted the 12th China International Aviation & Aerospace Exhibition, also called "Air Show China", in Zhuhai-Guangdong, that showcased new weapon systems and capabilities of China's booming manufacturing industry – indicating a significant transformation of China's long-ailing military-industrial complex. In the Air Show, China's Aerospace Science and Industry Corp (CASIC), the nation's largest maker of missiles, displayed the CM-401 supersonic anti-ship ballistic missile, said to be the "first of its kind" in the international market, to buyers seeking a reliable and affordable deterrent against threats from the sea.[82] Arguing so, Wu Peixin, defence industry observer in Beijing states:

> "the ultrafast anti-ship ballistic missiles like the CM-401 can potentially become a game changer in modern naval operations because it is very difficult for existing air-defence radars and weapons on ships to intercept such missiles due to their unique trajectories and hypersonic speeds. Therefore users will be able to effectively deter an enemy's vessels, especially aircraft carriers, from approaching their coast".[83]

This Chinese perspective highlights four key emerging patterns in PRC's defence industry: First, a departure from reverse engineering to innovating its own. Second, a commitment towards China's rapid military modernisation. Third, an increasing defence spending in research and development. And lastly, a building capacity of self-reliance to reduce dependency on foreign imports of arms and technology. These aspects are a clear indication of the significant transformation undergone by China's defence industry from being 'backward and dependent' to that of becoming 'new age and self-reliant', as in the past, the industry was highly centralised and characterised by a lack of access to capital and technology. Besides, it is also argued that, in the past, China's defence industry did not benefit from opening up to the West, as noted that except for few "islands of competence", China's military-industrial complex remained "a sea of mediocrity, backwardness, and redundancy".[84]

But, in the current times, with China's defence industry manufacturing new age weapons and weapon systems, it would be a faulty assessment to suggest that with the state-of-the-art military technology and hardware, China has produced little of significance, as current developments suggest otherwise. While PRC's defence industry has evolved; however, China has also been accused, mainly by the USA and Russia of reverse engineering, unauthorised copying of other countries' military hardware, technology thefts and others. For instance, in 2019, Russian defence conglomerate Rostec accused China of unauthorised copying of Russian military hardware such as aircraft engines, Sukhoi planes, deck jets, air defence systems, portable air defence missiles and analogues of the Pantsir medium-range surface-to-air systems.[85]

What is noteworthy is that despite these accusations, China's defence industry has qualified in the group of global arms exporters. For instance, in 2018, Chinese defence-related SOEs were listed for the first time in the *Defence News Top 100* defence companies, as also successively in the 2019 list.[86] The global indexing of Chinese corporations highlights the increasing size and scope of China's MIC - characterised to be one of the largest and most diversified military-industrial complexes in the developing world. This is evident from China's rising prominence in the global defence industrial primes, as noted in Table 4.10 – wherein all the listed eight Chinese SOEs rank in the top 25; while three (AVIC, NORINCO and CASIC) rank in the top 10. A similar trend was also suggested by the SIPRI 2020 report, as discussed earlier.

Table 4.10: Ranking of 8 Chinese SOEs (2018-2019)

SOE Ranking	*Name of the SOE*	*Def News Ranking 2018*	*Def News Ranking 2019*	*Revenue from Defence (%)*
1	Aviation Industry Corporation of China (AVIC)	5	6	38
2	China North Industries Group Corporation Limited (NORINCO)	8	8	22
3	China Aerospace Science and Industry Corporation (CASIC)	10	11	32
4	China Shipbuilding Industry Corporation (CSIC)	11	14	20
5	China Electronics Technology Group Corporation (CETC)	12	15	31
6	China South Industries Group Corporation (CSGC)	14	18	31
7	China Aerospace Science and Technology Corporation (CASC)	19	20	21
8	China State Shipbuilding Corporation Ltd (CSSC)	22	24	16
	Total Value	US$ 95 b	US$ 97 b	

Note: In November 2019, CSSC and CSIC merged to form the China State Shipbuilding Corporation Ltd.

Source: Annotated by the Author with reference to *Defence News* (2020).[87]

Apart from the listed eight, the other key defence industry conglomerates of China include Aero Engine Corporation of China (AECC), Commercial Aircraft Corporation of China, China Electronics Corporation and China National Nuclear Corporation. Of all, the key focus areas of China's defence industry are noted in Table 4.11.

Table 4.11: Key Focus Areas of China's Defence Industry

Area of Focus	*Key SOEs*	*Profile of the SOEs*
Missile Technology	CASC and CASIC	Leading suppliers of missiles, carrier rockets and satellites.
Aviation Technology	AECC and AVIC	Primary suppliers of aviation technology to the PLA. AECC develops aircraft engines; AVIC supplies military aircraft to the PLA
Military Electronics	CETC	Leading manufacturer of military electronics such as radars and drone swarms. It is also a leading supplier of integrated surveillance systems, facial recognition cameras and mobile applications.
Nuclear Weapons Programme	Chinese Academy of Engineering Physics (CAEP)	Responsible for development and manufacturing of China's nuclear weapons. Also involved in developing lasers, directed energy weapons and conventional weapons.

Source: Annotated by the Author with reference to Joske (2019).[88]

Here, it is important to note that to acquire technologies and knowhow with military applications, China's SOEs' have forged linkages with foreign companies and universities, mainly in the USA, UK, Australia, Germany, Austria and Switzerland[89] – raising significant concerns over China's intentions. In this, the CPC has been accused of encouraging civilian enterprises and companies to undertake classified research and get involved in weapons production as well as adopt unlawful measures to bolster its own military capabilities. For instance, the U.S. State Department suggests that China is acquiring key technologies by means of: investment in private industries, talent recruitment programs, directing academic and research collaboration to military gain, forced technology transfer, intelligence gathering, and outright theft.[90]

Given this dynamic, it is argued that the joint research institutions, academia, and private firms are all being exploited to build the PLA's future military systems, often without their knowledge or consent.[91] Needless to say, the SOEs are a significant component of China's integrated military-civilian development under the 'military-civil fusion' strategy – major organisations that make China's MIC. Their specialised defence production is determined by the Chinese state's security and material requirements of its products and services, with the PLA being the main customer of China's MIC. Furthermore, it exemplifies the evolution of the MIC from a set of numbered machine-building industrial ministries (such as the Ministry of Heavy Industry in the beginning in 1950) to an array of civilian-run, profit-seeking corporations within horizontally integrated enterprise groups under the Chinese state, with the private sector accelerating the rise of China's best defence contractors.

According to the 2020 DoD Report, the two key observations on China's defence industry are:[92] First, many of China's missile programs are comparable to other top-tier producers; and second, China is the top ship-producing nation in the world by tonnage and has the capability to produce naval gas turbine and diesel engines, shipboard weapons and electronic systems—making it nearly self-sufficient for all shipbuilding needs.[93] What signifies China's MIC is that apart from the military and technological achievements, the other key objective is to reduce the level of the Chinese dependence on the import of foreign technologies. For instance, the MCF strategy seeks to advance China's self-reliance, as evident from "Made in China 2025", by which the PRC strives to achieve greater self-sufficiency in manufacturing key industrial technologies, equipment and materials, including those with dual-uses.

Chinese analysts argue that MCF is a "strategic requirement" [*zhanlüe xuqiu*, 战略需求] and the only way to build a military capable of winning informationized wars".[94] However, in providing some understanding of Xi's intent, one of the interpretations suggests that MCF can benefit China in four ways:[95] First, it can support China's transformation into a powerful nation with defence construction providing a boost to the slowed economic growth. Second, it can help China gain advantages in international technological and military competitions by closing the technological gap with other major powers such as the USA and even surpass them in S&T development. Third, it provides Beijing with an excellent opportunity to improve the PRC's governance system, integrating the military and civilian sectors and enabling the creation of a governing system across sectors, government bodies, and domains. And fourth, it supports the strategic goal of building a world-class military by gaining economic strength, scientific and technological strength, and comprehensive national strength.[96]

In view of this, from the current trends of China's arms exports, the following assessments can be drawn: First, it demonstrates China's departure from its past heavy leaning on Russia for supplies of advanced weapons, which continued through the 1990s. To cite an example, the *Shenyang* J-11 fighter was adopted from the Russian Su-27k and China's HQ-9 surface-to-air missiles were inspired by Russia's S-300 platform. But increasingly, Russian exports to China is declining, from 47.7 per cent of total sales in 2006 to 13.7 per cent in 2018.[97] To substantiate, through the 2000s, Russian arms sales to China averaged US$ 2.6 billion, reaching a peak of US$ 3.2 billion in 2005, with a significant drop averaging US$ 816 million between 2010 and 2018.[98] This trend is significant as it indicates that China has developed an advanced arms industry, thus, becoming less reliant on arms imports from Russia.

Second, arms production by China's defence conglomerates highlight the increasing priorities of China's military modernisation in domains of air, space and sea. For instance, AVIC, NORINCO, CASIC and CSIC remain to be the four top Chinese corporations that are involved in producing high-profile platforms and systems such as the CM-401 anti-ship ballistic missile system, the J-20 fighter aircraft, the *Shandong* aircraft carrier, and others – suggesting that arms production in China has become more specialised in nature. Unlike other major global arms producers, Chinese arms companies specialise primarily in one arms production sector; for example, AVIC produces mostly aircraft and avionics, CSIC deals with shipbuilding, and CASC is the largest maker of missiles. While its Western counterparts such as Lockheed Martin produce a wide range of military products across different sectors—land systems, aerospace, and shipbuilding within one company.

Third, the significant jump in the status of China's defence industry highlights the transition from its once backward status to that of creating its own military-industrial complex. The impetus to this was given by the Tiananmen era bans that led to the suspension of US and EU technological assistance to the PLA. As a result of this, an innovative and efficient domestic arms industry became the crucial need for the PRC to build a military force, capable of safeguarding its security claims. Justified by its increasing military spending, the growth of China's domestic arms industry reflects two important aspects: First, it has steadily reduced China's military imports; and second, it has transformed China into a top arms exporter, securing a competitive edge against its competitor, the USA.

Fourth, the trend highlights China's increasing ambition to transform its leading contractors such as AVIC, CSSC and others into the league of American defence industry giants such as Lockheed Martin, Boeing and Northrop Grumman Corp. or Britain's BAE Systems. This also clarifies the Chinese government's heavy investment in its state-owned and private defence companies, a move driven by Xi Jinping's quest to reduce the barriers between the two under its military-civil fusion strategy.

Fifth, it surfaces PRC's intention towards achieving military-civil fusion (as discussed in Chapter 3), wherein the so-called "Seven Sons of National Defence" (国防七子) (see Table 4.12), a group of leading universities subordinate to the MIIT, are driving China's military and defence industry.[99] For instance, one Chinese study on MCF in the university sector estimated that more than half the academics at the 'Seven Sons' have been involved in defence projects.[100] The seven universities are accredited at the institutional level to participate in research and the production of top secret weapons and defence equipment. In addition, China also has "Seven Sons of the Arms Industry" (兵工七子) (Table 4.12), a group of Chinese universities previously subordinate to the Ministry of Ordnance Industry (兵器工业部) until 1986.[101] Also to note that China's defence research goes beyond these 'sevens', as found in the 101 agreements signed between defence industry agency SASTIND (or its predecessor, COSTIND) and other agencies since 1999 to 'jointly construct' (共建) 61 universities subordinate to those agencies.[102] These universities are at the forefront of China's defence-related R&D and assist in major PLA projects – thus, significantly contributing to China's defence industry.

Table 4.12: Seven Sons of China's National Defence and Arms Industry

Seven Sons of National Defence	*Seven Sons of Arms Industry*
Beijing Institute of Technology	Beijing Institute of Technology
Beihang University	Changchun University of Science and Technology
Harbin Engineering University	Chongqing University of Technology
Harbin Institute of Technology	Nanjing University of Science and Technology
Nanjing University of Aeronautics and Astronautics	North University of China
Nanjing University of Science and Technology	Shenyang Ligong University
Northwestern Polytechnical University	Xi'an Technological University

Source: Annotated by the Author with reference to Joske (2019).[103]

Sixth, the civilian sector is becoming a potent source of major technological innovation in China's defence-industrial base. For instance, an analysis in *Qiushi* observed that "disruptive technological change in the 21st century now usually starts in the civilian sector".[104] To cite a few examples, some private companies working with the PLA in supporting the MCF include: *Yunzhou* Tech, a leader in unmanned surface vessels; *Ziyan*, a major player in drones and unmanned helicopters; and *Kuang-Chi* Technologies, which is applying machine learning to its research on military meta-materials amongst others.[105] Similarly, in the field of AI, Tianjin's new Artificial Intelligence Military-Civil Fusion Innovation Centre was established in partnership with the Academy of Military Science, while Qingdao has specialised in undersea robotics systems and is actively exploring applications of AI for this domain.[106]

Against these key assessments, the trend in Table 4.10 also highlights a drop in the ranking of Chinese SOEs from 2018 to 2019. Does this 'drop' hold any significance? What can rather be observed is that such a downward trend should not be treated as an underestimation of the Chinese defence technological and industrial base. To argue so, as above everything, the 2019 *Defence News* list clarifies that China is the second-largest market in total defence revenue terms at US$ 95 billion, behind that of the USA.[107] Adding to it, as per IISS calculations using 2019 US$ constant exchange rates, the total defence-related revenue of China's eight SOEs is US$ 97bn, just short of the total defence revenue of all European companies, which stands to be US$ 100bn.[108]

These indicators, therefore, suggest that a drop in the rankings should not lead to discounting of China's defence industry as a whole. Rather, their rankings in the top 25 and 10 exemplify the increasing strength of China's defence industrial base, which cannot be ignored at any cost. Most critically, it could mean the rise of a more (in military terms) technologically advanced China that would be increasingly prone to challenge for regional, even global, predominance.[109] In Richard Bitzinger's view, as China's military-industrial complex increasingly comes into its own, the "repercussions could be far-reaching and, to say the very least, disquieting" – suggesting that a "militarily self-confident China, coupled with its growing economic and soft power, could be more assertive".[110] Besides, there is also a looming concern over the security implications of China's MCF strategy. As one of the leading critiques of MCF, U.S. Secretary of State, Mike Pompeo suggested that MCF's:

> "goal is to ensure that the People's Liberation Army has military dominance. And the PLA's core mission is to sustain the Chinese Communist Party's grip on power—that same Chinese Communist Party that has led China in an increasingly authoritarian direction and one that is increasingly repressive as well...".[111]

Such an assumption is driven by the perception that the PRC's MCF constitutes "a major security challenge to US, its neighbours, and any country with a stake in the open international order".[112] That is, MCF can "make *any* technology accessible to *anyone* under the PRC's jurisdiction available to support the regime's ambitions" – while it "is in part about economic power, but also, quite centrally, about augmenting Beijing's *military* power" [emphasis added].[113] Therefore, under MCF, the scope of China's defence industry goes beyond public-private partnership, thus, holds critical implications.

II. China's Arms Exports

Over the years, PRC's economic rise coupled with its military modernisation has transformed China into a net arms exporter – exhibiting a departure from the long-held status of being an arms importer. As noted, in the last 12 years, China has exported 16.2 billion units of ammunition, mostly to countries in Asia, the Middle East and Africa.[114] The trend came into being with China becoming the world's third largest exporter of major weapons in 2012–16, having overtaken Germany, France and the UK; taking a departure from being ranked the seventh largest supplier in 2007-2011.[115] These shifts indicate that China has well-positioned itself as a lower-cost alternative for advanced weapon systems, and a main competitor to Russian hardware.

What is important to note is that for long China's 'arms exports' have been under scrutiny, given its supplies to rogue states such as North Korea and Iran. Besides, China was also not a signatory to the Arms Trade Treaty (ATT),[116] and only became a signatory in July 2020, with the Treaty coming into force on 4 October 2020.[117] Given this, China's official position states that its arms export policy adheres to three principles:[118] (a) conducive to the legitimate self-defence capability of the recipient country; (b) not undermine peace, security and stability of the region concerned and the world as a whole; and (c) non-interference in the internal affairs of the recipient country.[119]

However, as recent trends suggest, China has become a significant arms provider and top exporter of military equipment to countries across the globe, taking a departure from providing logistics to that of weapons and weapon systems. What makes China a major source of arms transfers is the availability, cheap pricing and easy to use and maintenance of Chinese weapons and weapon systems.

Figure 4.9: China's Share in Global Arms Exports (2015-2019)
(10 Top Exporters)

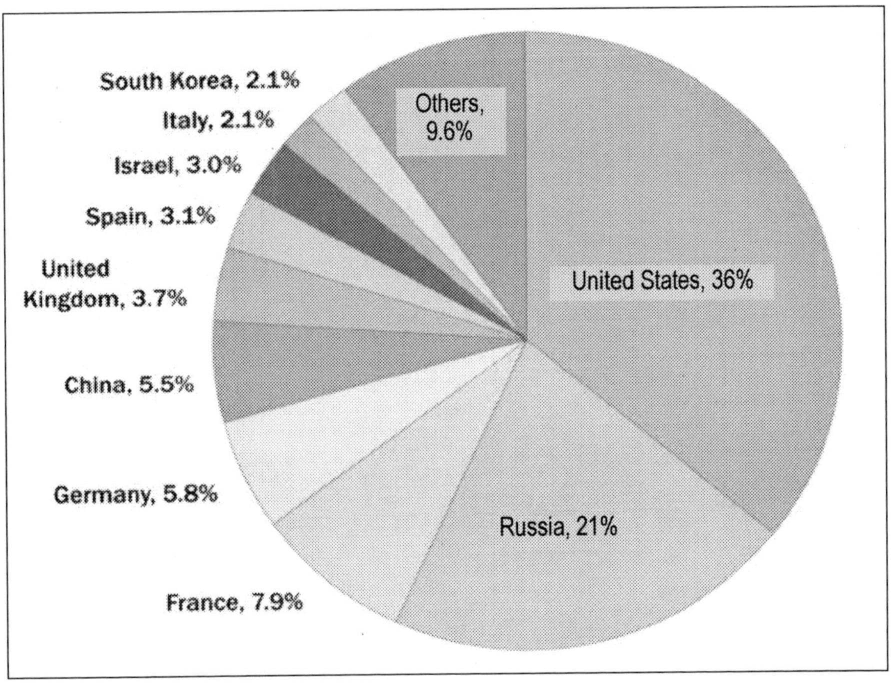

Source: Adapted from SIPRI (2020).[120]

Table 4.13: Top 25 Global Exporters of Major Arms and their Main Clients (2015-2019)

*(*Percentages below 10 are rounded to 1 decimal place; percentages over 10 are rounded to whole numbers.)*

	Exporter	*Share of arms exports (%)*		*Per cent change from 2010-14 to 2015-19*[a]	*Main clients (share of exporter's total exports, %), 2015-19*		
		2015-19	*2010-14*		*1st*	*2nd*	*3rd*
1	United States	36	31	23	Saudi Arabia (25)	Australia (9.1)	UAE (6.4)
2	Russia	21	27	–18	India (25)	China (16)	Algeria (14)
3	France	7.9	4.8	72	Egypt (26)	Qatar (14)	India (14)
4	Germany	5.8	5.3	17	South Korea (18)	Greece (10)	Algeria (8.1)
5	China	5.5	5.5	6.3	Pakistan (35)	Bangladesh (20)	Algeria (9.9)
6	United Kingdom	3.7	4.6	–15	Saudi Arabia (41)	Oman (14)	USA (9.1)
7	Spain	3.1	2.9	13	Australia (33)	Singapore (13)	Turkey (11)
8	Israel	3.0	1.8	77	India (45)	Azerbaijan (17)	Viet Nam (8.5)
9	Italy	2.1	2.7	–17	Turkey (20)	Pakistan (7.5)	Saudi Arabia (7.2)
10	South Korea	2.1	0.9	143	UK (17)	Iraq (14)	Indonesia (13)
11	Netherlands	1.9	2.0	–2.8	Indonesia (17)	USA (14)	Jordan (13)
12	Ukraine	1.0	2.8	–63	China (31)	Russia (20)	Thailand (17)
13	Switzerland	0.9	0.9	2.6	Australia (15)	China (14)	Saudi Arabia (14)
14	Turkey	0.8	0.5	86	Turkmenistan (25)	Oman (12)	Pakistan (12)
15	Sweden	0.6	1.8	–65	USA (22)	Algeria (12)	UAE (10)
16	Canada	0.6	0.9	–33	Saudi Arabia (34)	India (11)	UAE (10)
17	Norway	0.4	0.6	–30	Oman (35)	USA (20)	Finland (14)
18	UAE	0.4	0.2	86	Egypt (41)	Algeria (13)	Unidentified state (12)
19	Australia	0.3	0.3	11	USA (42)	Indonesia (18)	Canada (18)
20	Belarus	0.3	0.5	–23	Viet Nam (31)	Sudan (16)	Serbia (15)
21	Czechia	0.3	0.1	453	Iraq (39)	USA (17)	Ukraine (9.0)
22	South Africa	0.3	0.5	–36	USA (23)	UAE (20)	Malaysia (11)
23	India	0.2	0.0	426	Myanmar (46)	Sri Lanka (25)	Mauritius (14)
24	Brazil	0.2	0.2	6.8	Afghanistan (38)	Indonesia (17)	Lebanon (11)
25	Portugal	0.2	0.0	1239	Romania (95)	Uruguay (2.9)	Cabo Verde (1.2)

Note: [a]Figures show the change in volume of the total arms exports per exporter between the two periods.

Source: Adapted from SIPRI (2020).[121]

As per SIPRI data, the top 25 accounted for 99 per cent of the world's major arms exports in 2015–2019, of which North America and Europe accounted for 87 per cent of the total sales; while the five largest suppliers – USA, Russia, France, Germany and China, accounted for 76 per cent of all exports with combined arms exports 9.5 per cent higher than 2010-2014 (the top five remained the same).[122]

Specifically to note, China accounted for 5.5 per cent of total arms exports, with conventional arms sales surging from US$ 645 million in 2008 to US$ 1.04 billion in 2018.[123] Also to note, after an increase of 13.3 per cent between 2005–2009 and 2010–2014, Chinese arms exports grew by only 6.3 per cent between 2010–2014 and 2015–2019. Of the total arms transfers in 2015-2019, Asia and Oceania accounted for 74 per cent, 16 per cent flowed into Africa, and the Middle East accounted for 6.7 per cent – exemplifying a significant increase in the number of countries to which China delivers arms, which rose from 40 in 2010–2014 to 53 in 2015–2019.[124]

Table 4.14: China's Arms Exports (2012-2016)

Region	*Country*	*Share of China's Arms Exports (%)*
South Asia	Pakistan	35.10
	Bangladesh	17.85
South East Asia	Myanmar	10.07
	Indonesia	3.09
	Thailand	1.46
	Cambodia	0.62
	Laos	0.35
Central Asia	Turkmenistan	2.62
	Kazakhstan	0.07
Middle East	Iran	0.67
	Turkey	0.40
	Iraq	0.19
	Saudi Arabia	0.16
	Jordan	0.10
	UAE	0.07
	Syria	0.06
	Egypt	0.05
	Bahrain	0.05
Africa	Algeria	9.28
	Tanzania	2.82
	Cameroon	2.26
	Sudan	1.46
	Nigeria	1.31
	Zambia	0.87
	Namibia	0.70

Region	*Country*	*Share of China's Arms Exports (%)*
	Ethiopia	0.60
	Chad	0.44
	Ghana	0.40
	Mauritania	0.39
	Morocco	0.39
	Kenya	0.30
	Senegal	0.18
	Djibouti	0.16
	South Sudan	0.14
	Seychelles	0.11
	Burundi	0.06
Latin America and the Caribbean	Venezuela	4.53
	Bolivia	0.26
	Trinidad and Tobago	0.18
	Peru	0.15

Source: Annotated by the Author with reference to SIPRI (2017).[125]

As can be observed from Tables 4.13 and 4.14, the major recipients of Chinese arms are mainly Pakistan, Bangladesh, Myanmar and Algeria. This has been a consistent trend, of which, since 2007, China's top arms export countries by total units are: Pakistan (6.57 billion units), Bangladesh (1.99 billion units) and Myanmar (1.28 billion units); in 2018 alone China sold Bangladesh 75 million units, Myanmar 105 million units and 448 million units to Pakistan, as per SIPRI's calculations (see Figure 4.10).[126]

Figure 4.10: Arms Exported from China

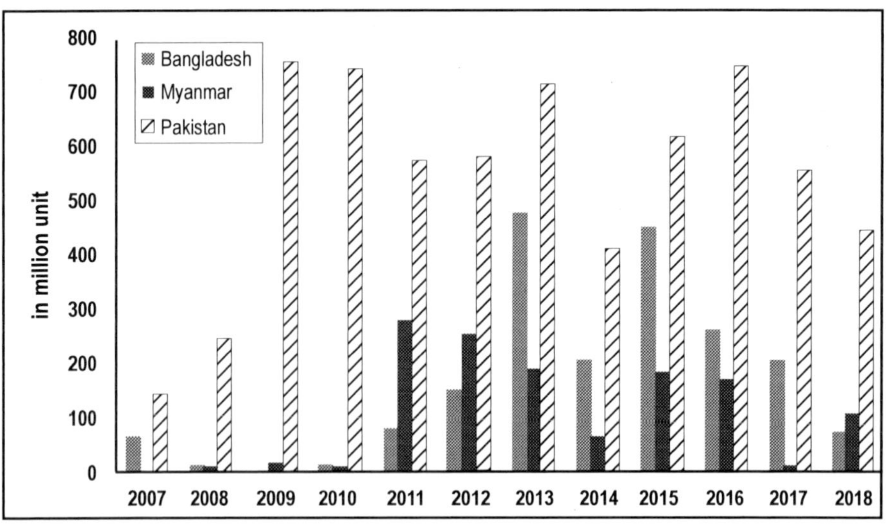

Source: Adapted from *CNBC* (2019).[127]

In recent times, China arms sales/projects to the three countries include:[128] Pakistan, sophisticated optical tracking systems for nuclear missiles with multiple warheads along with collaborations, such as the co-developed JF-17 aircraft and China's ongoing construction of the Type 054AP class warship for the Pakistani Navy. Bangladesh, mainly small arms such as rifles and pistols, and two used Type-035G Ming-class submarines. And Myanmar, includes 7 JF-17 aircraft, 12 Chinese Rainbow UAVs, two Type-43 Frigates, and 76 Type-92 armoured vehicles.[129] Owing to this trend, Timothy Heath anticipates that the "potential market" and "loose restrictions" in the developing world may make China "well positioned to become one of the world's largest arms exporters.[130]

While China's arms exports to other regions entail:[131] First, Chinese conventional weapons make up just 3 per cent of the combined North and South American arms import market, which is mainly dominated by the USA, 19 per cent; Russia, 3 per cent; and Germany, 12 per cent. Second, in Europe, the case is different as more than 99 per cent of China's total arms imports come from Europe, thus its exports is a paltry US$ 17 million of its own weapons to the continent. This is due to the fact that Russia supplies China with 68 per cent of its foreign arms, while France and Ukraine collectively supply an additional 20 per cent of these imports. And third, in Africa, since 2008, countries collectively purchased around 20 per cent (US$ 3.2 billion) of China's overall arms exports; wherein North Africa (49 per cent), Eastern Africa (21 per cent), and the remaining 30 per cent of the imports are divided between other areas of the continent.[132]

To put things in perspective, while China has emerged as one of the top five global arms exporters, but it has certain limitations as compared to its key competitors, such as the USA and Russia. To suggest: First, although Asia is the dominant receiver of Chinese arms, with sales across South and Southeast Asia growing from US$ 386 million in 2008 to US$ 1.3 billion in 2016 before falling to US$ 759 million in 2018, China still lags behind the USA, with exports amounting to US$ 13.8 billion since 2008. Second, while the number of countries to which Chinese exports has increased over time, major arms importers such as India, Australia, South Korea and Vietnam do not seek to procure arms from China.

Additionally, unlike other arms importers, China's arms sales call for scrutiny. Wherein, the scepticism is caused by two key features that characterise China's arms sales: First, is the nature of the recipients of Chinese arms transfers, that raises significant doubts over China's intention to act as 'a responsible global player'. To note, China is one of the few countries willing to transfer equipment and technology-related knowhow to states such as Iran, North Korea, and Myanmar; that other nations are unwilling to sell to. Second, is the aspect of 'duality' in China's arms exports, as Beijing's willingness to pass on technology related to nuclear and chemical weapons, and ballistic missiles runs contrary to its adherence to international agreements on regulating the sale and spread of weapons – thus, indicating China's failure to completely conform to the international norms. This is well-witnessed in China's arms transfer to Pakistan, North Korea, Iran and others. This Chinese practice holds significant global implications, such as: First, it adds a new player into the international arms market, as noted in China's emerging status as a top arms exporter. And second, it further complicates the international efforts to control the proliferation of conventional and nuclear weapons to unstable and rogue states, as already witnessed with China's assistance to Pakistan and North Korea's nuclear programme.

These aspects make it imperative to understand the motivations behind China's arms sales to such countries. For instance, Timothy Heath contends that:

> "China is likely to continue expanding its arms exports, especially to partner (Belt and Road) countries.... Arms exports provide an efficient, lower cost way for China to both improve security in countries featuring major Chinese investments and to minimize spending and commitments by the PLA".[133]

In view of this, China's arms sales can be explained by a combination of strategic and commercial motivations.[134] Wherein, the strategic concerns include:[135] First, a desire to strengthen the foes of China's rivals, such as arms transfer to Pakistan is aimed against India. Second, to expand China's political influence in regions, such as strong ties to Pakistan are aimed to facilitate Beijing's relations with countries in the Middle East – strengthening China's influence in the region. While commercial motivations in China's arms transfers apply in cases where Beijing's political interests are limited, mainly driven by economic interests. Here, the aim is to maintain its defence industries in the face of diminished domestic procurement, generate foreign exchange earnings for the country as a whole and for the defence industries in particular, subsidize research and development programs by including foreign recipients in the customer base, and stimulate technological progress by competing in foreign markets.[136]

Hence, China's growing profile as a net arms exporter calls for significant worry, as its strategic and political motivations outweigh the commercial considerations. This is justified by China's disputes in terms of Taiwan, the South China Sea, the East China Sea, the land border with India; and the increasing arms race in Asia. Therefore, China's arms exports raise significant concerns over its ambitious intentions.

PLA's New Age Weapons Inventory: Sharper and Stronger

On 1 October 2019, during the 70th anniversary of the founding of the PRC, China demonstrated an extravagant display of its military muscle in a grand parade. In showcasing its military prowess, the PLA staged a highly orchestrated display of China's military capabilities by exhibiting the PLA's diverse new, high-tech and strategic weapon systems related to electronic warfare, unmanned systems and precision guided munitions. These growing military capabilities reflect a prioritisation of the acquisition of the so-called concept of *shashoujian*, or "assassin's mace"[137] technologies to build a national defence mobilisation system that can meet the requirements of "winning informationized wars and responding to both emergencies and wars".[138] As defence intelligence analyst, Dan Taylor suggests:

> "China is rapidly building a robust, lethal force, with capabilities spanning ground, air, maritime, space and information domains, designed to enable China to impose its will in the region, and beyond".[139]

This argument is validated by the display of China's military prowess at the parade that introduced China's "new type informationised armed force,"[140] under four formations, consisting of 16 vehicles each, equipped with antennas in different shapes. This highlighted the PLA's quest towards gaining an upper hand in battlefields with complex electro-magnetic conditions; equipment for tactical electronic countermeasure; new mobile communication equipment that beefs up PLA's joint operations and trans-theatre combat capabilities based on the network and information system; and vehicles for meteorology and hydrology observation, topographical survey, forecast support, and mapping and navigation.[141]

Furthermore, apart from displaying China's military capabilities, the parade also represented China's growing self-reliance in military modernisation given the military equipment on display was "100 per cent made in China" – exhibiting a significant departure from its first military parade in 1949 when the equipment came from 98 factories in 24 countries.[142] As Chinese military analyst Tong Zhao argues, it shows:

> "how much progress it [China] has made, and how much more advanced it is compared to years before. Now, China has better capability to defend itself. It deserves equal and fair treatment from other powers".[143]

This trend further confirms the PLA's transformation from being antiquated to that of becoming a capable, modern force, both in terms of equipment and operational practice. In this regard, the most important weapons and weapon systems to watch out for in China's 'new age' inventory include new technology drones and missile systems that carry strategic implications in the current security environment. Hence, it is important to assess the capabilities of the weapons and weapon systems from the perspective of 'how they are used' or 'will be used' - excelling at both assault and defence. In view of this, some of the weapons that are of critical significance are as follows:

I. Drones: GJ-11, WZ-8 and HSU-001

The military parade exhibited unmanned aerial vehicle phalanxes that included reconnaissance drones in multi-range and multi-altitude, featuring a new-type combat force for future warfare. The most notable of the new drones are China's reconnaissance-strike drones, such as GJ-11 and WZ-8 as well as an unmanned underwater vehicle (UUV). Here, the imperative lies in understanding the significance of these new equipments.

Gongji-11(GJ-11)

The GJ-11[144] (*Gongji* ["attack"]-11), is a carrier-based stealth unmanned combat air vehicle based off the PLA's *Lijian* ("Sharp Sword") test bed.[145] Its significant capabilities entail:[146] first, it is intended as an attack aircraft so an internal weapons bay is included as part of the aircraft's makeup. And second, the design bestows stealth characteristic given its low profile and shrouded exhaust port.

In addition, the UCAV is also assumed to have autonomous capability along with maximised aerodynamic and fuel efficiency that becomes significant for operational ranges. These features provide the UAV with the capacity to "sneak" into enemy air space and attack targets of strategic value without being detected.[147] More specifically, the GJ-11 is designed to conduct long-range strikes and supply targeting information to Chinese missile forces.[148]

WZ-8

The WZ-8 is an air-launched supersonic drone. It is a high-altitude reconnaissance UAV that is likely to be able to fly at a high-supersonic speed added with stealth capabilities and is likely to be launched in the air via a bomber or transport aircraft.[149] The drone has been assigned to the PLAAF's 30th Air Regiment, which operates from Luhe-Ma'an air base near Nanjing; and is also speculated to have entered service with the PLA's Eastern Theatre Command that focuses on Taiwan and Japan.[150]

What makes this UAV significant is its capability to effectively gather intelligence in real time in a controllable way compared to other platforms like satellites, and provide more reliable reconnaissance data than satellites.[151] As noted, that despite not possessing loitering capability that helps aid missile targeting, the WZ-8 will help aid Chinese aircraft in locating and targeting enemy surface forces.[152] In Chinese view, the UAV acts as a "soft deterrence" that signals the message that the PLA can engage in reconnaissance on its targets, and can launch strikes on them.[153]

HSU-001 Unmanned Underwater Vehicle

The HSU-001 is China's first Large Displacement Unmanned Underwater Vehicle (LDUUV). In size and design, the UUV is analogous to the U.S. Navy's LDUUV, "Snakehead", aimed to carry out missions such as Intelligence preparation of the environment (IPOE) and anti-submarine warfare (ASW).[154] The size of the HSU-001 makes it large enough to carry smaller UUVs or, potentially sensors or mines.[155]

Given its design, the UUV's task would mainly entail carrying out wide-area intelligence, surveillance, and reconnaissance missions; hunt for mines and conduct underwater mapping and given its size, might evolve to carry new sensor payloads or even compact weapons.[156] Also, its twin screw-back propellers makes it optimised for slow speed cruising relatively near the surface as opposed to a deep-diving autonomous underwater vehicle (AUV).[157] With specific "battlefield environment reconnaissance" and "enemy surveillance" capabilities, the LDUUV would provide a significant boost to China's anti-submarine and underwater ISR capabilities.[158]

II. Missiles

The military parade displayed for the first time China's advanced missile systems from its inventory. This included three new cruise missiles: YJ-12B, YJ-18 and CJ-100; two ballistic missiles, JL-2 and DF-41; and a hypersonic glide vehicle, DF-17. The capabilities of each entail the following:

1. Cruise Missiles: YJ-12B, YJ-18 and CJ-100

YJ-12B

The YJ-12B (*YingJi* meaning 'Eagle Strike') is a land-based supersonic anti-ship cruise missile with a range of 295 nautical miles (545 km).[159] In terms of its capability, the Chinese claim that the missile can sink medium to large vessels during surprise attacks and thereby, act as a cornerstone to the PLA's naval defence system.[160] In addition, the missile could also be stationed in remote islands. As reported, China has already deployed the YJ-12B on the Fiery Cross Reef, Subi Reef and Mischief Reef in the Spratly Islands chain in the South China Sea, thus providing China with the ability to strike surface vessels within 295 nautical miles of the reefs.[161]

YJ-18

The YJ-18 is China's subsonic anti-ship missile with a cruise speed of about 600 miles per hour (mph) or Mach 0.8.2.[162] Given its speed, it is suggested that when the missile is about 20 nautical miles (nm) from its target, the warhead accelerates to supersonic speed, reportedly up to Mach 3.0.[163] The missile has a range between 220 and 540 km.[164] With a sea-skimming flight path, the YJ-18, by flying only a few metres above the sea, attempts to evade detection by surface radar until it breaks the radar horizon 16 to 18 nm from its target.[165] Given its supersonic speed and long range, the YJ-18 is likely to hold serious implications for the ability of US Navy surface ships to operate freely in the Western Pacific in a contingency.[166] The YJ-18 probably will be widely deployed on China's indigenously built ASCM-capable submarines and newest surface ships by 2020, and China could develop a variant of the YJ-18 to replace older missiles in its shore-based ASCM arsenal.[167]

CJ-100

CJ-100 (*Chang Jian*, "Long Sword"), also known as DF-100, is the PLA's third-generation ground-attack cruise missile with an expected range of 2,000 km.[168] Being the Chinese equivalent of the US "B" variant long-range anti-ship missile, the CJ-100 has a ceiling of 24,000 metres (79,000 feet), a cruising of speed Mach 4 and a top speed of Mach 4.5.[169] As speculated, the CJ-100 is a long-range supersonic cruise missile with a "near space" flight altitude, capable of speeds between three and four times the speed of sound.[170] However, Chinese state media called it "hypersonic" missiles, which make it at least five times faster the speed of sound.[171]

2. Ballistic Missiles: JL-2 and DF-41

JL-2

The JL-2 is a Sea-Launched Ballistic Missile (SLBM) with a minimum range of 2,000 km, and a maximum range greater than 8,000 km, carrying a payload of 1,050 to 2,800 kg and armed with a single 1 MT yield nuclear warhead and may also have an MIRV capability.[172] The missile uses an inertial guidance system with stellar updates and a Global Positioning Satellite (GPS) system and may also employ the Bei Dou navigational satellite system.[173]

This sea-based nuclear deterrent makes China capable of conducting nuclear strikes against Alaska if launched from waters near China; against Alaska and Hawaii if launched from waters south of Japan; against Alaska, Hawaii, and the western portion of continental USA if launched from waters west of Hawaii; and against all the 50 US states if launched from waters east of Hawaii.[174]

DF-41

DF-41 (Dong Feng-41) is China's Intercontinental Ballistic Missile (ICBM) estimated to have an operational range of 12,000-15,000 km with MIRV capability, rail-or road-mobility and is solid propelled with a payload capacity of 2,500 kg.[175] Its warheads can be a single 1 MT nuclear warhead or a selectable yield of 20, 90 or 150 kT on each MIRV. It uses inertial guidance, likely with stellar updates and a GPS system, which gives it an accuracy of 100-500 m CEP and uses a three-stage solid propellant engine.[176]

It is estimated to have a top speed of Mach 25 and will be capable of delivering up to 10 MIRVed warheads, projected to be able to strike continental USA within 30 minutes.[177] Chinese missile expert, Yang Chengjun strongly argues that the missile "can cover any corner on the earth. Anyone who dares to launch a nuclear strike against us [China] will face effective retaliation",[178] perceived to be as "balancing the power and security victory".[179]

3. DF-17

The DF-17 (Dong Feng-17) is the first missile designed for the operational deployment of a hypersonic glide vehicle (HGV) and named DF-ZH by the PLARF. It is a "short to medium-range" ballistic missile with an estimated range between 1,800 and 2,500 kilometres heavily based on the DF-16B short-range ballistic missile.[180] As noted, the DF-17 is likely to be the first or second HGV in the regular inventory of any military, given that Russia claimed to deploy an HGV in 2019.[181]

With its range, the DF-17 could reach South Korea and Japan, challenging their missile defence systems and penetrate the US missile shields in the region - transforming Beijing's previously defensive strategy of containing independence-leaning forces in the Taiwan Straits.[182]

China's Military Capabilities: Less Benign & More Strategic in Intention

In the backdrop of China's increasing ISR and conventional precision strike capabilities, PLA's new age weapons and weapon systems as displayed at the 2019 parade highlight certain key intentions of the PLA. This can be argued as:[183] First, augmenting its precision-guided strike complex with improved ISR capabilities; second, disrupting US communication and information networks, threatening US situational awareness and precision targeting; third, holding US and allied forces in the Asia-Pacific at risk with manoeuvring munitions that challenge existing US air and missile defences; and fourth, increasing undersea situational awareness, challenging the dominance of US submarines.

In this regard, based on an assessment of China's new age weapons inventory, four significant implications that Beijing's regional rivals and adversaries should take note of, are: First, such heavy display of network centricity exemplifies China's warfighting intent in the near future, suggesting that the focus lies on making the PLA 'informationised' combat ready under a joint combat system in fighting and winning informationised local wars. That is, the PLA envisions fighting multi-domain battles under the framework of "Integrated Network Electronic Warfare" (*wangdianyitizha*). Second, China's domestically built equipment highlight the self-reliance achieved in the development and production of armaments. This is also indicative of the civil-military integration that is bolstering the rapid build-up of China's military-industrial complex,[184] which for long has been argued to be one of the technologically backward defence industries in the world. Third, dispelling all doubts, the display at the parade affirms China's determination towards striving and attaining its key goals - military modernisation by 2035 and becoming a World Class Military by 2050. And finally, an increasing Chinese military budget is indicative of its growing military capabilities and undeterred military intentions, as also justified by the parade.

These four indicators thus, sound a strong message to the world at large and its adversaries in particular, of 'what China can do, if need be' to safeguard its own interests against any form of threat or challenge. As Wang Yiwei, pointedly argues: Such a military display reflects that "China's defence industry is independent and complete" and most importantly, "shows that China is not afraid of any evil pressure when it comes to the so-called China-US trade war".[185] This further justifies the significance of 'active defence' in Chinese military affairs and most importantly, its military preparedness to fight and win informationised local wars in the 21st century.

Conclusion

In an overall assessment, it can be rightly argued that China's rapid economic growth has transformed it into a strong military power. The testimony to this lies in the upward swing in China's defence expenditure, which invariably indicates Beijing's increasing military capabilities and undeterred military intentions. That is to say, given China's growing need for power projection, an increased defence spending is an indicator of its quest to secure its strategic space, both regionally as well as globally. This further exemplifies China's overall development in terms of updating its doctrine, improving the quality of its personnel in war fighting, and better equipped with advanced weaponry.

Moreover, unlike its antiquated past, in the current times, China's military-industrial complex is increasingly bridging the weaponry and defence technology gap with the West. This is evident from China's growing capabilities in hypersonics, AI, precision strikes and anti-satellite capabilities – areas where China is also taking the lead. This new military hardware is also indicative of China's ascending military superiority. However, with the strategic goal to become a 'World Class Military', sustaining a modern PLA comes with critical challenges. Here, the pressure point is that, in all circumstances, China needs to grow economically to sustain and increase its military spending in order to fuel its defence industry to produce sophisticated weaponry.

Furthermore, the expanded efforts also aim at shedding the old prejudice attached to the PLA of being characterised as 'backward and redundant', and replacing it with that of the PLA being called a 'battle-ready force'. Overall, the quest lies in building a strong China with a strong PLA – further validating the 'active' element of China's 'active defence'.

NOTES

1. Quoted in "Building a strong army through reform", *Xinhuanet*, 16 March 2016, http://www.xinhuanet.com//mil/2016-03/16/c_128804009.htm, accessed online 5 April 2020.
2. "Full Text: China's National Defense in the New Era", *Xinhuanet*, 24 July 2019, http://www.xinhuanet.com/english/2019-07/24/c_138253389.htm, accessed online 20 March 2020.
3. The 70th Anniversary of the Founding of the People's Republic of China (2019), "No force can stop Chinese people, nation from marching forward: Xi", 1 October 2019, http://www.xinhuanet.com/english/2019-10/01/c_138438667.htm, accessed online 20 July 2020.
4. See, Tara Copp and Aaron Mehta (2019), "New defense intelligence assessment warns China nears critical military milestone", *Defense News*, 15 January 2020, https://www.defensenews.com/news/your-military/2019/01/15/new-defense-intelligence-assessment-warns-china-nears-critical-military-milestone/, accessed online 27 July 2020.
5. Office of the Secretary of Defense (2020), "Annual Report to Congress: Military and Security Developments involving the People's Republic of China 2020", https://media.defense.gov/2020/Sep/01/2002488689/-1/-1/1/2020-DOD-CHINA-MILITARY-POWER-REPORT-FINAL.PDF, accessed online 4 September 2020.
6. Ibid.
7. Stockholm International Peace Research Institute (2020), "Global military expenditure sees largest annual increase in a decade-says SIPRI-reaching $1917 billion in 2019", 27 April 2020, https://www.sipri.org/research/armament-and-disarmament/arms-and-military-expenditure/military-expenditure, accessed online 27 May 2020.
8. Stockholm International Peace Research Institute (2020), "New SIPRI data reveals scale of Chinese arms industry", 27 January 2020, https://www.sipri.org/media/press-release/2020/new-sipri-data-reveals-scale-chinese-arms-industry, accessed online 20 June 2020.

9. Zhao Lei (2020), "Defense budget increase is lowest in 32 years", *China Daily*, 22 May 2020, http://www.chinadaily.com.cn/a/202005/22/WS5ec73de1a310a8b241157994.html, accessed online 10 June 2020.
10. Ibid.
11. Amrita Jash (2019), "China's Military Budget 2019: Numbers Do Matter When Intentions Remain Strong", Centre for Land Warfare Studies, 15 March 2019, https://archive.claws.in/1985/china's-military-budget-2019-numbers-do-matter-when-intentions-remain-strong-dr-amrita-jash.html, accessed online 20 May 2020.
12. Liu Xuanxun (2020), "China slows defense budget growth to 6.6 % in 2020", *Global Times*, 22 May 2020, https://www.globaltimes.cn/content/1189146.shtml, accessed online 10 June 2020.
13. The State Council of the People's Republic of China (2020), "Full Text: Report on the Work of the Government", 30 May 2020, http://english.www.gov.cn/premier/news/202005/30/content_WS5ed197f3c6d0b3f0e94990da.html, accessed online 15 June 2020.
14. Liu Xuanxun (2020), "China slows defence budget growth", n. 12.
15. "Xi Focus: Xi emphasizes strengthening national defense, armed forces", *Xinhuanet*, 26 May 2020, http://www.xinhuanet.com/english/2020-05/26/c_139089760.htm, accessed online 20 June 2020.
16. Liu Xuanxun (2020), "China slows defence budget growth", n. 12.
17. Ibid.
18. Andrew S. Erickson (2020), "China's Official 2020 Defense Budget to Rise 6.6% to $178 Billion (1.27 Trillion Yuan): Lowest Growth Rate Since 1988 Exceeds All Other Major Nations'", 22 May 2020, https://www.andrewerickson.com/2020/05/chinas-official-2020-defense-budget-to-rise-6-6-percent-to-178-billion-1-27-trillion-yuan-lowest-growth-rate-since-1988-exceeds-all-other-major-nations/, accessed online 10 June 2020.
19. "Full Text: China's National Defense in the New Era", *Xinhuanet*, n. 2.
20. "U.S. Defense Secretary Donald Rumsfeld On Pacific Security Issues: Why Is China's Defense Spending Growing?, 2005", USC US-China Institute, 4 June 2005, https://china.usc.edu/us-defense-secretary-donald-rumsfeld-pacific-security-issues-why-chinas-defense-spending-growing, accessed online 10 June 2020.
21. Quoted in Keith Crane et al. (2005), *Modernizing China's Military: Opportunities and Constraints*, Santa Monica, CA: RAND Corporation, p. 92, https://www.rand.org/content/dam/rand/pubs/monographs/2005/RAND_MG260-1.pdf, accessed online 25 May 2020.
22. "China has no "hidden military spending": spokesperson", *Xinhuanet*, 21 May 2020, http://www.xinhuanet.com/english/2020-05/21/c_139076274.htm, accessed online 20 June 2020.
23. Adam P. Liff and Andrew S. Erickson (2013), "Demystifying China's Defense Spending: Less Mysterious in the Aggregate", *The China Quarterly*, Vol. 216, p. 815.
24. "Full Text: China's National Defense in the New Era", *Xinhuanet*, n. 2.
25. Quoted in Michael Martina and Ben Blanchard (2019), "Rise in China's defence budget to outpace economic growth target", *Reuters*, 5 March 2019, https://www.reuters.com/article/us-china-parliament-defence-idUSKCN1QM03Y, accessed online 20 May 2020.
26. Liu Xuanxun (2020), "China slows defence budget growth", n. 12.
27. Cited in "China boosts defense spending for 2018", *DW*, 5 March 2018, https://www.dw.com/en/china-boosts-defense-spending-for-2018/a-42826549, accessed online 15 March 2020.

28. Full Text: China's National Defense in the New Era", *Xinhuanet*, n. 2.
29. Ibid.
30. Ibid.
31. Ibid.
32. Stockholm International Peace Research Institute (2020), "Global military expenditure", n. 7.
33. Amrita Jash (2019), "China's Military Budget 2019", n. 11.
34. "Full Text: China's National Defense in the New Era", *Xinhuanet*, n. 2.
35. Ibid.
36. Liu Xuanzun (2019), "China likely to see steady increase in 2019 defense budget", *Global Times*, 12 February 2019, http://www.globaltimes.cn/content/1138581.shtml, accessed online 15 May 2020.
37. "Full Text: China's National Defense in the New Era", *Xinhuanet*, n. 2.
38. Dong Ryul Lee (2019), "The Prospect and Trend of Military Spending and Strategy in Rising China", EAI Working Paper, 8 January 2019, p. 4, http://www.eai.or.kr/main/english/publication_01_view.asp?intSeq=9913&board=eng_report, accessed online 20 May 2020.
39. See, Brian Wang (2018), "China defense budget increases by 8.1% but police state budget is still 20% more", Nextbigfuture, 7 March 2018, https://www.nextbigfuture.com/2018/03/china-defense-budget-increases-by-8-1-but-police-state-budget-is-still-20-more.html, accessed online 15 June 2020.
40. "What Does China Really Spend on its Military?", China Power, https://chinapower.csis.org/military-spending/, accessed online 20 May 2020.
41. Ibid.
42. Dong Ryul Lee (2019), "The Prospect and Trend of Military Spending", n. 38, pp. 1-2.
43. See, "What Does China Really Spend on its Military?", China Power, n. 40.
44. Ibid.
45. Ibid.
46. "Full Text: China's National Defense in the New Era", *Xinhuanet*, n. 2.
47. Adam P. Liff and Andrew S. Erickson (2013), "Demystifying China's Defense Spending", n. 23, p. 815.
48. Ibid.
49. Ibid. p. 811.
50. Keith Crane et al. (2005), *Modernizing China's Military*, n. 21, pp. 102-103.
51. Ibid.
52. Ministry of National Defense of the People's Republic of China (2002), "China's National Defense in 2002", http://eng.mod.gov.cn/Database/WhitePapers/2002.htm, accessed online 20 May 2020.
53. Keith Crane et al. (2005), *Modernizing China's Military*, n. 21, p. 103.
54. Ibid.
55. Dong Ryul Lee (2019), "The Prospect and Trend of Military Spending", n. 38, p. 2.
56. Stockholm International Peace Research Institute (2020), "International Arms Transfers", March 2020, https://www.sipri.org/sites/default/files/2020-03/fs_2003_at_2019.pdf, accessed online 20 June 2020.
57. Stockholm International Peace Research Institute (2017), "The state of major arms transfers in 8 graphics", 22 February 2017, https://www.sipri.org/commentary/blog/2017/state-major-arms-transfers-8-graphics, accessed online 20 June 2020.

58. Apart from Russia, Ukraine also provides China with propulsion systems. In 2011, Beijing acquired Ukrainian turbofans for trainer and combat aircraft, along with 50 diesel-powered tank engines and three refurbished IL-78 air-refuelling planes. A sizable portion of China's orders from France are also for engines. In addition, China has sourced French-built diesel engines, such as the 16PC2.5 and 12PA6, for outfitting its naval vessels.
59. Stockholm International Peace Research Institute (2020), "International Arms Transfers", n. 56, p. 6.
60. Ibid., p. 9.
61. "How Dominant is China in the Global Arms Trade?", China Power, 26 April 2018, https://chinapower.csis.org/china-global-arms-trade/, accessed online 20 July 2020.
62. Sean Chen and John Feffer (2010), "China's Military Spending: Soft Rise or Hard Threat?", *Foreign Policy In Focus*, 6 May 2010, https://fpif.org/chinas_military_spending_soft_rise_or_hard_threat/, accessed online 20 May 2020.
63. Stockholm International Peace Research Institute (2020), "International Arms Transfer", n. 56.
64. "Is China a Global Leader in Research and Development?", China Power, 31 January 2018, https://chinapower.csis.org/china-research-and-development-rnd/, accessed online 20 September 2020.
65. Xi Jinping (2017), "Secure a Decisive Victory in Building a Moderately Prosperous Society in All Respects and Strive for the Great Success of Socialism with Chinese Characteristics for a New Era", Delivered at the 19th National Congress of the Communist Party of China, 18 October 2017, http://www.xinhuanet.com/english/download/Xi_Jinping's_report_at_19th_CPC_National_Congress.pdf, accessed online 20 July 2020.
66. Adam P. Liff and Andrew S. Erickson (2013), "Demystifying China's Defence Spending", n. 23, p. 816.
67. Ibid.
68. Ibid., pp. 817-819.
69. Ibid.
70. Dong Ryul Lee (2019), "The Prospect and Trend of Military Spending", n. 38, p. 2.
71. Liangyu (2019), "China's limited defense spending poses no threat to any other country: spokesperson", *Xinhuanet*, 4 March 2019, http://www.xinhuanet.com/english/2019-03/04/c_137867991.htm, accessed online 14 May 2020.
72. For details see, The State Council of the People's Republic of China (2014), "State Administration for Science, Technology and Industry for National Defence", 6 October 2020, http://english.www.gov.cn/state_council/2014/10/06/content_281474992893468.htm, accessed online 14 May 2020.
73. David Shambaugh (2004), *Modernizing China's Military: Progress, Problems, and Prospects*, New Delhi: Book Mart Publishers, p. 234.
74. Stockholm International Peace Research Institute (2020), "New SIPRI data reveals scale of Chinese arms industry", n. 8.
75. For details of the Top 100 companies, see, Susan T. Jackson (2012), "Arms production and military services", in *SIPRI Yearbook 2012: Armaments, Disarmament and International Security*, pp. 251-256, https://www.sipri.org/yearbook/2012/05, accessed online 20 June 2020.
76. Ibid., p. 251.

77. Stockholm International Peace Research Institute (2020), "New SIPRI data reveals scale of Chinese arms industry", n. 8.
78. Ibid.
79. Tai Ming Cheung (2019), "From Big to Powerful: China's Quest for Security and Power in the Age of Innovation", EAI Working Paper, April 2019, p. 3, https://igcc.ucsd.edu/_files/great-powers/gp_reading_cheung.pdf, accessed online 12 March 2020.
80. Ibid.
81. Richard A. Bitzinger (2008), "China's Military-Industrial Complex: Is It (Finally) Turning a Corner?", RSIS Commentary CO08121, 21 November 2008, https://www.rsis.edu.sg/rsis-publication/rsis/1141-chinas-military-industrial/#.X3IXbC2B1QI, accessed online 20 July 2020.
82. "Ultrafast anti-ship missiles offered for sale", *China Military Online*, 25 December 2018, http://english.chinamil.com.cn/view/2018-12/25/content_9388061.htm, accessed online 22 June 2020.
83. Ibid.
84. David Shambaugh (2004), *Modernizing China's Military*, n. 73, p. 230.
85. "Furious Russia Blasts China Over Unauthorized copying of Russian Military Hardware", *The Eurasian Times*, 23 December 2029, https://eurasiantimes.com/furious-russia-blasts-china-over-unauthorized-copying-of-russian-military-hardware/, accessed online 20 September 2020.
86. "Top 100 for 2020", *Defense News*, https://people.defensenews.com/top-100/, accessed online 20 September 2020.
87. Ibid.
88. Alex Joske (2019), "The China Defense Universities Tracker", Policy Brief, Report No. 23, Australian Strategic Policy Institute, November 2019, pp. 17-20, https://s3-ap-southeast-2.amazonaws.com/ad-aspi/2019-11/The%20China%20Defence%20Universities%20Tracker_0.pdf, accessed online 15 November 2020.
89. Ibid., pp. 16-20.
90. U.S. Department of State, "Military-Civil Fusion and the People's Republic of China", https://www.state.gov/wp-content/uploads/2020/06/What-is-MCF-One-Pager.pdf, accessed online 20 September 2020.
91. Ibid.
92. Office of the Secretary of Defense (2020), "Annual Report to Congress", n. 5, p. 143.
93. Ibid.
94. Brian Lafferty (2019), "Civil-Military Integration and PLA Reforms", in Phillip C. Saunders et al. (eds.) *Chairman Xi Remakes the PLA: Assessing Chinese Military Reforms*, Washington DC: National Defense University Press, p. 628.
95. Alex Stone and Peter Wood (2020), *China's Military-Civil Fusion Strategy: A View from Chinese Strategists*, Montgomery, AL: China Aerospace Studies Institute, Air University, pp. 25-26, https://www.airuniversity.af.edu/Portals/10/CASI/documents/Research/Other%20topics/CASI%20China's%20Military%20Civil%20Fusion%20Strategy-%20Full%20final.pdf?ver=2020-06-15-152810-733, accessed online 12 September 2020.
96. Ibid.
97. "How Dominant is China in the Global Arms Trade?", China Power, n. 61.
98. Ibid.
99. Alex Joske (2019), "The China Defense Universities Tracker", n. 88, p. 6.
100. Ibid., p. 7.

101. Ibid.
102. Ibid., p. 8. For details, also see "Appendix: Universities supervised by SASTIND", pp. 25-26.
103. Ibid., pp. 6-8.
104. Brian Lafferty (2019), "Civil-Military Integration and PLA Reforms", n. 94, p. 635.
105. Elsa B. Kania (2019), "In Military-Civil Fusion, China Is Learning Lessons From the United States and Starting to Innovate," *Real Clear Defense*, 27 August 2019, https://www.realcleardefense.com/articles/2019/08/27/in_military-civil_fusion_china_is_learning_lessons_from_the_united_states_and_starting_to_ innovate_114699.html, accessed online 19 September 2020.
106. Ibid.
107. Top 100 for 2020", *Defense News*, n. 86.
108. Meia Nouwens (2020), "China's defence-industry rankings: down but by no means out", IISS (Analysis), 17 August 2020, https://www.iiss.org/blogs/analysis/2020/08/china-defence-industry-rankings, accessed online 20 September 2020.
109. Richard A. Bitzinger (2008), "China's Military-Industrial Complex", n. 81.
110. Ibid.
111. Michael R. Pompeo (2020), "Silicon Valley and National Security," U.S. Department of State, 13 January 2020, https://www.state.gov/silicon-valley-and-national-security/, accessed online 18 September 2020.
112. Christopher Ashley Ford (2020), "The PRC's "Military-Civil Fusion" Strategy Is a Global Security Threat," U.S. Department of State, 16 March 2020, https://www.state.gov/the-prcs-military-civil-fusion-strategy-is-a-global-security-threat/, accessed online 20 September 2020.
113. Ibid.
114. "How Dominant is China in the Global Arms Trade?", China Power, n. 61.
115. For details, see Paul Holtom et al. (2012), "International arms transfers" in *SIPRI Yearbook 2012: Armaments, Disarmament and International Security*, p. 266, https://www.sipri.org/yearbook/2012/05, accessed online 20 June 2020.
116. See United Nations, "Arms Trade Treaty", at https://www.un.org/disarmament/convarms/arms-trade-treaty-2/, accessed online 1 October 2020.
117. Permanent Mission of the People's Republic of China to the United Nations Office at Geneva and other International Organizations in Switzerland (2020), "Statement of the People's Republic of China to the Sixth Conference of States Parties to the Arms Trade Treaty", 17 August 2020, http://www.china-un.ch/eng/dbtxwx/t1807021.htm, accessed online 1 October 2020.
118. Ibid.
119. Ibid. In addition, in confirming to the other ATT requirements, China also suggests: First, it has promulgated a series of domestic laws and regulations, and exercises strict and effective control on all arms exports accordingly. They include the Law on the Administration of Firearms, the Regulation on Administration of Military Products Exports and its annexed Military Products Export Control List, and etc. Second, China conducts arms trade with sovereign states only, and requires the end-user and end-use certificates by the recipient governments, with commitments not to transfer the arms imported from China to any third party without the prior consent of the Chinese Government. China does not permit arms exports to non-state actors, which goes beyond the requirements of the ATT and demonstrates China's strong sense of responsibility.

120. Stockholm International Peace Research Institute (2020), "International Arms Transfers", n. 56, p. 3.
121. Ibid., p. 2.
122. Ibid.
123. "How Dominant is China in the Global Arms Trade?", China Power, n. 61.
124. Stockholm International Peace Research Institute (2020), "International Arms Transfers", n. 56, p. 5.
125. Stockholm International Peace Research Institute (2017), "The state of major arms transfers", n. 57.
126. Grace Shao (2019), "China, the world's second largest defense spender, becomes a major arms exporter", *CNBC*, 26 September 2019, https://www.cnbc.com/2019/09/27/china-a-top-defense-spender-becomes-major-arms-exporter.html, accessed online 20 July 2020.
127. Ibid.
128. "How Dominant is China in the Global Arms Trade?", China Power, n. 61.
129. Ibid.
130. Grace Shao (2019), "China, the world's second largest defense spender", n. 126.
131. "How Dominant is China in the Global Arms Trade?", China Power, n. 61.
132. Ibid.
133. Quoted in Grace Shao (2019), "China, the world's second largest defense spender", n. 126.
134. Daneil Bynam and Roger Cliff (1999), *China's Arms Sales: Motivations and Implications*, Santa Monica, CA: RAND Corporation, pp. 26-30, https://www.rand.org/pubs/monograph_reports/MR1119.html, accessed online 20 September 2020.
135. Ibid., pp. 27-28.
136. Ibid., pp. 28-30.
137. While the exact meaning of the term remains elusive, however, as per the Pentagon report "assassin's mace" is used to designate a wide array of technologies that might afford an inferior military an advantage in a conflict with a superior military power. See, "The Assassin's Mace: China's Growing Military Might", The New Atlantis, Summer 2004, p. 108, https://www.thenewatlantis.com/docLib/TNA06-State%20Of%20The% 20Art-Assassins%20Mace.pdf, accessed online 5 January 2020.
138. The State Council of The People's Republic of China (2015), "China's Military Strategy", 27 May 2015, http://english.gov.cn/archive/white_paper/2015/05/27/content_281475115610833.htm, accessed online 30 June 2020.
139. Quoted in Jim Garamone (2019), "DIA's China Military Power Report Details Leaders' Strategy", U.S. Department of Defense, 15 January 2019, https://www.defense.gov/Explore/News/Article/Article/1732657/dias-china-military-power-report-details-leaders-strategy/, accessed online 25 June 2020.
140. Xiaoxia (2019), "China's new-type informationized armed forces debut at National Parade", *Xinhuanet*, 1 October 2019, http://www.xinhuanet.com/english/2019-10/01/c_138439073.htm, accessed online 30 June 2020.
141. Ibid.
142. "Chinese parade injects confidence to safeguard world peace", *China Military Online*, 3 October 2019, http://eng.chinamil.com.cn/view/2019-10/03/content_9643397.htm, accessed online 27 June 2020.
143. Quoted in Helen Regan and James Griffiths (2019), "No force can stop China's progress, says Xi in National Day speech", *CNN*, 1 October 2019, https://edition.cnn.com/

2019/09/30/asia/china-oct-1-national-day-intl-hnk/index.html, accessed online 27 June 2020.

144. The specifications are: length 38.22 ft; width 203.41 ft; height 10.17 ft; weight (empty) 6,350 kg; weight (MTOW) 20,215 kg; power 1x air breathing turbofan engine; speed 1,000 kph; ceiling 12,500 m and range 4,000 km. For details see, "Gongji-11 (GJ-11)", Military Factory, 2 October 2019, https://www.militaryfactory.com/aircraft/detail.asp?aircraft_id=2219, accessed online 1 January 2020.
145. Ibid.
146. Ibid.
147. Ibid.
148. Ian Williams (2019), "More Than Missiles: China Previews its new Way of War", CSIS Briefs, Center for Strategic and International Studies, 16 October 2019, https://www.csis.org/analysis/more-missiles-china-previews-its-new-way-war, accessed online 15 June 2020.
149. Yang Sheng and Liu Xuanzun (2019), "China unveils new high-altitude, high-speed reconnaissance drone WZ-8", *Global Times*, 1 October 2019, http://www.globaltimes.cn/content/1165936.shtml, accessed online 15 June 2020.
150. Andreas Rupprecht, Mainz (2019), "Images suggest WZ-8 UAV in service with China's Eastern Theatre Command", Jane's Defence Weekly, 4 October 2019, https://www.janes.com/article/91701/images-suggest-wz-8-uav-in-service-with-china-s-eastern-theatre-command, accessed online 1 January 2020.
151. Yang Sheng and Liu Xuanzun (2019), "China unveils new high-altitude", n. 149.
152. Ian Williams (2019), "More Than Missiles", n. 148.
153. Yang Sheng and Liu Xuanzun (2019), "China unveils new high-altitude", n. 149.
154. David R. Strachan (2019), "China enters the UUV Fray", The Diplomat, 22 November 2019, https://thediplomat.com/2019/11/china-enters-the-uuv-fray/, accessed online 2 June 2020.
155. H.I. Sutton (2019), "Chinese HSU-001 LDUUV Large Displacement Unmanned Underwater Vehicle", Covert Shores, 2 October 2019, http://www.hisutton.com/Chinese_LDUUV.html, accessed online 2 June 2020.
156. Joseph Trevithick (2019), "Four of the Biggest Revelations From China's Massive 70th Anniversary Military Parade", The Drive, 1 October 2019, https://www.thedrive.com/the-war-zone/30119/four-of-the-biggest-revelations-from-chinas-massive-70th-anniversary-military-parade, accessed online 2 June 2020.
157. H.I. Sutton (2019), "Chinese HSU-001 LDUUV", n. 155.
158. Ian Williams (2019), "More Than Missiles", n. 148.
159. "China Deploys YJ-12B and HQ-9B Missiles on South China Sea Islands", *Navy Recognition*, 4 May 2018, https://www.navyrecognition.com/index.php/news/defence-news/2018/may-2018-navy-naval-defense-news/6190-china-deploys-yj-12b-and-hq-9b-missiles-on-south-china-sea-islands.html, accessed online 4 June 2020.
160. Chris Pleasance (2019), "'The world's most powerful nuke' that can hit the US in 30 minutes, hypersonic drones and 'carrier killer' missiles: China shows off bristling array of new military technology during 70th anniversary parade", *Mail Online*, 1 October 2019, https://www.dailymail.co.uk/news/article-7523979/The-worlds-powerful-nuke-array-new-weapons-unveiled-China.html, accessed online 2 June 2020.
161. "Why China's New Missiles in the South China Sea Should Scare the Navy and Air Force", The National Interest, 5 May 2018, https://nationalinterest.org/blog/the-

buzz/why-chinas-new-missiles-the-south-china-sea-should-scare-the-25718, accessed online 4 June 2020.

162. Michael Pilger (2015), "China's New YJ-18 Antiship Cruise Missile: Capabilities and Implications for U.S. Forces in the Western Pacific", US-China Economic and Security Review Commission, 28 October 2015, p. 2, https://www.uscc.gov/sites/default/files/Research/China's%20New%20YJ-18%20Antiship%20Cruise%20Missile.pdf, accessed online 4 June 2020.
163. Ibid.
164. Ian Williams (2019), "More Than Missiles", n. 148.
165. Michael Pilger (2015), "China's New YJ-18 Antiship", n. 162.
166. "YJ-18 Eagle Strike CH-SS-NX-13", Global Security.org., https://www.globalsecurity.org/military/world/china/yj-18.htm, accessed online 4 June 2020.
167. Ibid.
168. Minnie Chan and Liu Zhen (2019), "China's new supersonic arsenal could give bomber force greater reach", *Inkstone*, 12 November 2019, https://www.inkstonenews.com/china/chinas-new-supersonic-arsenal-could-give-h-6-bomber-force-greater-reach/article/3037318, accessed online 4 June 2020.
169. Ibid.
170. Sebastien Roblin (2019), "China's New DF-100 Missile: Designed to Kill U.S. Navy Aircraft Carriers?", The National Interest, 5 October 2019, https://nationalinterest.org/blog/buzz/chinas-new-df-100-missile-designed-kill-us-navy-aircraft-carriers-85931, accessed online 4 June 2020.
171. Ibid.
172. Missile Defence Project, "JL-2 (Ju Lang-2/CSS-NX-14)", Missile Threat, Center for Strategic and International Studies, 12 August, 2016, last modified 7 October 2019, https://missilethreat.csis.org/missile/jl-2/, accessed online 7 June 2020.
173. Ibid.
174. Brian Wang (2014), "China new nuclear JL-2 and DF-41 missiles will cover all US territory", Next Big Future, 30 December 2014, https://www.nextbigfuture.com/2014/12/china-new-nuclear-jl-2-and-df-41.html, accessed online 7 June 2020.
175. "Dong Feng-41 (CSS-x-20)", Missile Defense Advocacy Alliance,https://missiledefenseadvocacy.org/missile-threat-and-proliferation/missile-proliferation/china/df-41/, accessed online 7 June 2020.
176. Missile Defence Project, "DF-41 (Dong Feng-41 /CSS-X-20)", Missile Threat, Center for Strategic and International Studies, 12 August 12, 2016, last modified 8 October 2019, https://missilethreat.csis.org/missile/df-41/, accessed online 7 June 2020.
177. Ibid.
178. Quoted in Zhao Lei (2017), "New ballistic missile that covers globe nearly ready", *China Daily*, 29 November 2017, https://www.chinadaily.com.cn/china/2017-11/29/content_35119000.htm, accessed online 20 June 2020.
179. Quoted in Hans M. Kristensen (2019), "Military Might Takes Center Stage at Chinese 70-Year Anniversary Parade", Federation of American Scientists, 1 October 2019, https://fas.org/blogs/security/2019/10/china-military-parade/, accessed online 20 June 2020.
180. "Dong Feng-17", Missile Defense Advocacy Alliance, https://missiledefenseadvocacy.org/missile-threat-and-proliferation/missile-proliferation/china/dong-feng-17/, accessed online 20 June 2020.

181. David Axe (2019), "Check Out China's New DF-17 Hypersonic Glide Vehicle: A Real Killer?", The National Interest, 1 October 2019, https://nationalinterest.org/blog/buzz/check-out-chinas-new-df-17-hypersonic-glide-vehicle-real-killer-84946, accessed online 20 June 2020.
182. Minnie Chan (2019), "Will hypersonic DF-17 missile transform Beijing's Taiwan strategy?", *South China Morning Post*, 16 November 2019, https://www.scmp.com/news/china/military/article/3037972/will-hypersonic-df-17-missile-transform-beijings-taiwan, accessed online 20 June 2020.
183. Ian Williams (2019), "More Than Missiles", n. 136.
184. It is to note that apart from the USA, China is one of the few countries in the world to produce a full range of military equipment, from small arms to armoured vehicles to fighter aircraft to warships and submarines, in addition to nuclear weapons and intercontinental ballistic missiles.
185. Quoted in Anna Fifield (2019), "China rolls out its military firepower with emphasis on 'Cold War-style' nuclear might", *The Washington Post*, 1 October 2019, https://www.washingtonpost.com/world/asia_pacific/china-rolls-out-its-military-firepower-with-emphasis-on-cold-war-style-nuclear-might/2019/10/01/243d5302-e168-11e9-be7f-4cc85017c36f_story.html, accessed online 20 June 2020.

5

China's Behaviour at the LAC

"We fought a war with old Chiang [Kai-shek]. We fought a war with Japan, and one with America. During none of these, did we fear. And in each case, we won. Now the Indians want to fight a war with us. Naturally, we don't have fear. We cannot give ground; once we give, it would be tantamount to letting them seize a big piece of land equivalent to Fujian province. [...] Since Nehru sticks his head out and insists on us fighting him, for us not to fight with him would not be friendly enough. Courtesy emphasizes reciprocity".

—Mao Zedong (1962)[1]

"No one should expect us to swallow the bitter fruit that is harmful to our sovereignty, security or development interests".

—Xi Jinping (2017)[2]

A famous Chinese saying suggests that 'one mountain cannot contain two tigers' *(yî shân bù róng èr hô)*, and this logic often seems to be true when contrasted with China's quest to occupy strategic space in Asia; and particularly along the Himalayan border with India. This is exemplified by the 2020 military stand-off in Eastern Ladakh, which took a violent turn when troops of the Indian Army and the Chinese PLA clashed in the Galwan Valley on June 15 - resulting into casualties in over 45 years. This brings into perspective the aspect of China's military activism in securing its territorial claims, which the PRC justifies on the grounds, as Xi Jinping notes:

> "The Chinese people love peace. We will never seek aggression or expansion, but we have the confidence to defeat all invasions. We

> will never allow any people, organization or political party to split any part of Chinese territory out of the country at any time, in any form".[3]

Xi's remarks resonate with Chinese actions, as in recent years, China has become actively engaged in its quest to occupy strategic space in Asia. Rather than aiming for superpower status, Beijing's primary objective lies in strengthening its regional supremacy by dislodging US influence in Asia. In doing so, China's actions are guided by taking incremental steps by adopting salami-slicing tactics. China's strategy in this direction have been evident in securing its control by creating artificial islands in the South China Sea since 2014, unilateral establishment of an Air Defence Identification Zone (ADIZ) in the disputed East China Sea against Japan in 2013; and in 2017, this tactic came into play in the unilateral construction of a road through the disputed Doklam Plateau at the India-China-Bhutan tri-junction—resulting in the 73-day Doklam stand-off with India. Events in Doklam highlight China's implementing of salami-slicing tactics on land.

More strikingly, China's increasing adventurism against India at the Line of Actual Control (LAC) amidst the COVID-19 pandemic has failed to tone down China's intentions. The Eastern Ladakh crisis gravely hindered the celebratory spirit of the 70 years of India-China ties with 2020 marked as "Year of India-China Cultural and People to People Exchanges". What is noteworthy is that in the 70 years, the biggest dilemma has been of finding a solution to the contested border. To which, even the pandemic failed to make any difference, rather the tensions only got flared up to a new degree at the LAC. Despite various levels of engagement (diplomatic, political and military) between India and China, the increasing trends of transgressions and stand-offs have only made the dispute intense over time. Of all, it is the violent clash in Galwan Valley that claimed lives of 20 Indian soldiers (the casualties on the Chinese side remain unknown),[4] has resurfaced the debate over the potency of the 'hard power' component in the relatively 'peaceful border'. Here, one needs to ask: Was the Galwan Valley incident unexpected? To which, one can strongly argue that, if not unexpected, it was indeed a watershed! But the query remains: *What called for Chinese adventurism in Eastern Ladakh in times of the COVID-19 crisis?*

In recent times, what has also provided the momentum to the border dimension is Xi's emphasis on the PLA's battlefield readiness and gaining more operational experience, especially in the high-altitude areas. This has raised concerns over the possibility of even inadvertent conflicts, especially with regard to the PLA's activities in the Western Theatre Command (WTC) that holds specific implications for India. This is further compounded by the increasing military build-up by the two countries along the border, which has heightened the security dilemma. As both countries have failed to find a mutually agreed border settlement, the lack of a consensus has turned the border into a potential hotspot. This is to suggest that the complexities have raised the unwarranted risks of escalation between the two countries caused by aggressive patrolling that has resulted in periodic episodes of face-offs between the troops from both sides. Of which, the violent border clash at the Galwan Valley—being the first case of fatalities along the LAC since the 1975 Tulung La incident,[5] and one of the biggest military confrontations since the Sumdorong Chu stand-off—has resurfaced the fears of a conflict between the two nuclear-armed neighbours. To this conundrum, as John Garver rightly argues, the border has become a "protracted contest" between India and China.

In this context, the present chapter aims to study the India-China boundary dispute from the vantage of China's military behaviour at the LAC. In doing so, this chapter will examine the patterns in Chinese behaviour along the border. Here, the crux lies in assessing China's perceptions of the LAC, its military actions in the name of safeguarding its core interest of 'sovereignty and territorial integrity', and the implications of it for India.

Differing Perceptions & Contradictions on the Border

India and China share a border of 3,488 km, which runs from northwest of the Karakoram Pass and ends at Arunachal Pradesh, without any demarcation on the ground. Due to which, the territorial dispute primarily owes its existence to the absence of an internationally accepted boundary between India and China, and lack of an agreement on where does the de facto 'Line of Actual Control' actually lie.

This makes the border not fully demarcated, and the LAC, neither clarified nor confirmed by the two countries. As a result of which, the border is disputed in three sectors, namely: the Western, Middle and Eastern sectors (see Figure 5.1 and Table 5.1)

Figure 5.1: The Disputed Border between India and China

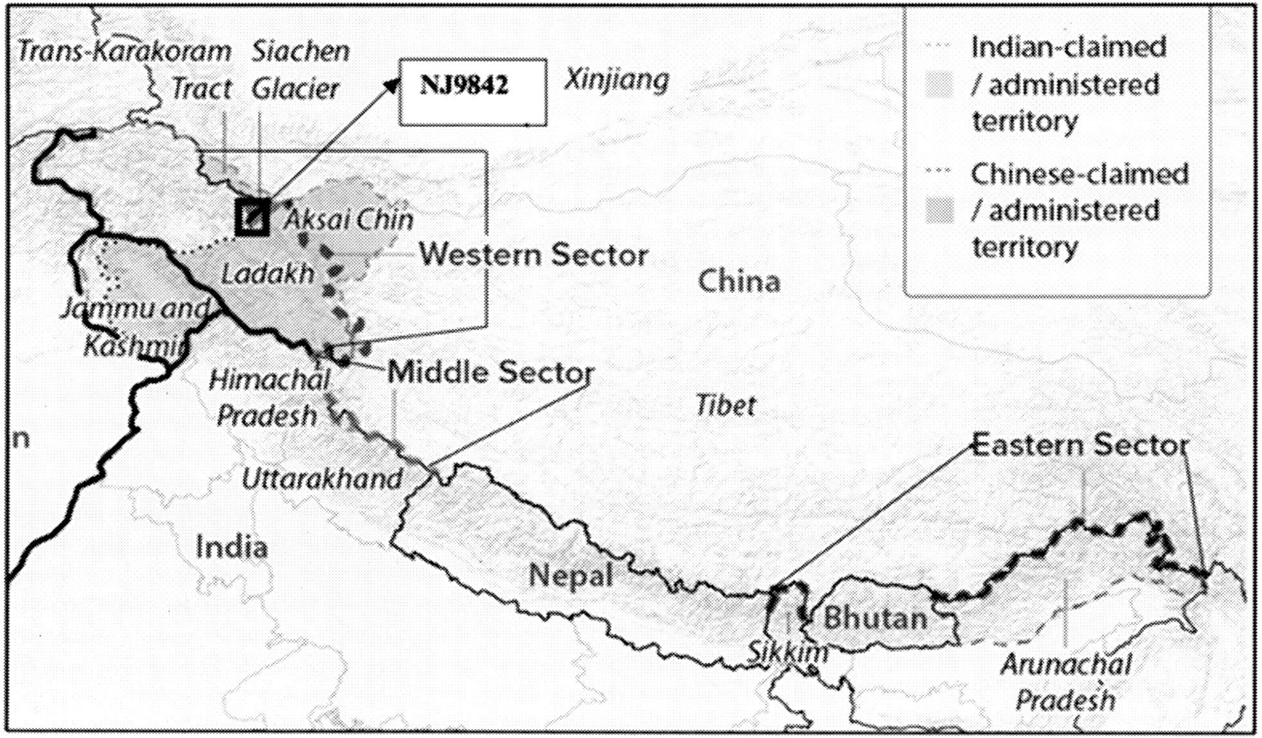

Source: Adapted from Sen (2020),[6] and annotated by the Author (Not to Scale).

Table 5.1: Areas under Dispute/Frequent Transgressions across the LAC

Sector	*Areas*	*Status of the Dispute*	*Key Disputed and Sensitive Areas*	*China's Position/ Claims*	*India's Position/Claims*
Western	Aksai Chin	Disputed (Second largest area of dispute covering over 38,000 sq. km.)	Samar Lungpa Trig Heights Depsang Pangong Tso Dumchele Demchok Chumar	Administered by China	Claimed by India
Middle*	Himachal Pradesh	Disputed (dispute covers around 2,000 sq. km.)	Kaurik Shipkila	Parts claimed by China	Administered by India
	Uttarakhand		Barahoti Pulam Sumda		
Eastern	Sikkim	Undisputed	—	In 2003, China recognised Sikkim as part of India	Administered by India
	Arunachal Pradesh	Disputed (Largest disputed area covering around 90,000 sq. km.)	Namka Chu Sumdorong Chu Yangtse Asaphila Longju Fish Tail-1 & 2 in Dibang Valley Dichu	Claimed by China as so-called "South Tibet"*	Administered by India

Note: On Arunachal Pradesh, China's claims have grown over the decades. Earlier, Beijing only claimed a region called Tawang. However, in the 2000s, it started claiming all of Arunachal Pradesh, which it calls "South Tibet".

* The middle sector is the least disputed of the three sectors.

Source: Author.

These are areas where claims of both sides overlap and through agreement, both refrain from any permanent occupation. In this regard, any unilateral action on either side along the LAC becomes a bone of contention between New Delhi and Beijing. This overlap in claims necessitates the understanding of the Indian and Chinese perception of the border. To note, except for the middle sector, the mutual exchange of maps about their respective perceptions on the other two sectors have not taken place between the two countries. In this regard, it becomes imperative to understand two key perspectives that contribute to the dispute: First, the divergence over the McMahon Line between India and China; and second, the dilemma over the LAC.

On the aspect of the 'McMahon Line',[7] Beijing contradicts New Delhi's stance on accepting it as the boundary between China and India. Calling it "illegal" and "unacceptable", China rejects the McMahon Line on the following grounds: First, that the Sino-Indian boundary had never been formally delimited and that no treaty or agreement had been concluded between the Chinese Central government and the Government of India. Second, the McMahon Line is an 'imperialist legacy' wherein Beijing discounts the 1914 Simla Convention between Great Britain, China and Tibet, contending that Tibet was not a sovereign state and therefore, had no power to conclude treaties.

While China rejects India's stand, Beijing's such an attitude calls for scrutiny. As to note, there is a dichotomy in China's handling of border issues. That is, Beijing practices a 'selective' approach, wherein China's exceptionalism towards India is founded on two contradictions: First, on China's acceptance of the 1914 Simla Convention and the McMahon Line. China has de facto accepted the same McMahon Line extending into Burma (now Myanmar) and settled the border issue with Myanmar in 1960; however, in the case of India, China rejects the same Convention and same map.[8] Second, on the demarcation of land boundaries based on the 'Watershed Principle', China settled the boundary with Nepal in 1960 by dividing Mount Everest by the Watershed Principle; however, with India, China rejects the McMahon Line that followed the Watershed Principle and to all extent possible, ran along the highest ridges of the eastern Himalayan ranges.[9] Given this dichotomy in China's behaviour, one needs to ask: Why does China maintain such a discrepancy on the border with India?

While on the de facto LAC, China affirms its position by reiterating that "China-India border LAC is very clear, that is the LAC on November

7, 1959". Here, the "LAC on November 7, 1959" is a reference to the proposal made by Chinese Premier Zhou Enlai,[10] to Indian Prime Minister Jawaharlal Nehru in his 7 November 1959 letter. In which, positing that the "Sino-Indian boundary has never been delimited", Zhou suggested:[11]

> "In order to maintain effectively the status quo of the border between the two countries, to ensure the tranquillity of the border regions and to create a favourable atmosphere for a friendly settlement of the boundary question, the Chinese government proposes that the armed forces of China and India each withdraw 20 kilometres at once from the so-called McMahon Line in the east, and from the line up to which each side exercises actual control in the west, and that the two sides undertake to refrain from again sending their armed personnel to be stationed in and patrol the zones from which they have evacuated their armed forces, but still maintain civil administrative personnel and unarmed police there for the performance of administrative duties and maintenance of order".[12]

Defying China's 'so-called LAC', India's former National Security Advisor Shivshankar Menon in his book *Choices – Inside the Making of India's Foreign Policy*, suggests that China has always described the so-called 1959 LAC "only in general terms on maps not to scale".[13] In arguing so, Menon states that:

> "In both 1959 and 1962, India had rejected the concept of a Line of Actual Control, arguing that the Chinese concept was a disconnected series of points on a map that could be jointed up in many ways; the line should omit gains from aggression in 1962 and therefore should be based on the actual position on September 8, 1962, before the Chinese attack; and the vagueness of the Chinese definition left it open for China to continue its creeping attempt to change facts on the group by military force". [14]

Accordingly, India's official position suggests that it has "never accepted the so-called unilaterally defined 1959 Line of Actual Control (LAC)",[15] given Nehru rejected Zhou's proposal in a reply dated 16 November 1959, stating that:

> "A proper understanding of the facts in regard to the Sino-Indian boundary is essential to the consideration of any proposal that is made for the avoidance of border clashes".[16]

Officially, the Indian position has been that the LAC should be the line that divided the two forces on the eve of the war on 8 September 1962. However, by default, the LAC that India has had to accept was the one that China had created through war since Indian forces did not return to the area for several years.[17] At present, in the western sector, the LAC represents the line that separates the Indian areas of Ladakh from Aksai Chin, which is concurrent with the Chinese Aksai Chin claim line. However, what preceded the LAC in this area was two proposed borders by the British Empire, namely, the Johnson Line and the MacDonald Line.[18]

What China has largely maintained is its '1960 claim line', which in any case was different from the supposedly definitive line of 1956, as reiterated in 1959.[19] To which, India's former Foreign Secretary Shyam Saran posits that China has also retained 3,000 sq km of additional territory occupied in the Chip Chap Valley, Pangong Tso and Spanggur areas.[20] Given these variations, one can rightly argue that China's perception of the border, as proposed by Zhou[21] has significantly shifted over the years, which has consistently been rejected by India.

More precisely, as per the *Report of the Officials of the Governments of India and the Peoples' Republic of China on the Boundary Question* [published by India's Ministry of External Affairs (MEA) in 1961], Chinese officials posited that "The Sino-Indian boundary has never been formally delimited and there is only a traditional customary boundary line between the two countries".[22] In providing clarifications to the Indian side, the Chinese officials put forward the following latitude and longitude, suggesting that from the Karakoram Pass, the boundary ran eastward to a point east of 78° 05′ E, and that the line turned southwest to a point 78° 1′ E and 35° 21′ N where it crossed the Chip Chap river. After this, it turned southeast along the mountain ridge and passed through two peaks 6,845 metres (78°12′ E and 34° 57′N) and Peak 6,598 metres (78° 13′ E 34° 54′ N). *(misprinted in report as 68°). Thereafter, it crossed the Galwan River at 78° 13′E, 34° 46N. Thereafter it passes through Peak 6,556 (approximately 78° 262′ E, 34° 322′ N), and runs along the watershed between the Kugrang Tsangpo River and its tributary, the Changlung River, to approximately 78° 532′ E, 34° 222′ N where it crosses the Changlung River and reaches the Kongka Pass. It reached the Pangong Lake at 78° 49′ E, 33° 44′N and crossed the southern bank of the Lake at 78° 43′ E, 33° 40′ N.[23] However, China's current claims and actions run contrary to the aforementioned coordinates,[24] causing 'new differences' to the old dispute.

The bottom line is that there does not exist any formal version of the LAC that has been surveyed and delineated on maps; and hence, no demarcation on the ground thus, calling for the dispute along the LAC.

As a result of which, the border is patrolled and managed by the military forces of both sides. In this respect, what causes the discord, as India's Ministry of External Affairs categorically suggests:

> "[A]s there is no commonly delineated Line of Actual Control (LAC) in the border areas between India and China, from time to time, on account of differences in the perception of the LAC, situations have arisen on the ground that could have been avoided if we had a common perception of the LAC".[25]

This very statement brings into perspective the 'fault line'. Given that the LAC is not demarcated on the ground, it leads to incidental fallouts, with both armies carrying out patrolling to their respective LAC perception points. Therefore, it is the lack of consensus over the LAC that results into the perception gap wherein, the misperceptions foster the strategic distrust in the India-China ties.

The Context of 'Relative Peace' in the Disputed Border

It is an accepted fact that territorial disputes bear on a state's "national sovereignty and territorial integrity, its core interests" being the most common issue over which "states collide and go to war".[26] Similarly, in the case of India and China, after the 1962 War, it was in 1967 that the two countries got engaged in a border skirmish in the Sikkim sector, which was followed by the biggest face-off in Samdurong Chu in 1986-1987. However, since then, both sides did succeed in avoiding any form of armed conflict but have failed to scale down the tensions. With the increasing volatility in the recent times, the final settlement of the dispute on a 'win-win' formula has become a 'dilemma' – with no way forward any time soon.

In view of this, the question remains: How sustainable is the existing 'relative peace'? The significance of this query lies in the fact that the unsettled nature of the border makes it a potent hotspot. Unlike in the past, the disputed border is increasingly showing signs of becoming 'active' at all ends. That is, both sides have build-up armed forces and war-waging arsenals opposite each other in all the three sectors of the border- western, middle, and eastern. To which, the Eastern Ladakh stand-off has triggered a massive escalation of the already volatile border, resulting into a military stalemate.

What makes the 2020 stand-off in Eastern Ladakh significant is the fact that it occurred in the aftermath of two "Informal Summits" held between Chinese President Xi Jinping and Indian Prime Minister

Narendra Modi-2018 in Wuhan and 2019 in Mamallapuram. The very aim of the "Informal Summits" was to quell the future risks of a contingency. Owing to which, the 'Summits' called for strategic and long-term perspective in handling the boundary predicament in a peaceful manner. To note, as per the consensus reached in Wuhan (also known as the "Wuhan spirit"), both sides affirmed the need for the two countries:

> "to intensify [the] efforts to seek a fair, reasonable and mutually acceptable settlement. The two leaders underscored the importance of maintaining peace and tranquillity in all areas of the India-China border region in the larger interest of the overall development of bilateral relations. To this end, they issued strategic guidance to their respective militaries to strengthen communication in order to build trust and mutual understanding and enhance predictability and effectiveness in the management of border affairs".[27]

What is important to note is that the "Wuhan Spirit" reiterates the principles of the existing agreements as signed between India and China to stabilise the LAC and normalise their relationship in other areas. This brings into perspective the role of confidence building measures (CBMs) in the India-China border dispute. Here, the point of query is: Have the CBMs helped to quell the risks?

Confidence Building between India and China: Agreements and Mechanisms

Since the 1962 War, India and China have signed various bilateral agreements (Table 5.2), as CBMs to prevent any form of escalation at the border.

Of which, the 2005 accord between India and China is the most significant given it laid down the parameters to the settlement. Of which, the three key guidelines to the settlement process entails that:[29] (a) Both sides will make meaningful and mutually acceptable adjustments to their respective positions on the boundary question, so as to arrive at a package settlement to the boundary question. (b) The boundary settlement must be final, covering all sectors of the India-China boundary. (c) Both sides will give due consideration to each other's strategic and reasonable interests, and the principle of mutual and equal security. In this case, the stumbling block is the 'win-win' dynamic of the 'consensus', making the settlement a dilemma for the two countries. More strikingly, the increasing number of skirmishes and stand-offs between the Indian and Chinese military forces along both disputed and settled parts of the border have evidently surfaced concerns over the efficacy and relevance of these agreements in resolving the boundary dispute.

Table 5.2: Bilateral Agreements Signed between India and China on the LAC

Year/Place	*Agreement Signed*	*Key Points of Agreement*
7 September 1993 *Signed in Beijing*	*Agreement on the Maintenance of Peace and Tranquility along the Line of Actual Control in the India-China Border Areas*	• Respect and abide by the LAC. • Continue implementing confidence building measures in the military field along the line of actual control. • Maintain peace and tranquility in areas along the LAC in the India-China border areas. • Neither side shall use its military capability against the other side and that their respective military strengths shall not be used to attack the other side. • Neither side shall use or threaten to use force against the other by any means or seek unilateral military superiority. • The two sides shall safeguard due interests of their settled populations in the border areas.
29 November 1996 *Signed in New Delhi*	*Agreement Between the Government of the Republic of India and the Government of the People's Republic of China on Confidence-Building Measures in the Military Field Along the Line of Actual Control in the India-China Border Areas*	
11 April 2005 *Signed in New Delhi*	*Agreement between the Government of the Republic of India and the Government of the People's Republic of China on the Political Parameters and Guiding Principles for the Settlement of the India-China Boundary Question*	
17 January 2012 *Signed in New Delhi*	*India-China Agreement on the Establishment of a Working Mechanism for Consultation and Coordination on India-China Border Affairs*	
23 October 2013 *Signed in Beijing*	*Agreement between the Government of the Republic of India and the Government of the People's Republic of China on Border Defence Cooperation*[28]	

Source: Annotated by the Author with reference to sources available in the website of the Ministry of External Affairs (Government of India) and the UN Peacemaker database.

While India and China maintain a relatively peaceful border, this peace is only temporary, as verified by the Eastern Ladakh crisis. The border being unsettled carries an inherent danger of an unwarranted risk of an escalation, as also proven by the 2020 stand-off. This criticality of the situation highlights the failure of the agreements in bringing a constructive outcome to the boundary question. On the contrary, it can be said that these agreements have rather transformed the boundary into a long-term predicament between India and China. To argue so, such agreements only act as constructive binders on either side thus, preventing one from taking any form of unwarranted action against the other. For instance, as part of the 1996 agreement, Indian and Chinese troops are not allowed to carry firearms on the LAC, a preventive measure to reduce tensions. As to note, Article VI of the 1996 agreement clearly states that:[30]

> "Neither side shall open fire, cause bio-degradation, use hazardous chemicals, conduct blast operations or hunt with guns or explosives within two kilometres from the line of actual control. This prohibition shall not apply to routine firing activities in small arms firing ranges". [...]
>
> "If the border personnel of the two sides come in a face-to-face situation due to differences on the alignment of the line of actual control or any other reason, they shall exercise self-restraint and take all necessary steps to avoid an escalation of the situation [...]".[31]

However, these protocols failed to prevent the violence at the Galwan Valley, as to argue: First, at the Galwan Valley clash, if not firearms were used but the protocol still stands breached due to the use of stones, iron rods, and other makeshift weapons by the Chinese side that led to fatalities; and second, as reported, shots were fired in September at Pangong Tso. Both these incidents, being the firsts since the 1975 Tulung La incident, violated the very essence of the 1996 and other agreements. Therefore, unlike the tensions in the past, the turn of events in the Eastern Ladakh crisis have successively proved the agreements to be 'null and void'. Hence, this situation calls for the need to ponder: Have these agreements lost their significance in managing the dispute?

It is also necessary to note that to further enhance the protocols, both India and China have also adopted various bilateral mechanisms for managing peace and stability at the border. These CBMs are practiced to maintain checks and control over any unilateral behaviour along the disputed border. The key mechanisms at play at the political and military levels are listed in Tables 5.3 and 5.4.

Table 5.3: Bilateral Mechanisms at the Political Level between India and China

Institutional Mechanism	*Year*	*Objective*	*Meetings Held*	*Focus*
Special Representatives Talks	2003	Mechanism to explore the framework of a boundary settlement	22 Rounds of Talks (last held in December 2019)	To find a solution to the settlement of the boundary
Annual Defence Dialogue (ADD)	2007	Mechanism for consultation and co-operation on defence and security issues between the two countries	9 Rounds of Dialogue (last held in 2018)	To improve ties between the Armed Forces of India and China as well as exchange views on regional and global security issues of mutual concern
Working Mechanism for Consultation and Coordination on India-China Border Affairs (WMCC)	2012	Mechanism for consultation and co ordination for management of India-China border areas as well as exchange views on strengthening communication and cooperation, including between the border security personnel of the two sides	20 Meetings (of which 6 virtual meetings; last held in December 2020)	To manage relations between the troops on the ground in border areas

Source: Author.

Table 5.4: Bilateral Mechanisms at the Military Level between India and China

Institutional Mechanism	Border Personnel Meeting between Indian Army and the PLA- Held at the Formation Commander-level					
Year	Meetings have been held since 1990s					
Meeting Points	**5 Meeting Points** *(The meeting points were established after signing of the BDCA agreement in 2013)*					
	Name of the Point	Samarlungpa	Chushul	Nathu La	Bum La	Kibithu
	Indian State/UT	UT of Ladakh	UT of Ladakh	Sikkim	Arunachal Pradesh	Arunachal Pradesh
	Chinese Prefecture	Ngari Prefecture in TAR	Ngari Prefecture in TAR	Xigaze in TAR	Nyingchi in TAR	Nyingchi in TAR
	2 Proposed Meeting Points					
	Name of the Point	Lipulekh Pass	Chumar/Demchok			
	Indian State/UT	Uttarakhand	UT of Ladakh			
Objective of BPMs	Mechanism to facilitate cooperation and peace at the disputed border through consultation and interaction between the two armies.					
Conduct of BPMs (2 Types of BPMs)	**Ceremonial Meetings** These meetings are held yearly to commemorate five key occasions. This is customary in nature.					
	Date	1 January	26 January	14 April	15 May	15 August
	Event	New Year	Republic Day of India	Harvest Festival	PLA Day of China	Independence Day of India
	Flag Meetings These meetings are held between the two sides at the local/unit commander level to register their protest over any incident of transgression as well as other areas of mutual concern given the differing perception of the LAC between the two countries. This is conducted as per circumstances and situations of crisis without any fixed agenda unlike BPMs.					
Intention	To resolve local issues of border incidents arising out of the patrolling of the disputed areas, prevention of flare-ups and fostering confidence amongst troops guarding the border on both sides.					

Note: UT – Union Territory
Source: Author.

Furthermore, both the Indian and Chinese armies also have a 'hotline' at the local commander-level in order to communicate and coordinate the meetings and BPMs. In addition, both India and China also hold joint military exercises to further add to the trust building between the two countries, as noted in Table 5.5.

Table 5.5: Military Exercises between the Indian Army and the PLA (2007-2019)

Institutional Mechanism	Joint Military Hand-in-Hand Exercise	
Year	2007	
Objective	Mechanism to conduct company level joint training on counter-terrorism operation in semi-urban terrain under United Nations mandate	
No. of Exercise Conducted	8 Military Exercises	
Timeline of Exercise	*Year*	*Place*
	2007	Kunming, China
	2008	Belgaum, India
	2009-2012	Suspended due to staple visa row
	2013	Chengdu, China
	2014	Pune, India
	2015	Kunming, China
	2016	Pune, India
	2017	Suspended due to Doklam Stand-off
	2018	Chengdu, China
	2019	Meghalaya, India
Intention	To improve the capabilities in fighting terrorism and promoting mutual understanding between the two armies.	

Note: In 2020, no military exercise was held, due to the Eastern Ladakh crisis.
Source: Author.

Given these mechanisms at play, one can state that while the CBMs did fail to 'resolve' the dispute, but have been instrumental in advocating 'dialogue' between the two parties in times of crisis. For example, until December 2020, interactions under various mechanisms such as Special Representative level talks, WMCC meetings and Commander-level talks have been held between India and China to de-escalate the tensions.

To which, one can suggest that, if not quelling the risks altogether, the CBMs have acted as an incremental fix over time to the protracted boundary dispute. The mechanisms have certainly helped in management of the dispute by ensuring relative peace amidst border tensions, as also evident from the crisis in Eastern Ladakh. However, the fact remains that 'peace' at the border is temporary. What is worrisome is that the boundary between India and China is not just disputed, but is increasingly exhibiting signs of being volatile thus, making the LAC a flashpoint in South Asia. Here, the query to ask is: Is China seeking to settle the border with India? The answer is 'No'.

To settle the border, the precursor is set by Article III of the 2005 Agreement between India and China, which categorically mentions that:

> "Both sides should, in the spirit of mutual respect and mutual understanding, make meaningful and mutually acceptable adjustments to their respective positions on the boundary question, so as to arrive at a package settlement to the boundary question. The boundary settlement must be final, covering all sectors of the India-China boundary".[32]

In this context, it is imperative to note that except for India and Bhutan, China has settled the border disputes with 12 of its neighbours and got 'differences' resolved on its own terms and conditions. This is the legacy that the treaties of Argun (1858) and Peking (1860) have bestowed upon China: "never bargain from a position of weakness".[33] This is also the reason why China has taken such a long time to resolve its border disputes with its neighbours.

Interestingly, two patterns are found in China's border settlement behaviour:[34] First, it is a harder bargain when China's own security interests or economic interests have been the prime concern (Russia). And second, it compromises only when its internal stability is threatened (Central Asia).[35] Specifically, in the case of India, China is sensitive to the strategic significance of the border, that is, the eastern sector is sensitive due to the large Tibetan population; the middle sector is an area that has some key mountain passes between Tibet and India on the western side of Nepal; and the western sector is strategically important as it connects Xinjiang to Tibet. This strategic component thereby explains China's attitude of seeking concessions from India on the border. For instance, one of the biggest sticking point to the resolution is China's insistence that the status of Tawang in Arunachal Pradesh, the birthplace of the sixth Dalai Lama, is 'non-negotiable'. As Ananth Krishnan in his book *India's China Challenge* notes:[36]

> "In a 2017 article, Dai [Bingguo][37] suggested that a resolution would be possible only if India made some concessions in the eastern sector, with both sides having ruled out a status-quo resolution. Tawang, he wrote, was an 'inalienable' part of Tibet and that a boundary

> settlement would not be possible unless India agreed to make concessions over here. But if India did so, China would also make concessions in Aksai Chin, according to Dai. 'The major reason the boundary question persists is that China's reasonable requests [in the east] have not been met. If the Indian side takes care of China's concerns in the eastern sector of their border,' he said, 'the Chinese side will respond accordingly and address India's concerns elsewhere'".[38]

This Chinese perspective clearly highlights Beijing's prioritisation of its strategic interests when it comes to the border, and rightly brings into perspective as to why it is not in the Chinese interest to concede to India. Rather, China thinks otherwise. However, the Eastern Ladakh stand-off has not just exposed Beijing's hardened stand but has also clarified China's reluctance to concede even in Aksai China – thus, defying Dai Bingguo's proposition.

In this context, what makes the settlement of the boundary an imperative concern can be understood in a three-fold perspective: First, the 22 rounds of talks have failed to reach a constructive resolution. More importantly, unlike 2005, when the two countries signed the *Political Parameters and Guiding Principles for the Settlement of the India-China Boundary Question*, the border talks have become more customary between India and China without any remarkable progress. Second, the increasing episodes of transgressions and stand-offs exemplify that "maintaining peace and tranquillity at the border" has become a rhetoric. These incidental fallouts have constantly put the status quo at check, indicating the growing instability along the LAC. And third and most important, the increasing phenomenon of 'upped ante' given the elevated military build-up by the two countries along the border, has heightened the security dilemma, further increasing the stakes on either side.

Notwithstanding these factors, one cannot dismiss China's own growing insecurities vis-à-vis India. That is, China can no longer afford to underestimate India's military competitiveness, which has caused a significant shift in China's attitude towards India. Unlike in the past, India now is a potential threat for China and can be called as China's new found territorial 'insecurity', as evident from the Chinese public opinion highlighted in Figure 5.2 below. Here, the two significant observations to note, are: First, India ranks third in order after USA and

Japan in Chinese perception of countries that pose a military threat to China. Second, the threat perception towards India has increased. This change of perception towards India can be argued to be a direct outcome of India's intervention at Doklam in 2017 and more specifically, a strong resistance at Eastern Ladakh in 2020. To which, one can rightly argue that India's strong retaliation has significantly raised China's own security concerns. Wherein, for China, its policy of settlement of the borders (as noted in 12 countries with which it has resolved the borders) mostly on its own 'terms and conditions', has become a hard bargain in case of India. Therefore, this complexity calls for China's military activism at the LAC.

Figure 5.2: Chinese Public Opinion on Countries/Regions Posing a Military Threat to China

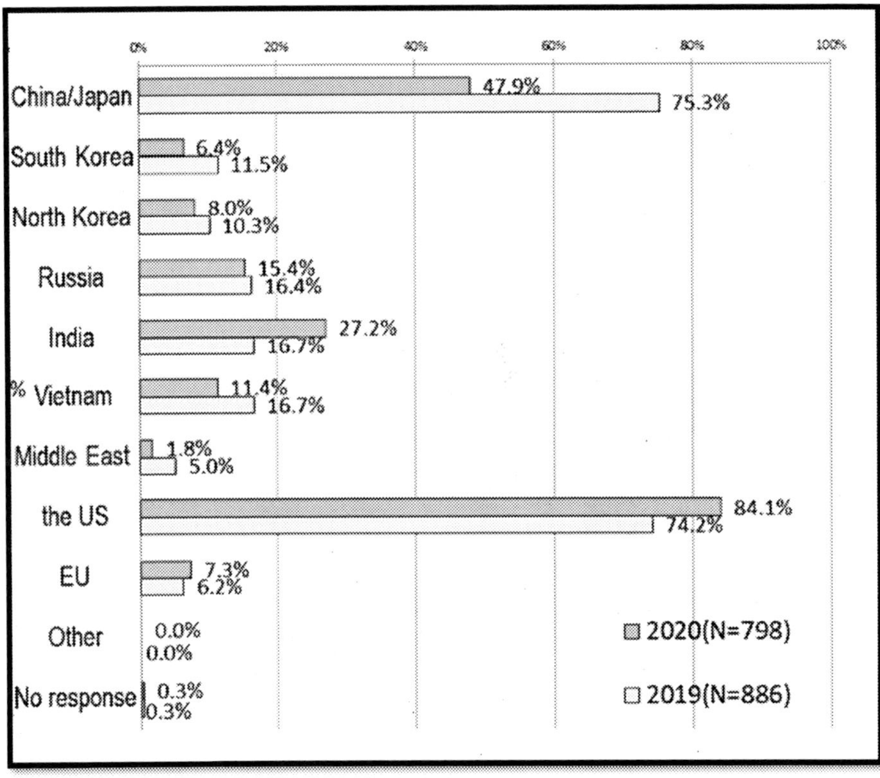

Source: Adapted from The Genron NPO (2020).[39]

How China Acts & Reacts on the Border

What is striking to note, China is now encroaching in areas that were earlier not disputed, as evident from the PLA's recent advances at the LAC in Eastern Ladakh. This has caused new additions to the existing key areas of dispute along the LAC, such as the 'Galwan Valley', where, so far no such dispute existed. But, in the aftermath of the clash in June, Beijing asserted sovereignty over the "entire" Galwan Valley, "a new claim and a significant change to the territorial status quo".[40]

Manoj Joshi notes that as per the relevant historical maps where China shows Aksai Chin as being within its border, both the Chip Chap and the Galwan river valleys are on the Indian side of the LAC.[41] However, in the current times, China is exemplifying a departure from its long-held position. For instance, on 19 June 2020, in his statement on the 'events in the Galwan valley', Chinese spokesperson Zhao Lijian stated:

> "Galwan Valley is located on the Chinese side of the Line of Actual Control in the west section of the China-India boundary. For many years, the Chinese border troops have been patrolling and on duty in this region. Since April this year, the Indian border troops have unilaterally and continuously built roads, bridges and other facilities at the LAC in the Galwan Valley".[42]

On the contrary, on 20 June 2020, India's Ministry of External Affairs issued a statement at the "All Party Meeting of 19 June" suggesting that the violence in Galwan was a result of the Chinese side "seeking to erect structures just across the LAC and refused to desist from such actions".[43] In refuting China's position on 'Galwan valley', the MEA issued another statement suggesting:

> "The position with regard to the Galwan Valley area has been historically clear. Attempts by the Chinese side to now advance exaggerated and untenable claims with regard to Line of Actual Control (LAC) there are not acceptable. They are not in accordance with China's own position in the past. Indian troops are fully familiar with the alignment of the LAC in all sectors of the India-China border areas, including in the Galwan Valley".[44]

The shifts in China's LAC perceptions only clarifies its intention to alter the LAC in the Galwan area, a similar approach to its earlier advances in the case of Pangong Tso and Depsang. That is to suggest, China is exploiting the ambiguity on where its version of the LAC lies for purposes that are not quite clear but could well have little to do with the border itself.[45]

Here, two observations can be made on China's behaviour:[46] First, China practices a very subtle way of intruding and then claiming any land which it considers to be part of its territory while China encroaches towards unclaimed boundaries and starts construction activities and when challenged, Beijing retaliates and justifies its actions under the pretext of safeguarding 'its' territory. Second, China adopts punishing its neighbours with punitive action in order to take the pressure off its internal instability.[47] This is evident from China's growing military activities along the LAC through transgressions, stand-offs, infrastructure build-up, conduct of military drills in Tibet, and similar such actions. These Chinese activities have made the LAC 'active' over time – thus, calling for India to be on the alert.

I. China's Actions: Transgressions,[48] Stand-offs, and Political Opposition

In asserting its claims, the PLA's behaviour along the India-China border is demonstrated by encroaching moves that exemplify its intention of physically occupying certain areas of the LAC, and preventing the movement of Indian patrols. It is evident from the increasing trend of Chinese transgressions along the LAC and episodes of stand-offs, mainly in areas where claims of the two countries overlap, as noted in Tables 5.6, 5.7, and 5.8, respectively.

Table 5.6: Incidents of Chinese Transgressions (2013-2020)

Year	*No. of Incidents*
2013	411
2014	334
2015	350
2016	273
2017	426
2018	326
2019	663 [49]
2020*	170 (130 in Ladakh) as on May 2020

Note: The transgressions are recorded from 2013 as it marked the DBO-Chumar stand-offs- first since the 1987 Sumdorong Chu stand-off.

*In 2020, the rate of Chinese transgression is expected to be higher, given the stand-off in Eastern Ladakh.

Source: Annotated by the Author based on data collected from various sources such as the Ministry of External Affairs and Indian newspapers.

Table 5.7: Major Sites of Chinese Transgressions on the LAC (2015-2019)

Location	*2015*	*2016*	*2017*	*2018*	*2019*	*Total*	*% Overall*
Pangong Tso	164	77	112	72	142	567	25
Trig Heights	92	64	127	99	116	496	22
Burtse	67	50	75	83	157	432	19
Dichu*	69	65	90	37	68	329	14.5
			Minor Sites				
Galwan River	0	1	4	1	0	6	-
Naku La*	0	0	0	2	2	4	-

Note: *Eastern Sector; the rest all Western Sector. The 2020 transgression record will be higher.

Source: Adapted from Singh (2020).[50]

Table 5.8: Major Episodes of Stand-offs (1962-2020)

Year	*War/Stand-off/Incident*	*Sector*
1962	Sino-Indian Border War	Multiple Sectors
1967	Nathu La and Cho La Skirmishes	Eastern Sector
1975	Tulung La Incident	Eastern Sector
1986-87	Sumdorong Chu Stand-off	Eastern Sector
2013	DBO and Chumar Stand-offs	Western Sector
2014	Demchok Stand-off	Western Sector
2015	Burtse Incident	Western Sector
2017	Doklam Stand-off	Eastern Sector
2020	Naku La Incident and Eastern Ladakh Stand-off	Eastern Sector and Western Sector

Source: Author.

Here, it is significant to note that in addition to the transgressions and stand-offs, China also asserts its claims, especially in the eastern sector by lodging routine protests on visits of Indian leaders and the Dalai Lama to Arunachal Pradesh, as noted in Table 5.9.

Based on an overall assessment of the pattern of Chinese actions along the LAC, some of the key observations made, are as follows: First, the frequency of China's transgressions in recent times reflect the ineffectiveness of the 2013 Border Defence Cooperation Agreement that enumerates various mechanisms to maintain peace and stability at the LAC. Arguably, the episodes of Chinese transgressions not just showed an uptick but have also intensified in due course of time both in scope and scale.

Second, the PLA's forays along the LAC are exhibiting transgressions in new areas, a tactic to further reify Beijing's claims. For instance, the areas under dispute were mainly: Namka Chu, Sumdorong Chu, Asaphila, Longju and Yangste in Arunachal Pradesh; Barahoti in Uttarakhand; and Trig Heights and Demchok in Ladakh. However, in recent times, China's transgressions are mainly witnessed in areas such

Table 5.9: China's Reaction to Visits of Indian Leaders and the Dalai Lama to Arunachal Pradesh (2013-2020)

Month-Year	*No. of Visits/Leadership*	*China's Official Response*
Nov. 2013	1 Visit: President Pranab Mukherjee	Beijing opposes the 'visits' on the following three points: (a) China's position on the eastern sector of the China-India boundary is consistent and clear. (b) The Chinese government has never recognised "Arunachal Pradesh". (c) India should refrain from taking action that complicate the boundary question but take action to uphold peace and tranquillity of the border area.
2014	No Visit	
Feb. 2015	1 Visit: Prime Minister Narendra Modi	
2016	No Visit	
2017	2 Visits	
Apr. 2017	Dalai Lama	
Nov. 2017	President Ram Nath Kovind	
2018	2 Visits	
Feb. 2018	Prime Minister Narendra Modi	
Jul. 2018	The Dalai Lama	
2019	2 Visits	
Feb. 2019	Prime Minister Narendra Modi's Visit	
Nov. 2019	Union Defence Minister Rajnath Singh	
Feb. 2020	1 Visit: Union Home Minister Amit Shah's Visit	

Source: Annotated by the Author with reference to data collected from the MEA, Chinese Government sources, and Indian and Chinese newspapers.

as DBO, Depsang, Galwan, Gogra Post, Hot Springs, Pangong Tso, Demchok and Chumar in the western sector; and Dichu areas in the eastern sector-thus, adding new areas to China's old claims.

Third, in recent years, as compared to Arunachal Pradesh, China's transgressions have mainly risen in the Ladakh area, as evident in the major stand-offs since 2013 in DBO, Demchok and Chumar (as noted in Table 5.7). This trend highlights that Eastern Ladakh is a major flashpoint between India and China along the LAC, as evident from the 2020 stand-off. Furthermore, it also clarifies China's strong intention in safeguarding Aksai Chin, which is under Beijing's control, unlike Arunachal Pradesh which is controlled by India. Owing to this asymmetry, one can argue that Beijing's such a stance is guided by the acceptance that 'abandon what you cannot have'.

Fourth, Sikkim and Himachal Pradesh, which remain comparatively less disputed, are exhibiting new signs of Chinese ingress-making the LAC 'active' at all points.

Fifth, China's behavioural pattern along the India-China border also complies with its 'salami-slicing' strategy as witnessed in the case of South China Sea, wherein it encroaches and takes control of disputed areas. In this case, China's repeated acts of transgression can be attributed to its 'bit-by-bit' policy of securing its claims, a way to increasingly test India's resolve.

And finally, China's intention lies in changing the territorial status quo by asserting sovereignty over new claims.

II. China's Adventurism in Eastern Ladakh: An Assessment

Of all the incidents in the past, the Eastern Ladakh stand-off has emerged as the longest and most intensified since the 1986-87 Samdorong Chu stand-off and the 73-day Doklam stand-off in 2017. It is significant to note that the signs of China's adventurism in Eastern Ladakh began in April-May 2020 with the PLA's heightened activities in the Tibetan plateau, resulting in transgressions across the LAC at multiple junctions, mainly Pangong Tso, Hot Springs, Galwan Valley and Depsang Plateau.

On 5 May, around 250 Indian and Chinese troops clashed at Finger 5 on the northern bank of the Pangong Tso. This was followed by an incident near Naku La Pass in the Sikkim sector. More importantly, India's state-led Intelligence agencies reported two episodes of incursion by PLA helicopters in India's air space in the LAC; the first one recorded on 11 April, almost 7-9 miles into the Samdho region of Lahaul-Spiti district, and the other on 20 April, in the same region.[51] In addition, on 12 May, it was reported that Chinese military choppers flew close to the LAC in North Sikkim.

Figure 5.3: Flashpoints along the LAC in Eastern Ladakh

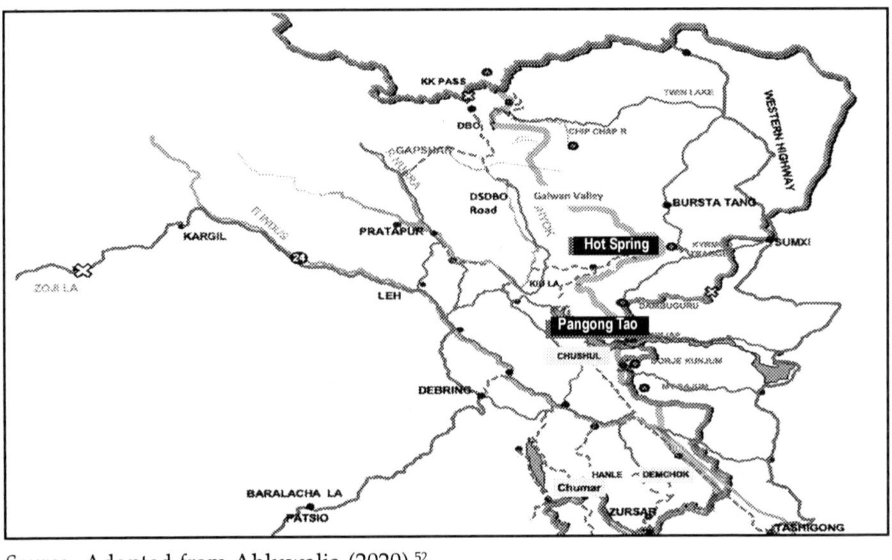

Source: Adapted from Ahluwalia (2020).[52]

Table 5.10: The Unfolding of the Eastern Ladakh Stand-off (May-December 2020)

Date	*LAC Flashpoints*
May	Violent clash between Indian and Chinese patrols on the northern bank of Pangong Tso. Confrontation between Indian and Chinese soldiers in north Sikkim's Naku La area. Tensions simmer in northern bank of Pangong Tso and its 'Fingers', Galwan Valley and Hot Springs
June	Indian and Chinese soldiers engage in a violent clash at Galwan Valley Tensions simmer in Galwan Valley, Hot Springs and Gogra Post
August	Tensions simmer in southern bank of Pangong Tso

Exchanges to Mitigate Tensions (June-December 2020)

Political	*Diplomatic*	*Military*
Special Representatives Talks One Virtual Talk between India's National Security Advisor Ajit Doval and Chinese State Councillor and Foreign Minister Wang Yi. 5 Jul *Both sides agreed for "earlier complete disengagement".*	**17 June 2020** Telephonic conversation between Indian External Affairs Minister S. Jaishankar met Chinese Foreign Minister and State Councillor Wang Yi *Both sides agreed that "the overall situation would be handled in a responsible manner".* **14 August 2020** India's Ambassador to China, Vikram Misri met Major General Ci Guowei of the CMC and Director of the office of international military cooperation, and Liu Jianchao, deputy director of the CPC's central committee's foreign affairs commission, in Beijing. *Provided a brief on India's stance vis-a-vis the situation on the borders in eastern Ladakh.*	**Commander-level Talks** Eight rounds of talks held between India and China 6 Jun, 22 Jun, 30 Jun, 14 Jul, 2 Aug, 22 Sep, 13 Oct, and 6 Nov *Talks failed to break the deadlock* *Ninth round of talks on the agenda*
WMCC Meetings 6 Virtual Meetings of the WMCC 24 Jun, 10 Jul, 24 Jul, 20 Aug, 30 Sep, 18 Dec *No significant breakthrough*	**4 September 2020** Indian Defence Minister Rajnath Singh met Chinese Defence Minister Wei Fenghe on the sidelines of SCO Summit. *Details of the meeting not available.* **10 September 2020** Indian External Affairs Minister S. Jaishankar met Chinese State Councillor and Foreign Minister Wang Yi in Moscow on the sidelines of SCO Summit. *Both sides agreed on a "Five Point Consensus".*[53]	

Source: Annotated by the Author based on data collected from the MEA, Chinese Government sources, and Indian and Chinese newspapers.
Note: The data has been recorded only till 31 December 2020.

Specifically, India's Ministry of Defence (MoD) reported that Chinese aggression along the LAC has been on the rise, especially in Galwan Valley, since 5 May, with transgressions noted in the areas of Kurang Nala, Gogra and the north bank of Pangong Tso on 17-18 May.[54] In assessing the situation on the ground, the report pointedly stated that the "present situation arising from unilateral aggression" by China continues to be sensitive, and the present stand-off "is likely to be prolonged".[55] Highlighting the intensity of the situation, in early June, Indian Defence Minister Rajnath Singh acknowledged that China had moved troops in "significant numbers".[56]

What makes China's transgressions in Eastern Ladakh an important case in point is the 'changing pattern' of the PLA's behaviour that exhibits a clear departure from the past routine stand-offs. To argue so, as in Eastern Ladakh, PLA's behaviour was orchestrated with engagement at multiple points over a wide front with large-scale regular forces, deliberate transgressions, violent physical confrontations and resultant casualties.[57] In addition, China also opened another front almost 1,500 km away in Sikkim at Naku La on 9 May. At the foremost, the 2020 skirmishes represented a direct manifestation of Beijing's assertive foreign policy, especially as it evolved under the COVID-19 pandemic under its "Wolf Warrior Diplomacy"; but a close watch of the events that unfolded since April/May 2020, certainly pointed towards "more of a [Chinese] design than a default".[58] Highlighting this aspect, the 2020 Annual Report of the U.S.-China Economic and Security Review Commission categorically states:

> "Some evidence suggested the Chinese government had planned the incident, potentially including the possibility for fatalities. For instance, several weeks prior to the clash Defense Minister Wei made his statement encouraging Beijing to "use fighting to promote stability". [...] Satellite images depicted a large Chinese build-up in the Galwan Valley, including potentially 1,000 PLA soldiers, the week before the deadly skirmish".[59]

In this regard, China's action along the LAC resonates Wei's statement, as it indicates Beijing's intention to proactively initiate military tensions with its neighbours [India] to project an image of strength amidst its deteriorating external security environment.[60] In addition, former Indian Foreign Secretary Shyam Saran posits that the skirmish can be interpreted as a bid by Beijing to "warn New Delhi" against aligning more closely with Washington on geopolitical matters.[61] To validate, in May 2020, China's state-run media *Global Times* in its editorial warned India of not engaging in "US-China confrontation", by stating:

> "If in a new Cold War, India leans towards the US or becomes a US pawn attacking China, the economic and trade ties between the two Asian neighbors will suffer a devastating blow".[62]

In view of this 'warning', it is interesting to note that against China's actions; India not just responded militarily but also by other means such as by banning popular Chinese apps and imposing restrictions on Chinese imports.

Undeniably, it can be argued that Chinese actions highlight an 'expansionist design' that aims to bring new territorial enclaves under its control. This is evident from China's intention of keeping the LAC active simultaneously at different points, such as on the northern bank of the Pangong Tso, at the Hot Springs, and in the Galwan Valley, all along the LAC in Eastern Ladakh. If China's goal, as Tanvi Madan, argues, was :

> ""to acquire territory ... [the Chinese government] might deem the moves a success." However, if Beijing intended to dissuade India from building infrastructure on its side of the LAC or warn it against aligning with the United States, however, "then the Chinese moves have been ineffective, if not counterproductive"".[63]

Most importantly, it is argued that China's current act by design suggests that Beijing seeks to eventually control the entire Aksai Chin plateau (on which parts of Ladakh are located). China has laid claim to this region since the 1950s, but as India-China rivalry intensified after the Cold War, Beijing attempted to gradually bring bits and pieces of the disputed frontier under its de facto authority.[64] Here, as the term "de facto authority" appears to be inadequate, given the absence of maps that clearly delineate which areas each side actively controls, China's creeping appropriation of territory cannot be either contested or contained except by physical Indian obstruction.[65]

Specifically with reference to the 'intensity' of the stand-off, the query remains: What explains China's provocation in Eastern Ladakh? In assessing the various perspectives, one factor that looms large is China's increasing insecurity and anxiety over Aksai Chin. In light of which, China's provocative behaviour at the LAC can be explained under two aspects: At the foremost, it is China's anxiety over India's infrastructure build-up in close proximity to the LAC, especially the 255-km long Darbuk-Shyok-DBO (DSDBO) road that runs almost parallel and at places very close to the LAC, that extends up to the base of the Karakoram Pass. In view of this, China's actions are largely perceived as pre-emptive designs in responding to its own insecurity. To suggest so, as Lieutenant General V. K. Ahluwalia, former Army Commander of India's Central Command, argues that China's actions highlight two key aspects:[66] First, that China is apprehensive over a threat to Aksai Chin; mainly to the 179-km long part of China's Western Express Highway (G219) through Aksai Chin that connects Kashgar in Xinjiang to Lhasa in Tibet. Second, by simultaneously inching westwards ahead of the LAC, China wants to further dominate India's DSDBO road, and its feeder roads to the LAC.[67]

What makes China sensitive is the DSDBO's close alignment to the LAC near Galwan Valley, wherein important communication arteries to the China-Pakistan Economic Corridor (CPEC) over Khunjerab Pass, and the G219 lie immediately to the north of the Karakoram Pass.

Figure 5.4: Strategic Alignment of the DSDBO Road

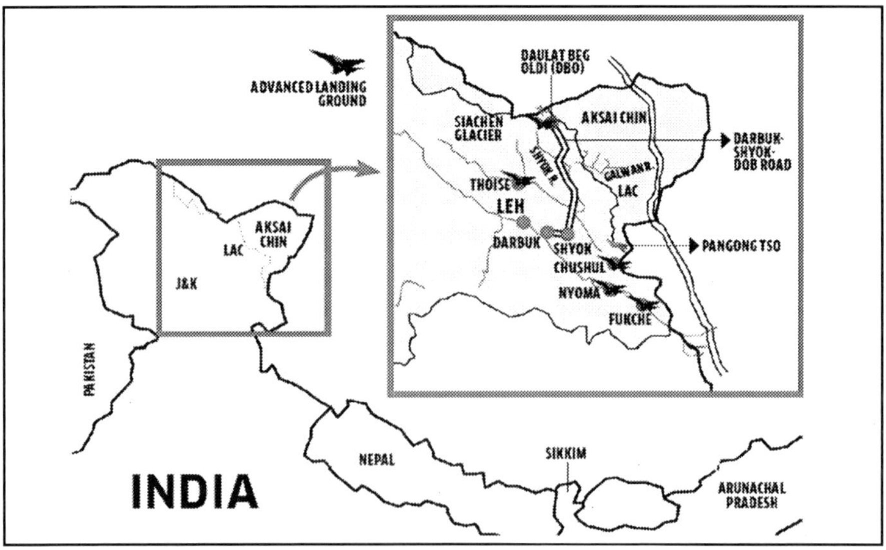

Source: Adapted from Guhathakurta (2020).[68]

This further justifies that the Chinese provocation in the Galwan Valley was an attempt to seek strategic domination in these areas that give access to the Aksai Chin plateau. Besides, China's activities are also bolstered by its Belt and Road Initiative, given to the west of the DBO is the region where China comes in proximity to Gilgit-Baltistan in Pakistan Occupied Kashmir (PoK). Furthermore, this area is also critical for Beijing as it is where the CPEC is getting constructed in PoK – which has also been one of the key objections raised by India in opposing the China-led BRI.

While the other aspect that explains China's provocative behaviour is India's declaration of Ladakh as a Union Territory in 2019. In this case, China's antagonism can be attributed to Beijing's perception of 'Ladakh' as a "Chinese territory in the western section of the China-India boundary".[69] To note, on 5 August 2019, India abrogated Article 370 of the Indian Constitution and gave assent to the Jammu and Kashmir Reorganization Act, 2019. As a result of this, the former state of Jammu & Kashmir was reorganised as the new Union Territory of Jammu and Kashmir and the new Union Territory of Ladakh on 31 October 2019. Officially, on 2 November 2019, India's Ministry of Home Affairs released a new map of India depicting the two new Union Territories, as noted below.

Figure 5.5: Map of the Union Territory of Jammu & Kashmir and Union Territory of Ladakh

Source: Adapted from *PIB* (2019).[70]

In raising opposition against India's move, China's Foreign Ministry issued a statement, saying:

> "China deplores and firmly opposes this. India is challenging China's sovereign rights and interests by unilaterally revising domestic law and administrative division. This is illegal, null and void. It will neither change the fact that the relevant region is under China's actual control nor produce any effect".[71]

China also opposed the subsequent publication of maps depicting the entire Aksai Chin as part of Ladakh as well as India's infrastructure build-up along the LAC.

To note, as on 31 December 2020, the tensions in Eastern Ladakh remain escalated. Given the stalemate situation, the de-escalation can only result after complete disengagement between the two armies at the LAC. In assessing the crisis, Srikanth Kondapalli argues that "China is trying to use a war of attrition to wear down the Indian forces".[72] While the stalemate still there, but one can rightly posit that the tensions will get diffused eventually, as neither side wants war and nor can settle in for a long haul. But the truth is, once the peace is restored at the LAC, it would be fragile. Henceforth, this would require India and China to handle the border with greater responsibility.

III. China's Reactions: 'Blame It' on India

The other aspect of China's behaviour on the border is found in Beijing's tendency to turn the opponent's actions as a precondition to its choice of reactions. In case of India, since 1962, at every instance of escalation or tension at the border, China has accused India to justify its own actions, – what can be called as China's 'blame it' on India syndrome. This was evident when China, under the leadership of Mao Zedong, meticulously turned Jawaharlal Nehru's 'Forward Policy of November 1961' into their goodwill by taking the adversary (India) by strategic surprise with its 'self-defence counter attack' on 20 October 1962. For instance, in the statement calling for a unilateral ceasefire in 1962, the Chinese government warned that if India violated the ceasefire, then:

> "China reserves the right to strike back in self-defense, and the Indian Government will be held completely responsible for all the grave consequences arising there from. The people of the world will then see even more clearly who is peace-loving and who is bellicose,

> who upholds friendship between the Chinese and Indian peoples and Asia-African solidarity and who is undermining them, who is protecting the common interests of the Asian and African peoples in their struggle against imperialism and colonialism and who is violating and damaging these common interests".[73]

What further adds to the element of 'putting the onus' on India is the Chinese reiteration of the fact that India should draw 'lessons from the 1962 War'. This was testified by Chinese media's propaganda offensive in the event of the 2017 Doklam stand-off, wherein a message to India pointedly stated "[r]emember your defeat in 1962 and accept China's position in the current stand-off at the Sikkim border".[74] This Chinese warning was met with a strong Indian response, as India's then Defence Minister Arun Jaitley remarked saying "[i]f they [Chinese] are trying to remind us, the situation in 1962 was different, the India of today is different".[75]

Furthermore, a *People's Daily* editorial titled "If This Can Be Tolerated, What Cannot?" on 22 September 1962 warned of serious consequences for India if the conflict lingered, stating that the "Chinese people would not tolerate the provocation by the Indian Army".[76] In view of this, the Chinese predominantly argue that it was Indian Prime Minister Jawaharlal Nehru's misunderstanding and miscalculation of the border situation that pushed China, then reeling under the impact of large-scale famine, into war with India.[77] More specifically, the Chinese pointedly argue that:

> "It was Nehru's 'Forward Policy'[78] of wanting to define the border unilaterally and go beyond the McMahon Line that really provoked China. Finally, Chinese leadership got irritated. The language used at that time (by leaders of the Communist Party of China (CPC) was something like 'teach (India) a lesson'".[79]

Likewise, in the case of the 2017 Doklam stand-off, China's reactive response towards India exemplified a similar response, that is, putting the onus on India, as China stated:

> "The Indian military's trespass into Chinese territory is a blatant infringement on China's sovereignty, which should be immediately and unconditionally rectified. [...] The withdrawal of Indian troops from Doklam remains a precondition for bilateral peace, and China will take all necessary measures to ensure its territorial integrity. [...] India should rectify its mistakes and show sincerity to avoid an even more serious situation creating more significant consequences".[80]

Similarly, commenting on the violent scuffle at the Galwan Valley, China stated that:

> "On the early morning of May 6, the Indian border troops crossed the LAC by night, trespassed into China's territory and built fortification and barricades, which impeded the patrol of Chinese border troops. They deliberately made provocations in an attempt to unilaterally change the status quo of control and management. The Chinese border troops were compelled to take necessary measures to respond to the situation on the ground and strengthen management and control in the border areas".[81]

What further adds to China's 'blame on India' attitude, is the tendency of putting the onus solely on India to 'abide by the agreements and avoid unilateral actions'. For whenever there is a discord along the border, China's position on India mainly reiterates the following:

> "China urges India to abide by the provisions of relevant conventions and treaties, earnestly follow the 1959 LAC, strictly restrict the activities of its border troops and faithfully maintain the peace and stability of the boundary areas of the two countries".[82]

Likewise, on India's declaration of 'Ladakh as a Union Territory', China's Foreign Ministry categorically stated:

> "Recently India has continued to undermine China's territorial sovereignty by unilaterally changing its domestic law. [...] We urge India to exercise prudence in words and deeds concerning the boundary question, strictly abide by relevant agreements concluded between the two sides and avoid taking any move that may further complicate the boundary question".[83]

This Chinese tendency of 'accusing India' in order to justify its own actions highlight the fact that even after over five decades of the 1962 War, the Chinese attitude towards India remains unchanged, as validated by the Chinese perception that the violence at Galwan Valley was the result of an Indian encroachment. This further proves that in Beijing's view, the onus of any and every crisis at the border rests with India, even when China is on the 'wrong side'. Besides, it also clarifies that the two countries have failed to build a consensus on the disputed territory.

China's Military Preparedness in the Western Theatre Command

Out of the five TCs, the WTC is geographically the largest TC within China, comprising a complex terrain including desert and high mountains, long borders, and challenging social conditions. Its jurisdiction includes Sichuan, Tibet, Gansu, Ningxia, Qinghai, Xinjiang and Chongqing. The WTC's theatre missions include supporting the PAP in maintaining internal stability in the restive Tibet and Xinjiang regions and disaster relief requiring liaison with civilian organisations; while its external responsibilities include responding to possible unrest in Central Asia under the auspices of the Shanghai Cooperation Organization (SCO).[84]

Under this new command structure, two provincial military commands, namely, Tibet and Xinjiang operate, wherein the Tibet Military Command (TMC) looks after the eastern (Sikkim, Bhutan and Arunachal Pradesh) and central sectors (Uttarakhand, Uttar Pradesh and Nepal) on the India-China border while the Xinjiang Military Command (XMC) looks after the western part of the border between the two countries, mainly Ladakh and possibly Himachal Pradesh. The WTC headquarters includes a joint operations command centre also located in Chengdu and the theatre Army headquarters based in Lanzhou; while the Strategic Logistics Support Force's subordinate Joint Logistics Support Centre is located in Xining for the WTC.[85]

Primarily, the WTC is responsible for responding to a conflict with India and terrorist and insurgent threats to and within western China. In its contingency planning, the PLA units located within the WTC include two group armies, other army units under the region's two military districts (Tibet and Xinjiang), three air force bases, and one rocket force base (as noted in Figure 5.6). Besides, the PAP units responsible for Xinjiang operations are also likely under the control of the WTC.

Figure 5.6: Western Theatre Command

Source: Adapted from the DoD Report (2020).[86]

The very fact that the WTC is 'India-centric' is both symbolic and significant to imply a substantial threat to India's security. As to note, the WTC covers the entire boundary with India from the northern tip of the Siachen Glacier to the tri-junction of India, China and Myanmar at Diphu Pass in Arunachal Pradesh, holding grave implications for India. These new dispensations are argued as signals of a new command structure being put into place to confront and pressurise India and embark upon another era of expansionism.[87]

Given this contingency, the WTC becomes important as it is responsible for mountain warfare at the border area with India, wherein the TMC holds special relevance for India. Specially, in the aftermath of the elevation in TMC's status, the strategic implications of it are far more significant. To note, in May 2018, the TMC was elevated to a level higher than other provincial military commands,[88] and also raised in authority by placing it under the direct jurisdiction of the PLA Ground Forces, an obvious move to advance TMC's operational potential and battle readiness. While the other 28 provincial military commands were put under the control of the newly-established National Defense Mobilisation Department of the CMC, which succeeded the former General Staff Department Mobilisation Department, a second-level (Corps Leader–grade) department, under the reorganisation of the four headquarters of the PLA.[89] The other exceptions were the Beijing Weifang District,[90] and the Xinjiang Military Command, which unlike the TMC are not yet under the jurisdiction of the PLA Army.

What also qualifies WTC's military preparedness is that it is a key beneficiary of China's military modernisation, as evident from the weapons and weapon systems stationed in the TMC (as explained in detail in the next section). In addition, China's combat readiness in the WTC is also witnessed in the training activities of the PLA. To note, the theatre contains the combined arms tactical training bases (CATTB)[91] located at Xichang and Qingtongxia.[92] These CATTBs are highly developed training facilities for both combined arms and joint training with the PLAAF wherein the Qingtongxia CATTB, established around 2000, includes an urban warfare training village, electromagnetic environment simulation, monitoring and control systems, as well as a 1:500 scale (900 meters × 700 meters) mock-up of the contested Aksai Chin border region.[93] In addition, the WTC contains joint training coordination zones for conducting joint exercises in the Tianshan Mountains, in Gansu Province, and in the Chongqing area.[94]

Figure 5.7: WTC and TMC under the Command and Control of the CMC

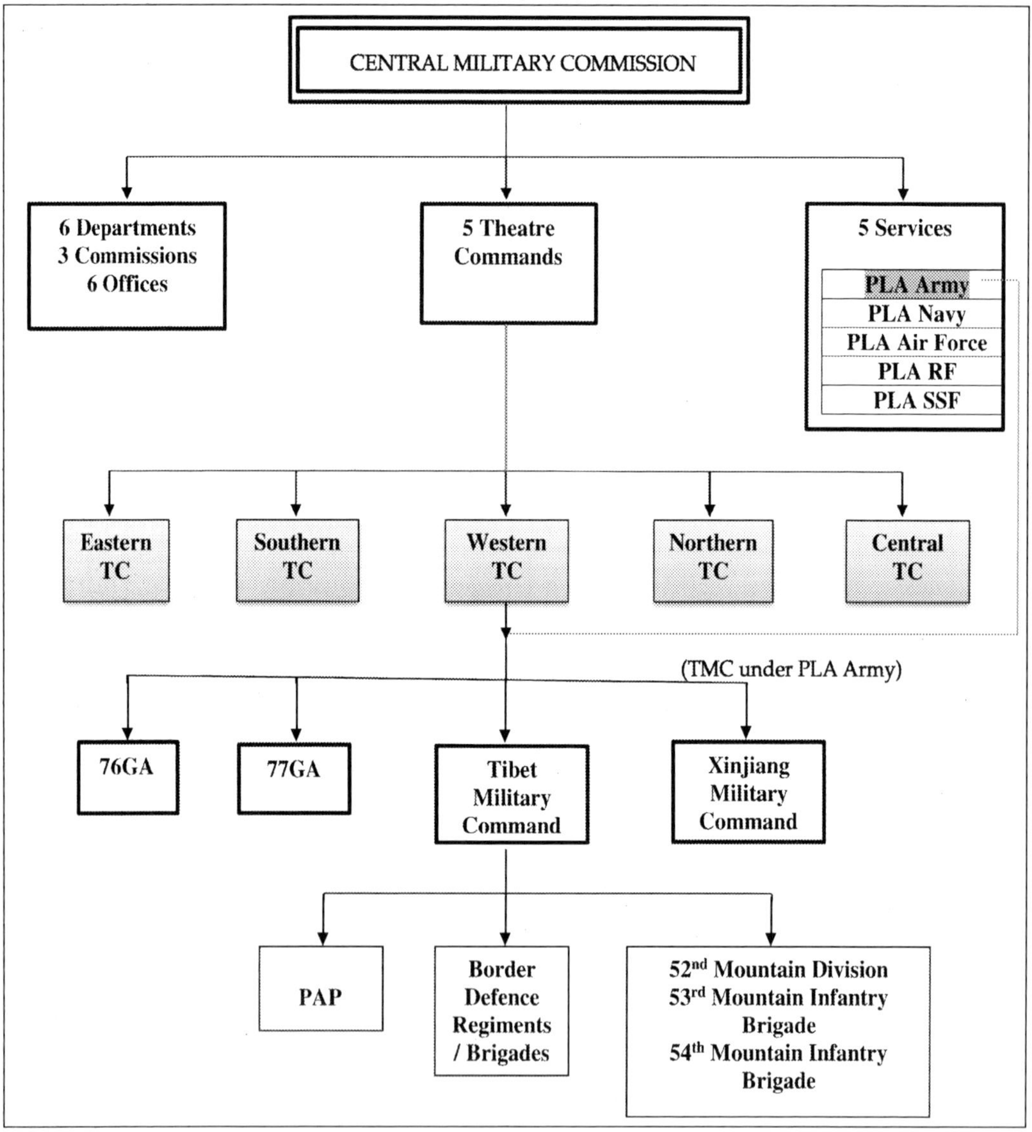

Note: GA—Group Army

Source: Adapted from Jash (2019).[95]

Table 5.11: Composition of the Tibet Military Command

Units Directly under Tibet Military District
15th Engineer Brigade (Dazi, Lhasa); Unit-77619, 308 Artillery Regiment, Lhasa; Unit-77611, 65th Air Defense Division, Lhasa; Unit-77616, 16th Vehicle Regiment, Lhasa; Communications Battalion, Lhasa; Special Operations Division, Lhasa; Unit-77606, Lhasa
52nd Mountain Division
Bayi village, Linzhi County), Unit-77675; Artillery Regiment (Nixi, Bayi village, Linzhi County) Unit-77678; 1st Battalion (Bujiu village, Linzhi County); 2nd Battalion (Yongjiu village, Linzhi County); 3rd Battalion (Yongjiu village, Linzhi County); 4th Battalion (Bujiu village, Linzhi County).
53rd Mountain Infantry Brigade
(Linzhi City, Milin County), Unit-77680; Artillery Regiment (Jiage village, Linzhi City, Milin County) Unit-77683; First Battalion (Wolong village, Linzhi City, Milin County); Second Battalion (Gangga village, Linzhi County); 3rd Battalion (Linzhi County);4th Battalion (Wolong village, Linzhi City, Milin County).
54th Mechanised Infantry Brigade (High Plateau Cavalry)
(Lhasa City, Duilongdeqing County), Unit-77625; an Artillery Regiment; a mechanized infantry First Battalion; a mechanized infantry 2nd Battalion; a mechanized infantry 3rd battalion; Tank Battalion; Chemical Warfare Battalion.
The Border Defence Regiments under the TMC
1st Border Defense Regiment (Shannan City, Longzi County) Unit-77629: China-India and China-Bhutan Border
2nd Border Defense Regiment (Shannan City, Cuona County) Unit-77635: China-India, China-Bhutan Border
Luoza County 5th Independent Battalion (Shannan City, Luoza County): China-Bhutan Border
3rd Border Defense Regiment (Shigatse City, Tingri County) Unit-77639: China-India and China-Nepal Border
5th Border Defense Regiment (Shigatse City, Saga County) Unit 77646: China-Nepal Border
6th Border Defense Regiment (Shigatse City, Yadong County) Unit-77649: China-India and China-Bhutan Border (Nathula outpost is the first outpost of South West, Zhangniangshe Outpost of the 6th Border Defense Regiment is the Yunzhong outpost)
Gyantse 1st Independent Battalion (Shigatse City, Gyantse County) Unit -77655: China-India and China-Bhutan Border
Gangba 2nd Independent Battalion (Shigatse City, Gangba County) Unit-77656: China-India Border (Chaguola Outpost is the High Plateau Red Border Defense Troops)
4th Border Defense Regiment (Chayu, Linzhi), Unit-77643: China-India Border
Medog County 3rd Independent Battalion (Beibeng village, Linzhi City, Medog County) Medog Garrison , Mofan BattalionÿUnit-77659: China-India Border
Milin 4th Independent Battalion (Nanyi Township, Linzhi City, Milin County): China-India Border

Note: There can be some changes to this composition since the restructuring of the PLA.
Source: Prepared by the Author with reference to Ranade (2015).[96]

I. Tibet Military Command & Preparedness Against India

The elevation of the TMC under the larger command and control structure of the PLA (as noted in Figure 5.7) calls for significant deliberation. This reform signifies two important implications: First, the amalgamation of the provincial military commands under one department has diminished their importance. And second, most importantly, the elevation of the TMC's political rank and bringing it under the PLA Army clarifies its exceptional status as well as its greater role in PLA's joint operations to conduct combat missions.

Specific to the TMC, apart from being the Tibet Military Region, its status has evolved since its inception, such as: in 1952, it came into force on the basis of the 18th Army of the Chinese PLA wherein it was a second-level border defence military region under the Southwest Military Region; in 1955, it was reorganised into a large military region; and in 1968 it was adjusted to a military rank under the command of the Chengdu Military Region.[97] The present elevation in the status of the TMC is both symbolic and most importantly, significant. Wherein, it denotes the priority China attaches to Tibet in its national security calculus, which is directly linked to its territorial and boundary dispute with India, and further aggravated by a challenge to China's sovereignty claims from the pro-Tibet independence forces.

Besides the elevated political status of the TMC, China has also revamped its military activities that exemplify its core concentration on combat missions. This can be assessed from the key developments in terms of new military equipment deployment, infrastructure build-up and military activities taking place in Tibet that significantly contribute to the enhancement of the combat capability of the TMC, as explained below.

On 27 December 2018, China's Ministry of National Defense revealed that a new "Type 15 lightweight Tank" has been commissioned by the PLA Ground Forces.[98] What makes it significant in China's combat missions are its three key features: First, unlike the PLA's other main battle tanks such as Type 99 and Type 96, Type 15 is significantly lighter with about 32 to 35 tonnes weight. In addition, its engine is capable of 1000 horsepower driving force, about twice that of the Type 62 tank it is replacing.[99] Second, in terms of firepower, Type 15 uses a new 105-mm tank gun, which is superior to the Type 88A tank and Type 59D tank equipped Type 94 105-mm tank gun. Wei Dongxu, a Chinese military expert, stated that "the Type 15 is equipped with a 105-millimeter main gun capable of firing armour-piercing rounds and gun launched missiles, making its firepower not much inferior to a heavier main battle tank".[100] Third and most importantly, the Type 15 tank is mainly meant for the rugged and mountainous terrain of the Himalayan region. Chinese analysts argue that this lightweight tank can "outperform" other Chinese tanks in combat operations in plateau areas like Tibet. To note, it has been categorically suggested that the Type 15 can be quickly deployed in Tibet "if border dispute reoccurs".[101] This implies the effective manoeuvrability of Type 15 to operate in high-altitude combat missions in Tibet, in case of any possible outbreak between India and China.

While in January 2019, the PLA Ground Forces in the TMC have been equipped with new vehicle-mounted howitzers, which Chinese analysts speculate to be the PLC-181 vehicle-mounted howitzer.[102] The howitzer has a 52-caliber cannon with a range of over 50 km and shoots laser-guided and satellite-guided projectiles. This characteristic feature, as argued by Song Zhongping, will significantly "boost the high-altitude combat capability of the PLA in Tibet".[103] To further add to the TMC's military preparedness, the other equipment that holds significance are a 10-ton Z-20 medium lift rotary-wing aircraft[104] and GJ-2 attack UAVs.[105] Furthermore, two KJ-500 Airborne Early Warning (AEW) aircraft are now deployed permanently in the Lhasa Gonggar airport,[106] seen as a fallout of the 2017 Doklam stand-off.[107] While the PLAAF's latest J-20 stealth aircraft has not yet been noticed in the skies above Tibet or Xinjiang, the latest J-10s (8), J-11s (20) and Mi17-IVs (8) are now deployed in the Western Theatre.[108] Besides, Chengdu J-20 air-superiority fighters have been noticed in the training missions on the Tibetan Plateau,[109] and amidst the tensions with India in Eastern Ladakh, H-6 bombers and Y-20 large transport aircraft attached to the PLA Central Theatre Command Air Force have been deployed in the Tibetan plateau region for training missions.[110]

The other critical aspect to note is China's stepped up infrastructure build-up activities in the Tibet region to enhance the PLA's military preparedness in terms of mobility and manoeuvrability of troops, equipment and logistics for undertaking combat missions. That is, given its quest for mechanisation, deployment of military equipment at high-altitude terrain such as Tibet require greater access, that is, greater communication with surrounding areas in the border region. Owing to this, China has upgraded roads, railways and air bases in Tibet. To note, there are 14 airbases in the WTC, of which the key bases are- Hoping, Bangda, Shiquanhe, Bayixincun and Kongka. In addition, there are two airfields in Lhasa, and in the aftermath of Doklam, China upgraded Tibet's four airbases including the Shigatse airbase and the Lhasa Gonggar, Qamdo Bamda, and Nyingchi airports;[111] and commissioned seven new helipads in frontier areas.[112] Besides, the airfield in Gar Gunsa, in the Ngari prefecture of Tibet, is a dual-use civil-military airfield. It is also reported that China is going to build three new airfields in the Tibetan areas of Lhoka, Xigaze and Ngari, bordering India, Bhutan and Nepal.[113]

Apart from airfields and airbases, China is also strengthening its capabilities by building connectivity through roads and railways. China has constructed 96,000 km of roads in Tibet by 2018, with over 4,000 km of highways added per year since 2012.[114] This includes the 409 km Lhasa-Nyingchi Highway (north of Arunachal Pradesh) built at a cost of US$ 5.8 billion that was commissioned in 2017 and a 135-km Yaán-Kangding expressway that was constructed at a cost of $ 3.3 billion making a second expressway from Sichuan to connect to Tibet after National Highway 318 which links up with Lhasa.[115] In addition, apart from the Gormud to Lhasa railway line commissioned in 2006, China also began construction of the 435 km Lhasa-Nyingchi railway line to be completed by 2021. And in 2018, China announced the 1,700 km long Sichuan-Tibet Railway project at a cost of US$ 36 billion to be completed by 2026 (see Figure 5.8).[116] This makes it the second such railway into Tibet after the Qinghai-Tibet Railway. The railway project consists of three major sections: the Chengya Railway (Chengdu-Ya'an), YaNying Railway (Ya'an-Nyingchi), and LaNying Railway (Lhasa-Nyingchi). Wherein, it is planned to run from Chengdu through Ya'an and Kangding and enter Lhasa via Qamdo (or Chamdo in Chinese) and Nyingchi.[117] It is to note, amidst tensions with India, in November 2020, Xi Jinping urged to advance construction of the Sichuan-Tibet Railway by calling the project "a major measure", with it playing a key role in facilitating the CPC's plans for governing Tibet as well as in safeguarding national unity, and consolidating border stability.[118]

Figure 5.8: Sichuan-Tibet Railway Project

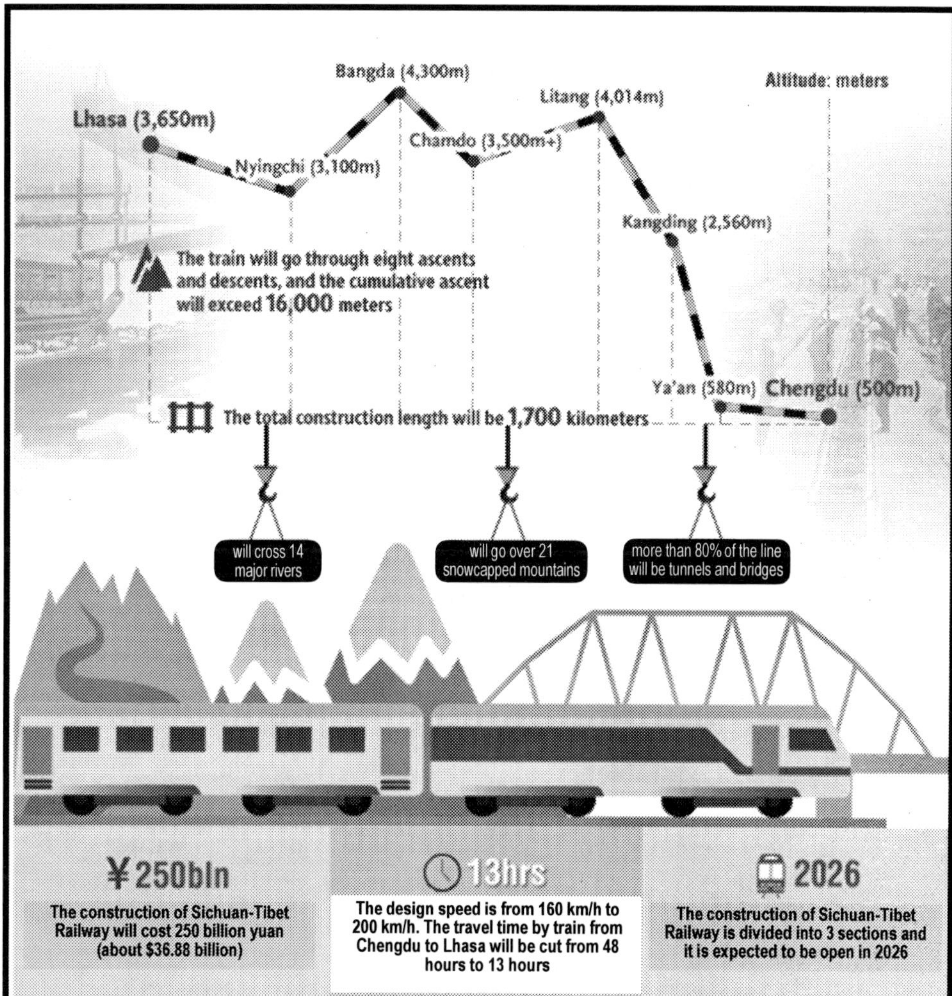

Source: Adapted from *Global Times* (2018).[119]

Primarily, China's heavy infrastructure build-up in Tibet is aimed at securing border stability. Specifically, it gives Beijing a strategically advantageous position to rapidly move additional forces to the border, to potentially strike at India at a time of its choosing.[120] For instance, Chinese analysts argue that with the Sichuan-Tibet railway, TAR will have "stronger capabilities in material transportation and logistical supplies" and mainly in a scenario of crisis with India, the railway will help with the "delivery of strategic materials" right up to the disputed India-China border.[121] As evident, in the initial phase of the 2020 stand-off, given the advantage of the infrastructure and mainly the connectivity of the Western highway and other state roads, the PLA was able to mobilise faster and gained numerical strength over Indian security forces deployed in Eastern Ladakh.[122] This further proves that China's infrastructure build-up in Tibet is mainly aimed at: troop mobilisation, deployment of military hardware (even strategic assets, if needed) and sustenance – with an objective to beef up China's military presence in TAR at large, and mainly in the forward areas of the disputed border with India.

These Chinese activities demonstrate the way active defence is played out at the LAC. Wherein, it clearly reflects intention as well as its increasing ability to effectively intervene at any sector of the LAC, at a time of its choosing – thus, raising significant security concerns for India.

II. Security Implications for India

The very fact of transforming to a Theatre Command structure in peacetime entails China's determination to hone its integrated joint operations capability. In this perspective, the TMC's elevated political status under the WTC added with the significant military developments both in terms of equipment deployment as well as training signify that this Chinese theatre ranks high in China's joint operational missions. Specifically, it remains prone to high-altitude warfare, as witnessed in the 1962 Sino-Indian war. The above preparations highlight China's active military preparedness, a direct outcome of Xi Jinping's defined guideline for the PLA to 'fight and win'. As noted, in the 19th Party Congress report, Xi clearly instructed the PLA for "military preparedness for all strategic directions" and combat readiness in "both traditional and new security fields".[123]

Specific to the TMC, China's contingencies are far more profound. To say so, in the Chinese perspective, in the 1962 war with India, China "failed to protect its fruits of victory due to poor logistics support" and lack of sustainable support from the local Tibetan residents, who "provided soldiers only temporary support".[124] In view of this, PLA's training drills conducted with the local population in Tibet is mainly aimed at testing the capabilities in terms of logistics, armament support capabilities and most importantly, civil-military integration in times of crisis given the longstanding internal divide due to the pro-Tibet independence forces.

To avert such risks, the PLA has stepped up its drills in terms of live-firing exercises to test the ability of the troops. For instance, in 2015, to avoid health contingencies due to high-altitude sickness, the PLA built oxygen stations in Tibet mainly for medical purposes; however, these stations are now being used for regular training.[125] PLA's training exercises in the WTC have featured offensive and defensive mountain and cold weather warfare training and long-distance movement of units. Specifically, the WTC focuses on relevant campaign scenarios to train troops for potential combat operations that include Anti-terrorism Stability Maintenance operations to combat internal unrest; Joint Border Counterattack Campaigns to defend against an attack (assuming that India would take the lead in launching an offensive) and regain lost territory; Mountain Offensive Campaigns; and Joint Fire Strike Campaigns[126] usually supporting another campaign, but also independent by themselves.[127]

For instance, in 2017, amidst the Doklam crisis, the PLA conducted an armoured brigade live-fire assault exercise in the Qinghai-Tibet plateau. It was carried out at 5,100 metres above sea level for the first time and included the PLA's most advanced battle tank, the Type 96B, aimed at testing "full combat readiness".[128] A *China Daily* report stated that the exercise was conducted by a ground combat brigade of the TMC and involved scenarios such as rapid deployment and multi-unit joint strike and anti-aircraft defence.[129] Commenting on the exercise, Beijing-based military analyst Zhou Chenming said that with the exercise, "PLA wanted to demonstrate [that] it could easily overpower its Indian counterparts" as against India, "China has a clear advantage in terms of speed of movement, fire power and logistics".[130]

While in 2018, the PLA conducted a military drill in the TAR to test the logistics and armament support capabilities and, most importantly, to test military-civil integration.[131] It was a first exercise of its kind in the region since the Doklam stand-off, and as argued, was aimed to "realise the country's goal of building a strong military in the new era".[132] In 2020, there has been an uptick in China's war games in Tibet amidst the tensions with India in Eastern Ladakh, as noted in Table 5.12.

Table 5.12: China's Major Military Drills (June-September 2020)

Month	*Military Drill*
June	PLA Tibet Military Command had "conducted a post-enemy penetration and attack drill. *The exercise involved anti-tank rockets, mortars, and grenade launchers to fire live ammunition under the full tactical background
	PLA conducted a night drill at an elevation of 4,700 meters in the foothills of Nyenchen Thangla (Chinese: Nianqing Tangulla) Mountains, located to the north of the Tibetan capital Lhasa. *PLA's 76th brigade, under the WTC, fired "more than 2,000 munitions, including mortar shells, rifle grenades and rockets" Tibet Military Region held comprehensive exercises in high-altitude regions
August	Tibet Military Command conducted a round-the-clock combined brigade strike exercises at an elevation of over 4,500 meters.
	Xinjiang Military Command conducted a tactical training by combined arms battalion in the hinterland of Tianshan Mountains.
September	At an average altitude of 5,000 metres in Tibet, a combined army brigade of the Tibet Military Command and the latest ground strikers of the PLAAF practised air-ground joint assault and control of enemy-occupied grounds. *It was the first-ever air-ground joint exercise.

Source: Annotated by the Author with reference to various sources available online.[133]

What do these military drills imply? Strategically, it can be argued that China is preparing for a worst-case scenario at the Himalayan border with India. To suggest so, preparations of this kind make the PLA more familiar with the high-altitude and further improves their combat capability and tactics if a contingency arises; also, the cost will be low when one is prepared. While tactically, China's provocative military drills can be seen as a way to build pressure on India.

Apart from the drills, the PLA also officially launched five militia groups, codenamed Snow Eagle Air Patrol, Snow Dove Polar Communication Team, Snow Wolf Extreme Climbing Team, Snow Fox Alpine Express Team, and Snow Mastiff Plateau Resistance Team – which are to take part in patrolling, communication and fighting.[134] This can be seen as a move to further push China's military-civil fusion in fighting against India at the border.

Besides, China has also cited the need to strengthen the control of airspace over the mountainous region. Calling it an urgent need to deal with any current threat from India, China has been strengthening the 3.5-generation fighter jets or even stationing more advanced fighters in the WTC, and as argued, will continue to do so.[135] These activities highlight China's increasing militarisation of Tibet through mobilising forces that include bombers, air defence troops, artillery, armoured vehicles, special forces and infantry units, paratroopers and others – a move to exemplify the PLA's capability and force projection against India. That is, the growing number of PLA's military exercises in Tibet is an indicator of the alarming threat that India faces at the LAC.

In training the TMC units for wartime operational missions, China seeks to decrease the need for pre-war preparations. Specifically, it enhances the combat effectiveness of forces in the WTC. In doing so, the TMC's agenda aims at achieving military-civil integration and advancing China's logistics support capabilities in the high-altitude to fight a contingency along the border with India. As Xi categorically remarked: "[i]mplementing the strategy of military-civilian integration is a prerequisite for building integrated national strategies and strategic capabilities and for realizing the Party's goal of building a strong military in the new era".[136] The leveraging of the civilian sector to boost the PLA's military's capabilities is the top priority in the agenda of what China calls its 'military-civil fusion' strategy.

To note, China's strategy is well-witnessed in the form of building Chinese settlements along the India border, a tactic to strengthen its territorial claims. For instance, amidst the stand-off in Eastern Ladakh, satellite imagery from Planet Labs (a US agency) suggested that China has constructed at least three villages in an area about five kilometres from Bum La Pass in western Arunachal Pradesh.[137] China's 'settlement' strategy resonates with Xi's 2017 urge to the herdsmen from a Tibetan settlement bordering Arunachal Pradesh to "set down roots in the border area" to safeguard "Chinese territory".[138] Explaining this 'civilian aspect', Brahma Chellaney argues:

> "China has been using a strategy of settling Han Chinese and Tibetan members of the Communist Party along the Indian border to strengthen its territorial claims and escalate border intrusions. Like it [China] used fishermen in the South China Sea, China uses civilian resources—herders and grazers—as the tip of the spear to intrude into Indian-patrolled Himalayan areas".[139]

In this perspective, the elevation of the TMC's profile and stepped-up military activities in the WTC holds key relevance for India. It is mainly centred on the strategic implications that these developments entail with regard to the future role of the TMC. To argue so, as Zhao Zhong, deputy director of the Political Work Department of the TMC stated, as quoted by *Global Times* "[t]he elevation of the authority level is not only an improvement for the troops' designation but also an expansion of their function and mission".[140] This rationale stands valid given the increasing military investment in TMC as noted in terms of induction of the new Type 15 tank and deployment of the PLC-181 vehicle-mounted howitzer, which were used in an artillery brigade in Tibet during the Doklam stand-off.[141] What also adds to the mechanisation is the stepped up infrastructure development to attain greater manoeuvrability in the high mountains, to support military operations in times of conflict.

These strategic developments further clarify the TMC's significant role in China's core objective to conduct joint operations rather than limited to being focused on mobilisation of national defence, as practised by the other provincial military commands. With training, manoeuvres and drills involving all arms and services, the PLA's military preparedness in the WTC is driven by Xi Jinping's core objective that calls for the armed forces to be able to respond quickly and effectively to contingencies, asking them to upgrade commanding capability of joint operations, foster new combat forces, and improve military training under combat conditions.[142] That is to suggest, such combat readiness signifies the future possibilities of the TMC undertaking combat missions and trans-regional operations, which then becomes a primary concern for India. This further makes it imperative for India to revise its own combat effectiveness against China. Although China has dismissed such India-centric intentions; however, for India, China's intentions in this regard cannot be outlawed. To argue so, in China's territorial quest, the border with India is the only theatre where a high-altitude war can take place in the 21st century, if at all.

India's China Policy: Need for a Change

There should not be any doubt in reading the Chinese intention, which aims at changing the status quo along the border in favour of Beijing. The recurrent ingress is a sign of Beijing's reluctance to resolve the boundary dispute with New Delhi, be it now or in the future. This is further exemplified by the fact that China's acts of transgressions are are increasingly becoming tactics to test India's resolve. Besides, deception is an integral part of China's military strategy, which is well-witnessed in case of China's military activism at the LAC.

In this regard, Galwan was another litmus test that significantly clarified Beijing's intention to keep the LAC active despite talks on seeking a resolution. New Delhi can no longer afford to overlook these red flags while reading between the lines and therefore, a change of policy towards the handling of the disputed border is needed more than ever. For, it can be strongly argued that China has no desire to either resolve the dispute or implement the key clauses of the agreements that call for the creation of a mutually acceptable LAC – hence, pending the resolution of the dispute. The truth is, the change of status quo at the LAC has significantly raised the risk of confrontation between the two nuclear powers, making the India-China border a potent regional hotspot.

With these dynamics at play, India's China policy needs a serious re-thinking. This calls for a change in the mindset by dismantling the old ways of dealing with China. This would require India to change its perception such as: First, as there are no permanent friends, or enemies but only permanent interests, India too needs to address China based on its own national interest, wherein a firm, non-compromising stand along the border should be the first policy principle. Second, Chinese acts of transgressions should not be treated as 'local' and 'normal'. It is to understand that China believes in 'testing the resolve', as already witnessed in Doklam and Galwan. Third, China's actions along the border with India are guided by the logic of 'salami slicing'- incremental approach towards securing its claims. Thus, in the near future, new differences will be added to the old claims. So, India should be prepared for Chinese adventurism along any sector and at any time. Fourth, China's actions are pre-mediated and top driven and thereby, not to be perceived as a fallout of a local misadventure. Sixth, 'deception' is the most important tool of Chinese warfare thus, a duality in 'what is said and what is done' should not be a surprise. Not to forget, this is the bottom line principle of China's 'art of war', which remains to be a constant in Chinese strategic military thinking. Therefore, the change in New Delhi's outlook is imperative, especially in the event of the Eastern Ladakh crisis.

To deal with the 'China challenge', New Delhi needs to step up its own activities. This can be done by: First, militarily, India needs to take four key measures: (a) strengthen its own defences by building infrastructure on its territory at the border; (b) strengthen its force structure and capabilities in both forward and depth areas; (c) boost up the modernisation process of the Indian Armed Forces under the *Atmanirbhar Bharat* initiative to meet the demands of multi-domain warfare; and (d) be prepared to simultaneously fight at the LAC and Line of Control (LoC) against the China-Pakistan nexus. These imperatives are necessary as when it comes to securing one's (India's) sovereignty, the choice is not to seek an 'alternative' but to remain firm in 'safeguarding one's own claims'.

Second, apart from the border, India needs to become more active in its own 'sphere of influence'- the Indian Ocean Region. There should be no doubt that while China seeks to lay its foothold, India is strongly anchored in the region and has a strategic advantage.

Third, India needs to make concerted efforts in maintaining coordinated and stable ties with its regional and extended neighbourhood. In this process, India should build defence and strategic partnerships and security dialogue mechanisms with friendly foreign countries.

Fourth, India needs to strengthen its strategic weight in the Indo-Pacific region by leveraging ties with its QUAD as well as QUAD-Plus (New Zealand, South Korea and Vietnam) partners. 'Non-alignment' is no more a policy option. In this regard, New Delhi has already taken its first steps by conducting the India-US bilateral tri-service amphibious military exercise "Tiger Triumph" in 2019; upgrading its ties with Australia to a "Comprehensive Strategic Partnership" signed under nine arrangements that include "Mutual Logistics Support" for their militaries in 2020; and most importantly, signing of the Basic Exchange and Cooperation Agreement (BECA) with the USA, promoting greater interoperability between the two militaries as well as transfer of high-end technology. These choices made by India validate the fact that hard power still calls the shots. For, it is no more balance of power but balance of threat compounded with balance of interests that tops the security and strategic agenda.

And fifth, India also needs to seize the opportunity as it is in a position to benefit from a potential shift in global supply chains from China. Concerted efforts should be made towards making India a preferred destination of foreign investments to capitalise on the growing demand from international manufacturers under the *Atmanirbhar Bharat* initiative.

Hence, India needs to seriously consider its China policy in the context of the Eastern Ladakh crisis, wherein the tensed border compounded with China's increasing power projection capabilities in South Asia and the IOR will have critical implications for India.

Conclusion

With no resolution reached, the boundary predicament between India and China has evolved from being 'protracted to that of becoming increasingly volatile', as evident from the Eastern Ladakh stand-off. In the long-term, there are little prospects that the two sides would settle their border differences. To say so, as the unwillingness to compromise has led to irreconcilable positions, and managing of the boundary question has taken precedence over resolution. Thus, the tensions at the LAC will only get intensified with time.

Specifically, the emerging situation at the LAC has aggravated China's territorial 'insecurity' that carries significant implications for India. The security dilemma is likely to get much heightened and will automatically result in attempts by China to change the status quo at the border, making India wary of Chinese activities. Here, two key observations can be made in terms of China's behaviour along the border: First, China's acts will only get aggressive towards India, if not diffident. As a result of which, border flare-ups will only get intensified, wherein one cannot dismiss Beijing's willingness to use force to neutralise the opposing force. Second, while 'limited' use of force cannot be ruled out but a 'war' against India is not on the Chinese agenda, not until Beijing has realised the Chinese Dream, which can only be achieved under a peaceful and stable neighbourhood. Besides, India's nuclear power status also significantly adds to the Chinese reluctance. Hence, the tensions at the border will remain.

While situational fallouts are increasingly becoming a norm at the border, but what plays the trick in the dispute is the lack of consensus between New Delhi and Beijing on the LAC, that has increasingly contributed to one's distrust in the intentions of the other. To which, only a timely check on each other's perceptions can help avoid a misadventure cropped from 'assuming the worst' out of a situation. This complexity calls for the need for the two countries to strictly adhere to the protocols to prevent any form of exchange of fire at the border.

It is, therefore, in the best interests of the two nuclear powers to refrain from adding new differences to the old dispute, for it only makes the case complicated and the boundary settlement gets further delayed. Thus, whether a packaged deal or a sector-wise settlement, it is time that the two countries take a step forward towards the resolution of the boundary dispute.

NOTES

1. Cited in John W. Garver (2006), "China's Decision for War with India in 1962" in Alastair Ian Johnston and Robert S. Ross (eds.) *New Directions in the Study of China's Foreign Policy*, Stanford, CA: Stanford University Press, p. 115.
2. Quoted in Liangyu (2017), "Xi: China loves peace, but never compromises on sovereignty", *Xinhuanet*, 1 August 2017, http://www.xinhuanet.com//english/2017-08/01/c_136490361.htm, accessed online 20 August 2020.
3. Ibid.
4. China has not confirmed casualties on its side. However, the Indian media reported that the PLA lost more than 43 soldiers. See, "China suffered 43 casualties in violent face-off in Galwan Valley, reveal Indian intercepts", *Hindustan Times*, 17 June 2020, https://www.hindustantimes.com/india-news/china-suffered-43-casualties-in-violent-face-off-in-galwan-valley-reveal-indian-intercepts/story-7JhOt8tC6cf C9bx3CUzrTI.html, accessed online 5 August 2020.
5. According to India, in October 1975, PLA soldiers ambushed an Indian patrol (of Assam Rifles) along the LAC in Arunachal Pradesh (then NEFA) resulting in the deaths of four Indian soldiers, while no Chinese deaths were reported. India blamed Chinese troops for crossing into Indian territory while China claims that it acted in self-defence and that Indian soldiers attacked Indian positions. For details, see Srijan Shukla (2020), "1975 Arunachal ambush-the last time Indian soldiers died in clash with China at LAC", *The Print*, 16 June 2020, https://theprint.in/india/1975-arunachal-ambush-the-last-time-indian-soldiers-died-in-clash-with-china-at-lac/442674/, accessed online 5 August 2020.
6. Joydeep Sen (2020), "India and China will avoid war but grow further apart", Oxford Analytica, 23 June 2020, https://dailybrief.oxan.com/Analysis/DB253456/India-and-China-will-avoid-war-but-grow-further-apart, accessed online 8 December 2020.
7. The McMahon Line was named after Lieutenant Colonel Sir Arthur Henry McMahon who, in the 1914 Simla Accord, proposed the 'line' to separate Tibet from India in the eastern sector.
8. Major Nirvikar Singh (2020), "China & the international law", *The Daily Guardian*, 7 November 2020, https://thedailyguardian.com/china-the-international-law/, accessed online 8 December 2020.
9. Ibid.
10. Post the letter of 1959, during his high-profile visit to New Delhi in 1960, Zhou Enlai had used the phrase "LAC" during a press conference, stating: "There exists between the two counties a line of actual control up to which each side exercises administrative jurisdiction," he said as part of a six-point proposal to maintain peace at the border. Furthermore, Zhou also specified that both sides should keep to the "[...] line of actual control and should not put forward territorial claims as pre-conditions, but individual adjustments may be made". For details, see Sutirtho Patranobis (2020), "China makes it official, wants to revert to 1959 LAC India has rejected many times", *The Print*, 29 September 2020, https://theprint.in/diplomacy/china-makes-it-official-wants-to-revert-to-1959-lac-india-has-rejected-many-times/512584/, accessed online 30 September 2020.
11. "Premier Chou En-lai's [Zhou Enlai's] Letter to Prime Minister Nehru", 7 November, 1959, History and Public Policy Program Digital Archive, Documents on the Sino-Indian Boundary Question (Peking: Foreign Language Press, 1960), p. 15, https://digitalarchive.wilsoncenter.org/document/175959.pdf?v=1e8bdb140ea 9671eecba1c 252bca0865, accessed online 10 September 2020.

12. Ibid., p. 16.
13. Shivshankar Menon (2016), *Choices: Inside the making of India's Foreign Policy*, New Delhi: Penguin/Allen Lane, p. 31.
14. Ibid.
15. Quoted in "After China Brings up '1959 LAC Alignment', India Says That Proposal Wasn't Accepted", *The Wire*, 29 September 2020, https://thewire.in/diplomacy/after-china-brings-up-1959-lac-alignment-india-says-that-proposal-wasnt-accepted, accessed online 1 October 2020.
16. Ministry of External Affairs, Government of India, "Notes, Memoranda and letters Exchanged and Agreements signed between The Governments of India and China", WHITE PAPER III, November 1959 - March 1960, http://www.archieve.claudearpi.net/maintenance/uploaded_pics/Corres_Nov59_Mar60.pdf, accessed online 10 August 2020. See, the section on "Letter from the Prime Minister of India to the Prime Minister of China, 16 November 1959".
17. See Manoj Joshi (2020), "Sino-Indian Border Deadlock: Time to rewrite India playbook", ORF Occasional Paper 269, Observer Research Foundation, 31 August 2020, https://www.orfonline.org/research/sino-indian-border-deadlock-time-to-rewrite-india-playbook-72495/, accessed online 15 September 2020.
18. The Johnson Line shows Aksai Chin to be under Indian control whereas the MacDonald Line places it under Chinese control while India considers the Johnson Line as the correct, rightful national border with China; however, China considers the MacDonald Line as the correct border with India.
19. Manoj Joshi (2020), "Sino-Indian Border Deadlock", n. 17.
20. Ibid. For details, see Shyam Saran (2017), *How India sees the world: Kautilya to the 21st century*, New Delhi: Juggernaut, pp. 131-138.
21. To note, on 23 January 1959, Zhou for the first time informed Nehru "that the Sino-Indian boundary has never been formally delimited", and stated that "there are certain differences" over the border; and proposed that the two sides maintain the status quo, "each side keep for the time being to the border areas at present under its jurisdiction and not go beyond them". Adding further, on 17 December 1959, Zhou told Nehru that "the line up to which each side exercises actual control in this sector is very clear, just as it is in the other sectors of the Sino-Indian border".
22. Report of the Officials of the Governments of India and the Peoples' Republic of China on the Boundary Question, Ministry of External Affairs, Government of India, http://www.archieve.claudearpi.net/maintenance/uploaded_pics/OR_Part_1.pdf, accessed online 20 September 2020. See the section on "The Chinese description of the Location and Terrain Features of the Traditional, Customary Sino-Indian Boundary line".
23. Noted in Manoj Joshi (2020), "Sino-Indian Border Deadlock", n. 17. For greater details, see Report of the Officials of the Governments of India and the Peoples' Republic of China on the Boundary Question, n. 13, section on "Clarifications sought by the Indian side".
24. Ibid.
25. Ministry of External Affairs (2018), Sino-India Relations including Doklam, Border Situation and Cooperation in International Organizations", Twenty Second Report, Committee on External Affairs (2017-18), Sixteenth Lok Sabha, 4 September 2018, p. 26, http://164.100.47.193/lsscommittee/External%20Affairs/16_External_Affairs_22.pdf, accessed online 9 March 2020.

26. M. Taylor Fravel (2008), *Strong Borders, Secure Nation: Cooperation and Conflict in China's Territorial Disputes*, Princeton, NJ: Princeton University Press, p. 10.
27. Ministry of External Affairs, Government of India (2018), "India-China Informal Summit at Wuhan", 28 April 2018, https://mea.gov.in/press-releases.htm?dtl/29853/IndiaChina_Informal_Summit_at_Wuhan, accessed online 5 July 2020.
28. The signing of the BDCA was spurred by the 2013 stand-off between the two militaries at DBO in Eastern Ladakh.
29. Ministry of External Affairs, Government of India (2005), "Agreement between the Government of the Republic of India and the Government of the People's Republic of China on the Political Parameters and Guiding Principles for the Settlement of the India-China Boundary Question", 11 April 2005, https://www.mea.gov.in/bilateral-documents.htm?dtl/6534/Agreement+between+the+Government+of+the+ Republic +of+India+and+the+ Government+of+the+Peoples+Republic+of+China+on+the+ Political +Parameters+and+Guiding+Principles+for+the+Settlement+of+the+ India China+Boundary+Question, accessed online 20 July 2020.
30. See "Agreement Between the Government of the Republic of India and the Government of the People's Republic of China on Confidence-Building Measures in the Military Field Along the Line of Actual Control in the India-China Border Areas", https://peacemaker.un.org/sites/peacemaker.un.org/files/CN%20IN_961129_Agreement %20between%20China%20and%20India.pdf, accessed online 20 July 2020.
31. Ibid.
32. Ministry of External Affairs, Government of India (2005), "Agreement between the Government of the Republic of India and the Government of the People's Republic of China on the Political Parameters and Guiding Principles for the Settlement of the India-China Boundary Question", 11 April 2005, https://www.mea.gov.in/bilateral-documents.htm?dtl/6534/Agreement+between+the+Government+of+the+Republic+of+ India+and+the+ Government+of+the+Peoples+Republic+of+China+ on+the+ Political+Parameters+and+Guiding+Principles+for+the+Settlement+of+the+ India China+Boundary+Question, accessed online 11 August 2020.
33. Major Akshat Upadhyay (2013), "China's Border Wars", *Journal of the United Service Institution of India*, Vol. CXLII, No. 591, January-March 2013, https://usiofindia.org/publication/usi-journal/chinas-border-wars/, accessed online 1 December 2020.
34. Ibid.
35. Ibid.
36. Ananth Krishnan (2020), *India's China Challenge: A Journey Through China's Rise and What It Means for India*, India: Harper Collins, p. 251.
37. Dai Bingguo was China's Special Representative in the over 15 rounds of boundary talks with India between 2003-2013.
38. Ananth Krishnan (2020), *India's China Challenge*, n. 36.
39. The Genron NPO (2020), *The 16th Joint Public Opinion Poll: Japan-China Public Opinion Survey 2020*, November 2020, p. 7, https://www.genron-npo.net/en/201117_en.pdf, accessed online 10 December 2020.
40. *2020 Report to Congress of the U.S.-China Economic and Security Review Commission*, Washington: U.S. Government Publishing Office, 1 December 2020, p. 363, https://www.uscc.gov/sites/default/files/2020-12/2020_Annual_Report_to_Congress.pdf, accessed on 10 December 2020.
41. Manoj Joshi (2020), "Sino-Indian Border Deadlock", n. 17.
42. Ministry of Foreign Affairs of the People's Republic of China (2020), "Foreign Ministry

Spokesperson Zhao Lijian's Regular Press Conference on June 19, 2020", 19 June 2020, https://www.fmprc.gov.cn/mfa_eng/xwfw_665399/s2510_665401/2511_665403/t1790521.shtml, accessed online 20 August 2020.

43. Ministry of External Affairs, Government of India (2020), "Statement on All Party Meeting of 19th June 2020", 20 June 2020, https://mea.gov.in/press-releases.htm?dtl/32775/Statement_on_All_Party_Meeting_of_19th_June_2020, accessed online 20 August 2020.
44. Ministry of External Affairs, Government of India (2020), "Official Spokesperson's response to media queries seeking comments on the statement issued on 19 June by the Chinese Spokesperson on the events in the Galwan valley area", 20 June 2020, https://www.mea.gov.in/response-to-queries.htm?dtl/32770/Official_ Spokes persons_ response_ to_ media_queries_seeking_comments_on_the_statement_issued_ on_19_June_by_the_Chinese_Spokesperson_on_the_events_in_the_, accessed online 20 August 2020.
45. Manoj Joshi (2020), "Sino-Indian Border Deadlock", n. 17.
46. Major Akshat Upadhyay (2013), "China's Border Wars", n. 33.
47. Ibid.
48. Here, 'transgression' refers to when one party goes to the other side of the border, assuming that it is their own territory
49. 2019 witnessed a 75 per cent spike in the western sector and 55 per cent spike in the eastern sector. Noted in Sushant Singh (2020), "Big surge in Chinese transgressions, most of them in Ladakh", *The Indian Express*, 22 May 2020, https://indianexpress.com/article/india/aksai-chin-army-big-surge-in-chinese-transgressions-most-of-them-in-ladakh-6421674/, accessed online 28 May 2020.
50. Sushant Singh (2020), "Chinese troops focus on 4 LAC locations, test new areas in Ladakh", *The Indian Express*, 23 May 2020, https://indianexpress.com/article/india/chinese-transgression-line-of-actual-control-indian-territory-galwan-river-6423131/, accessed online 9 December 2020.
51. "CID, intelligence agencies submit report on Chinese choppers entering 15 kms into India's Lahaul-Spiti", *Times Now Digital*, 17 July 2020, https://www.timesnow news.com/india/article/cid-intelligence-agencies-submit-report-on-chinese-choppers-entering-15-kms-into-indias-lahaul-spiti/593165, accessed online 20 August 2020.
52. V. K. Ahluwalia (2020), "India-China Border Quandary: The Cyclical Conundrum", Centre for Land Warfare Studies, 8 June 2020, https://www.claws.in/india-china-border-quandary-the-cyclical-conundrum/, accessed online 20 August 2020.
53. For details, see Ministry of External Affairs, Government of India (2020), "Joint Press Statement - Meeting of External Affairs Minister and the Foreign Minister of China (September 10, 2020)", 10 September 2020, https://www.mea.gov.in/pressreleases.htm?dtl/32962/Joint_Press_Statement__Meeting_of_External_Affairs_Minister_and_the_Foreign_Minister_of_China_September_10_2020, accessed online 20 September 2020.
54. Cited in Dinakar Peri (2020), "LAC standoff | Defence Ministry takes down report on Chinese transgressions beginning early May", *The Hindu*, 6 August 2020, https://www.thehindu.com/news/national/mod-takes-down-report-on-chinesetrans gressions-into-indian-territory/article32284188.ece, accessed online 20 August 2020.
55. Ibid.
56. Ibid.
57. V. K. Ahluwalia (2020), "China's Adventurism in Eastern Ladakh - A Strategic

Miscalculation", Wilson Center, 20 July 2020, https://www.wilsoncenter.org/article/chinas-adventurism-eastern-ladakh-strategic-miscalculation, accessed online 20 August 2020.

58. Ibid.
59. *2020 Report to Congress of the U.S.-China Economic and Security Review Commission*, n. 40, p. 362.
60. Will Green (2020), "Conflict on Sino-Indian Border: Backgrounder for Congress", U.S.-China Economic and Security review Commission, 2 July 2020, p. 2, https://www.uscc.gov/research/conflict-sino-indian-border-background-congress, accessed online 20 July 2020.
61. Kunal Purohit (2020), "China using border tensions to warn India not to side with the US: ex-foreign secretary Shyam Saran", *South China Morning Post*, 1 June 2020, https://www.scmp.com/week-asia/politics/article/3087030/china-using-border-tensions-warn-india-not-side-us-ex-foreign, accessed online 20 July 2020.
62. "Advisable for India not to engage in US-China confrontation", *Global Times*, 31 May 2020, https://www.globaltimes.cn/content/1190096.shtml, accessed online 20 July 2020.
63. Quoted in *2020 Report to Congress of the U.S.-China Economic and Security Review Commission*, n. 40, p. 362.
64. Ashley J. Tellis (2020), "Hustling in the Himalayas: The Sino-Indian Border Confrontation", Carnegie Endowment for International Peace, 4 June 2020, https://carnegieendowment.org/2020/06/04/hustling-in-himalayas-sino-indian-border-confrontation-pub-81979, accessed online 20 August 2020.
65. Ibid.
66. V. K. Ahluwalia (2020), "Counter China's Design on India – China Border", Centre for Land Warfare Studies, 2 October 2020, https://www.claws.in/counter-chinas-design-on-india-china-border/, accessed online 3 October 2020.
67. Ibid.
68. Himanshu Guhathakurta (2020), "Will there be a limited war between India and China?", Wretchedmind, 15 September 2020, https://wretchedmind.com/what-is-going-on-between-india-china/, accessed online 28 September 2020.
69. Embassy of the People's Republic of China in the Republic of Trinidad and Tobago (2019), "Foreign Ministry Spokesperson Hua Chunying's Remarks on the Indian Government's Announcement of the Establishment of the Ladakh Union Territory Which Involves Chinese Territory", 6 August 2019, http://tt.china-embassy.org/eng/zt/fyrth/t1686549.htm, accessed online 18 August 2020.
70. "Maps of newly formed Union Territories of Jammu Kashmir and Ladakh, with the map of India", *PIB*, 2 November 2019, https://pib.gov.in/PressReleasePage.aspx?PRID=1590112, accessed online 20 August 2020.
71. Huaxia (2019), China urges India to respect its territorial sovereignty", *Xinhuanet*, 1 November 2019, http://www.xinhuanet.com/english/2019-11/01/c_138519114.htm, accessed online 20 August 2020.
72. Quoted in Murali Krishnan (2020), "India-China Himalayan conflict: Does Beijing have an advantage after talks stall?" *DW*, 10 November 2020 , https://www.dw.com/en/india-china-military-standoff-continues/a-55553845, accessed online 5 December 2020.
73. Quoted in Amrita Jash (2018), "Mao Zedong's Art of the 1962 War: Perception of Opportunity Versus Perception of Threat", Manekshaw Paper No. 76, Centre for Land Warfare Studies, p. 2, https://www.claws.in/static/MP76_Mao-Zedong's-Art-of-the-

1962-War-Perception-of-Opportunity-Versus-Perception-of-Threat.pdf, accessed online 20 August 2020.

74. "Remember 1962 defeat: Chinese media warns India again amid Sikkim standoff", *Business Standard*, 13 July 2017, https://www.business-standard.com/article/current-affairs/remember-1962-defeat-chinese-media-warns-india-again-amid-sikkim-standoff-117071300376_1.html, accessed online 20 July 2020.
75. "India of 2017 different from that of 1962: Jaitley to China", *The Times of India*, 1 July 2017, https://timesofindia.indiatimes.com/india/india-of-2017-different-from-that-of-1962-jaitley-to-china/articleshow/59394967.cms, accessed online 20 July 2020.
76. Quoted in "People's Daily to India: Borderline is bottom line", *People's Daily Online*, 11 July 2017, http://en.people.cn/n3/2017/0711/c90000-9240280.html, accessed online 15 July 2020.
77. Sutirtho Pratnabis (2012), "China blames Jawaharlal Nehru for 1962 war", *Hindustan Times*, 7 October 2012, https://www.hindustantimes.com/world/china-blames-jawaharlal-nehru-for-1962-war/story-cFv9MZjltsWjCGy8HmuxVO.htmlccessed, accessed online 15 July 2020.
78. Forward Policy was designed to secure the entire Sino-Indian frontier in Ladakh in the west to the North-East Frontier Agency in the east. This policy move was decided upon in a meeting in New Delhi on 2 November 1961, less than a year before the 1962 war. It is argued that Nehru's Forward Policy was not aimed at provoking the Chinese but to reassert what the Indians considered to be the traditional boundary and to check the continuing Chinese advance by connecting all the gaps and plugging the holes along the frontier by establishing new outposts and sending out patrols even to the remotest parts of Ladakh and the NEFA. In view of this, action was to be taken only if there were any new Chinese army camps south of where the Indians had decided that the McMahon Line should be. See Bertil Lintner (2018), *China's India War: Collision Course on the Roof of the World*, New Delhi: Oxford University Press, pp. xi, 98-99.
79. Ibid.
80. "Commentary: India must understand borderline is bottom line", *Xinhuanet*, 10 July 2017, http://www.xinhuanet.com/english/2017-07/10/c_136432645.htm, accessed online 15 July 2020.
81. Consulate-General of the People's Republic of China in Mumbai (2020), "Foreign Ministry Spokesperson Gave a Step-by-Step Account of the Galwan Valley Incident", 20 June 2020, http://mumbai.china-consulate.org/eng/zxhd/t1790663.htm, accessed online 15 July 2020.
82. Ministry of Foreign Affairs of the People's Republic of China (2017), "Foreign Ministry Spokesperson Hua Chunying's Regular Press Conference on August 21, 2017", 21 August 2017, https://www.fmprc.gov.cn/mfa_eng/xwfw_665399/s2510_665401/t1486314.shtml, accessed online 20 August 2020.
83. Embassy of the People's Republic of China in the Republic of Trinidad and Tobago (2019), "Foreign Ministry Spokesperson Hua Chunying's Remarks", n. 69.
84. Kevin McCauley (2017), "Snapshot: China's Western Theater Command", *China Brief*, Vol. 17, Issue 1, 13 January 2017, https://jamestown.org/program/snapshot-chinas-western-theater-command/#sthash.SBpcZHmo.dpuf, accessed online 20 August 2020.
85. Ibid.
86. Office of the Secretary of Defense (2020), "Annual Report to Congress: Military and Security Developments involving the People's Republic of China 2020", p. 106, https:/

/media.defense.gov/2020/Sep/01/2002488689/-1/-1/1/2020-DOD-CHINA-MILITARY-POWER-REPORT-FINAL.PDF, accessed online 4 September 2020.

87. Mandeep Singh Bajwa (2020), "Military Digest | Poised Against India: The PLA's Western Theatre Command", *The Indian Express*, 27 July 2020, https://indianexpress.com/article/india/military-digest-poised-against-india-the-plas-western-theatre-command-6526051/, accessed online 20 August 2020.
88. The provincial military region/command is a military-level organisation set up by the PLA in all provinces, autonomous regions and municipalities directly under the Central Government. It leads a number of military divisions and a certain number of troops and is responsible for the military work in the province where the military is located. The main tasks are to lead reserve forces, militia, military service and mobilization. Earlier to the 2016 military reform, provinces had been led by the seven military regions.
89. National Defense Mobilisation Department looks at conscription, military sources for military forces, and guidance reserve forces such as militia and reserve forces.
90. The Beijing Weifang district is assigned to the Central Theatre Command. It is under the dual leadership of the former Beijing Military Region and the Beijing Municipal Party Committee and Government. Its main task is to be responsible for military security, garrison duty, anti-terrorism and stability in the Beijing area, carry out militia, military service and mobilisation work, maintain the military discipline of the capital, and assist local maintenance of public security.
91. CATTBs typically contain direction, evaluation and simulation facilities. Exercise umpires, multiple integrated laser engagement systems (MILES), data collection systems, and opposing forces (OPFOR) are employed to promote training realism and evaluation.
92. Kevin McCauley (2017), "Snapshot", n. 84.
93. Ibid.
94. Ibid.
95. Amrita Jash (2019), "Tibet Military Command: People's Liberation Army's combat Role in High Altitude", Issue Brief No. 181, Centre for Land Warfare Studies, May 2019, p. 3, https://www.claws.in/publication/tibet-military-command-peoples-liberation-armys-combat-role-in-high-altitude/, accessed online 20 August 2020.
96. Jayadeva Ranade (2015), "China's Focus on Military Activities in Tibet", Vivekananda International Foundation, 18 September 2015, https://www.vifindia.org/article/2015/september/18/china-s-focus-on-military-activities-in-tibet, accessed online 20 August 2020.
97. "National Defense Mobilization Department after the military reform", sina.com.cn, 22 November 2016, http://finance.sina.com.cn/roll/2016-11-22/doc-ifxxwrwk1646007.shtml, accessed online 5 August 2020.
98. Yang Yi (2018), "China's type 15 lightweight tank commissioned", *Xinhuanet*, 27 December 2018, http://www.xinhuanet.com/english/2018-12/27/c_137702935.htm, accessed online 7 July 2020.
99. Mark Episkopos (2019), "Introducing China's New Type 15 Tank. Here's What You Need To Know", The National Interest, 1 January 2019, https://nationalinterest.org/blog/buzz/introducing-chinas-new-type-15-tank-heres-what-you-need-know-40297, accessed online 20 July 2020.
100. Quoted in Liu Xuanzun (2018), "Light-weight Type 15 better suited for mountain warfare, island landing", *Global Times*, 25 November 2018, http://www.globaltimes.cn/content/1128943.shtml, accessed on 16 July 2020.

101. Ibid.
102. Chen Zhuo (2019), "Mobile howitzers help Tibet border defense", *China Military Online*, 8 January 2019, http://english.chinamil.com.cn/view/2019-01/08/content_9398635.htm, accessed online 17 July 2020.
103. Ibid.
104. China's Z-20 helicopter is often compared to America's UH-60 Black Hawk. The 10 ton-class medium-lift rotary-wing aircraft is the first Chinese helicopter to use domestically developed anti-icing and de-icing technology for rotors, making China the fourth country to possess such technology. It features domestic engines powerful enough for it to fly in low-oxygen plateaus. See "China Inducts Black Hawk Comparable Chopper, Z-20 into Tibet Military Command", Defense world.net, 14 December 2020, https://www.defenseworld.net/news/28536/China_Inducts_Black_Hawk_Comparable_Chopper__Z_20_into_Tibet_Military_Command, accessed online 15 December 2020.
105. "China to replace Black Hawk Choppers with 'CopyHawk' Harbin Z-20", *Indian Defence News*, 2 September 2018, http://www.indiandefensenews.in/2018/09/china-to-replace-black-hawk-choppers.html, accessed online 8 August 2020.
106. Rajeswari Pillai Rajagopalan and Pulkit Mohan, "PLA Joint Exercises in Tibet: Implications for India", *ORF Occasional Paper No. 238*, Observer Research Foundation, February 2020, https://www.orfonline.org/research/pla-joint-exercises-in-tibet-implications-for-india-61735/#_edn40, accessed online 20 September 2020.
107. Mandeep Singh Bajwa (2020), "Military Digest", n. 87.
108. Ibid.
109. Ibid.
110. Liu Xuanzun (2020), "PLA bombers, air defense troops, paratroopers deployed in plateau region amid border tensions", *Global Times*, 9 September 2020, https://www.globaltimes.cn/content/1200374.shtml, accessed online 20 September 2020.
111. Rajeswari Pillai Rajagopalan and Pulkit Mohan, "PLA Joint Exercises in Tibet", n. 105.
112. Mandeep Singh Bajwa (2020), "Military Digest", n. 87.
113. "Tibet to build more airports near border", *Global Times*, 10 June 2018, https://www.globaltimes.cn/content/1106374.shtml, accessed online 25 July 2020.
114. Srikanth Kondapalli (2019), "Is India ready? China steps up military build-up in Tibet as America passes law of Reciprocal Access", *Financial Express*, 14 January 2019, https://www.financialexpress.com/defence/is-india-ready-china-steps-up-military-build-up-in-tibet-as-america-passes-law-of-reciprocal-access/1443394/, accessed online 25 July 2020.
115. Ibid.
116. Lobsang Tenchoe (2018), "Shortcut to Tibet; China's new ambitious railway project worth over $36 billion", *The Tibet Express*, 12 October 2018, https://tibetexpress.net/9148/shortcut-to-tibet-chinas-new-ambitious-railway-project-worth-over-36-billion/ accessed online 25 July 2020.
117. "Investment in high-speed rail continues", *Ecns.cn*, 3 January 2019, http://www.ecns.cn/news/economy/2019-01-03/detail-ifzcitha9949856.shtml, accessed online 25 July 2020.
118. Huaxia (2020), "Xi Focus: Xi stresses building high-quality Sichuan-Tibet Railway", *Xinhuanet*, 8 November 2020, http://www.xinhuanet.com/english/2020-11/08/c_139500425.htm, accessed online 20 November 2020.
119. "Sichuan Tibet Railway: China builds world's most challenging railway", *Global Times*,

19 October 2018, https://www.globaltimes.cn/content/1123663.shtml, accessed online 10 December 2020.

120. Brahma Chellaney (2013), "Rising Powers, Rising Tensions: The Troubled China-India Relationship", *SAIS Review*, Vol. 32, No. 2, January 3, http://chellaney.net/2013/01/03/rising-powers-rising-tensions-the-troubled-china-india-relationship/, accessed on 25 August 2020.

121. Fan Anqi and Li Qingqing (2020), "Construction of Sichuan-Tibet railway to boost local development and border stability", *Global Times*, 31 October 2020, https://www.globaltimes.cn/content/1205235.shtml, accessed online 5 November 2020.

122. To note, China used troops that were engaged in a war game on the Chinese side and rushed them to the border with India in trucks used to ferry mud for an airbase project not far off from Indian areas. See Manjeet Negi (2020), "China deceives India in Ladakh; mobilises forces on mud trucks", *Business Today*, 27 May 2020, https://www.businesstoday.in/current/economy-politics/china-deceives-india-in-ladakh-mobilises-forces-on-mud-trucks/story/405130.html, accessed on 20 August 2020.

124. Xi Jinping (2017), "Secure a Decisive Victory in Building a Moderately Prosperous Society in All Respects and Strive for the Great Success of Socialism with Chinese Characteristics for a New Era", *Xinhuanet*, 18 October 2017, p. 48, http://www.xinhuanet.com/english/download/Xi_Jinping's_report_at_19th_CPC_National Congress.pdf, accessed online 20 August 2020.

124. Cao Siqi (2018), "PLA holds high-altitude drill on plateau in Tibet", *Global Times*, 28 June 2018, http://www.globaltimes.cn/content/1108770.shtml, accessed online 28 July 2020.

125. "China equips troops along India-Tibet border with mobile howitzers: Report", *Dailyhunt*, 8 January 2019, https://m.dailyhunt.in/news/india/english/wion+news-epaper-wionnew/china+equips+troops+along+india+tibet+border+with+mobile+howitzers+report-newsid-105836817, accessed online 8 August 2020.

126. A joint fire strike campaign is a long-range precision strike by missile and air-power forces with the mission to destroy important enemy targets, paralyse the enemy's operational systems, weaken the will to resist through terror attacks and destroy war potential in the form of resources.

127. Kevin McCauley (2017), "Snapshot", n. 84.

128. "PLA armoured brigade holds 'high altitude drill' in Tibet with most advanced tank", *Tibet Environmental Watch*, 21 July 2017, http://tew.org/pla-armoured-brigade-holds-high-altitude-drill-in-tibet-with-most-advanced-tank/, accessed online 10 August 2020.

129. It is noted that before the exercise, the brigade mobilized all its members and equipment and took six hours to transport them from the barracks to the drill zone at an altitude of 5,000 metres on the plateau. See Zhao Lei (2017), "Qinghai-Tibet Plateau site of PLA war games", *China Daily*, 17 July 2017, http://www.chinadaily.com.cn/china/2017-07/17/content_30133519.htm, accessed online 20 August 2020.

130. Liu Zhen (2017), "China flexes its military muscle in Tibet, close to border dispute with India", *South China Morning Post*, 17 July 2017, https://www.scmp.com/news/china/diplomacy-defence/article/2102965/china-flexes-its-military-muscle-tibet-close-border, accessed online 20 August 2020.

131. Yao Jianing (2018), "PLA holds high-altitude drill on plateau in Tibet," *China Military Online*, 29 June 2018, http://eng.chinamil.com.cn/view/2018-06/29/content_8074859.htm, accessed online 18 August 2020.

132. Ibid.

133. For details, see Liu Zhen (2020), "PLA reveals five-fire drill in eastern Tibet mountains as China-India border dispute claims at least 20 lives", *South China Morning Post*, 17 June 2020, https://www.scmp.com/news/china/military/article/3089388/pla-reveals-live-fire-drill-eastern-tibet-mountains-china-india, accessed online 20 July 2020. Smriti Chaudhary (2020), "WARNING FOR INDIA: Chinese Army & Air Force Hold Joint Military Drills Near LAC", *The Eurasian Times*, 14 September 2020, https://eurasiantimes.com/warning-for-india-chinese-army-air-force-for-1st-time-hold-combined-military-drills-near-indian-border/, accessed online 20 September 2020.
134. "China increases military drills in Tibet amid tensions with India", International Campaign for Tibet, 25 June 2020, https://savetibet.org/china-increases-military-drills-in-tibet-amid-tensions-with-india/, accessed online 10 September 2020.
135. "Citing threat from India, China Stations 3.5 Gen Fighter Jets in Tibet," *Tibetan Review*, 21 February 2018, http://www.tibetanreview.net/citing-threat-from-india-china-stations-3-5-gen-fighter-jets-in-tibet/, accessed on 18 August 2020.
136. Zhou Xin (2018), "Xi calls for deepened military-civilian integration", *Xinhuanet*, 12 March 2018, http://www.xinhuanet.com/english/2018-03/12/c_137034168.htm accessed online 17 August 2020.
137. One image from Planet Labs dated 17 February 2020 showed only one village with some 20 structures in the area; while a second image dated 28 November 2020 showed three additional villages in the same area with a total of about 50 structures. For details, Vishnu Som (2020), "Exclusive: China Sets Up 3 Villages Near Arunachal, Relocates Villagers", *NDTV*, 6 December 2020, https://www.ndtv.com/india-news/exclusive-china-sets-up-3-villages-near-arunachal-pradesh-relocates-villagers-2334869, accessed online 8 December 2020.
138. Central Tibetan Administration (2017), "Tibetan Herdsmen to become Guardians of Chinese Territory bordering Arunachal Pradesh: Xi Jinping", 1 November 2017, https://tibet.net/tibetan-herdsmen-to-become-guardians-of-chinese-territory-bordering-arunachal-pradesh-xi-jinping/, accessed online 8 December 2020.
139. Quoted in Vishnu Som (2020), "Exclusive: China Sets Up 3 Villages", n. 137.
140. Kou Jie (2016), "China Raises Tibet Military Command's power rank", *Global Times*, 13 May 2016, http://www.globaltimes.cn/content/982843.shtml, accessed online 24 July 2020.
141. Liu Caiyu and Ji Yuqiao (2019), "Mobile howitzers help Tibet border defense", *Global Times*, 7 January 2019, http://www.globaltimes.cn/content/1134945.shtmln, accessed online 19 August 2020.
142. Chengcheng (2019), "Xi orders armed forces to enhance combat readiness", *Xinhuanet*, 4 January 2019, http://www.xinhuanet.com/english/2019-01/04/c_137720169.htm, accessed online 11 August 2020.

Conclusion

The purpose of this book has been to unveil the essence of China's Military Strategy despite the lack of a formal document. In doing so, the aim has been to offer an understanding of China's 'National Military Strategy' from an analytical perspective, wherein the assessment is based on a comprehensive approach rather than being limited to a stated understanding of what the China's People's Liberation Army intends to achieve in terms of its military objectives and goals.

In analysing a country's military strategy, it becomes imperative to understand how states perceive their security environment. That is to ask: Is it just informed by threats or are there other factors that come into play? At the bottom line, in international relations, a state's behaviour is constructed given the way it defines the international environment. It is thereby, the definition of the security environment defines the interests and objectives that underpin the state's military strategy.

Taking this as the point of reference, the present study aimed to address the nature of China's military strategy. It has set out with an emphasis on three key aspects: (a) How does China perceive its security environment? (b) How do these perceptions impact China's strategic military thinking? (c) What are the PLA's ambitions and how does it seeks to achieve it? Wherein, the aim is to understand by uncovering the core, that is, China's Military Strategy. In finding the answers, this study adopted a top-down approach of the Chinese understanding of 'strategy' to explain China's military strategy by drawing a linkage from its national and national security strategy. The simple reason being that these concepts are mutually constitutive, wherein a change in one affects the other.

While there is extensive literature on China's military strategy and the PLA, but significant gaps still exist in terms of an overall framework that can conceptualise as to what constitutes China's military strategy. This is evident from the very debate on whether China has a military strategy. To add further, there remains very limited understanding of the concept of 'Active Defence' in these studies. This aspect forms the base of this book, wherein much of the analyses have concentrated on the content and context that characterises the concept of 'active defence' in China's military strategy. This template is helpful as: it provides a comparative understanding of Chinese definitions as against Western understanding; highlights the essence of China's military strategy as embedded in the national military strategic concepts; and finally, brings into perspective the similarities and differences in the PLA's strategic and military thinking vis-à-vis the universal paradigm. Simplistically put, it forces one to think: How different is the PLA?

In doing so, this book demystifies China's defensive military posture. More significantly, it highlights the essence of 'active defence' as one of the principal 'strategic concepts' that define and shape China's military strategy. However, this comes with an understanding that China's military strategy, like that of any other country, is dynamic and subject to change, with significant changes and minor adjustments caused by the Chinese perception of the security environment. Given this context, the findings of this book suggest the following:

First, the lack of an official Chinese document on 'military strategy' should not be treated as lack of a 'strategy'. Such simplistic deductions only call for ill-informed ideas. In the case of China, the starting point lies in decoding the Chinese formulation of national strategy as Beijing has its own way of projecting its 'strategy', wherein the ambition lies in realising "the great rejuvenation of the Chinese nation", commonly called the "Chinese Dream" by applying the theorem of "Socialism with Chinese Characteristics". This very goal has set the course of China's policy milestones and laid out the objectives for making the PLA a 'modern force'.

To achieve this objective, China's national security strategy aims to safeguard sovereignty, security and development interests which form the key tasks of the PLA, permeating the security factor into the military strategy. This brings into perspective the interconnectedness of China's national strategy with that of national security strategy and national military strategy, wherein the Chinese Dream of the 'great rejuvenation' is complemented by building a 'strong military'.

Thereby, it can be rightly argued that China has a national military strategy that is guided by the "military strategic guideline" of "winning informationised local wars" and informed by the strategic concept of "active defence". To which, the significance lies in understanding the difference between strategic concept and strategic guideline in China's military strategy.

Second, the concept of 'active defence' is a key determinant of China's national military strategy with changes in the meaning and operational applications overtime. Earlier active defence was mainly functional against a perceived attack, that is, against an invasion; however, in the current times, as China faces no threat of invasion, the very applicability of active defence has changed. That is, China has moved beyond the 'counter-attack' and 'no aggression' policies of active defence, as evident from China's growing military posture and power projection capabilities, which suggest otherwise. That is to argue, China has moved away from its strategy of 'luring the enemy in deep'. As a result of which, active defence has taken the form of 'forward defence' wherein, China is expanding the battlespace beyond its borders and coasts. Besides, China today aims and strives to 'win informationised local wars', wherein 'invasion' is no more a causal factor for active defence. Furthermore, as the 'military strategic guidelines' are susceptible to change given the strategic shifts in the international security environment as perceived by China, it also impacts the 'type of war' that the PLA would have to fight in the future.

Besides, what also makes 'active defence' significant is that although the concept is a relatively stable component in China's military thinking, but it is not static in nature. For while it is interpreted to be defensive in orientation, one cannot dismiss the element of offence and pre-emption that makes it dynamic in nature. This makes active defence an 'operational concept', which calls for quick reaction before the adversary launches a strike, calling for the PLA to be 'mobile, flexible and deceptive' by using the element of surprise.

Therefore, 'active defence' is neither China's strategic guideline or military strategy, but is the primary 'strategic concept' that lies at the core of the PLA's thinking which informs, defines and shapes China's national military strategy at any given period of time. Most importantly, the defining character of active defence is not the much-stated 'defensive posture' but the underlying 'offensive element' that does not necessitate an attack to be kinetic to warrant a countermeasure. Thus, it is what the PRC perceives to be an attack, not just military but political or economic, which be responded with "active defence".

Third, the rapid pace of China's military modernisation has not just spurred the debate on China's military capabilities in terms of war fighting and deterrence; it has also raised red alarms on China's military intentions. Specifically, it has further clarified that the PRC does have a national military strategy, which is not simply defensive. That is to argue, one cannot ignore that modernisation aims at building military capabilities, which is not just about defence, but very much for offence as well. This adds to the Chinese dimension of 'active defence' that currently is focussed on the PLA carrying out joint operations, with both operational and strategic preparedness in all domains of threat – land, air, water, space, cyber and electromagnetic spectrums. Furthermore, there remains little doubt to state that China's military capabilities hold severe security implications as manifested in the PLA's growing power projection and expeditionary capabilities to fight the opponent beyond China's borders and coasts.

In this regard, it can be strongly stated that the PRC's military calculus aims at making China a security maximising state, wherein by building its military means, Beijing aims to meet the goal of a strong national security state. This is guided by the vision of becoming a 'world-class military' with the expected outcome of the PLA playing a greater role in shaping China's future by securing the strategic space, both regionally and globally. To achieve this ambition, it is essential for the PRC to transform the PLA into a more professional and modern fighting force that is combat-ready to quell the risks of the contingencies, at any given time. The intention therefore, lies in improving the PLA's ability to conduct joint operations in fighting multi-domain warfare, with the PLA better positioned to impose costs on its adversaries in achieving China's strategic aims. This is exemplified by China's modernisation efforts that have created a favourable asymmetry in the military strength between China and the others. Owing to which, China can pose a serious challenge to its adversaries and aim at potential targets for pre-emption and disruption, adding to the dimension of active defence. Therefore, China's military modernisation and reforms increasingly highlight the intention of the PLA to be 'battle-ready', wherein one cannot dismiss the possibility of China acting first against an opponent.

Fourth, it can be rightly argued that China's rapid economic growth has transformed China into a strong military power. This is exemplified by China's increasing defence expenditure, which is an indication of its increasing military capabilities and its military intentions. That is to argue, an increased defence spending is an indicator of Beijing's intentions to secure its strategic space both regionally as well as globally by building power projection and expeditionary capabilities. This intention is reflected in China's overall development in terms of updating its doctrine and improving the quality of its personnel in warfighting by equipping the PLA with better and advanced weaponry.

Moreover, unlike its antiquated past, in the current times, China's military-industrial complex is increasingly bridging its weaponry and defence technology gap with the West. This is evident from China's emerging capabilities in hypersonics, AI, precision strikes, anti-satellite capabilities and drone technologies. With China increasingly taking the lead in these new areas of military hardware under its RMA, one cannot dismiss the fact that China is inching towards military superiority. However, with the strategic goal to become a 'world-class military', sustaining a modern PLA is what calls for the challenge for China. Here, the pressure point is that in all circumstances, China needs to grow economically to continue its military spending in order to fuel and sustain its defence production and industry. Hence, it can be rightly argued that the PRC's defence spending is directly proportional to the growth of its defence industry - which can no longer be overlooked.

Fifth, as no resolution has been reached, the boundary predicament between India and China has evolved from being 'protracted' to that of becoming 'volatile'. With the risks higher than ever, both countries are now in a position of seeing eyeball-to-eyeball. Primarily, China's military activism in Eastern Ladakh and specifically, the Galwan Valley clash has exposed China's 'territorial 'insecurity'. More precisely, it has clarified China's perception of viewing India as a potential threat and the likely implications it holds.

There remains no doubt to suggest that the tensions along the LAC will only get intensified. This also comes with the assessment that China will be reluctant to engage itself in any form of full-scale war with India. A 'war' against India is not on the Chinese agenda given its primary goal is to realise the Chinese Dream, which can only be achieved under a peaceful and stable neighbourhood. Besides, as India is a nuclear power, it significantly adds to the deterrence.

In view of this, the possible outcome to expect is that of tensions in all the three sectors of the LAC. More significantly, if the ties take a further downturn under the current stalemate in Eastern Ladakh, border flare-ups will only get intensified. To which, one can argue that China's strategic behaviour towards India will only get aggressive, if not diffident. Moreover, in all likelihood, China will increasingly make forays along the LAC to change the status quo at the border. In doing so, China will create new differences to the old sensitive areas under dispute at the LAC. This will further heighten the security dilemma and increasingly make one wary of the other's intentions. This will call upon war preparedness, leaving less room for any form of compromise between India and China. As a result, the resolution of the border issue will only be further delayed. In this scenario, to avert the contingency of an unwarranted risk, both New Delhi and Beijing need to maintain a timely check on each other's perceptions to avoid a misadventure cropping from 'assuming the worst' scenario. It is, therefore, in the best interests of both the countries to maintain the status quo at the border and refrain from adding new differences to the old dispute. Thereby, the starting point lies in strictly adhering to the agreements and protocols to maintain peace and stability at the contested border.

Based on these findings, this book would like to make seven significant claims: First, active defence is a crucial aspect of China's military strategy that should not be met with an oversight. What China claims to be defensive holds the potential of being offensive. The possibility of which is triggered by China's perception of a threat or challenge. Wherein, an act of pre-emption which calls for the offence is not just limited to a military action but can be triggered by anything that China perceives as a threat. Therefore, all is not defence in active defence.

Second, threats from China should not be just assumed to be necessarily in the form of direct military action. The threat can be manifested in various forms that demands 'no use of force'. In this perspective, China's Belt and Road Initiative and Military-Civil Fusion strategy are significant in furthering China's national interests and most specifically, safeguarding its core interests. In this process, China's growing military-industrial complex, and its power projection and expeditionary capabilities, need to be carefully watched to assess the scope and scale of the threat posed by China to its adversaries, such as the USA and neighbouring countries such as India, Japan and others with whom China has territorial and maritime disputes.

Third, much as China would like to follow Sun Tzu's dictum of subduing the enemy without fighting, but the new guidance for the PLA is to 'fight and win'. This explains China's increasing quest to achieve combat readiness. This is driven by the PLA's ambition to fulfil the strategic target-centric goals with the ultimate aim of becoming a 'world-class military'. This is exemplified by robust reforms and rapid military modernisation of the PLA, which are dedicated to the first and foremost objective of enhancing the PLA's real combat capabilities. Here, the onus lies on the PLA to perfect the art of being 'battle-ready' to carry out joint operations in fighting an 'intelligentised war' with greater offensive military capabilities.

Fourth, PRC's assertive and aggressive dispositions are clear signifiers of China's non-compromising attitude when it comes to its national or, rather core interests. To which, one can specifically argue that China will not compromise in areas of 'strategic interests'. In this scenario, in the case of the border with India, China surely seeks no resolution if not in alignment with China's interests. This also applies to the South China Sea dispute and the Diaoyu/Senkaku islands and maritime disputes with Japan in the East China Sea. Therefore, a win-win settlement of the disputes is not on Beijing's cards, as it does not meet the Chinese interests.

Fifth, there remains little doubt to state that a modern and combat-ready PLA will be the reality in the near future. In this respect, to deliberate on whether the PLA is modernising will hold less credence; rather investigating on what capabilities China is building and what ends it seeks to meet would be the key watch areas. This, thereby, makes it imperative for the USA and China's neighbours, especially India and Japan, to keep a close watch on China's actions given their respective disputes in the South China Sea, the border with India, the East China Sea and the IOR. This will invariably become vital to assess whether the USA and China's neighbours have the ability to quell the risks posed by

China. That is to suggest, what capabilities one needs to possess to fight the Chinese threat.

Sixth, specifically to the context of India, greater competition between the two Asian powers is an evitable fact. With no quick fix solution for the unsettled border and increasing incidents of transgressions and stand-offs, China's military activism will only get heightened over time. China is expected to walk by design along the LAC – thus, stand-offs will not only become recurrent but also harder to resolve. The boundary predicament will only get complicated with time, wherein unlike the past, it is management of tensions at the border that will become the new dilemma.

The change in dynamics necessitates India to build its own defences in fighting against China's designs. This makes it imperative for New Delhi to be aware of the fact that apart from engaging in stand-offs, Beijing will also play by the book of 'Unrestricted Warfare'. Wherein, China will employ two key means: First, application of "Three Warfares Strategy" to wage psychological warfare against India; and second, wage an integrated network-centric warfare in compliance with ground warfare under the command of the PLASSF. With the increasing possibility of confrontation, if a conflict occurs, the PLA would use all its arms and services. Hence, to avert a contingency, India needs to build its own military preparedness in fighting a multi-domain warfare with China – more specifically, an 'intelligentised warfare'.

In this perspective, what adds to India's concerns over China's encroachment into its territory is the need to be alert and aware of the other corresponding threats emanating from the broader strategic context. Especially with regard to the regional context, the five key areas that would require India's significant attention are:

(a) China's infrastructure build-up in TAR and in areas adjacent to the LAC. In this regard, India needs to pay close attention to the upcoming Sichuan-Tibet Railways, that will be instrumental in consolidating Beijing's border stability. By connecting Chengdu to Lhasa and cutting down on the travel time, the railways will enhance PLA's military presence in TAR as well as its combat readiness as a whole - providing a critical advantage for China along the LAC.

(b) China's military ties with countries neighbouring India, of which, at the apex lies Sino-Pakistan ties. Wherein, increasing military cooperation between the two countries against increasing tensions with India at the LAC and LoC, one cannot discount the increasing possibility of a 'two-front war' scenario against India. This also holds true given China's own stakes in Pakistan under the huge investments in CPEC. To safeguard its strategic assets as well as a countermeasure against India, in the future, one can expect Gwadar to become one of the potential military bases for the PLA—both to project power as well as to operate as an expeditionary force.

(c) China's defence exports to India's neighbours, especially to Pakistan, Bangladesh and Myanmar. Undeniably, China's arms exports to these countries will only increase, given the flux in the regional security environment.

(d) China's activities in South Asia, especially in terms of Beijing's public diplomacy. Wherein, apart from Pakistan, China's infrastructure build-up in terms of port activities, radar posts, rail and road links with countries such as Nepal, Sri Lanka and Bangladesh will be one of the prominent areas for India to watch.

(e) PLA Navy's greater presence in the Indian Ocean and the Bay of Bengal. This will witness a hike in China's maritime activities in the region as well as combined activities with countries friendly to Beijing (Pakistan, Bangladesh, Sri Lanka and Myanmar) in terms of basing, logistics, and refuelling facilities—further adding to PLA's power projection and expeditionary capabilities.

And finally, one of the key area's to watch in the near future is the applicability of China's 'military-civil fusion' strategy. It is essential to note that the scope of MCF is much broader than simply being 'public-private partnerships—as clarified by the very prioritisation of putting 'military' before 'civil' in MCF, which calls for scrutiny. More specifically, with no barriers between civil and military under MCF, China's civil sector will get completely integrated into the country's military-industrial complex; wherein China's research institutes, academic institutions and private firms will be heavily invested in modernisation of the PLA. This 'dual-use' nature of MCF holds strategic ramifications for the globe at large and China's adversaries in particular thereby, making 'MCF' another manifestation of the growing 'China Challenge'.

These claims signify the possible implications of China's military strategy and the way 'active defence' will be played out. At the foremost, to assume that China will only act in defence will be a critical error. As China calls upon the PLA to be battle-ready, it also applies to the other nations, especially to countries in dispute with China, to be militarily prepared at all times to quell the risks posed by China. For, one cannot rule out that when China strikes, it will be decisive; until then it will keep testing the opponent's resolve by its 'salami-slicing' tactic. Thus, offence is very much on China's strategic military thinking.

On the whole, there remains no doubt to state that China's rise is equated with the China threat. This is demonstrated by China's increasing unilateral behavioural dispositions. It would not be wrong to posit that one is dealing with an aggressive and assertive China. With the 'China Challenge' becoming the new reality of the 21st century, the expanded efforts by the PRC call for shedding the old prejudices attached to the PLA. That is, the old perception of PLA being 'backward and redundant' needs to be replaced with that of the PLA being a 'battle-ready force'. Needless to say, the quest is to build 'a strong China with a strong PLA'.

In view of which, apart from acting in defence, to claim its strategic space China would also act with offence; thus, playing by the rule book of 'active defence'. Hence, this will be determined by the threats and challenges that will provoke China to pre-empt – as 'offence is the best defence'.

Index

*